the
ART
of
PROBLEM
SOLVING

Volume 1:
the *BASICS*

Sandor Lehoczky
Richard Rusczyk

Published by Greater Testing Concepts/Sandor Lehoczky and Richard Rusczyk, P. O. Box 5014, New York, NY 10185-5014.

ISBN: 1-885875-01-0

This book was produced as camera ready copy using the TeX and LaTeX typesetting systems.

To Ameyalli, for laughter clear as your lake, for spirit strong and serene as your skyline, for all that you have taught and learned in four winters. And to Mrs. Wendt, who is still by far the best teacher I ever had.

—SL

For my desert flower Vanessa. We'll make it there eventually.

—RR

Special thanks to the following people who helped make this possible: William and Claire Devlin, Sandor L. and Julianne G. Lehoczky, Steve and Ann Rubio, Richard and Claire Rusczyk, Stanley Rusczyk.

To Students

Unless you have been much more fortunate than we were, this book is unlike anything you have used before.

The information in this book cannot be learned by osmosis. What the book teaches is not *facts*, but *approaches*. To learn from a section, you have to read—and comprehend—the text. You will not gain from just looking for the key formulas.

Since subjects are ordered by topic, important ideas may be in seemingly out-of-the-way places, where someone skimming might miss them. Similarly, don't expect to find a uniform difficulty level. When you need to, read slowly, spending minutes on a single line or equation when you need to. Fly when you can. There will be times for both, so don't get impatient.

Some very important concepts are introduced only in examples and exercises. Even when they are simply meant to increase your comfort with the idea at hand, the examples and exercises are the key to understanding the material. Read the examples with even more attention than you pay to the rest of the text, and, no matter what kind of hurry you are in, take the time to do the exercises thoroughly.

This book is about methods. If you find yourself memorizing formulas, you are missing the point. The formulas should become obvious to you as you read, without need of memorization. This is another function of the examples and exercises: to make the methods part of the way you think, not just some process you can remember.

Most of all, this book is about problems. We have gone to great lengths to compile the end-of-chapter problems and other problems in the book. Do them, as many as you possibly can. Don't overload on a single subject, though, or you'll forget everything in a week. Return to each subject every now and then, to keep your understanding current, and to see how much you've grown since you last thought about that subject.

If you have trouble with the problems, don't get neurotic, GET HELP! Consult other students, consult your teachers and, as a last resort, consult the Solution Manual. Don't give up too quickly and begin using the Solution Manual like a text. It should be referred to only after you've made a serious effort on your own. Don't get discouraged. Just as importantly, if these last sentences don't apply to you, you should be the one other students can come to for help.

The book thus comes with one warning: you will not learn if you don't do the problems. Cultivate a creative understanding of the thought processes which go into solving the problems, and before too long you will find you can do them. At that same instant you'll discover that you enjoy them!

To Teachers

This book is our conception of what a student's introduction to elementary mathematics should be.

We strongly feel that a student should learn all subjects simultaneously. There are two reasons for this. First, it helps to convey the interconnectedness of it all; how geometry naturally leads to coordinates and how those coordinates make it easy to define conic sections and the complex plane; how counting leads to probability, the binomial theorem, and number theoretical ideas. Second, it all sinks in better. Overloading on a single subject can cause students to acquire a surface understanding which doesn't connect to any deeper comprehension, and is thus rapidly lost.

You may be surprised at some of the things we do or do not include in this first volume. We put great emphasis on geometry, which we feel is the most neglected subject in many curricula: students take a year of geometry, then don't ever see it again. It is widely felt that American students are very weak in geometry. Other subjects in which our treatments may surprise you are basic number theory and counting, which many would put in an intermediate, rather than an elementary, text. The intuitive appeal of the subjects convinces us that they are excellent introductory material, while other subjects which are less intuitively striking are moved to our second text.

Our notation sometimes diverges from the accepted notation. In these cases, however, our decisions have been made with full deliberation. We strive to use symbols which evoke their meanings, as in the use of the less-popular $\lfloor \rfloor$ to denote the greatest integer function instead of the usual $[\,]$.

Each chapter of the text is meant to feel like the discussion of a subject with a friend. In one aspect of such a discussion, the text must fail: the answering of questions. This weakness must be repaired by teachers or strong students who are able to assume a leadership role. Teachers are crucial to the process of the book, whether teaching the material directly or simply being available for explanation.

We urge teachers using this in a classroom or club setting to encourage students who understand certain areas to explain the subjects to the rest of the class, or perhaps rotate such responsibility among a large group of willing students. This will not only give the other students a different view, and perhaps one closer to their own thought process, but it also greatly enhances the teaching student's understanding of the subject. Furthermore, the teaching student will have a chance to see the rewards that come from teaching.

We also suggest that after covering each subject, students attempt to write problems using the principles they have learned. In writing a problem, one does much more math than in solving one. This further inspires the creative drive which is so essential to problem solving in math and beyond, and if students are asked to take a crack at each others' creations, the competitive urge will also be tickled.

In closing, this book is about methods, not memory. The formulas we prove are important ones, but we intend for our explanations to be such that memorization is not necessary. If a student truly understands why a formula is true, then the formula can be internalized without memorization. However you choose to use this book, we hope that the focus remains that students understand *why* formulas work. Only in this way can they understand the full range of the formulas' applications and the full beauty of the mathematics they are learning.

Possible Curricula

Ordering the chapters of this textbook was an especially hard task due to the wide range of uses we expect it to be put to. The order we finally settled on was an attempt to make the book the easiest to use for the greatest number of people; however, many different curricula are possible, depending on the reader's experience and goals. Here are a few possibilities.

A totally integrated approach, with no clumping together of similar topics, is satisfying from a purely educational point of view. Alternating between geometry and non-geometry topics would force greater retention on the part of the student and emphasize the interconnectedness of the topics. Those teachers using the book in math team or club settings and those students using the book for rigorous self study might consider covering the elementary material with a chapter order like

$$1 \rightarrow 9 \rightarrow 10 \rightarrow 2 \rightarrow 11.1\text{-}11.4 \rightarrow 3 \rightarrow 4 \rightarrow 11.5\text{-}11.9$$
$$\rightarrow 5 \rightarrow 6 \rightarrow 12 \rightarrow 13 \rightarrow 14 \rightarrow 7 \rightarrow 15 \rightarrow 17 \rightarrow 8 \rightarrow 18.$$

However, from a classroom point of view such an ordering of chapters would present grave difficulties. We decided to group the chapters so that teachers using the book as a primary or secondary text in an Algebra or Geometry course would have fewer problems. An Algebra curriculum might be

$$1 \to 2 \to 3 \to 4 \to 6 \to 7 \to 22 \to 21 \to 24 \quad (5, 8, 23, 25, 26),$$

where the chapters in parentheses might be covered if there is time. A Geometry curriculum might be

$$9 \to 10 \to 11 \to 12 \to 13 \to 14 \to 15 \to 17 \to 18 \to 20 \quad (16, 19).$$

A third approach is for students already done with ordinary Algebra and Geometry, but with little experience in math outside the classroom. This curriculum would begin by solving several end-of-chapter problems from the familiar chapters, to get used to solving more advanced problems, then turning to a sequence like the following to extend into the more interesting material:

$$2 \to 5 \to 7 \to 8 \to 11.9 \to 12.7 \to 17 \to 19 \to 20 \to 21$$
$$\to 22 \to 24 \to 25 \to 26 \to 27 \to 28 \to 29 \quad (16, 23, 27).$$

A fourth and final approach to the book is from a pleasure-seeker's point of view—that of someone who knows most of the math and is reading the book just to see some interesting concepts and solve some interesting problems. For such casual readers we would recommend a sequence like

$$4.3 \to 5.5 - 5.7 \to 7 \to 8 \to 11.8 \to 16.1 - 16.2$$
$$\to 19 \to 20 \to 23 \to 25.3 \to 28 \to 29$$

as well as the difficult problems in every chapter and the *BIG PICTURE*s.

Of course, we don't here cover all the possible curricula one might create with the book; and even the ones we present here are at best templates, needing modifications to fit any specific situation. Good luck in coming up with your own approach!

Thanks

A large number of individuals and organizations have helped make *the ART of PROBLEM SOLVING* possible. All of the following people and groups made very significant contributions, and we offer our deepest gratitude to them all.

Samuel Vandervelde. Sam is our partner in producing The Mandelbrot Competition; his work in producing the Team Tests still astounds us. In addition to writing these tests, Sam has also written questions for the U.S.A. Mathematical Olympiad. Sam is a 1993 graduate of Swarthmore College and is currently attending the University of Chicago as a graduate student in mathematics. He was a member of the 1989 U.S. International Mathematics Olympiad team, and was a grader for three years at the Math Olympiad Program, a seminar which determines and prepares that team. Many times when trying to find a proof for some theorem, we'll call on Sam and he'll give us three or four. We owe Sam many thanks for his contributions as a mathematician, our partner, and our friend.

Mu Alpha Theta (MAΘ) is a national honor society for high school and junior college mathematics students. Every year, Mu Alpha Theta holds a national convention attended by over 600 students from all over the country. The conventions include competitions, speakers, and the opportunity to meet many fascinating people; many questions included in *the ART of PROBLEM SOLVING* are from convention tests. The location of the convention varies from year to year; some recent sites were New Orleans, LA; Honolulu, HI; Princeton, NJ; and Huntsville, AL. As participants in Mu Alpha Theta conventions throughout high school, the authors highly recommend that students attend. We would also like to thank Mu Alpha Theta for their continued support of The Mandelbrot Competition and give a special thanks to Diane Rubin, who has given us much help and excellent advice. For more information on Mu Alpha Theta, write Mu Alpha Theta, 601 Elm Avenue, Room 423, Norman, OK 73019.

MATHCOUNTS is a nationwide seventh and eighth grade mathematics competition. The competition has three levels—local, state, and national—with the top students from each round proceeding to the next. Over 8,000 schools and 30,000 students are involved each year nationwide. MATHCOUNTS was the starting point in mathematics for one of the authors, and is a great entry into mathematics for seventh and eighth graders. To Barbara Xhajanka, Assistant Director of MATH-COUNTS, we offer an extra thank you for her help. For more information, write to MATHCOUNTS, 1420 King Street, Alexandria, VA 22314-2794.

The Mandelbrot Competition, started in 1990, is produced by Sam Vandervelde and the authors. It is a five round high school competition designed to teach students not only common classroom subjects, but also subjects which usually aren't taught in high school, like number theory and proof techniques. Each round of the competition consists of an Individual Test and a Team Test. The Individual Test is in a short answer format while the Team Test is a series of proofs designed to enhance participants' knowledge of a particular subject area. There are two divisions of the competition, one for beginners and one for more advanced problem solvers. For more information regarding The Mandelbrot Competition, write us at Greater Testing Concepts, P. O. Box 5014, New York, NY 10185.

Dr. George Berzsenyi. We could go on for pages about Dr. Berzsenyi's many contributions to mathematics education through his involvement in competitions and summer programs. He has been involved in writing the AHSME, AIME, and USAMO as well other independent competitions. His current work is the *U.S.A. Mathematics Talent Search* and its international counterpart, in which participating students are given a month to prepare full solutions to five problems in each of four rounds. These solutions are graded by Dr. Berzsenyi and other professors and comments on the papers are returned to the students. The USAMTS is an excellent way for students to learn how to write proofs. For more information on the USAMTS, write to Dr. George Berzsenyi, Department of Mathematics, Rose-Hulman Institute of Technology, 5500 Wabash Ave., Terre Haute, IN 47803.

Dr. Berzsenyi is also an editor and contributor of the **Mathematics and Informatics Quarterly** (M&IQ). In addition to many practice problems, M&IQ contains articles written (in English) by professors all over the world, on various subjects of interest to the high school mathematician. While entirely within the reach of the average student, the articles are fascinating and have shown this text's authors many new approaches to various fields of mahtematics. For more information on M&IQ, write to Dr. George Berzsenyi, Department of Mathematics, Rose-Hulman Institute of Technology, 5500 Wabash Ave., Terre Haute, IN 47803.

The **American Regions Mathematics League** (ARML) is an annual competition in which 15-member teams representing schools, cities, and states compete in short answer, proof, and relay contests. The authors of this text were teammates on the Alabama team at ARML in 1988 and 1989. We highly recommend this experience to students, as they will learn not only about mathematics but also about teamwork. ARML's primary question writers for the tests from which we have drawn are Gilbert Kessler and Lawrence Zimmerman. For more information on ARML, contact Mark Saul, 711 Amsterdam Avenue, New York, New York, 10025.

Mathematical Association of America. The MAA produces the *American High School Mathematics Examination* (AHSME), the *American Invitational Math Exam* (AIME), and the *U.S.A. Math Olympiad* (USAMO). These tests are used to select a group of 24 students to attend the Math Olympiad Program, a one month training seminar which determines the six-student national team. For more information regarding these competitions, contact Dr. Walter Mientka, Executive Director, American Mathematics Competitions, Department of Mathematics and Statistics, University of Nebraska, Lincoln, NE 68588-0658.

Key Curriculum Press produces **The Geometer's Sketchpad**, which was used to generate most of the diagrams in this text. The Sketchpad is an amazing program which forces students to learn geometry while producing fascinating visual output. The Sketchpad can be used to do everything from teaching simple geometric principles in an interactive way to generating complex fractals. For more information on the Geometer's Sketchpad, contact Key Curriculum Press, P.O. Box 2304, Berkeley, CA 94702.

We'd also like to thank **Kai Huang** and **Lauren Williams**, two excellent high school mathematicians, for helping us edit this second edition.

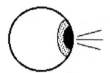 The eye will be found looking at especially important areas of the text. When you see it, pay extra attention.

 The threaded needle indicates particularly difficult problems or concepts. If your hands are too shaky, you may need help from someone else.

 The bomb signals a warning. If you see it, tread lightly through the material it marks, making sure you won't make the mistakes we warn against.

Contents

1 Exponents and Logarithms   **1**

1.1   Integer Exponents 1

1.2   Fractional Exponents 4

1.3   Simplifying Radical Expressions 7

1.4   Rationalizing Denominators 9

1.5   Logarithms 13

2 Complex Numbers   **17**

2.1   The Square Root of -1 17

2.2   Complex Number Operations 18

3 Linear Equations   **22**

3.1   What is a Linear Equation? 22

3.2   One Equation, One Variable 23

3.3   Two Equations, Two Variables 24

3.4   Word Problems 28

4 Proportions   **36**

4.1   Direct and Inverse 36

4.2   Manipulating Proportions 39

4.3   Conversion Factors 40

4.4   Percent 43

5 Using the Integers   **51**

5.1   Divisibility   51
5.2   Number Bases   52
5.3   The Last Digit   55
5.4   Modular Arithmetic   55
5.5   Tricks   59
5.6   Primes   61
5.7   Common and Uncommon Factors   63

6   Quadratic Equations   **69**
6.1   What's a Quadratic?   69
6.2   Factoring Quadratics   69
6.3   The Quadratic Formula   74
6.4   Variations on a Theme   78
      6.4.1   Rearrangements   78
      6.4.2   Substitutions   80
6.5   Square Roots of Irrationals and Imaginaries   81
6.6   Beyond Quadratics   84

7   Special Factorizations and Clever Manipulations   **89**
7.1   Factorizations   89
7.2   Manipulations   93

8   What Numbers Really Are   **99**
8.1   Integers and Rationals   99
8.2   Lowest Terms and Irrationals 102
8.3   Complex and Beyond 104

9   An Introduction to Circles   **107**

10 Angles   **111**
10.1 Lines, Rays, and Segments 111
10.2 Classification and Measurement 111
10.3 Angles and Parallel Lines 113
10.4 Arcs, Segments, Sectors, and Angles 115

10.5 Angles Formed By Lines Intersecting a Circle 116

10.6 The Burden of Proof 119

11 Triangles, a.k.a. Geometry   123

11.1 Classifying Triangles 123

11.2 Parts of a Triangle 124

11.3 The Triangle Inequality 127

11.4 The Pythagorean Theorem 128

11.5 Congruent Triangles 131

11.6 Similar Triangles 135

11.7 Introduction to Trigonometry 139

11.8 Area of a Triangle 144

11.9 A Handful of Helpful Hints 149

12 Quadrilaterals   157

12.1 The Fundamentals 157

12.2 Trapezoids 158

12.3 Parallelograms 160

12.4 Rhombuses (Rhombi?) 162

12.5 Rectangles and Squares 163

12.6 Hints and Problems 165

13 Polygons   169

13.1 Types of Polygons 169

13.2 Angles in a Polygon 170

13.3 Regular Polygons 171

13.4 Regular Hexagons 173

14 Angle Chasing   176

15 Areas   179

15.1 Similar Figures 179

15.2 Same Base/Same Altitude 180

15.3 Complicated Figures 182

16 The Power of Coordinates **189**

   16.1 Labeling the Plane 189

   16.2 What's it Good For? 191

   16.3 Straight and Narrow 192

   16.4 Plotting a Line 197

   16.5 The Distance Formula and Circles 198

   16.6 Went Down to the Crossroads... 200

   16.7 ...Fell Down on My Knees 201

17 Power of a Point **205**

   17.1 Introduction 205

   17.2 Power of a Point Proofs 208

18 Three Dimensional Geometry **211**

   18.1 Planes, Surface Area, and Volume 211

   18.2 Spheres 212

   18.3 Cubes and Boxes 213

   18.4 Prisms and Cylinders 217

   18.5 Pyramids and Cones 219

   18.6 Polyhedra 221

   18.7 How to Solve 3D Problems 223

19 Shifts, Turns, Flips, Stretches, and Squeezes **228**

   19.1 Translation 228

   19.2 Rotation 229

   19.3 Reflection 231

   19.4 Distortion 233

   19.5 Dilation 233

   19.6 The More Things Change... 235

   19.7 Transformation Proofs 236

20 A Potpourri of Geometry **239**

21 Functions **246**

21.1 Welcome to the Machine 246

21.2 Graphing Functions 247

21.3 Inputs and Outputs 248

21.4 Even and Odd 250

21.5 Some Special Functions 252

    21.5.1 Absolute Values 252

    21.5.2 Floored 253

    21.5.3 Split Up 254

21.6 Transforming a Function 255

22 Inequalities   **259**

22.1 What They Do 259

22.2 Linear Inequalities 261

22.3 Quadratic Inequalities 262

22.4 Absolute Value Inequalities 265

22.5 A Trivial Inequality 266

23 Operations and Relations   **270**

23.1 What is an Operation? 270

23.2 Properties of Operations 271

23.3 Relations 273

24 Sequences and Series   **277**

24.1 Arithmetic Series 277

24.2 Geometric Series 279

24.3 Infinite Series 280

24.4 $\displaystyle\sum_{i=1}^{n}$ 282

24.5 Sequences 284

24.6 Sequences and Means 286

25 Learning to Count   **291**

25.1 What's to Learn? 291

25.2 Multiplication 292

25.3 Example: The Number of Divisors 293

25.4 Restrictions on Multiplication 294

25.5 Permutations, Arrangements, and ! 296

25.6 Mixing it Up 299

25.7 Counting the Wrong Thing, Part I 301

25.8 Counting the Wrong Thing, Part II 301

25.9 Doing it Another Way 306

25.10 The Binomial Theorem 306

26 Statistics and Probability   **311**

26.1 Statistics 311

26.2 Probability and Common Sense 313

26.3 Multiplying Probabilities 316

26.4 Casework 318

26.5 Odds 319

26.6 What Did You Expect? 320

27 Sets   **325**

27.1 Some Definitions 325

27.2 Operating on Sets 326

27.3 Venn Diagrams 327

27.4 Subsets 330

28 Prove It   **334**

28.1 Words, Words, Words 334

28.2 Contradiction 338

28.3 Converses Aren't Necessarily True 338

28.4 Mathematical Induction 339

28.5 Shooting Holes in Pigeons 341

28.6 Convincing But Wrong 342

29 Parting Shots   **348**

Chapter 1

Exponents and Logarithms

1.1   Integer Exponents

Multiplication is simply a shorthand for repeated addition. Instead of writing $2 + 2 + 2 + 2 + 2$, we can write $5 \cdot 2$. Similarly, $x + x + x + x = 4x$.

Just as we have a shorthand for repeated addition, we have a simple way of writing repeated multiplication. Instead of writing $2 \cdot 2 \cdot 2 \cdot 2 \cdot 2$, we can write 2^5 to mean the product of five 2's. Similarly, $x \cdot x \cdot x \cdot x$ is x^4, the product of four x's.

In an expression like 2^5, the 2 is called the **base** and the 5 is the **exponent** or **power**. This is sometimes read "Two to the fifth power" or "Two raised to the fifth power." A number which is raised to the second power is said to be **squared** and to the third power is said to be **cubed**. When you study finding the area of squares (page 164) and the volume of cubes (page 213), you'll understand the source of these names. Let's examine some properties of powers.

EXAMPLE 1-1   What is $2^5 \cdot 2^6$?

Solution: The first term in the product is the product of five 2's and the second is the product of six 2's, so altogether, we have the product of eleven 2's. Thus $2^5 \cdot 2^6 = 2^{11} = \textbf{2048}$.

EXAMPLE 1-2   What is $\dfrac{3^{15}}{3^{12}}$?

Solution: Evaluating the numerator and denominator and then performing the division is long, tedious, and leaves much room for error. We instead note that the twelve 3's on the bottom cancel with twelve of the fifteen threes on top (because $\frac{3}{3} = 1$), leaving three 3's on the top:

$$\frac{3 \cdot 3 \cdot 3 \cdot 3 \cdot 3 \cdot 3 \cdot 3 \cdot 3 \cdot 3 \cdot 3 \cdot 3 \cdot 3 \cdot 3 \cdot 3 \cdot 3}{3 \cdot 3 \cdot 3 \cdot 3 \cdot 3 \cdot 3 \cdot 3 \cdot 3 \cdot 3 \cdot 3 \cdot 3 \cdot 3} = \frac{3 \cdot 3 \cdot 3}{1} = \mathbf{27}.$$

From these examples we see that when we multiply two expressions with the same base, we *add* their exponents, and when we divide two expressions with the same base we *subtract* exponents. This is analogous to the relationship between multiplication and addition. (Do you see why?)

What about $3^6/3^8$? Following our above rules, this equals $3^{6-8} = 3^{-2}$, an expression with a negative exponent! What has happened here is that the six 3's on top cancel with six on the bottom, leaving two on the bottom. Thus, a negative exponent means the extra numbers are in the denominator. This means

$$\frac{3^6}{3^8} = 3^{6-8} = 3^{-2} = \frac{1}{3^2} = \frac{1}{9}.$$

When dealing with problems involving multiplication and division of expressions with negative exponents, we can treat them just as the expressions with positive exponents, for example $x^3 x^{-2} = x^1 = x$ and $x^3/x^{-2} = x^{3-(-2)} = x^5$.

Now you should be comfortable multiplying and dividing exponential expressions with integer exponents. WARNING: We can only apply our rules regarding multiplication and division when the bases of the expressions are the same.

EXAMPLE 1-3   What is the difference between $\dfrac{5^5 + 5^2}{5}$ and $\dfrac{(5^5)(5^2)}{5}$?

Solution: The difference here is a very important one. In the first expression, 5 must be divided into each term of the numerator, so we write the expression as

$$\frac{5^5 + 5^2}{5} = \frac{5^5}{5} + \frac{5^2}{5} = 5^4 + 5.$$

In the second, the 5 in the denominator need only be divided into one of the factors, and the expression can be written

$$\frac{(5^5)(5^2)}{5} = 5^5\left(\frac{5^2}{5}\right) = (5^5)(5).$$

You will see the importance of this when you start working with expressions like $(3 + x)/3$ and $3x/3$. The first is not reducible, but the second equals x, as the 3's cancel.

EXERCISE 1-1   Evaluate each of the following.

    i. 3^4

   iii. $5^{-3}5^55^{-1}$

    v. $2^7/2^2$

  vii. $2^53^22^{-3}$

    ii. 2^52^2

   iv. $4^3/4$

   vi. $(3^43^{-2})/(3^53^{-2})$

  viii. $5^23^{-1}2^45^{-1}2^{-2}$

What if an exponent is 0? Consider 3^0. This could result from $3^3/3^3 = 3^{3-3} = 3^0$. Clearly, the numerator and denominator of the initial fraction are the same, so the initial fraction equals 1. Thus any nonzero number raised to the zero power equals 1. WARNING: What about 0^0? We can't determine that it is 1 with the above method, because we can't let 0 be in the denominator of a fraction. Thus, 0^0 is undefined. Similarly, zero raised to any negative power is undefined. Of course, 0 raised to any positive power is always 0 because the product of any number of 0's is always zero.

How about $(2^3)^5$? This is the product of five 2^3's; we multiply three 2's five times, for a total of fifteen 2's. Thus $(2^3)^5 = 2^{15}$. Hence, when an exponential expression is raised to a power, we multiply the exponent of the expression by the power to which the expression is raised.

EXAMPLE 1-4   Evaluate $(3^5)^2$ and $(4^{-3})^{-2}$.

    Solution:

$$(3^5)^2 = 3^{5\cdot2} = \mathbf{3^{10}}.$$

$$(4^{-3})^{-2} = 4^{(-3)(-2)} = \mathbf{4^6}.$$

EXAMPLE 1-5   What is the difference between 2^{3^4} and $(2^3)^4$?

   Solution: In 2^{3^4}, the exponent itself is raised to the fourth power, while in $(2^3)^4$, the entire expression 2^3 is raised to the fourth power. Thus,

$$2^{3^4} = 2^{81}, \quad \text{but} \quad (2^3)^4 = 2^{3 \cdot 4} = 2^{12}.$$

Clearly these expressions are different. WARNING: Always be sure you know which is intended! Expressions like 2^{3^4} are rare, but when they occur, know what they mean.

1.2   Fractional Exponents

Now we've covered all possible integer exponents, but what about fractional exponents? For example, what is $25^{1/2}$? We know that $5^2 = 25$, and if we take the leap of faith that all our previous rules hold for fractional powers as well, we can raise each side to the $1/2$ power:

$$(5^2)^{1/2} = 25^{1/2}.$$

Since $(5^2)^{1/2} = 5^{2(1/2)} = 5^1 = 5$, we then have $25^{1/2} = 5$.

   The exponent $1/2$ has a special name, the **square root**, and it also has a special symbol associated with it, $\sqrt{}$. (This symbol is called a **radical**.) Thus we write

$$25^{1/2} = \sqrt{25} = 5.$$

When asked for the square root of a number, say 81, we find the number which, when squared, equals 81. Since we get 81 when we square 9, $\sqrt{81} = 9$.

EXAMPLE 1-6   Which two integers is $\sqrt{55}$ between?

   Solution: Since $\sqrt{49} = 7$ is smaller than $\sqrt{55}$ and $\sqrt{64} = 8$ is larger, we know that $\sqrt{55}$ is between **7** and **8**.

When dealing with other powers which are reciprocals of integers, like 1/3, 1/4, 1/5, and so on, we proceed just as with square roots. When asked for the fifth root of 100000, we want the number which, when raised to the fifth power, equals 100000. Since $10^5 = 100000$, we have $100000^{1/5} = 10$. We can adapt the radical sign to use with other roots by writing $\sqrt[n]{\ }$ for the nth root. For example, $8^{1/7}$ is $\sqrt[7]{8}$. (When no number is written where the 7 is, then the symbol is assumed to be the square root.) As with square roots, numbers raised to the 1/3 power have a special name, **cube roots**.

When working with fractional powers in which the numerator is not 1, we use our rule for raising exponential expressions to powers *backwards*. This is a little tricky, and it looks like this:

$$8^{2/3} = 8^{(1/3)(2)} = (8^{1/3})^2 = (2)^2 = 4.$$

We find the fractional root first, then we raise the result to the power of the numerator, even if the numerator is negative. This takes practice, but you'll soon be able to handle expressions like this in your head quite swiftly.

EXAMPLE 1-7   Consider the following examples:

   i. $8^{5/3} = (8^{1/3})^5 = 2^5 = \mathbf{32}$.

   ii. $(\sqrt{8})^{2/3} = (8^{1/2})^{2/3} = 8^{(1/2)(2/3)} = 8^{1/3} = \mathbf{2}$.

   iii. $\sqrt[4]{81^{-3}} = 81^{-3/4} = (81^{1/4})^{-3} = 3^{-3} = \dfrac{1}{3^3} = \dfrac{\mathbf{1}}{\mathbf{27}}$.

   iv. $\left(\dfrac{1}{8}\right)^{2/3} = \dfrac{1^{2/3}}{8^{2/3}} = \dfrac{1^2}{2^2} = \dfrac{\mathbf{1}}{\mathbf{4}}$.   (Note that 1 raised to *any* power is always 1.)

EXAMPLE 1-8   Evaluate $\dfrac{(4^{2/3})(2^{1/6})(3^{3/2})}{(2^{-1/2})(3^{1/2})}$.

Solution: Just because the exponents are fractions doesn't mean we can't use all our rules for multiplication and division. First, we convert all the expressions to the simplest base possible (by writing $4^{2/3} = (2^2)^{2/3} = 2^{4/3}$), then we simplify the expression using our rules for multiplication and division of expressions with a common base:

$$\frac{(4^{2/3})(2^{1/6})(3^{3/2})}{(2^{-1/2})(3^{1/2})} = \frac{(2^{4/3})(2^{1/6})(3^{3/2})}{(2^{-1/2})(3^{1/2})} = 2^{4/3+1/6-(-1/2)}3^{3/2-1/2} = (2^2)(3) = \mathbf{12}.$$

EXERCISE 1-2   Try these.

i. $9^{3/2}$

ii. $\left(\sqrt[3]{81}\right)^{3/2}$

iii. $64^{-4/3}$

iv. $\sqrt[5]{100000^3}$

v. $(4/9)^{(-3/2)}$

vi. $\sqrt[4]{(1/16)^{-3}}$

WARNING: You may have realized that 5 is not the only number which, when squared, equals 25. In fact, -5 squared equals 25 as well. So, if you are asked for the square root of 25, what will you answer? In general, always give the positive root.

A good rule of thumb is: if the radical sign or the fractional power was in the problem to start with, then we are only looking for the positive root; if we force the problem to have a fractional exponent, then we must find all answers. The difference is the phrasing of the question. If asked for the square root of 25, we answer 5, because the problem involves a fractional power. If asked what number squared is 25, we give 5 and -5 as the answers, because the problem involves no fractional powers. Also, when asked to "find *all* values," we obviously include both positive and negative solutions. This is a ticky-tacky detail at best, but it is best to remove all confusion as early as possible.

EXAMPLE 1-9   What is the difference between $x^2 = 9$ and $x = \sqrt{9}$?

Solution: In the first, we are asked what numbers squared are 9, so x can be 3 or -3. We write this as $x = \pm 3$. In the second, $x = 3$, because x is *the* square root of 9, which implies the positive value. This is just another example of our rule that *if the radical sign or fractional power is already there, only give the positive solution; if not, give all solutions.*

We only run into the difficulty of multiple real roots for even powers. For odd powers there is no confusion, because negative numbers raised to an odd power are negative and positive numbers raised to an odd power are positive. For example, the only real number which cubed equals 8 is 2, because -2 cubed is -8.

EXAMPLE 1-10   What is the difference between $(-1)^{1/2}$ and $-1^{1/2}$?

Solution: The first denotes the square root of -1, while the second asks for the negative of the square root of 1. This is very clear if we write the two in radical notation: the first is $\sqrt{-1}$, while the second is $-\sqrt{1}$. There is a big difference between the two. There is no real number which equals the first, while the second is equal to -1.

EXERCISE 1-3   Find all real x in each of the following.

i. $x = (-2)^5$ ii. $x = \sqrt[3]{-1/8}$
iii. $x^6 = 64$ iv. $x^3 = 64$
v. $x = (-27)^{-2/3}$ vi. $x^{5/3} = 243$

1.3   Simplifying Radical Expressions

What is the square root of 8? After thinking for a moment, you'll decide that there is no integer that can be squared to give 8. Perhaps we could just write $\sqrt{8}$ and go on. However, since $8 = 4 \cdot 2$, we could write

$$\sqrt{8} = (8)^{1/2} = (4 \cdot 2)^{1/2} = 4^{1/2} \cdot 2^{1/2} = 2 \cdot 2^{1/2} = 2\sqrt{2}.$$

We almost always write $2\sqrt{2}$ rather than $\sqrt{8}$ because, for one thing, simplifications such as $\sqrt{8}/2 = (2\sqrt{2})/2 = \sqrt{2}$ are much easier to see this way.

In a radical expression, all factors that can be removed from the radical should be removed. We do this by writing the prime factorization (page 62) of the number under the radical. (The number under the radical is called the **radicand**.) Thus to find $\sqrt{96}$ we write

$$\sqrt{96} = \sqrt{2^5 \cdot 3}.$$

If the expression isn't already in exponential notation (rather than using the radical sign), we write it as such:

$$\sqrt{2^5 \cdot 3} = (2^5 \cdot 3)^{1/2}.$$

We next apply the root (1/2 in the above example) to each factor separately:

$$(2^5 \cdot 3)^{1/2} = (2^5)^{1/2} \cdot 3^{1/2} = 2^{5/2} \cdot 3^{1/2}.$$

We then evaluate any of the resulting expressions which have integral exponents. If any of the powers of the remaining factors are greater than one, we split the expression into a product of the factor with an integer exponent and the factor with a fractional coefficient less than one. Thus $2^{5/2}$ becomes $(2^2)(2^{1/2})$. We evaluate all parts with integer exponents, then combine everything with fractional exponents into a single expression.

Completing our example,

$$2^{5/2} \cdot 3^{1/2} = 2^2 \cdot 2^{1/2} \cdot 3^{1/2} = 4 \cdot 2^{1/2} \cdot 3^{1/2} = 4(2 \cdot 3)^{1/2} = 4\sqrt{6}.$$

With practice, you'll be able to do this much more quickly.

Here's how I would simplify $\sqrt{96}$ in my mind: I try to find perfect squares which divide 96. I know $96 = 16(6)$, so $\sqrt{96} = \sqrt{16(6)} = \sqrt{16}\sqrt{6} = 4\sqrt{6}$. Since I know there are no squares besides 1 that divide 6, I know I'm done. You'll agree that this method is quicker than the above step-by-step method, but our first method never fails, whereas the "inspection" method we've described is unreliable until you become experienced. Try some of the following examples using the rigorous method, then by inspection. It shouldn't take long to become pretty good at these.

EXAMPLE 1-11 Simplify $\sqrt{1440}$, $\sqrt[3]{\dfrac{144}{125}}$, and $\sqrt[6]{6912}$.

Solution: The prime factorization of 1440 is $2^5 \cdot 3^2 \cdot 5$. Following the method we have described, we have

$$\begin{aligned}
\sqrt{1440} &= (2^5 \cdot 3^2 \cdot 5)^{1/2} = (2^5)^{1/2}(3^2)^{1/2}(5)^{1/2} = (2^{5/2})(3^{2/2})(5^{1/2}) \\
&= (2^{5/2})(3^1)(5^{1/2}) = 3\left[(2^2)(2^{1/2})(5^{1/2})\right] = 3(4)2^{1/2}5^{1/2} = \mathbf{12\sqrt{10}}.
\end{aligned}$$

By inspection, since 144 is a perfect square which divides 1440, we obtain $\sqrt{1440} = \sqrt{144}\sqrt{10} = 12\sqrt{10}$. Much quicker.

Let's move on to the second one. When dealing with a fraction, first simplify the fraction, then work on the numerator and denominator separately. Thus,

$$\begin{aligned}
\sqrt[3]{\frac{144}{125}} &= \frac{\sqrt[3]{144}}{\sqrt[3]{125}} = \frac{(2^4 \cdot 3^2)^{1/3}}{(5^3)^{1/3}} = \frac{(2^{4/3})(3^{2/3})}{5^{3/3}} \\
&= \frac{2^1 \cdot 2^{1/3} \cdot 3^{2/3}}{5^1} = \left(\frac{2}{5}\right)\left((2^{1/3})(3^{2/3})\right) = \frac{2}{5}\sqrt[3]{(2)(3^2)} \\
&= \mathbf{\frac{2}{5}\sqrt[3]{18}.}
\end{aligned}$$

How would you attack this by inspection?

For the third one, inspection is at a loss. We turn to our method:

$$\sqrt[6]{6912} = (2^8 \cdot 3^3)^{1/6} = 2^{4/3} \cdot 3^{1/2} = 2(2^{1/3} \cdot 3^{1/2}) = 2(2^{2/6} \cdot 3^{3/6}) = 2\sqrt[6]{4(27)} = \mathbf{2\sqrt[6]{108}}.$$

Notice that we reduced the fractional exponents ($8/6 = 4/3$) before removing the integer parts; this keeps us from missing simplifications of expressions like $\sqrt[4]{9} = (3^2)^{1/4} = 3^{1/2} = \sqrt{3}$. If we don't simplify the $2/4$, we might come to the erroneous conclusion that $\sqrt[4]{9}$ is irreducible.

EXERCISE 1-4 Find the following.

    i. $\sqrt{27}$ ii. $\sqrt[3]{128}$

  iii. $\sqrt[4]{1600}$ iv. $\sqrt{9095625}$

   v. $\sqrt[3]{\dfrac{36000}{243}}$ vi. $\sqrt{\dfrac{56}{126}}$

1.4   Rationalizing Denominators

Rationalizing denominators is exactly what it sounds like: making the denominators of fractions rational. A rational number is a number which can be expressed as the ratio of two integers, i.e. a fraction. When rationalizing denominators, we usually make the denominator an integer. For example, consider the expression $1/\sqrt{2}$. If we multiply the numerator and the denominator by $\sqrt{2}$, we have

$$\frac{1}{\sqrt{2}} = \frac{1}{\sqrt{2}} \cdot 1 = \frac{1}{\sqrt{2}} \cdot \frac{\sqrt{2}}{\sqrt{2}} = \frac{\sqrt{2}}{2}.$$

As you can see, multiplying the numerator and denominator of a fraction by the same value doesn't change the value of the fraction because it is the same as multiplying by 1. Remember this fact, for we will use it often. Although the expressions $1/\sqrt{2}$ and $\sqrt{2}/2$ are equal, we will almost always use $\sqrt{2}/2$ as the preferred expression because its denominator is a rational number.

We've seen how to handle square roots in the denominator; just multiply the top and the bottom of the fraction by the square root and the denominator is rationalized. For other roots, we must be more crafty. First, we reduce the radical as in the previous section. Then, we split the expression under the radical in the denominator into its prime factors and treat each factor separately. Consider $1/\sqrt[3]{12}$. From our first two steps, we have

$$\frac{1}{\sqrt[3]{12}} = \frac{1}{\sqrt[3]{2^2}\,\sqrt[3]{3}}.$$

To get rid of the $\sqrt[3]{2^2}$, we multiply top and bottom by $\sqrt[3]{2}$:

$$\frac{1}{\sqrt[3]{2^2}\,\sqrt[3]{3}}\left(\frac{\sqrt[3]{2}}{\sqrt[3]{2}}\right) = \frac{\sqrt[3]{2}}{\sqrt[3]{2^3}\,\sqrt[3]{3}} = \frac{\sqrt[3]{2}}{2\sqrt[3]{3}}.$$

To rationalize the $\sqrt[3]{3}$, we multiply by $\sqrt[3]{3^2}$ to make the denominator $2\sqrt[3]{3^3}$:

$$\frac{1}{\sqrt[3]{12}} = \frac{\sqrt[3]{2}}{2\sqrt[3]{3}}\left(\frac{\sqrt[3]{3^2}}{\sqrt[3]{3^2}}\right) = \frac{\sqrt[3]{2}\,\sqrt[3]{3^2}}{2\sqrt[3]{3^3}} = \frac{\sqrt[3]{18}}{2\cdot3} = \frac{\sqrt[3]{18}}{6}.$$

As you may have guessed, we have chosen our multiplying factors to make the exponent of the factor under the radical equal to the root. For example, in our final step above the power of 3 under the radical in $\sqrt[3]{3}$ is 1. To make that power 3, we must multiply by $\sqrt[3]{3^2}$, so that $\sqrt[3]{3}\,\sqrt[3]{3^2} = \sqrt[3]{3^3} = 3$, a rational number. (Remember to multiply the numerator by this factor too.)

EXAMPLE 1-12   Rationalize the denominator of $\dfrac{2\sqrt{5}}{3\sqrt[4]{72}}$.

Solution: First we split everything into prime factors:

$$\frac{2\sqrt{5}}{3\sqrt[4]{72}} = \frac{2\sqrt{5}}{3\sqrt[4]{2^3}\,\sqrt[4]{3^2}}.$$

For the factor 2, we must multiply by $\sqrt[4]{2}$, to get $\sqrt[4]{2^4}$. Likewise, for the factor 3, we multiply by $\sqrt[4]{3^2}$ to get $\sqrt[4]{3^4}$.

$$
\begin{aligned}
\frac{2\sqrt{5}}{3\sqrt[4]{72}} &= \frac{2\sqrt{5}}{3\sqrt[4]{2^3}\,\sqrt[4]{3^2}}\cdot\frac{\sqrt[4]{2}}{\sqrt[4]{2}} = \frac{2\sqrt{5}\,\sqrt[4]{2}}{3\sqrt[4]{2^4}\,\sqrt[4]{3^2}}\\[2mm]
&= \frac{2\sqrt{5}\,\sqrt[4]{2}}{3\cdot2\sqrt[4]{3^2}}\cdot\frac{\sqrt[4]{3^2}}{\sqrt[4]{3^2}} = \frac{2\sqrt{5}\,\sqrt[4]{2}\,\sqrt[4]{3^2}}{6\sqrt[4]{3^4}} = \frac{\sqrt[4]{25}\,\sqrt[4]{2}\,\sqrt[4]{9}}{3\cdot3}\\[2mm]
&= \frac{\sqrt[4]{450}}{9}.
\end{aligned}
$$

Don't feel bad if you need to go through all those equations more than once!

EXERCISE 1-5 Express the following as fractions with rational denominators.

   i. $3/\sqrt{3}$ ii. $\sqrt{2}/\sqrt{6}$
  iii. $2/\sqrt[3]{24}$ iv. $1/\sqrt[4]{1800}$
   v. $5^{1/3}/5^{5/3}$ vi. $(3^{1/2}2^{2/3})/(3^{1/6}2^{3/2})$

What if we have an expression like $1/(1 + \sqrt{2})$? Multiplying top and bottom by $\sqrt{2}$ does little good, as the result is $\sqrt{2}/(\sqrt{2} + 2)$, which still has an irrational denominator. There is, however, a way to rationalize this denominator: we multiply top and bottom by $1 - \sqrt{2}$. What happens? We will see if we expand the product $(1 + \sqrt{2})(1 - \sqrt{2})$, to get

$$(1 + \sqrt{2})(1 - \sqrt{2}) = 1(1 - \sqrt{2}) + \sqrt{2}(1 - \sqrt{2}) = 1 - \sqrt{2} + \sqrt{2} - 2 = -1.$$

The result is rational, and we have

$$\frac{1}{1 + \sqrt{2}} \cdot \frac{1 - \sqrt{2}}{1 - \sqrt{2}} = \frac{1 - \sqrt{2}}{(1 - \sqrt{2})(1 + \sqrt{2})} = \frac{1 - \sqrt{2}}{-1} = \sqrt{2} - 1.$$

The quantity $1 - \sqrt{2}$ is called the **conjugate radical** of $1 + \sqrt{2}$. We find the conjugate radical of a two-term expression by changing the sign in front of one radical term. Multiplying top and bottom by the conjugate radical of an expression in the denominator will always make the denominator rational. This only works for square roots, and only for two-term expressions like $1 + \sqrt{2}$, $3 - 4\sqrt{2}$, $\sqrt{2} - \sqrt{3}$, etc.

EXAMPLE 1-13 Show that the product of $a\sqrt{b} + c\sqrt{d}$ and $a\sqrt{b} - c\sqrt{d}$ is always rational if a, b, c, and d are rational.

Proof: We simply multiply and show that there are no radical signs in the result:

$$\begin{aligned}(a\sqrt{b} + c\sqrt{d})(a\sqrt{b} - c\sqrt{d}) &= a^2b + (a\sqrt{b})(-c\sqrt{d}) + (c\sqrt{d})(a\sqrt{b}) - c^2d \\ &= a^2b - ac\sqrt{bd} + ac\sqrt{bd} - c^2d \\ &= a^2b - c^2d\end{aligned}$$

The result is rational. We can now see why our method of rationalization works: the two terms involving radicals in the expression cancel each other.

EXAMPLE 1-14   What is $\dfrac{\sqrt{2}}{5 - \sqrt{2} - \sqrt{3}}$ when its denominator is rationalized?

Solution: Although the denominator is not a two-term expression, we can treat it like one to get rid of one of the radicals by writing $5 - \sqrt{2} - \sqrt{3}$ as $(5 - \sqrt{2}) - \sqrt{3}$. This suggests multiplying by $(5 - \sqrt{2}) + \sqrt{3}$, which results in

$$\frac{5\sqrt{2} - 2 + \sqrt{6}}{(5 - \sqrt{2})(5 - \sqrt{2}) + (5 - \sqrt{2})(\sqrt{3}) + (-\sqrt{3})(5 - \sqrt{2}) + (-\sqrt{3})(\sqrt{3})}.$$

In the new denominator, we see that the center two terms cancel each other, leaving the outer two terms. Evaluating these we find that we have cleared the denominator of all irrationals except $\sqrt{2}$. (Multiply it out yourself.) Our expression now is

$$\frac{5\sqrt{2} - 2 + \sqrt{6}}{24 - 10\sqrt{2}}.$$

To rationalize the denominator of this expression, we multiply top and bottom by the conjugate of $24 - 10\sqrt{2}$, or $24 + 10\sqrt{2}$. After some simplification, we find that the fraction is

$$\frac{\mathbf{13 + 25\sqrt{2} + 5\sqrt{3} + 6\sqrt{6}}}{\mathbf{94}}.$$

EXERCISE 1-6 Rationalize the denominators of each of the following expressions.

i. $\dfrac{1}{\sqrt{7} + \sqrt{3}}$

ii. $\dfrac{6}{\sqrt{15} - \sqrt{6}}$

iii. $\dfrac{\sqrt{2}}{\sqrt{6} - 2}$

iv. $\dfrac{1}{\sqrt{1 + \sqrt{2}}}$ (Hint: First multiply top and bottom by $\sqrt{1 + \sqrt{2}}$.)

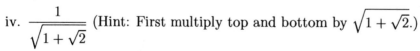

v. $\dfrac{1}{2 - \sqrt[4]{2}}$ (Hint: Let $\sqrt[4]{2} = \sqrt{\sqrt{2}}$.)

As you can see, the previous examples and exercises extend what we have learned about two-term expressions involving square roots to a variety of other types of problems. This is what mathematics is all about: extending one's knowledge in creative ways to solve different types of problems.

1.5 Logarithms

When someone writes $\log_2 8$, they mean the power you have to raise 2 to in order to get 8. Since $2^3 = 8$, we write $\log_2 8 = 3$. This is read, "The logarithm of 8 base 2 is 3." Similarly, since $3^5 = 243$, we can write $\log_3 243 = 5$.

Logarithms are just another way of writing expressions like $3^2 = 9$. Instead of writing that, we can write $\log_3 9 = 2$. To help answer the nagging question of why anyone would want logarithms, see *the BIG PICTURE* which follows this chapter.

The first step in becoming proficient with logarithms is learning how to switch back and forth from **logarithmic notation**, $\log_5 25 = 2$, to **exponential notation**, $5^2 = 25$. The number that is raised to some power in exponential notation (5 in the above example), the **base**, is the small lowered number (the **subscript**) of the logarithm. The exponent (2 above) is the result of the logarithm, and the result of the exponential equation (25 above) is the **argument** of the logarithm. (Don't worry if this seems complicated; it'll make sense when you've played with some logarithms yourself.)

EXERCISE 1-7 Convert the following exponential equations to logarithmic equations.

    i. $3^3 = 27$

   ii. $16^{1/4} = 2$

  iii. $x^z = y$

EXERCISE 1-8 Convert the following logarithmic equations to exponential equations.

    i. $\log_{36} 6 = 1/2$

   ii. $\log_3(1/9) = -2$

  iii. $\log_x y = z$

Solving logarithms is quite simple. We change one question, "What is $\log_7 343$?", to a more understandable one, "To what power do we have to raise 7 to get 343?" The answer is 3. If you don't see this right away, write $x = \log_7 343$ and convert this to exponential notation: $7^x = 343$. Now what is x?

WARNING: The base and the argument of the logarithm must both *always* be positive if the result of the logarithm is to be a real number. As for why arguments can't be negative, consider $\log_3(-3)$. For this to be true, there must be some x such that $3^x = -3$, but any power of a positive number is positive, so this is impossible. Also, when log appears without a base, it is usually assumed to be base 10.

The result of a logarithm, however, can be negative. For example, $\log_2 0.5 = -1$. (Do you see why?)

EXAMPLE 1-15 Evaluate $\log_3 \frac{1}{243}$ and $\log_8 2$.

Solution: Putting the first expression in exponential notation yields $3^x = 1/243$. Since $1/243 = (3)^{-5}$, we have $x = \mathbf{-5}$.

Putting the second expression in exponential notation gives $8^x = 2$. Solving this as in the prior section, we write $8 = 2^3$, so

$$(2^3)^x = 2,$$

yielding $2^{3x} = 2^1$. Two expressions with the same base are equal only if their exponents are equal, so $3x = 1$ and $x = \mathbf{1/3}$.

EXERCISE 1-9 Find each of the following.

   i. $\log_5 625$ ii. $\log_{1/2} 2$
   iii. $\log_9 \sqrt{3}$ iv. $\log_{\sqrt{5}} \sqrt[3]{5}$

Problems to Solve for Chapter 1

(If you do not have experience solving linear equations, read Chapter 3 before attempting problems 9-16.)

1. Find the value of $\log_5 \frac{(125)(625)}{25}$. (AHSME 1950)

2. What is the logarithm of $27\sqrt[4]{9}\sqrt[3]{9}$ base 3? (AHSME 1953)

3. Express $2 + \sqrt{2} + \dfrac{1}{2+\sqrt{2}} + \dfrac{1}{\sqrt{2}-2}$ in simplest form. (AHSME 1958)

4. Find $(-3)^{-2} + (-2)^{-1} + (-1)^0 + 0^1 + 1^2 + 2^3 + 3^4$.

5. Simplify the expression $81^{-(2^{-2})}$. (AHSME 1965)

6. Find, with a rational common denominator, the sum

$$\left(\frac{1}{2}\right)^{-1/2} + \left(\frac{3}{2}\right)^{-3/2} + \left(\frac{5}{2}\right)^{-5/2}$$

7. Write $\dfrac{\sqrt{2}}{\sqrt{2}+\sqrt{3}-\sqrt{5}}$ with a rational denominator. (AHSME 1952)

8. Find $\log_{\sqrt{3}}\sqrt[3]{9}$.

9. Solve for n: $\sqrt{1+\sqrt{2+\sqrt{n}}} = 2$. (MATHCOUNTS 1991)

10. Find x if $2^{16^x} = 16^{2^x}$. (Mandelbrot #3)

11. Solve the equation $\log_{2x} 216 = x$, where x is real. (AHSME 1960)

12. Suppose A and B are positive real numbers for which $\log_A B = \log_B A$. If neither A nor B is 1 and $A \neq B$, find the value of AB. (MAΘ 1992)

13. The formula $N = 8 \cdot 10^8 \cdot x^{-3/2}$ gives, for a certain group, the number of individuals whose income exceeds x dollars. What is the smallest possible value of the lowest income of the wealthiest 800 individuals? (AHSME 1960)

14. Show that if $a \neq c$, $a^x = c^q$ and $c^y = a^z$, then $xy = qz$. (AHSME 1951)

15. Given that $\log_3 2 = 0.631$, find the smallest positive integer a such that $3^a > 2^{102}$. (Hint: Show that $\log_3 2^{102} = 102\log_3 2$.) (Mandelbrot #3)

16. Show that $\log_6 2 + \log_6 3 = 1$.

─the BIG PICTURE─

Although they later came to have all sorts of uses, logarithms were first invented as a trick to do multiplication! John Napier realized in the early 1600's that instead of having to multiply two large numbers M and N, he could, if he knew their logarithms, simply add, because $\log MN = \log M + \log N$. So by constructing a table of logarithms, Napier was actually constructing a simple calculator.

Believe it or not, this technique worked! Tables of logarithms were a standard part of many people's lives for a long time, and the slide rule also operates on this principle.

Besides converting multiplication to addition, logarithms also convert powers to multiplication, as in $\log x^2 = 2 \log x$. This is the basis for logarithmic graph paper: instead of drawing some crazy curve for $y = 2^x$, I can just plot y against the logarithm of the right side, or $x \log 2$, which gives a straight line.

This property of logs also helps us to think about quantities which differ by a huge amount. For example, suppose we had some unit of loudness, the Spinal Tap or ST, such that a normal speaking voice was 1000 ST. Then a whisper might be only 100 ST, while a jet engine could be 1,000,000,000,000 ST. These numbers are just too far apart to think about. So we could take the log base 10 of the quantities instead, so that the voice would be 3 ST, the whisper 2 ST, and the jet 12 ST. Much easier to sink your teeth into. This is the basis for the **decibel**, the usual unit of loudness. The only difference is that decibels (written dB) are for some reason multiplied by 10, so that a whisper is 20 dB and a jet engine 120 dB.

I recently read an article in a newspaper which asserted that a jet engine is *6 times louder* than a whisper. Do you understand the error? How many times louder is the jet really? Spread some mathematical literacy today!

Chapter 2

Complex Numbers

2.1   The Square Root of -1

The study of complex numbers begins when we are bold enough to ask a very childish question: what is the square root of -1? Forbidden by sixth grade teachers the world over, the expression $\sqrt{-1}$ is nevertheless the key to a whole branch of math.

Historically, people were led to write $\sqrt{-1}$ by the quest to solve equations. Clearly, an equation like

$$x^2 + 1 = 0 \qquad (2.1)$$

has only the solutions $x = \pm\sqrt{-1}$. In order to be able to solve *all* equations, it was decided to accept $\sqrt{-1}$ as a legitimate number.

The square root of -1 is usually written as i. This weird number shows its weird properties almost from the beginning, as we shall see. It is not a real number in the mathematical sense. This is not to say it is not real, at least any less than negatives are. If we multiply i by a real number like 2 or π, we get a number like $2i$ or πi; there is no way to simplify this product. Numbers like this, formed by multiplying i by a real, are called **pure imaginary numbers**, though you should not let this prejudice of name keep you from accepting them as regular numbers. Treat the word imaginary as a purely mathematical definition.

If we multiply i by itself, we get $\sqrt{-1}\sqrt{-1} = (\sqrt{-1})^2 = -1$, as we would expect. But notice that if we try to combine the radicals and write $\sqrt{-1}\sqrt{-1} = \sqrt{(-1)^2} = 1$, we will get the wrong answer. Manipulations like this are forbidden.

If we keep taking powers of i we get $i^3 = ii^2 = -i$, $i^4 = ii^3 = i(-i) = -i^2 = 1$,

$i^5 = ii^4 = i$, $i^6 = -1$, etc. The powers of i go in cycles of 4: i, -1, $-i$, 1, i, -1, $-i$, 1, etc.

EXERCISE 2-1   What is i^{17}? How about i^{69}? i^{1972}?

2.2   Complex Number Operations

The so-called **complex numbers** are just the numbers you get when you add a real to an imaginary, like $\sqrt{2} + 3i$ or $-17 + \frac{17}{2}i$. Every real number is also a complex number; the imaginary component is just 0. Those complex numbers which are not real are called **imaginary numbers**. (This is not exactly the same as pure imaginary numbers; can you write a number which is imaginary but not pure imaginary?)

EXAMPLE 2-1   Let's clear up these confusing definitions by looking at some examples. 3 is both real and complex, but not imaginary. $3i$ is not real, but is complex, imaginary, and pure imaginary. $3 + 3i$ is neither real nor pure imaginary, but is imaginary and complex. (We realize this is unnecessarily complicated, but they *are* called complex numbers...)

Complex variables are usually designated by z or w, for no other reason than that letters near the end of the alphabet are best for variables, and x and y are already typically used for reals.

To add two complex numbers together, all we have to do is add their real and imaginary parts separately, as in the following examples.

EXAMPLE 2-2   Let's add $3 + 4i$ to $-3 + 8i$. The sum is just $3 - 3 + 4i + 8i = \mathbf{12i}$.

EXERCISE 2-2   What is $\left(-\frac{1}{4} + i\right) + \left(2 - \frac{3}{4}i\right)$?

EXERCISE 2-3   Find the general formula for the sum $(z_1 + z_2 i) + (w_1 + w_2 i)$.

Subtraction follows easily from addition. Furthermore, we can multiply two complex numbers with the distributive law.

EXAMPLE 2-3 Let's multiply $3 + 4i$ by $-3 + 8i$. The product is

$$
\begin{aligned}
(3 + 4i)(-3 + 8i) &= 3(-3 + 8i) + 4i(-3 + 8i) \\
&= (3)(-3) + (3)(8i) + (4i)(-3) + (4i)(8i) \\
&= -9 + 24i - 12i - 32 = \mathbf{-41 + 12i}.
\end{aligned}
$$

(Note the negative sign of the 32; it comes from i times i.)

EXERCISE 2-4 What is $\left(-\frac{1}{4} + i\right)\left(2 - \frac{3}{4}i\right)$?

EXERCISE 2-5 Find the general formula for the product $(z_1 + z_2 i)(w_1 + w_2 i)$.

EXERCISE 2-6 Simplify $(z_1 + z_2 i)(z_1 - z_2 i)$.

When we divide two complex numbers, we clear all instances of i from the denominator in exactly the same way as rationalizing a denominator which contains square roots. We use the fact that the complex number $a + bi$ multiplied by $a - bi$ is real, just as $a + \sqrt{b}$ multiplied by $a - \sqrt{b}$ gets rid of the square root. (You showed this in Exercise 2-6 above, right?)

EXAMPLE 2-4 Let's divide $3 + 4i$ by $-3 + 8i$. The quotient is

$$
\frac{3 + 4i}{-3 + 8i} = \frac{3 + 4i}{-3 + 8i} \cdot \frac{-3 - 8i}{-3 - 8i} = \frac{23 - 36i}{73} = \frac{\mathbf{23}}{\mathbf{73}} - \frac{\mathbf{36}}{\mathbf{73}}i.
$$

EXERCISE 2-7 What is $\dfrac{-\frac{1}{4} + i}{2 - \frac{3}{4}i}$?

EXERCISE 2-8 Find the general formula for the quotient $(z_1 + z_2 i)/(w_1 + w_2 i)$.

We can do more complicated operations, like taking square or cube roots of complex numbers, but we'll let that wait for now. We should define a couple of basic notations, however. Consider an arbitrary complex number $z = a + bi$. We denote the number $a - bi$ by $\bar{z}$, and call it the **conjugate** of z. We call the number a the **real part** of z, and denote it by $\operatorname{Re}(z)$. Similarly, the number bi is the **imaginary part** of z. WARNING: The expression $\operatorname{Im}(z)$ refers to the real coefficient of this imaginary part, not the imaginary part itself. Thus $\operatorname{Im}(a + bi) = b$, NOT bi.

EXERCISE 2-9   Prove that $\overline{\overline{z}} = z$ for all complex z.

EXERCISE 2-10   What is the conjugate of a real number a? of a pure imaginary number bi?

EXERCISE 2-11   Show that $\overline{z + w} = \overline{z} + \overline{w}$ for all z and w. Does this fact surprise you?

EXERCISE 2-12   Show that $\overline{zw} = \overline{z}\,\overline{w}$ for all z and w. Does this surprise you?

EXERCISE 2-13   How about $\overline{(z/w)}$? Surprising?

EXAMPLE 2-5   Consider $\text{Im}(z) + \text{Im}(\overline{z})$. Let $z = a + bi$, so that $\overline{z} = a - bi$. Then $\text{Im}(z) = b$ and $\text{Im}(\overline{z}) = -b$, so that $\text{Im}(z) + \text{Im}(\overline{z}) = 0$, no matter what z is.

EXERCISE 2-14   What is $\text{Re}(z) + i\,\text{Im}(z)$?

Problems to Solve for Chapter 2

17. Find $\dfrac{1 + i}{3 - i}$. (MAΘ 1987)

18. Which are true? (MAΘ 1987) (Don't look back at the text!)

$$
\begin{aligned}
&\text{i)} && \overline{z_1 + z_2} = \overline{z_1} + \overline{z_2} \\
&\text{ii)} && \overline{z_1 z_2} = \overline{z_1}\,\overline{z_2} \\
&\text{iii)} && \overline{z_1 / z_2} = \overline{z_1}/\overline{z_2}
\end{aligned}
$$

19. Evaluate $\sqrt{-1}\left(\sqrt{-1}\right)^2\sqrt{(-1)^2}$. (MAΘ 1991)

20. Find $i^{-18} + i^{-9} + i^0 + i^9 + i^{18}$. (MAΘ 1991)

21. Find $\text{Re}\left[(a + bi)(c + di)\right]$ in terms of a, b, c, and d. (MAΘ 1991)

22. Evaluate $(2 + i)^3$. (MAΘ 1991)

23. Find $(1 + i)^4(2 - 2i)^3$. (MAΘ 1987)

24. Simplify $\dfrac{\sqrt{-6}\sqrt{2}}{\sqrt{3}}$. (MAΘ 1990)

25. If $F(x) = 3x^3 - 2x^2 + x - 3$, find $F(1+i)$. (MAΘ 1990)

26. Which of the following are true? (MAΘ 1987)

$$\text{i)} \quad \overline{z + 3i} = z - 3i$$
$$\text{ii)} \quad \overline{iz} = -i\overline{z}$$
$$\text{iii)} \quad (2+i)^2 = \overline{3 - 4i}$$

Chapter 3

Linear Equations

3.1 What is a Linear Equation?

Any time we write something with an equal sign, we write an equation. Any quantity in an equation which we do not know is called a **variable**, while anything in an equation which can take on only one value is called a **constant**. When a variable term is multiplied by a constant, the constant is called the term's **coefficient**. For example, in the equation $3x + y = 2$, x and y are variables, 2 is a constant term, and 3 is the coefficient of x.

The **degree** of a term is the sum of the powers of the variables in that term. For example, the degree of x is one, and the degree of xy^2 is three. The degree of an equation is the highest degree of the terms in the equation.

The simplest type of equation is the **linear equation**. A linear equation is an equation whose degree is one. There are also no variables raised to fractional powers. For example, $x + \sqrt{x} = 3$ is not linear.

EXAMPLE 3-1 Which of these equations are linear?

  i. $x^2 + y = 4$

This equation has degree two, so it is not linear.

  ii. $xy = 4$

This equation also has degree two, so is not linear.

  iii. $x + y + z + w = 0$

This has degree one and thus is linear.

iv. $3^x + y = 0$

Because of the 3^x term, we can't define a degree for this equation, and it is not linear. This is also true of equations with trigonometric functions (page 139) and logarithms.

3.2   One Equation, One Variable

Let's start with linear equations in one variable, like $x + 4 = 5$ and $3y + 4 = -5$. We solve these with two steps: first move all the constants to one side of the equation and the variable to the other by subtraction and addition; then divide both sides by the coefficient of the variable.

EXAMPLE 3-2   Solve the equation $3x + 5 = 11 + x$ for x.

Solution: First, subtract 5 from both sides to get

$$3x = 6 + x.$$

Now subtract x from both sides to get

$$2x = 6.$$

Finally, divide by the coefficient, 2, of x to get

$$x = \mathbf{3}.$$

This gives the solution to our equation. It's a good idea to check the answer once you have solved an equation. To do this, just substitute 3 for x in the equation and make sure it works: $3(3) + 5 = 14 = 11 + 3$, so our answer is correct.

EXAMPLE 3-3   Solve the equation $ax + b = c$ for x, where a, b, and c are constants.

Solution: Remember that a, b, and c are just constants here, even though they are letters. Our first step is to subtract b from both sides to get

$$ax = c - b;$$

then we divide by a to get

$$x = \frac{c - b}{a}.$$

EXAMPLE 3-4   Solve for y:

$$\frac{1+y}{y} = 3.$$

Solution: Although this isn't linear, we can make it so my multiplying both sides of the equation by y, getting

$$1 + y = 3y.$$

Collecting y terms on one side yields $2y = 1$, so dividing by 2 yields $y = \mathbf{1/2}$.

EXERCISE 3-1   Solve for y: $3y + 2 = y - 3 + 4y$.

EXERCISE 3-2   Solve for y: $\dfrac{2y}{3} - 3 = y$.

3.3   Two Equations, Two Variables

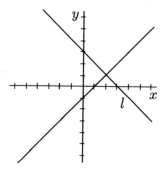

Now that we can solve one variable equations, we move on to equations with two variables. For example, try solving the equation $x + y = 3$ for x and y. We write a solution to this equation as an **ordered pair** (x, y). Thus, we see that $(3, 0)$ works for the equation, but so does $(0, 3)$, $(6, -3)$, and $(1, 2)$. In fact, there are infinitely many solutions to this equation. As discussed on page 192, when all the solutions to $x + y = 3$ are plotted on a grid as shown at right, line l is formed.

Now, suppose we say that in addition to $x + y = 3$, we also know that $x - y = 1$. Both of these equations describe lines (as discussed on page 197), which are shown to the right. The only place where both equations are true is where the two lines meet.

There are two standard ways to solve these **systems of equations**.

Substitution

The method of substitution involves solving one equation for one of the variables in terms of the other. For our problem, this means solving for x in the equation $x + y =$

3. When we say "solve for x", we mean put the equation in the form

$$x = \text{something not involving } x.$$

We do this just like in our one variable problems before. Thus $x+y = 3$ becomes $x = 3-y$. If we substitute this in place of x in the other equation, we get $(3-y)-y = 1$, so $y = 1$ and $x = 3 - y = 2$.

Elimination

The elimination method involves adding multiples of the two equations together to cancel one of the variables. For example, if we simply add the equations $x + y = 3$ and $x - y = 1$, we get

$$(x + y) + (x - y) = 3 + 1,$$

or

$$2x = 4.$$

Thus, $x = 2$ and we can substitute this in either of the original equations to get $y = 1$. As you see, we have "eliminated" y from the two equations by adding them together to get an equation involving only x.

Usually elimination is not as simple as just adding the equations together. In most cases, we must modify one or both of the equations before adding them together.

EXAMPLE 3-5 Solve the system

$$
\begin{aligned}
2x + 3y &= -1 \\
3x - 4y &= 7
\end{aligned}
$$

by both elimination and substitution.

Solution: We'll try elimination first. Simply adding these equations gives $5x - y = 6$, which doesn't help us at all; we must first modify the equations. If we multiply the first by -3 and the second by 2, we will get

$$
\begin{aligned}
-6x - 9y &= 3 \\
6x - 8y &= 14.
\end{aligned}
$$

Adding these gives $-17y = 17$, so $(x, y) = (1, -1)$. We can check this by substituting $x = 1$ and $y = -1$ into both the equations and making sure they both hold.

If we do this problem by substitution, we have

$$x = -1/2 - 3y/2$$

from rearranging the first equation. Substituting in the second equation yields

$$3(-1/2 - 3y/2) - 4y = 7,$$

from which we find y and then x.

In the elimination portion of the prior example, how did we decide to multiply the first equation by -3 and the second by 2? In general, when you have two equations, if you multiply the second by the coefficient of one of the variables in the first, and multiply the first by the *negative* of the coefficient of that variable in the second equation, you will then be able to eliminate that variable by adding the resulting equations. (Read that sentence closely and compare it to the example.)

To prove this in general, let the two equations be $a_1 x + a_2 y = a_3$ and $b_1 x + b_2 y = b_3$, where all the a's and b's are constants. Multiply the first equation by $-b_1$ and the second by a_1. Add the resulting equations. What happens?

When using elimination, you can solve the problem by eliminating either variable, just as with substitution you can substitute for either variable.

Now, there are two special cases of systems of two equations in which we cannot always find a single pair (x, y) to solve the equation. These two cases are demonstrated in the following examples.

EXAMPLE 3-6   Solve the system of equations

$$\begin{aligned} 2x - 4y &= 7 \\ x - 2y &= 2. \end{aligned}$$

Solution: If we try elimination we will get the astonishing result $0 = 3$. (Try it.) Since this can never be true, we deduce that there are never any solutions to this system. Indeed, if we graph the lines, we will find that they are parallel. Since parallel lines never intersect, the system can have **no solutions**.

EXAMPLE 3-7   Solve the system of equations

$$2x - 2y = 6$$
$$x - y = 3.$$

Solution: If we try elimination here, we get $0 = 0$. This means that the equations are identical; in fact, the first equation is exactly twice the second. They describe the same line! All the solutions to one equation are also solutions to the other, so there are **infinitely many** solutions.

A system of two equations will always fall into one of these categories if we can multiply one equation by some number to make its coefficients the same as the other equation. In the two examples above, the coefficients of the first equation are double those of the second. This means the lines described by the two equations are parallel; hence, they either never intersect (the first example) or they are the same line (the second).

WARNING: Always substitute your solution back into the original equations to check that your answer is correct.

EXAMPLE 3-8   Find (x, y) such that $2x = 2y - 4$ and $2y = 2 + x$.

Solution: First, we group all the x terms together and all the y terms together on one side as shown:

$$2x - 2y = -4$$
$$-x + 2y = 2.$$

(Make sure you see that these two equations are the same as the original equations.) We see that adding these together will eliminate y, to give $x = -2$, so $y = 0$. Thus $(x, y) = (\mathbf{-2}, \mathbf{0})$.

EXAMPLE 3-9   Find all (x, y) such that

$$2\sqrt{x} + 4\sqrt{y} = 10$$
$$2\sqrt{x} - 3\sqrt{y} = 3.$$

Solution: Even though these are not linear equations, we can solve them as linear equations for $\sqrt{x}$ and $\sqrt{y}$ rather than for x and y. (Then, we can just square these results to get x and y.) Subtracting the second equation from the first, we find $7\sqrt{y} = 7$, so $\sqrt{y} = 1$. Thus $2\sqrt{x} + 4 = 10$ and $\sqrt{x} = 3$. Squaring these equations for $\sqrt{x}$ and $\sqrt{y}$ yields $(x, y) = (\mathbf{9}, \mathbf{1})$. Just because the equations are not linear in terms of the variables does not always mean they cannot be solved as linear equations!

EXERCISE 3-3   Solve for (x, y).

i.
$$\begin{aligned} 3x &= 5 + 2y \\ 2x - 2y &= 7 \end{aligned}$$

ii.
$$\begin{aligned} \frac{x}{2} + 3y &= 4 \\ x + 6y &= 9 \end{aligned}$$

iii.
$$\begin{aligned} 0.1x + y &= 3 \\ 0.5x - 3y &= 7 \end{aligned}$$

iv.
$$\begin{aligned} x - y &= 2x + 3 \\ x - 2y &= 5 - 3y \end{aligned}$$

3.4   Word Problems

Word problems are just equations which are written with words rather than with variables. To solve a word problem, we must interpret the words as a set of equations and then use the principles of the last two sections to solve them. (The equations are very often linear, which is why we address word problems in this chapter.)

To show you how to solve the most common types of word problems, we will work through a couple of examples and then leave a few exercises for practice. In our examples we will follow a three step procedure.

> *Step 1*: Define all the variables.
> *Step 2*: Write the equations described by the problem.
> *Step 3*: Solve the equations.

EXAMPLE 3-10 Johnny is twice as old as Gina. Johnny is five years older than Gina. How old is Johnny?

Solution: First, we define our variables: let Johnny's age be J and Gina's be G. Second, we determine the equations. Since Johnny is twice as old as Gina, J must be twice G, so $J = 2G$. Because Johnny is five years older than Gina, then J must be 5 more than G, so $J = G + 5$. Solving this system, we find $(J, G) = (10, 5)$, so Johnny is **10** years old.

EXAMPLE 3-11 The units digit in a two-digit number is three times the tens digit. If the digits are reversed, the resulting number is 54 more than the original number. Find the original number. (MAΘ 1990)

Solution: Let the t be the tens digit and u the units digit. The value of the number is then $10t + u$. Since the units digit is three times the tens digit, $u = 3t$. If the digits are reversed, the resulting number has value $10u + t$. Thus $10u + t - (10t + u) = 9u - 9t = 54$, so $u - t = 6$. Since $u = 3t$, we have $u - t = 2t = 6$. Finally, $t = 3$ and the number is **39**.

EXERCISE 3-4 Adult tickets to a football game were $3.25 and student tickets were $1.75. If 1350 fans paid a total of $2700 to attend the game, how many adults attended? (MAΘ 1992)

The following set of problems includes samples of various types of word problems. Work through all of them, as each one is an example of a very common class of problems.

EXAMPLE 3-12 Jim drives to his mother's house, which is 40 miles away, and then drives back. On the way there he drives 40 miles an hour, but on the way back he drives only 20 mph. What is his average speed for the whole trip?

Solution: The answer is NOT 30 mph. Since Jim's mother's house is 40 miles away, it takes him one hour to get there and two to get back, so the whole trip takes 3 hours. The round trip is eighty miles, so his average speed is $80/3 = \mathbf{26\frac{2}{3}}$ mph.

All of these "moving" problems, whether they involve driving, walking, rowing a boat, or flying a plane, can be solved using the basic formula

$$\text{rate} \times \text{time} = \text{distance}.$$

This simply means that the rate (speed) you travel times the time you travel is the distance you travel. If you understand this you can do *all* of these problems.

EXERCISE 3-5   Jim drives 40 mph to his mother's house and 20 mph on the way back. Show that his average speed for the trip is $26\frac{2}{3}$ mph regardless of the distance to his mother's house.

EXAMPLE 3-13   A frog swims 8 miles downstream in 2 hours. She returns upstream in 14 hours. How fast does the frog swim in still water? (MAΘ 1987)

Solution: The current helps the frog swim downstream and hinders her swimming upstream. Let the frog's rate in still water be x and the current be y. Thus, swimming downstream the frog's rate is $x+y$, while swimming upstream it is $x-y$. Now apply rate times time equals distance: downstream, we have

$$(x+y)(2) = 8,$$

and upstream gives

$$(x-y)(14) = 8.$$

Solving these equations, we find that $(x,y) = (16/7, 12/7)$. Thus, the frog's rate in still water is **16/7** miles per hour.

EXAMPLE 3-14   Pipe A can fill a pool in 5 hours, while pipe B can fill it in four. How long will it take for the two to fill the pool if both are operating at the same time?

Solution: In one hour, pipe A can fill 1/5 of the pool. (Make sure you see why.) Similarly, pipe B can fill 1/4. The two together can thus fill $1/4 + 1/5$ of the pool in one hour. If the two are on for x hours, they fill the fraction $x(1/4 + 1/5)$ of the pool. When this fraction is 1, the pool is full. Thus, we solve

$$x\left(\frac{1}{4} + \frac{1}{5}\right) = 1.$$

Solving yields $x = 20/9$, so it will take **$2\frac{2}{9}$** hours to fill the pool if both pipes are operating.

EXAMPLE 3-15   Tom and Huck paint a fence for four hours, after which Jim helps them and they finish two hours later. If Jim had not helped them, it would have taken them 5 more hours to paint the fence. How long would it take for Jim to paint the fence alone?

Solution: We'll use the same basic method as in the prior example. Let T, H, and J be the number of hours it would take for Tom, Huck, and Jim, respectively, to paint the fence alone. Hence, $1/T + 1/H$ is the fraction of the fence Tom and Huck together can paint in an hour. (If you don't quite follow this, compare it to the previous example.) Since we are told that the two together can paint the entire fence in 9 hours, we have

$$9\left(\frac{1}{T} + \frac{1}{H}\right) = 1.$$

The fraction of the house Tom and Huck have painted in four hours is $4(1/T + 1/H)$. Since $1/T + 1/H + 1/J$ represents the fraction of the fence the three can paint in one hour, 2 times this is the amount the three can paint in 2 hours. The sum of these contributions is the entire fence, so

$$4\left(\frac{1}{T} + \frac{1}{H}\right) + 2\left(\frac{1}{T} + \frac{1}{H} + \frac{1}{J}\right) = 1.$$

Since $(1/T + 1/H) = 1/9$, we have

$$\frac{4}{9} + 2\left(\frac{1}{9} + \frac{1}{J}\right) = 1.$$

Solving for J we find that $J = 6$, so Jim can paint the fence alone in **6 hours**.

All problems involving some combination of two or three people or things performing a task in some amount of time can be solved using this method. Choose variables representing the total time for each person to do the job and write the problem as equations. These equations are always of the form

(time at work)(fraction of work in one unit of time) = (fraction of job done).

You'll find that this looks quite similar to the familiar rate times time equals distance. It should, for it is exactly the same concept; rate of work times time working equals total work done.

EXERCISE 3-6 A canoeist paddled upstream for 2 hours, then downstream for 3. The rate of the current was 2 mph. When she stopped, the canoeist realized she was 20 miles downstream from her starting point. How many hours will it take her to paddle back to her starting point? (MAΘ 1992) If you can do this problem, you should be able to handle any problems involving current.

EXERCISE 3-7   One knight can storm a castle in 15 days. He and his partner can do it in 10 days. How long does it take the partner to storm the same castle alone? (MAΘ 1987)

Problems to Solve for Chapter 3

27. At a dance party a group of boys and girls exchange dances as follows: one boy dances with 5 girls, a second boy dances with 6 girls, and so on, the last boy dancing with all the girls. If b represents the number of boys and g the number of girls, then find b in terms of g. (AHSME 1958)

28. The tens digit of a two-digit number exceeds its units digit by 4. The number exceeds twice the number obtained by reversing the digits of the original number by 10. What is the original number? (MAΘ 1987)

29. There are 16 coins in a bank. If the coins are all nickels and dimes and they total $1.05, how many nickels are there? (MATHCOUNTS 1990)

30. George Washington was born 11 years before Thomas Jefferson. In 1770 Washington's age was 3 more than 7 times the age of Jefferson in 1748. What was the sum of the two men's ages in 1750? (MAΘ 1991)

31. The number 66 is divided into smaller numbers. One number is 3 more than twice the other number. Find the larger of the two numbers. (MATHCOUNTS 1990)

32. Four pounds of onions costs the same as 2 pounds of string beans. At the same time, 1 pound of string beans costs 3 times as much as a pound of potatoes, while 1 pound of onions costs 4 cents less than 2 pounds of potatoes. What is the total cost (without tax) of 1 pound of each of the vegetables? (MAΘ 1991)

33. Find two consecutive odd integers such that 1/3 the smaller plus twice the larger equals 7 more than the sum of the two numbers. (MAΘ 1990)

34. In a basketball game, the United States has four times as many points as Croatia. A Croatian makes a basket for three points, at which point the United States only has three times as many points. How many points does the United States have? (Mandelbrot #3)

35. Mike and Joey bought identical loaves of bread and packages of bologna. Mike made sandwiches with 5 slices of bologna and had 4 slices of bread left when he ran out of meat.

Joey made sandwiches with 4 slices of bologna and had 4 slices of meat when he ran out of bread. How many slices of bread were in each loaf? (MAΘ 1992)

36. Sue has $3.08 in pennies, nickels, and quarters. She has four more pennies than quarters and one more nickel than pennies. How many nickels does she have? (MAΘ 1990)

37. Solve for c in terms of a and b given that

$$\sqrt{a + \frac{b}{c}} = a\sqrt{\frac{b}{c}}.$$

(AHSME 1955)

38. K takes 30 minutes less time than M to travel a distance of 30 miles. K travels $\frac{1}{3}$ mile per hour faster than M. If x is K's rate of speed in miles per hour, then find K's time for the distance in terms of x. (AHSME 1952)

39. What is the value of x if 1 minus the reciprocal of $(1 - x)$ equals the reciprocal of $(1 - x)$? (MAΘ 1992)

40. A train traveling from Aytown to Beetown meets with an accident after 1 hour. The train is stopped for 30 minutes, after which it proceeds at four-fifths of its usual rate, arriving at Beetown 2 hours late. If the train had covered 80 miles more before the accident, it would have been just one hour late. What is the usual rate of the train? (AHSME 1955)

41. Adam can do a job in 10 days, while Brenda takes 15 days to do it. After Brenda works alone for 3 days, Adam and Brenda work together to finish the job. How many days did Adam work? (MAΘ 1990)

42. A car travels 120 miles from A to B at 30 miles per hour but returns the same distance at 40 miles per hour. What is the average speed for the round trip? (AHSME 1950)

43. One car left a city at 2:00 PM and traveled at an average speed of 40 miles per hour. A second car left at 4:00 PM, traveled the same route and overtook the first car at 9:00 PM. What was the average speed in miles per hour of the second car? (MATHCOUNTS 1991)

44. A man can do a job in 9 days and his son can do the same job in 16 days. They start working together. After 4 days the son leaves and the father finishes the job alone. How many days does the man take to finish the job? (MAΘ 1991)

45. Twenty-five women did 1/5 of a job in 8 days. Then, because of an emergency, it became necessary to complete the job in the next 20 days. How many additional women needed to be added to the crew of 25 to accomplish this? (MATHCOUNTS 1989)

46. Two bicyclists are seven-eighths of the way through a mile-long tunnel when a train approaches the closer end at 40 mph. The riders take off at the same speed in opposite directions, and each escapes the tunnel as the train passes them. How fast did they ride? (Mandelbrot #3)

47. A train, x meters long, traveling at a constant speed, takes 20 seconds from the time it first enters a tunnel 300 meters long until the time it completely emerges from the tunnel. One of the stationary ceiling lights in the tunnel is directly above the train for 10 seconds. Find x. (MAΘ 1992)

48. Two men starting at a point on a circular 1-mile race track walk in opposite directions with uniform speeds and meet in 6 minutes, but if they walk in the same direction, it requires one hour for the faster walker to gain a lap. What is the rate of the slower walker? (MAΘ 1991)

49. A crew of 30 people can build a certain road in 60 days. After the tenth day the plans are changed; the company wants the road built in 30, not 60, days. How many more people must be hired? (MAΘ 1992)

50. Jack and Jill went up the hill at a rate of 8 units per minute. They came tumbling down at a rate of 8 units per second. What was their average rate, in units per minute, for the round trip? (MAΘ 1992)

51. Two dogs, each traveling 10 ft/sec, run toward each other from 500 feet apart. As they run, a flea flies from the nose of one dog to the nose of the other at 25 ft/sec. The flea flies between the dogs in this manner until it is crushed when the dogs collide. How far did the flea fly? (MAΘ 1992)

52. Find the ordered pair (x, y) that is the solution of the system   (MAΘ 1990)

$$\frac{x + 2y}{xy} = \frac{11}{12}$$
$$\frac{2x - 3y}{xy} = \frac{2}{3}.$$

53. Find the value of x/y if $(3/\sqrt{y}) - (1/\sqrt{x}) = 2/(\sqrt{x} + \sqrt{y})$. (MAΘ 1992)

54. When three numbers are added two at a time, the sums are 29, 46, and 53. What is the sum of all three numbers? (MATHCOUNTS 1991)

55. Each valve A, B, and C, when open, releases water into a tank at its own constant rate. With all three valves open, the tank fills in 1 hour, with only valves A and C open it takes 1.5 hour, and with only valves B and C open it takes 2 hours. How long will it take to fill the tank with only valves A and B open? (AHSME 1973)

Chapter 4

Proportions

4.1 Direct and Inverse

Proportions are a method of relating one quantity to another. When we say that 5 apples cost 39 cents, we create a relationship between apples and money: 5 apples = 39 cents. If we let a be the number of apples and c be cost, we can write this relation as $a/c = 5/39$. This is read as, "The ratio of apples to cents is 5 to 39." From this we can then determine the price of any number of apples. This is an example of a **direct proportion**. In a directly proportional relationship, the quotient of the two quantities is a constant, so when one of the quantities increases, the other does also. The best way to solve proportion problems is to write the equation relating the two quantities:

$$\frac{\text{apples}}{\text{cost}} = \frac{5}{39}.$$

If we are ever given the number of apples or the cost, we simply substitute that in the appropriate place to get the other.

Ratios are not always written as fractions. Sometimes they are written with colons as $a : c = 5 : 39$, where the colon takes the place of the division sign. For example, we may say that the ratio of trucks to cars in a parking lot is $4 : 3$. This means that out of every 7 vehicles in the lot, 4 are trucks and 3 are cars, or 4/7 are trucks and 3/7 are cars. When working problems, it is always best to write the ratios as fractions rather than using colons.

Ratios are written using colons in part to allow us to consider the ratio of three quantities. For example, if Jim is 20 years old, Jane is 10, and Sam is 5, we can say that the ratio of their ages is 20 : 10 : 5, or 4 : 2 : 1. (Make sure you see why these two expressions are the same.) Clearly, we can't use fractions in a convenient way to express the relationship among more than two quantities.

EXAMPLE 4-1   A ten foot pole casts an eight foot shadow. How long is a pole which casts a twelve foot shadow?

Solution: Since the height of an object is directly proportional to the length of its shadow, we can write

$$\frac{\text{pole}}{\text{shadow}} = \frac{10}{8}.$$

We can simply substitute 12 in where 'shadow' is and get our answer:

$$\frac{\text{pole}}{12} = \frac{10}{8}.$$

Hence, the pole is **15 feet** long.

EXAMPLE 4-2   The ratio of boys to girls in a class is 3 : 2. If there are 35 students in the class, how many girls are there?

Solution: For every 3 boys there are 2 girls. Since out of every 5 students 2 are girls, we know that 2/5 of the students are girls. Thus, there are $35(2/5) = $ **14** girls.

EXERCISE 4-1   In 4 games, Michael Jordan scores 124 points. If he continues scoring at this rate, how many points will he score in the next 6 games?

EXERCISE 4-2   The ratio of wins to losses of the Yankees is 15 : 16. If the Yankees lost 64 games, how many games did they play?

If a quantity is directly proportional to more than one variable, it is **jointly proportional** to those values. In one of the ensuing examples you will see this.

A relationship where two quantities have a constant product is called an **inverse proportion**. When one quantity increases in an inverse proportion, the other decreases. For example, if the area of a rectangle is 40, the length and width are inversely proportional: $lw = 40$. If the length of the rectangle is doubled and the area is to remain the same, we must divide the width by 2.

The constant product in inverse proportions and the constant quotient in direct proportions are often called the **constant of proportionality**.

EXAMPLE 4-3 If x and y are inversely proportional and $x = 10$ when $y = 6$, what is x when $y = 4$?

Solution: We are told $xy = (6)(10) = 60$, so when $y = 4$, we have $xy = 4x = 60$ and $x = \mathbf{15}$.

EXAMPLE 4-4   Given that x is directly proportional to y and to z and is inversely proportional to w, and that $x = 4$ when $(w, y, z) = (6, 8, 5)$, what is x when $(w, y, z) = (4, 10, 9)$?

Solution: Because x is inversely proportional to w, when all other variables are constant, xw is constant. Similarly, when the other two variables are constant, each of x/y and x/z is constant. We can combine all these by saying xw/yz is constant. Thus, from the problem we have

$$\frac{xw}{yz} = \frac{(4)(6)}{(8)(5)} = \frac{3}{5}.$$

When $(w, y, z) = (4, 10, 9)$, we find

$$x = \frac{3yz}{5w} = \frac{\mathbf{27}}{\mathbf{2}}.$$

EXAMPLE 4-5   It takes 3 days for 4 people to paint 5 houses. How long will it take 2 people to paint 6 houses?

Solution: Is the number of houses directly proportional or inversely proportional to the number of days and the number of people? If we have more houses, we will need more time, so the number of houses is directly proportional to the number of days. Similarly, if we have more houses and keep time constant, we need more people, so the number of houses is directly proportional to the number of people as well.

Direct proportion means that the quotient is constant, so both days and people are on the opposite side of the fraction from houses. Thus, our relationship among the three is

$$\frac{\text{houses}}{(\text{people})(\text{days})} = \frac{5}{12},$$

and the number of days necessary is

$$\text{days} = \frac{12(\text{houses})}{5(\text{people})} = \frac{(12)(6)}{(5)(2)} = \frac{36}{5}.$$

EXAMPLE 4-6   It is four o'clock now. How many minutes will pass before the minute and hour hands of a clock are coincident (at the same exact place)?

Solution: The answer is NOT 20, because the hour hand moves as the minutes hand does. When the minute hand is at 20 minutes, the hour hand has moved $20/60 = 1/3$ of the way from 4 hours to 5 hours. Now, suppose x minutes have passed. The hour hand has gone $x/60$ of the way from 4 hours to 5 hours. Since 4 hours on a clock also represents 20 minutes and there are 5 minutes between the 4 and 5 hour marks on a clock, $x/60$ of the way from 4 to 5 is the same place as $20 + 5(x/60)$ minutes. (Check this by seeing what happens when x is 0, 30, or 60.) We seek the place where this equals the number of minutes passed, x:

$$x = 20 + 5\left(\frac{x}{60}\right).$$

Solving this equation yields $x = \mathbf{240/11}$ minutes.

Some sources might give you a formula for "clock problems," as these are called. Don't bother memorizing it! It is much more important that you learn the *method* to solve this type of problem.

EXERCISE 4-3   If 5 hens can lay 24 eggs in 5 days, how many days are needed for 8 hens to lay 20 eggs?

4.2   Manipulating Proportions

Now that we have learned how to use proportions in problems, we will discuss various ways of manipulating proportions. These manipulations are most useful in solving geometry problems involving ratios.

As a first example, we will prove that if $a/b = c/d$, then all of the following equalities hold:

$$\frac{a}{b} = \frac{c}{d} = \frac{a+c}{b+d} = \frac{a-c}{b-d} = \frac{a+kc}{b+kd}.$$

We can prove all of these by just showing the last, that if $a/b = c/d$, then $a/b = (a + kc)/(b + kd)$ for all k. (Using $k = 1$ and $k = -1$, we get the other equalities.) Since $a/b = c/d$, we have $d/b = c/a$ and

$$\frac{a + kc}{b + kd} = \frac{a(1 + k(c/a))}{b(1 + k(d/b))} = \frac{a}{b}\left(\frac{1 + k(c/a)}{1 + k(c/a)}\right) = \frac{a}{b}.$$

Thus, the above equalities are all true.

Another very common type of proportion manipulation is multiplying given proportions. For example, if we are given $x/y = 4/5$ and $z/y = 4/3$, we can find x/z as

$$\frac{x}{z} = \left(\frac{x}{y}\right)\left(\frac{y}{z}\right) = \left(\frac{4}{5}\right)\left(\frac{3}{4}\right) = \frac{3}{5}.$$

Note how we multiply the ratios to cancel the y's.

EXAMPLE 4-7 Find x/y if $\dfrac{x + 2y}{x - y} = \dfrac{3}{4}$.

Solution: Although we spent this short section discussing fancy manipulations, most problems still call for simple algebra. Getting rid of the fractions by multiplying both sides by $4(x - y)$ yields $4(x + 2y) = 3(x - y)$, and rearranging this yields $x + 11y = 0$. To get x/y we simply subtract $11y$, yielding $x = -11y$, and divide, so $x/y = \mathbf{-11}$.

EXERCISE 4-4 Find $2y/x$ if $x/3z = 3$ and $y/4z = 2$.

4.3 Conversion Factors

A week after arriving at college, I asked a new friend of mine, a Canadian, how tall he was, and he responded 180 centimeters. I stared dumbly then asked, "How many feet?" He didn't know. I was stunned. I remembered that one inch was about 2.54 centimeters and 1 foot was 12 inches. So, to convert his height in centimeters to feet, did I divide by 2.54 and multiply by 12, multiply by 2.54 then divide by 12, or what?

Conversion factors will always give you the right answer when trying to convert from one unit to another. It's very simple, and often used as a method to solve proportion problems. We write down the conversions we know:

$$1 \text{ inch} = 2.54 \text{ centimeters},$$
$$1 \text{ foot} = 12 \text{ inches}.$$

If we divide both sides of the first equation by 2.54 centimeters, we have

$$\frac{1 \text{ inch}}{2.54 \text{ centimeters}} = \frac{2.54 \text{ centimeters}}{2.54 \text{ centimeters}} = 1.$$

Similarly,

$$\frac{1 \text{ foot}}{12 \text{ inches}} = 1.$$

Thus, we can multiply 180 centimeters by these factors to convert them to equivalent lengths in other units:

$$180 \text{ centimeters} = 180 \text{ centimeters} \times \frac{1 \text{ inch}}{2.54 \text{ centimeters}} \times \frac{1 \text{ foot}}{12 \text{ inches}} \approx 5.9 \text{ feet}.$$

Why does this work? First, each of the fractions in the above expression equals 1, so multiplying by these doesn't change the length (because multiplying an expression by 1 doesn't change the value of the expression). Second, where did the centimeters and the inches go? The 'inches' in the numerator of one fraction cancelled with the 'inches' in the denominator of another. Similarly, the 'centimeters' in the original expression cancelled with those in the denominator of one of the fractions.

How did we decide to write

$$1 \text{ inch} = 2.54 \text{ centimeters}$$

as

$$\frac{1 \text{ inch}}{2.54 \text{ centimeters}} = 1$$

rather than

$$\frac{2.54 \text{ centimeters}}{1 \text{ inch}} = 1?$$

Both of these are true, but if we use the second in our conversion, we have

$$180 \text{ centimeters} \times \frac{2.54 \text{ centimeters}}{1 \text{ inch}}.$$

In this, the 'centimeters' do not cancel as they did before. We thus choose our conversion factor to make the 'centimeters' cancel.

Note that while we have succeeded in converting 180 centimeters to feet, I still don't have a clear idea of how tall my new friend is because I have determined that he is 5.9 feet tall. What is 0.9 feet? Americans don't have a common conception of 0.9 feet, so to put this in more common terms, we convert the 0.9 feet to inches, giving

$$0.9 \text{ ft} \times \frac{12 \text{ in}}{1 \text{ ft}} = 10.8 \text{ in.}$$

Thus, my new friend is about 5'11".

Now let's convert 5 square feet to square meters, given that 1 foot is about 0.3048 meters. Using conversion factors as before, we have

$$\frac{0.3048 \text{ m}}{1 \text{ ft}} = 1.$$

Multiplying 5 square feet by this conversion factor, we have

$$5 \text{ ft}^2 \times \frac{0.3048 \text{ m}}{1 \text{ ft}}.$$

What is the problem here? If we write 'ft^2' as 'ft·ft', we note that the 'ft' in the denominator of the fraction cancels with only one 'ft' in the 'ft^2' term. To get both of the 'ft', we multiply by the conversion factor twice:

$$5 \text{ ft}^2 = 5 \text{ ft}^2 \times \frac{0.3048 \text{ m}}{1 \text{ ft}} \times \frac{0.3048 \text{ m}}{1 \text{ ft}} = 5 \text{ ft}^2 \times \left(\frac{0.3048 \text{ m}}{1 \text{ ft}}\right)^2 \approx 0.4645 \text{ m}^2.$$

Sometimes units are written with negative exponents. For example, density is measured as mass per unit volume, such as kg/m^3 or kg m^{-3}. In such a case, to convert the cubic meters to cubic feet, we multiply by $(0.3048 \text{ m}/1 \text{ ft})^3$, so the m^3 in the numerator of our conversion factor cancels with the m^3 in the denominator of our density. Hence, we have

$$1 \frac{\text{kg}}{\text{m}^3} = 1 \frac{\text{kg}}{\text{m}^3} \left(\frac{0.3048 \text{ m}}{1 \text{ ft}}\right)^3 \approx 0.02832 \frac{\text{kg}}{\text{ft}^3}.$$

EXAMPLE 4-8   Given that 1 inch is 2.54 centimeters and 1 ounce is 28.35 grams, convert 16.2 in² oz^{-1} to centimeters and grams.

Solution: This is a bit tricky. We convert the inches to centimeters and ounces to grams separately. First we convert the inches to centimeters:

$$\left(16.2 \text{ in}^2 \text{ oz}^{-1}\right) \times \left(\frac{2.54 \text{ cm}}{1 \text{ in}}\right)^2 \approx 104.5 \text{ cm}^2 \text{ oz}^{-1}.$$

Now we deal with the ounces. Since 'oz' appears in the denominator of the expression (remember, oz^{-1} = 1/oz), we must have 'oz' in the *numerator* of our conversion factor in order to make it cancel.

$$104.5 \text{ cm}^2 \text{ oz}^{-1} \times \frac{1 \text{ oz}}{28.35 \text{ g}} \approx \mathbf{3.686 \text{ cm}^2 \text{ g}^{-1}}$$

EXAMPLE 4-9   If 4 gleeps are worth 3 glops and 2 glops are worth 5 glips, how many glips are worth the same as 10 gleeps?

Solution: Since we have no conversion factor to convert gleeps directly to glips, we convert the gleeps first to glops, and then the glops to glips:

$$10 \text{ gleeps} \cdot \frac{3 \text{ glops}}{4 \text{ gleeps}} = 7.5 \text{ glops};$$

$$7.5 \text{ glops} \cdot \frac{5 \text{ glips}}{2 \text{ glops}} = 18.75 \text{ glips}.$$

Thus, 10 gleeps are worth the same as **18.75 glips**.

4.4   Percent

Percent means 'per hundred'. Thus 30% means $\frac{30}{100}$, or 0.30. As you see, it is quite simple to convert a percent to a fraction or to a decimal.

EXAMPLE 4-10   Write $33\frac{1}{3}\%$ as a decimal and as a fraction.

Solution: First, we will write it as a fraction:

$$33\frac{1}{3}\% = \frac{33\frac{1}{3}}{100} = \frac{100/3}{100} = \frac{1}{3}.$$

In decimal representation, this is $\mathbf{0.\overline{3}}$.

EXAMPLE 4-11   Write 2/5 as a percent.

Solution: If $2/5 = x\%$, then

$$\frac{2}{5} = \frac{x}{100}.$$

Solving for x yields $x = 40$. Thus, $2/5 = \mathbf{40\%}$.

EXERCISE 4-5   Write each of the following as a decimal and a fraction.

   i. 35%   ii. 175%

 iii. $66\frac{2}{3}\%$ iv. $16\frac{2}{3}\%$

EXERCISE 4-6   Write the following fractions and decimals as percents.

   i. $\frac{5}{6}$ ii. $2\frac{3}{4}$

 iii. $0.\overline{1}$ iv. 3.5

Percent is simply a type of proportion. When we say that 5% of all people are left-handed, we mean that 5 out of 100 people are left-handed. Percent problems can be solved just like proportion problems, but also can be made much easier by realizing that the word 'of' means 'multiply' and both 'are' and 'is' mean 'equals'. For example, since 5% of all people are left handed, we have:

$$(0.05)(\text{all people}) = (\text{left handed people}).$$

Thus, if we are told there are 60 people, we would expect $(0.05)(60) = 3$ of them to be left handed.

This example of converting language to math works on fractions as well. If we know that 1/20 of all people are left handed, we can write

$$\frac{1}{20}(\text{all people}) = (\text{left handed people}).$$

What does it mean when a store has a sale in which everything is "25% off"? This means that the prices of the goods have had 25% of their price deducted. If a book was originally $22, when it is on sale at a 25% discount, the new price is less by $(0.25)(\$22) = \$5.50$, so the new price is $\$22 - \$5.50 = \$16.50$. A percent increase is the exact opposite of this percent decrease. If the price of the book is increased by 25%, then the resulting price is the original price plus 25% of the original:

$$\$22 + (0.25)(\$22) = \$22 + \$5.50 = \$27.50.$$

Interest is simply a type of percent increase. Suppose you have taken a loan of $2000 at 8% annual interest. This means that at the end of a year the amount you will owe increases 8%, to $\$2000 + (0.08)(\$2000) = 1.08(\$2000) = \$2160$. Notice how we have used the distributive law "backwards" to write the amount we owe as 1.08($2000). After a while, you will use this directly, without having to write $\$2000 + (0.08)(\$2000)$ first. For example, 75 increased by 30% is $(1 + 0.30)(75) = 1.3(75)$, and is decreased by 30% is $0.7(75)$.

EXAMPLE 4-12   75 is 20% of what number?

Solution: Let x be the desired number. Thus, 20% of x is 75, or $(0.20)x = 75$; solving this equation yields $x = $ **375**.

EXAMPLE 4-13   The price of a car is originally $10000. If the price is decreased by 25%, then increased by 25%, what is the resulting price?

Solution: The answer is *not* $10000! After the decrease, the price is

$$\$10000 - (0.25)(\$10000) = (0.75)(\$10000) = \$7500.$$

Then we increase $7500 by 25%; the result is $\$7500(1.25) = $ **$9375**.

EXAMPLE 4-14   Suppose you borrow $4000 at 5% annual interest. How much money will you owe after 4 years?

Solution: After one year, you owe $4000(1.05). At the end of the second year, you must pay 5% interest on this amount, so you owe $\$4000(1.05)(1.05) = \$4000(1.05)^2$. This is the amount $4000(1.05) increased by 5%. (Make sure you understand this.) Now you see why we did not multiply out the $4000(1.05) after the first year. Following the above reasoning, you owe $\$4000(1.05)^3$ after three years and $\$4000(1.05)^4$

after four years. Evaluating this rounded to the hundredths place (money is meaningless past the second decimal place), you owe **$4862.03**.

EXAMPLE 4-15   If two liters of a 20% acid solution are mixed with 8 liters of a 50% acid solution, what is the concentration of the resulting solution?

    Solution: The concentration of an acid solution is the amount of acid in the solution divided by the total volume of the solution. Two liters of 20% acid solution contains $2(0.2) = 0.4$ liters of acid, while the other solution contains $8(0.5) = 4$ liters of acid. For the solution which is a mixture of these two,

$$\text{Concentration} = \frac{0.4 + 4}{2 + 8} = \frac{4.4}{10} = \mathbf{44\%}.$$

EXERCISE 4-7   The price of a ring is decreased 40% and the resulting price is increased by 50%. The final price is $360. What was the original price?

EXERCISE 4-8 A car was originally $8000, but is on sale for $7000. What percent decrease in price does this represent?

EXERCISE 4-9   The U.S. is loaning 1.5 million dollars to France. What annual interest rate must the U.S. charge if they want France to owe 2 million dollars at the end of one year?

EXERCISE 4-10 A chemist has 80 ml of a solution containing 20% acid. How many ml must be removed and replaced by pure acid in order to obtain a 40% solution? (MAΘ 1992)

Problems to Solve for Chapter 4

56. What percent of 20 is 13?

57. The population of a town increases 25% during 1991. By what percent must it decrease the following year to return to the population it was at the beginning of 1991?

58. A number is increased by 50%, then the resulting number is decreased by 40%. What was the initial number if the final number is 8 less than the original?

59. A metric calendar has 1 metric year equivalent to our calendar year of 365 days. A metric year is divided into 10 equal metric months; a metric month is divided into 10 equal metric weeks; a metric week is divided into 10 equal metric days. To the nearest day of our calendar, how many days are there in 4 metric months, 5 metric weeks and 8 metric days? (MATHCOUNTS 1985)

60. If the ratio of $2x - y$ to $x + y$ is $2 : 3$, find the ratio $x : y$. (MAΘ 1992)

61. If a stack of 8 quarters is exactly one-half inch high, how many quarters will be needed to make a stack one foot high? (MATHCOUNTS 1991)

62. If y^2 varies inversely as x^3, and $y = 3$ when $x = 2$, find y when $x = 9$, assuming that $y > 0$. (MAΘ 1990)

63. The discount on a stereo system is $69, and the rate of discount is 15%. What was the original price of the system? (MAΘ 1990)

64. Given $\dfrac{x}{y} = \dfrac{2}{3}$ and $\dfrac{y}{z} = \dfrac{3}{2}$, find $\dfrac{x}{z}$. (MATHCOUNTS 1992)

65. A test has two parts. The first part is worth 60% and the second part is worth 40%. If a student gets 95% of part one correct, what exact percent correct must the student achieve on part two to average 90% for the whole test? (MATHCOUNTS 1988)

66. Jennifer had a bag of Gummy Bears. She gave 1/2 of them to Jessica, 1/3 of them to Jana, and 15 to Julie. If the bag was then empty, how many Gummy Bears were in the bag at the beginning? (MATHCOUNTS 1991)

67. A man can run x feet in y seconds. How many yards can he run in z minutes? (MAΘ 1992)

68. x is directly proportional to y and inversely proportional to z. If $x = 1/2$ when $y = 3/4$ and $z = 2/3$, find x when $y = 7/8$ and $z = 7/9$. (MATHCOUNTS 1989)

69. A woman has part of $4500 invested at 4% and the rest at 6%. If her annual return on each investment is the same, then what is the average rate of interest which she realizes on the $4500? (AHSME 1953)

70. The wages of 3 men for 4 weeks is $108. At the same rate of pay, how many weeks will 5 men work for $135? (MAΘ 1991)

71. Tennis coaches High Lob and Low Smash decided to share with their assistants (Love and Vantage) the money they earned from tennis lessons. They agreed on the following ratios: Lob : Love = 17 : 12, Love : Smash = 3 : 4, and Smash : Vantage = 32 : 15. If their earnings totaled $3,150, how much did Love receive? (MAΘ 1990)

72. In a closed bottle, the product of the pressure and volume is constant. By what percent must the volume be decreased to increase the pressure by 25%? (MATHCOUNTS 1992)

73. In a school election, candidate A got $33.\overline{3}\%$ of the votes cast, B got $9/20$ of the votes, C got $2/15$ of the votes, and the only other candidate, D, got the remaining 75 votes. How many students voted in the election? (MATHCOUNTS 1990)

74. Ms. A owns a house worth $10000. She sells it to Mr. B at 10% profit. Mr. B sells the house back to Ms. A at a 10% loss. How much money does Ms. A make? (AHSME 1955)

75. The rails of a railroad are 30 feet long. As a train passes over the point where the rails are joined, there is an audible click. The speed of the train in miles per hour is approximately the number of clicks heard in how many seconds? (AHSME 1953)

76. A town's population increased by 1,200 people, and then this new population decreased by 11%. The town now had 32 less people than it did before the 1,200 increase. What was the original population? (AHSME 1974)

77. The cost of living in each quarter (3 months) increased by 2% over the previous quarter. To the nearest tenth of a percent, to what annual percentage rate of increase does this correspond? (MAΘ 1990)

78. It is given that x varies directly as y and inversely as the square of z, and that $x = 10$ when $y = 4$ and $z = 14$. What is x when $y = 16$ and $z = 7$? (AHSME 1959)

79. Two joggers are running around an oval track in opposite directions. One jogger runs around the track in 56 seconds. They meet every 24 seconds. How many seconds does it take the second jogger to run around the track? (MATHCOUNTS 1986)

80. If x varies as the cube of y, and y varies as the fifth root of z, then x varies as the nth power of z. What is n? (AHSME 1954)

81. It is now between 10:00 and 11:00. Six minutes from now, the minute hand of a watch will be exactly opposite the place where the hour hand was three minutes ago. What is the exact time now? (MAΘ 1991)

82. If p is 50% of q and r is 40% of q, what percent of r is p? (Mandelbrot #1)

83. Country A has $c\%$ of the world's population and owns $d\%$ of the world's wealth. Country B has $e\%$ of the world's population and $f\%$ of its wealth. Assume that the citizens of A share the wealth of A equally, and that those of B share the wealth of B equally. Find the ratio of the wealth of a citizen of A to the wealth of a citizen of B. (AHSME 1993)

84. A, B, C, D, and E are consecutive points on a line. If $\dfrac{AB}{BC} = \dfrac{1}{3}$, $\dfrac{BC}{CD} = \dfrac{1}{4}$, and $\dfrac{CD}{DE} = \dfrac{1}{2}$, what is $\dfrac{AC}{BE}$? (MATHCOUNTS 1992)

85. From time $t = 0$ to time $t = 1$ a population increased by $i\%$, and from time $t = 1$ to time $t = 2$ the population increased by $j\%$. By what percent, in terms of i and j, did the population increase from time $t = 0$ to time $t = 2$? (AHSME 1991)

86. If for three distinct positive numbers x, y, and z,

$$\frac{y}{x-z} = \frac{x+y}{z} = \frac{x}{y},$$

then find the numerical value of x/y. (AHSME 1992)

the BIG PICTURE

As the simplest possible relation between two variables, proportions find their way into almost any mathematical formulation. For example, modern chemistry got an enormous boost around the year 1800 when Dalton used a simple proportion to deduce that matter was made up of atoms. (Such a theory was actually advanced several hundred years B.C. by the Greek Democritus, but he was unable to accumulate the physical evidence needed to convince his peers.) Dalton knew that in any sample of some pure substance, the ratios of the weights of constituent elements was always a constant. For example, if in a sample of water we let the weight of oxygen be O and the weight of hydrogen be H, experiment will always yield the proportion

$$\frac{H}{O} \approx 0.124.$$

From this Dalton guessed that substances are made up of units, and each of these is made up of a fixed ratio of atoms. Otherwise, why would the ratio always be the same?

Economics has its share of proportions as well. In some economies, the price P and the demand D for a given product may be inversely proportional, so that

$$PD = \text{constant.}$$

Thus as the price increases, the demand decreases. Of course, other relationships between price and demand are possible, but the simple proportion is an important case.

In thermodynamics, the pressure, volume, and temperature of a gas obey the proportion

$$\frac{PV}{T} = \text{constant,}$$

so that, for example, lower volume at a constant temperature yields higher pressure. (Does this seem right? Try squeezing a balloon.) This **Ideal Gas Law** is crucial to engines and other applications of thermodynamics.

In the more complicated humanities and social sciences, simple proportions are harder to come by, as many a politician has found out who expected a proportion between money spent and votes received.

Chapter 5

Using the Integers

In spite of their being a rather restricted class of numbers, the integers have a lot of interesting properties and uses. Math which involves the properties of integers is called **number theory**.

5.1   Divisibility

An integer n is **divisible** by a different integer m if n is an integral multiple of m. For example, 15 is divisible by 3 because $15 = 5 \cdot 3$. The numbers which divide a given integer are called its **divisors**; for example, the divisors of 12 are 1, 2, 3, 4, 6, and 12 (which divides itself because $12 = 12 \cdot 1$).

EXERCISE 5-1   Write down all the divisors of 20.

   Primes are integers which have no divisors except themselves and 1. For example, 7 is a prime, but 8 is not because 2 and 4 divide 8. Numbers like 8 which do have divisors other than 1 and themselves are called **composite**.

   WARNING: 1 is NOT considered prime! Unfortunately, it is not composite either. (The reasons for this are too complicated to get into now.) The primes less than 10 are thus 2, 3, 5, and 7.

EXERCISE 5-2   Write down all primes between 11 and 20 inclusive.

EXERCISE 5-3   How many even primes are there?

The notation for one number dividing another is to put a vertical line between them, as in 13|26 and 12|24. To indicate that the first number does not divide the second, we put a slash through the line: 11 $\nmid$ 23.

5.2 Number Bases

We can write the integer 7965841 as

$$7000000 + 900000 + 60000 + 5000 + 800 + 40 + 1.$$

That we can write it this way is a consequence of the fact that our usual number system is **base 10**, meaning we have 10 digits. Each digit represents a multiple of a power of 10, based on its position. To make this clearer we could write

$$7 \times 10^6 + 9 \times 10^5 + 6 \times 10^4 + 5 \times 10^3 + 8 \times 10^2 + 4 \times 10^1 + 1 \times 10^0.$$

Why do we count the way we do, following the number 9 with a new number consisting of a 1 and a 0? Having used 10 digits (0 through 9) to count to 9, we make a new "tens place," and assume that the digit in that position is the number of tens. For example, 57 is 5 tens and 7 ones. This saves us from needing a new digit for each number; we can stick to our original ten digits. When we get up to 99, we need to add another place, making the next position represent the number of hundreds.

Humans use 10 digits because we have ten fingers. However, what if we were cartoon characters, with only 8 fingers? Then we might only use the eight digits 0, 1, ..., 7. To go higher than 7, we would create an "eights place," so that 25 in our new number system would represent two 8's and five 1's, or $2(8) + 5 = 21$ in the base ten system. Higher positions would correspond to higher powers of 8; for example, 6543 means $6 \times 8^3 + 5 \times 8^2 + 4 \times 8 + 3$. To get rid of the confusion of going back and forth between the two bases, we use the notation that 47_{10} means the base 10 number 47 and 47_8 means the base 8 number 47. (What is this in base 10?) This notation carries over into other bases as well.

───────────────────────────────

EXAMPLE 5-1   What is the base 7 number 3456_7 in base 10?

Solution: All we have to do is write

$$3 \times 7^3 + 4 \times 7^2 + 5 \times 7^1 + 6 \times 7^0 = 3(343) + 4(49) + 5(7) + 6(1) = \mathbf{1266}.$$

EXAMPLE 5-2   Write the base 10 number 216 in base 4.

Solution: The first few powers of 4 are 1, 4, 16, 64, 256, ... Clearly we can't use 256 or any greater power. The highest power which is less than 216 is $64 = 4^3$. The multiples of 64 are 64, 128, and 192; since $192 = 64 \times 3$ is still less than 216, the first digit is 3. Why don't we just use 2 64's? If so we would need more than 3 16's, but we are only allowed 3 nonzero digits to represent the number of 16's. Try it and see! To find the second digit, we look at what is left once we have taken out three 64's, or $216 - 192 = 24$.

In general, to find how many times one number goes into another, we can divide the first by the second and throw out the remainder. Doing this with 24 and 16, the quotient is 1.5, so only one 16 is needed (two 16's are too many), and the second digit is 1. We subtract this 16 from what is left, to get $24 - 16 = 8$. Dividing this by $4^1 = 4$, the quotient is 2, so the third digit is 2. Subtracting $8 - 2 \cdot 4$, we get zero, so the remaining digit is zero since we don't need any 1's. The number in base 4 is **3120_4**.

EXERCISE 5-4   Find the base 10 representations of 47_8, 47_9, and 47_{16}.

EXERCISE 5-5   Find the base 8, 9, and 16 representations of 47_{10}.

The presence of base 16 in the previous exercises raises a new question: what if we want to use a base greater than 10? We will need more digits than the usual 10, so all we do is use some other symbols. The most common such case is base 16, or **hexadecimal** (six-plus-ten-imal). Here we use the digits

$$0, \ 1, \ 2, \ 3, \ 4, \ 5, \ 6, \ 7, \ 8, \ 9, \ A, \ B, \ C, \ D, \ E, \ F.$$

Thus $A_{16} = 10_{10}$ and $F_{16} = 15_{10}$. If we had a high enough base we might have to start using smiley faces and triangles for digits, but there would be little use for such a system.

EXERCISE 5-6   Find the base 10 equivalents of BEE_{16}, DEF_{16}, and $A1_{16}$.

At the opposite extreme from all these digits is the lowly base 2, or **binary**. Here the only two digits are 0 and 1, and counting looks like 1, 10, 11, 100, 101, 110, ...

EXERCISE 5-7   How do you multiply a number by 2 in base 2?

EXERCISE 5-8   Do some conversions into and out of binary.

EXAMPLE 5-3   Perform the addition $1001110_2 + 11001101_2$ without converting the two numbers to decimal. Check your answer by converting to decimal, adding, and converting back.

Solution: We can do the addition just like ordinary base 10 addition, writing the numbers one above the other like so:

$$
\begin{array}{ccccccccc}
 & 1 & 0 & 0 & 1 & 1 & 1 & 0 \\
1 & 1 & 0 & 0 & 1 & 1 & 0 & 1 \\
\hline
\end{array}
$$

If two 0's are in a column, a zero goes in the result in the same column. If a 1 and a 0 are in a column, a 1 goes below. If two 1's are together, the sum is 2, which in binary is 10_2. Thus we must carry the 1, and put a 0 below. The 'carrying' process works in base 2 just like in base 10. (Compare this process to adding 56 and 65 in base 10.) This carried 1 will add to the numbers in the next column, making 1 if both are 0, 2 (or 10_2) with a 1 and a 0, and 3 (or 11_2) with two 1's. For the latter two we will have to carry another 1, and so on. Using these rules we can fill in the digits of the result from right to left, as usual:

$$
\begin{array}{ccccccccc}
1 & 1 & & & 1 & 1 & & & \\
 & & 1 & 0 & 0 & 1 & 1 & 1 & 0 \\
 & 1 & 1 & 0 & 0 & 1 & 1 & 0 & 1 \\
\hline
1 & 0 & 0 & 0 & 1 & 1 & 0 & 1 & 1 \\
\end{array}
$$

We've placed the carried digits above the columns they're carried to. The result is $100011011_2 = 256 + 16 + 8 + 2 + 1 = 283_{10}$. To confirm this we convert the original numbers to decimal, getting $1001110_2 = 64 + 8 + 4 + 2 = 78_{10}$ and $11001101_2 = 128 + 64 + 8 + 4 + 1 = 205_{10}$, and note that $205_{10} + 78_{10} = 283_{10}$, as desired.

We have seen that the operation of carrying works in binary. This procedure works in any base. Say we are adding the base 7 numbers 235_7 and 114_7. When we add the two rightmost digits we get $9 = 12_7$, so we place a 2 below the line and carry the 1.

5.3   The Last Digit

No matter what number base we are using, often the most important digit of a number is the last digit. Why should the last digit be so important? There is a very simple reason: if we want to know the last digit of the sum or product of two numbers, all we have to do is find the sum or product of their last digits and take the last digit of that result.

EXERCISE 5-9 Convince yourself that the previous statement is true. Find the last digits of $34 \cdot 17$ and $34 + 17$, first by actually doing the multiplication and addition, then by taking the last digits and just multiplying or adding those. Explain why this works.

The method of the last digit works in any number base and can be used to prove some very useful facts.

EXERCISE 5-10   In base 10, what digits can the last digit of the square of an integer not be?

EXAMPLE 5-4   Find the units digit of $7^{42} + 42^7$.

Solution: To find the last digit of $7^{42} + 42^7$, we find the last digit of each of the two quantities in the sum. To find the last digit of 7^{42}, we break it up into a product of 7's. Since $7^2 = 49$, 7^2 ends in 9. Since $7^4 = 7^2 \cdot 7^2$, it ends in the same number as $9 \cdot 9$ ends in, or 1. Now we write $7^{42} = (7^4)^{10} \cdot 7^2$. Since 7^4 ends in 1, the last digit of $(7^4)^{10}$ is the same as the last digit of the product of ten 1's, or 1. Finally, since $(7^4)^{10}$ ends in 1 and 7^2 ends in 9, 7^{42} ends in $1 \cdot 9 = 9$.

In finding the last digit of 42^7, the tens digit is irrelevant because it does not contribute to the units digit of the product. Hence we are only concerned with 2^7. Since this is 128, the last digit of 42^7 is 8. (Make sure you see why the last digit of 42^7 is the same as that of 2^7.) Completing our problem, $7^{42} + 42^7$ ends in the same digit as $9 + 8$, or **7**.

5.4   Modular Arithmetic

Imagine we decide to do all arithmetic in base 5. Doing arithmetic in different number bases is not always easy; for example, you don't want to memorize a multiplication table for base 16. ($B \cdot C = 84$?!) So just to make it easier on ourselves, we will consider only the last digits. All numbers which have the same last digit in base 5 will be considered equal:

$$2_5 = 12_5 = 22_5 = 32_5 = \cdots$$

In base 10, this looks like

$$2 = 7 = 12 = 17 = \cdots$$

The usual way to show that we are using this system is to replace the $=$ with a $\equiv$, and also append the suffix (mod 5). We thus write, for example, $12 \equiv 7$ (mod 5). We say that **12 is congruent to 7 mod 5**.

Another way to look at mods is that 2, 7, 12, 17, etc. all have the same remainder (2) when divided by 5. This method of viewing modular arithmetic makes actual computation much easier. It is often useful to find the smallest nonnegative integer which is congruent to x mod y. (For example, the smallest integer congruent to 12 mod 5 is 2.) When we perform this task, we say that we 'mod out' the 12. Now you see how our second way of viewing mods is useful. To mod out 7631 in mod 7, we can either find 7631 in base 7 and look at the last digit, or we can divide by 7 and look at the remainder.

In this discussion of remainders, we have used mods to denote the amount more than a multiple of 5 a given number is. For example, 2, 7, 12, 17, etc. are all exactly 2 more than a multiple of 5. In the same way we can define negative mods as the amount less than a multiple of 5 a number is. Since 2, 7, 12, 17, etc. are all 3 less than the nearest multiple of 5, they are all congruent to -3 mod 5. Extending this reasoning, we can write in mod 5:

$$\cdots \equiv -13 \equiv -8 \equiv -3 \equiv 2 \equiv 7 \equiv 12 \cdots$$

Note that each term is five away from the one before it and after it. Think about why this is true.

EXAMPLE 5-5 Why does the remainder method described above work?

Solution: Consider 7631 in base 7. It is 31151_7, or

$$3 \cdot 7^4 + 1 \cdot 7^3 + 1 \cdot 7^2 + 5 \cdot 7 + 1.$$

When we divide this expression by seven, the seven evenly divides the first 4 terms of the sum and leaves the last term as the remainder, i.e. $7631/7 = 3 \cdot 7^3 + 1 \cdot 7^2 + 1 \cdot 7 + 5$, with a remainder of 1. Hence we see that the last digit of 7631 written in base 7 is the same as the remainder we have upon dividing 7631 by 7. This is why the remainder method works.

EXERCISE 5-11 Write down some numbers which are congruent to 3 mod 5.

EXERCISE 5-12 What is the largest integer less than 100 which is congruent to 3 mod 5?

EXAMPLE 5-6 How many positive integers less than 100 are congruent to 3 mod 5?

Solution: The smallest is obviously 3. In the previous exercise, you should have found that the largest is 98. How many are there in between? We have $3 = 0(5) + 3$ and $98 = 19(5) + 3$, and the other numbers congruent to 3 mod 5 will be $1(5) + 3$, $2(5) + 3$, and so on. The number by which 5 is multiplied can be 0, 1, 2, ..., 19, so there are **20** possibilities.

EXERCISE 5-13 How many integers are there between 50 and 250 inclusive which are congruent to 1 mod 7?

EXERCISE 5-14 Which numbers are congruent to 0 mod 5?

Once the principle of congruence is understood, we can move on to doing actual arithmetic with it. One thing which we can do with a congruence like

$$12 \equiv 7 \pmod 5$$

is add the same thing to both sides:

$$12 + 3 \equiv 7 + 3 \pmod 5.$$

We can do this because if the last digits in base 5 are the same before the addition, they will be the same after the addition. Clearly the same will be true for subtraction.

How about for multiplication? Again, the same should hold. If the last digits are the same before the multiplication, they will be the same after.

Not only can we multiply or add the same quantities to both sides, but if x and y have the same last digit in base 5, then we can add x to one side and y to the other in mod 5. For example, since 8 and 13 have the same last digit in base 5,

$$12 + 13 \equiv 7 + 8 \pmod 5.$$

Applying this concept to multiplication, since 12 and 7 are congruent mod 5, we can multiply one side by 12 and the other by 7, yielding

$$12^2 \equiv 7^2 \pmod{5}.$$

In this manner, we can raise the two sides to any positive integral power!

WARNING: Division is a much more complicated matter. For instance, clearly $5 \equiv 10 \pmod{5}$, but if we divide both sides by 5, we have $1 \equiv 2 \pmod{5}$, an obviously false relation. There is something wrong here, and that something will be investigated in the next volume. Just remember that division doesn't generally work in modular arithmetic.

In finding the last digit of a sum or product of two numbers, we don't need to do the entire sum or product, just the sum or product of the last digits of the two numbers. In mods, this is reflected by the fact that we can "mod out" before or after doing operations; the order doesn't matter. By this we mean that we can mod out the factors of a product and then multiply the results rather than having to mod out the product of the numbers. For example, since $9899 \equiv 4 \pmod{5}$ and $7677 \equiv 2 \pmod{5}$, we can say $9899 \cdot 7677 \equiv 4 \cdot 2 \equiv 8 \equiv 3 \pmod{5}$ rather than first multiplying 9899 and 7677 and modding out the product. Make sure you follow this; it is a very important technique. Try to use it to show that $9453 \cdot 6824 \equiv 6782 \cdot 5675341 \equiv 2 \pmod{5}$.

Let's summarize what we can do with congruences. If $a \equiv b \pmod{m}$, then for all positive integers c:

1. $a + c \equiv b + c \pmod{m}$

2. $a - c \equiv b - c \pmod{m}$

3. $ac \equiv bc \pmod{m}$

4. $a^c \equiv b^c \pmod{m}$

5. $(a + b) \pmod{m} \equiv a \pmod{m} + b \pmod{m}$

6. $ab \pmod{m} \equiv \big(a \pmod{m}\big)\big(b \pmod{m}\big)$

You may need to chew on those last two a bit, though they are among the most useful. They just restate the fact that we can mod out before or after we add or multiply.

EXAMPLE 5-7 If we are given that $a \equiv 0 \pmod{b}$, then the remainder when a is divided by b is 0. Thus we can conclude that a is a multiple of b.

EXERCISE 5-15 Find the smallest positive integer which 123 is congruent to mod 4. Find the smallest positive integer that 321 is congruent to mod 7.

EXERCISE 5-16 Show that the square of any integer is congruent to either 0, 1, or 4 mod 8.

5.5 Tricks

Even at this early stage in understanding divisibility, we can find some tricks to tell if one number divides another. We start with the obvious example: a number is divisible by 10 if and only if its last digit is 0. This seems trivial, but then so will the rest of the rules in this section when you've used them a few times.

We start with the basic concept that a number, x, is divisible by another number, y if and only if $x \equiv 0 \pmod{y}$. This just means that when we divide x by y, the remainder is zero.

First we examine divisibility by 2. A number is divisible by 2 if and only if it is congruent to 0 mod 2. We can write the number, say 7965841, as the sum of its last digit and the rest, as in $7965841 = 1 + 7965840$. Thus we can write $7965841 \equiv 1 + 7965840 \pmod{2}$. The second part ends with a zero, so is divisible by 10, or $7965840 = 10(\text{something})$. But $2|10$, so this means $7965840 = 2(\text{something else})$, so that 2 divides 7965840, and $7965840 \equiv 0 \pmod{2}$. Substituting this in above, we find that $7965841 \equiv 1 \pmod{2}$, or a number is congruent to its last digit mod 2. So to test for divisibility by 2, we just test the last digit, which must be 2, 4, 6, 8, or 0 if the number is to be divisible by 2. We went through this very long method of showing that $2|7965840$ to give a hint as to how we test for divisibility of other numbers.

For example, consider 4. A multiple of 10 is not necessarily a multiple of 4, but a multiple of 100 is. Thus, we can write

$$45376 \equiv 45300 \pmod{4} + 76 \pmod{4}$$

$$\equiv (453 \;(\mathrm{mod}\; 4))(100 \;(\mathrm{mod}\; 4)) + 0 \;(\mathrm{mod}\; 4)$$

$$\equiv (453 \cdot 0) \;(\mathrm{mod}\; 4) + 0 \;(\mathrm{mod}\; 4) \equiv 0 + 0 \;(\mathrm{mod}\; 4) \equiv 0 \;(\mathrm{mod}\; 4).$$

Notice how we used $100 \equiv 0 \;(\mathrm{mod}\; 4)$.

EXERCISE 5-17 Find a shortcut along the same lines to test for divisibility by 5.

EXERCISE 5-18 How about for 4, 8, and 20?

EXERCISE 5-19 Why is it so easy to test for divisibility by these numbers?

We can find a (slightly more complicated) rule to test for divisibility by 3. Let's use 7965. We divide it not into two parts as above, but many more, writing it as $7000+900+60+5$. Since $10 \equiv 1 \;(\mathrm{mod}\; 3)$, taking the sum mod 3 causes each factor of 10 to reduce to a 1. (For example, $100 \equiv 10 \cdot 10 \;(\mathrm{mod}\; 3) \equiv 1 \cdot 1 \;(\mathrm{mod}\; 3) \equiv 1 \;(\mathrm{mod}\; 3)$.) Hence we have

$$
\begin{aligned}
7965 &\equiv 7000 + 900 + 60 + 5 \quad (\mathrm{mod}\; 3) \\
&\equiv 7 \cdot 10 \cdot 10 \cdot 10 + 9 \cdot 10 \cdot 10 + 6 \cdot 10 + 5 \quad (\mathrm{mod}\; 3) \\
&\equiv 7 \cdot 1 \cdot 1 \cdot 1 + 9 \cdot 1 \cdot 1 + 6 \cdot 1 + 5 \quad (\mathrm{mod}\; 3) \\
&\equiv 7 + 9 + 6 + 5 \quad (\mathrm{mod}\; 3).
\end{aligned}
$$

Thus a number is congruent to the sum of its digits in mod 3! In general, then, a *number is divisible by 3 if and only if the sum of its digits is.*

EXERCISE 5-20 For the numbers 1717, 3451, and 173451, test for divisibility by 3 by the shortcut and by direct division.

EXERCISE 5-21 Find the divisibility shortcut for 9; recreate the discussion of divisibility by 3, except using $10 \equiv 1 \;(\mathrm{mod}\; 9)$.

EXERCISE 5-22 Which of the following is divisible by 3 but not by 9: 4995, 4996, 4997, 4998, 4999?

We have been able to get good divisibility rules for 10 and its divisors, and for 3 and 9. How about $10 + 1 = 11$? We can write $10 \equiv -1 \pmod{11}$ (does this make sense?) to simplify. Each power of 10 will thus be congruent to a power of -1 when we write the number in mod 11, e.g. $1000 \equiv (10)^3 \equiv (-1)^3 \equiv -1 \pmod{11}$. Hence

$$
\begin{aligned}
7964 &\equiv 7 \cdot 10^3 + 9 \cdot 10^2 + 6 \cdot 10 + 4 \pmod{11} \\
&\equiv 7 \cdot (-1)^3 + 9 \cdot (-1)^2 + 6 \cdot (-1) + 4 \pmod{11} \\
&\equiv -7 + 9 - 6 + 4 \pmod{11}
\end{aligned}
$$

Hence, *a number is divisible by 11 if and only if the sum of its digits* with alternating signs *is*.

What if the alternating sum is negative? If it is -11, -22, etc., the number is divisible, otherwise not. This is because -11, -22, etc. are all evenly divisible by 11. If the alternating sum is 0, then the number is divisible by 11, as 0 is divisible by all numbers. You might be uncomfortable with using negatives for divisibility, but they are fine in both divisibility and modular arithmetic, as in the example of $10 \equiv -1 \pmod{11}$ above.

EXERCISE 5-23   Which of the following are divisible by 11: 11, 111, 1111, 1716, 1761, 152637?

EXERCISE 5-24   Prove, using our rule, that a two-digit number is divisible by 11 if and only if its digits are the same.

EXAMPLE 5-8   How would you test a number for divisibility by 12?

Solution: We might try to build a rule similar to that for 11, but there is a much easier way. Since 12 factors into 4×3, a number is divisible by 12 if it is divisible by 4 and by 3; divisibility by these numbers can be easily tested.

This shows that in general composite numbers can be analyzed in terms of the numbers which divide them.

5.6   Primes

Primes are the most important integers. There is a simple reason for this: every other number can be broken down into a product of primes. For example, 15 can be written as $3 \cdot 5$, the product of the primes 3 and 5, or 48 as $16 \cdot 3 = 2^4 \cdot 3$, with the primes 2 and 3. By definition, primes cannot be broken down any further, for they have no divisors to split into. The splitting up of numbers into prime factors, or **prime factorization**, is extremely useful, because each number has only one distinct prime factorization. (Here distinct means that, for example, $2^4 \cdot 3$, $3 \cdot 2^4$, and $2 \cdot 2 \cdot 3 \cdot 2 \cdot 2$ are considered the same.)

EXERCISE 5-25   Write down the prime factorizations of all integers from 2 to 12.

EXERCISE 5-26   What is the prime factorization of 256?

Finding the prime factorization of small numbers is very easy using only trial and error. To factor larger numbers, however, we need to be a little more systematic. One important tool is the divisibility tricks we have derived. We can easily factor out all 5's and 2's, for example. We can then test for 3's and 11's. For many numbers, we will already be well on our way with just these few methods.

For others we have to resort to trial and error, going up through the primes and dividing by each to see if it works. A tool to limit the amount of searching we have to do is to think about what the largest primes involved can be. Call the number we intend to factor N. Clearly there cannot be more than one factor greater than $\sqrt{N}$, since if there were more than one, their product would exceed N. Similarly, if N is not prime, there must be at least one factor less than or equal to $\sqrt{N}$. Why? Since N is not prime, it must have at least two factors other than itself and 1. Either both are greater than $\sqrt{N}$, which we have shown is impossible, or at least one is less than or equal to $\sqrt{N}$. Hence if we cannot find a prime less than $\sqrt{N}$ which divides N, we know N is prime.

EXAMPLE 5-9 Let's see how all this works in practice by factoring 123420. We first get rid of all 10's, and convert them to 2's and 5's: $123420 = 10 \cdot 12342 = 2 \cdot 5 \cdot 12342$. Note that upon finding the prime factors 2 and 5 here, we divide 123420 by them and continue our job with the result, 12342. (How would not doing so affect our search for the prime factorization? Try it and see.)

Since the number left is divisible by 2, but not by any more 2's after that, we can take out one more 2: $2 \cdot 5 \cdot 12342 = 2^2 \cdot 5 \cdot 6171$. We then test the number which remains for 3's and 11's. The sum of the digits of 6171 is $6 + 1 + 7 + 1 = 15$, which is divisible by 3 but not 9, so we can take out exactly one 3 to get $2^2 \cdot 3 \cdot 5 \cdot 2057$. The alternating sum of the digits of 2057 is $2 - 0 + 5 - 7 = 0$, which is divisible by

11, so 2057 is divisible by 11, and we have $2^2 \cdot 3 \cdot 5 \cdot 11 \cdot 187$. Testing 187, we again find divisibility by 11, leaving $2^2 \cdot 3 \cdot 5 \cdot 11^2 \cdot 17$. Since 17 is prime, this is a complete factorization.

EXAMPLE 5-10   Find the prime factorization of 97.

Solution: Clearly 2 and 5 do not divide 97; 3 does not divide it because the sum of the digits, 16, is not divisible by 3; 7 does not divide it if we do the long division. But these are all the primes less than $\sqrt{97} \approx 10$, so 97 is a prime.

EXERCISE 5-27   Factor 141, 1441, and 14441.

At some point in the study of primes, the question arises: How many primes are there? (Do you have a guess?) It was shown by a Greek that there have to be infinitely many primes. The proof is an easy application of contradiction.

Proof: Assume for the sake of contradiction that there are only finitely many primes and call them p_1, p_2, ..., p_n. Now consider the number $P = p_1 p_2 \cdots p_n + 1$. Clearly this number is not divisible by any of the p_i, since dividing by any p_i will leave a remainder of 1. But since P has no prime factor, it has no factor. Thus P is prime; but this is a new prime, not one of the p_i, which we assumed were all the primes. This is a contradiction, so the original assumption of finitely many primes must be false. If you don't understand contradiction, read about it on page 338 and return.

5.7   Common and Uncommon Factors

Given two numbers m and n, it is often important to think about what factors they have in common. For example consider the numbers 84 and 112, which can be factored into $2^2 \cdot 3 \cdot 7$ and $2^4 \cdot 7$, respectively. What prime factors are in common? Exactly two 2's and one 7.

Given the prime factors that are in common, we can write down the composite common factors as well by combining the primes. In our example, the composite common factors are $2^2 = 4$, $2 \cdot 7 = 14$, and $2^2 \cdot 7 = 28$.

The largest factor shared by two numbers is called their **greatest common factor**, or GCF. The greatest common factor is found by multiplying together all the common prime factors, so that for 84 and 112 we have 28 as the GCF. Once we can do the prime factorizations of two numbers, finding the GCF is easy: just combine all the common prime factors. The GCF of two numbers is usually expressed by writing the numbers in parentheses separated by a comma; for example, $(84, 112) = 28$. (Yes, this does look uncomfortably like an ordered pair.)

What about two numbers which, like 28 and 15, have no common factors? In this case, the greatest common factor is 1. Such numbers are called **relatively prime**.

EXAMPLE 5-11   Find the GCF of 100 and 1000.

Solution: The numbers factor as $2^2 \cdot 5^2$ and $2^3 \cdot 5^3$, so they share two 2's and two 5's. The product of these common factors is $2^2 \cdot 5^2 = \mathbf{100}$.

EXERCISE 5-28   Find $(117, 165)$, $(102, 119)$, and $(96, 36)$.

EXERCISE 5-29   Prove that (a, b) must be less than or equal to a, b, and $a - b$, where $a > b$.

Having analyzed the common factors of two integers, we can next think about the factors which are *not* in common. The **least common multiple** (LCM) of two integers is the smallest number which both integers divide evenly.

To see how the LCM works, let's return to our original pair, $84 = 2^2 \cdot 3 \cdot 7$ and $112 = 2^4 \cdot 7$. If an integer is divisible by 84, it must be divisible by two 2's, a 3, and a 7; if it is divisible by 112, it must be divisible by four 2's and one 7. Since we want it to be divisible by both, the LCM must contain four 2's, one 3, and one 7. Moreover, the LCM should not be divisible by anything else, or it would be larger than $2^4 \cdot 3 \cdot 7 = 336$, which is already divisible by both 84 and 112.

To find the LCM, then, we have to factor each number and for each prime, take the largest power which appears in either of the factorizations. The resulting list of powers of primes is multiplied together to get the LCM.

The LCM of two numbers is often written by placing the pair in square brackets, as in $[84, 112] = 336$. Note also that if you add two fractions, the denominator of the new fraction will be the LCM of the denominators of the summed fractions—the process of finding the "least common denominator" is just finding the LCM in disguise.

EXAMPLE 5-12   Find the LCM of 100 and 1000.

Solution: The numbers factor into $2^2 \cdot 5^2$ and $2^3 \cdot 5^3$, so the LCM must have three 2's and three 5's. The product of these factors is $2^3 \cdot 5^3 = \mathbf{1000}$.

EXERCISE 5-30   Find $[117, 165]$, $[102, 119]$, and $[96, 36]$.

EXERCISE 5-31   Show that each pair of integers in the preceding example satisfies $(m, n)[m, n] = mn$.

EXERCISE 5-32   Prove the formula of the previous exercise. This formula can be used to solve problems like, "If the GCF of two numbers is 8 and the product of the numbers is 2880, what is the LCM of the numbers?" Using the above method, we don't even have to find the two numbers!

GCF's and LCM's of more than two numbers are also possible. Here the GCF is the largest factor which divides all the numbers, and the LCM is the smallest number divisible by all the numbers.

EXAMPLE 5-13   Find $[12, 54, 42]$.

Solution: The factorizations of our three numbers are $2^2 \cdot 3$, $2 \cdot 3^3$, and $2 \cdot 3 \cdot 7$. The largest powers encountered are 2^2, 3^3, and 7; multiplying these yields $2^2 \cdot 3^3 \cdot 7 = \mathbf{756}$.

EXERCISE 5-33   Prove that

$$(l, m, n)[lm, mn, nl] = lmn$$

for positive integers l, m, and n.

Problems to Solve for Chapter 5

You are not expected to be able to do all of these now. Do the ones you can, and return to the others after you have completed more of the book.

87. Find the GCF of 36, 27, and 45.

88. How many multiples of 7 are there between 100 and 200?

89. Find the units digit of 19^{93}.

90. Find the 1275th term of the series $1, 3, 5, \ldots, 15, 1, 3, 5, \ldots, 15, 1, \ldots$ (Mandelbrot #3)

91. Find the smallest positive integer which when divided by 10 leaves a remainder of 9, when divided by 9 leaves a remainder of 8, by 8 leaves a remainder of 7, etc., down to where, when divided by 2, it leaves a remainder of 1. (AHSME 1951)

92. Find the value of digit A if the five-digit number $12A3B$ is divisible by both 4 and 9, and $A \neq B$. (MATHCOUNTS 1986)

93. Find the units digit of $3^{1986} - 2^{1986}$. (MATHCOUNTS 1986)

94. In how many ways can a debt of $69 be paid exactly using only $5 bills and $2 bills? (MATHCOUNTS 1988)

95. Find the sum of all four digit natural numbers of the form $4AB8$ which are divisible by 2, 3, 4, 6, 8, and 9. (MATHCOUNTS 1988)

96. If a set of markers is placed in rows of 4 each, there are 2 markers left over; if in rows of 5 each, there are 3 left over; and if in rows of 7 there are 5 left over. What is the smallest number of markers that the set could contain? (MATHCOUNTS 1984)

97. When n is divided by 5, the remainder is 1. What is the remainder when $3n$ is divided by 5? (MATHCOUNTS 1991)

98. A six place number is formed by repeating a three place number; for example 256,256 or 678,678, etc. What is the largest integer that divides all such integers? (AHSME 1951)

99. A base-two numeral consists of 15 digits, all of which are ones. When tripled and written in base two, how many digits does this number contain? (MATHCOUNTS 1986)

100. What is the largest base 10 number that can be expressed as a 3-digit base 5 number? (MATHCOUNTS 1989)

101. How many natural numbers require 3 digits when written in base 12, but require 4 digits when written in base 9? (MATHCOUNTS 1989)

102. Given $9^6 = 531,441$, how would you represent $531,440$ in base 9? (MATHCOUNTS 1990)

103. Find the smallest positive integer greater than one which yields a remainder of one when divided by any single digit positive integer greater than 1. (Mandelbrot #3)

104. A store sold 72 decks of cards for $\$a67.9b$. Find $a + b$. (MAΘ 1991)

105. For each of $n = 84$ and $n = 88$, find the smallest integer multiple of n whose base 10 representation consists entirely of 6's and 7's. (USAMTS 1)

106. When the number n is written in base b its representation is the two-digit number AB where $A = b - 2$ and $B = 2$. What is the representation of n in base $(b - 1)$? (MAΘ 1991)

107. If $a \neq 1$ and $\sqrt[a]{10000_a} = 10_a$, find a. (MAΘ 1990)

108. Denote by p_k the kth prime number. Show that $p_1 p_2 \cdots p_n + 1$ cannot be the perfect square of an integer. (M&IQ 1992)

109. Prove that it is impossible for three consecutive squares to sum to another perfect square. (Mandelbrot #2)

the BIG PICTURE

One of the most interesting aspects of the world of mathematics is the existence of **conjectures**, assertions which many think may be true but which no one is able to prove—or disprove. Many famous conjectures are or were in the realm of number theory.

An early instance was the conjecture of Mersenne in the mid-1600's that all integers of the form $2^{2^n} + 1$, called **Mersenne numbers**, are prime. It looks true for the first few n: $n = 1$ yields 5; $n = 2$ yields 17; $n = 3$, 257. (Can you verify that 257 is prime?) The fourth Mersenne number, $2^{16} + 1$, is also prime; with no computers to do the complicated calculations, this was as high as anyone could go. However, in the mid-1700's Leonhard Euler was able to find an explicit factor of $2^{32} + 1$, the fifth Mersenne number, and the conjecture was proved false.

Other conjectures were more fortunate; many live on to this day. Christian Goldbach conjectured in the early 1700's that every even integer greater than 4 could be written as the sum of two primes. (For example, $6 = 3+3$, $8 = 5+3$, $36 = 19 + 17$, and $200 = 97 + 103$.) **Goldbach's conjecture**, as it has come to be called, is to this day an open question. The most powerful computers have been unable to find a counterexample, and the best mathematicians have been unable to prove it. Steps have been made toward a proof, and some feel it is in sight, but that is as far as it goes.

The most famous conjecture of all time was also in the field of number theory. **Fermat's Last Theorem** haunted mathematicians (and amateur solvers, who have flooded publications with bogus "proofs") for centuries. In 1993, Andrew Wiles, a professor at Princeton University, finally finished the theorem off, but he required seven years' unremitting labor, as well as a very large body of supporting work by others, to do it. Old conjectures die hard.

Chapter 6

Quadratic Equations

6.1 What's a Quadratic?

When you study the physics of moving objects, you'll start with objects moving at a constant rate. For example, if a rock is thrown from a 100 foot tower and travels 5 feet per second from the top of the tower to the ground, it takes 20 seconds for the rock to hit the ground. Unfortunately, the real world isn't so simple. Gravity causes the rock to accelerate. The actual height above the ground in feet of the rock at time t is better described by $100 - 5t - 16t^2$. (Take this on faith for now, or read the first couple chapters of a basic physics book.) Now how long does the rock stay in the air? To find this, we must solve $100 - 5t - 16t^2 = 0$, because we want the time at which the height is 0. This is a **quadratic equation** because it has degree 2. If we just solve this as a linear equation, we get $t = (100 - 16t^2)/5$, which doesn't really tell us anything about t.

In this chapter, we examine methods used to solve quadratic equations and the use of these methods on other types of problems.

6.2 Factoring Quadratics

How do quadratics occur? You could think of them as a product of linear factors, such as

$$(x + 2)(x + 3) = x(x + 3) + 2(x + 3) = x^2 + 5x + 6.$$

Suppose we are asked to find the solutions to $x^2 + 5x + 6 = 0$. From above, we know this quadratic is the product $(x+2)(x+3)$. The solutions to the equation are the values of x which make this product 0. Thus, either $x+2=0$ or $x+3=0$, and our solutions are -2 and -3.

If we can find the factored form of a quadratic as above, we can always find where the quadratic equals 0. Fortunately, any equation of the form $ax^2+bx+c=0$ (where a, b, and c are the **coefficients** of the quadratic) can always be **factored** as

$$ax^2 + bx + c = a(x-r)(x-s) = 0.$$

The quantities r and s are called the **roots**, **zeroes**, or solutions of the quadratic equation. As above, these are the solutions of the equation because the expression $a(x-r)(x-s)$ can only be zero when either $(x-r)=0$ or $(x-s)=0$ (remember $a \neq 0$). Thus the expression equals zero when x equals r or s. Before we discuss how to find the factored form of a quadratic equation, we should first review how to multiply general expressions like $(x-r)(x-s)$ via the distributive property:

$$(x-r)(x-s) = x(x-s) + (-r)(x-s) = x^2 - sx - rx + rs = x^2 - (r+s)x + rs.$$

Can you see the relationship between the sum and product of the roots and the coefficients of the quadratic?

This same method also works when there are more than two terms in the parentheses, and when there are more than two sets of parentheses.

EXAMPLE 6-1   Expand the expression $(x-a)(x-a-b)(x+a)$.

Solution: Let's call this expression $f(x)$. We start by multiplying the first two parentheses and then multiply the result by the third parentheses. It goes

$$\begin{aligned} f(x) &= [x(x-a-b) + (-a)(x-a-b)](x+a) \\ &= (x^2 - 2ax - bx + a^2 + ab)(x+a) \\ &= x^2(x+a) - 2ax(x+a) - bx(x+a) + a^2(x+a) + ab(x+a). \end{aligned}$$

By expanding the last expression above, we come to our final answer,

$$(x-a)(x-a-b)(x+a) = x^3 - ax^2 - bx^2 - a^2x + a^3 + a^2b.$$

 EXERCISE 6-1   Show that $(x+y)^3 = x^3 + 3x^2y + 3xy^2 + y^3$. You will see this again, many times.

Now we come to the question of how to factor quadratic equations. Sometimes we are fortunate and are able to guess the factorization of the quadratic; being good at factoring requires ingenuity, experience, and sometimes dumb luck. Although we have a few helping hints to guide us, factoring is largely a matter of trial and error.

Let's try to factor $x^2 - 3x + 2$. We wish to write this as $(x + u)(x + v)$. Writing this product as

$$(x + u)(x + v) = x(x + v) + u(x + v) = x^2 + (u + v)x + uv,$$

we can compare the coefficients of this general form to those of the original quadratic. From the constant terms of the two quadratics we get $uv = 2$, and from the coefficients of x, we have $u + v = -3$. (Make sure you see why.) Assuming u and v are integers, from $uv = 2$ we find that u and v are either 1 and 2 or -1 and -2. Using $u + v = -3$, we determine that the latter is correct. Thus,

$$x^2 - 3x + 2 = (x - 1)(x - 2).$$

As we have seen, factoring comes down to guessing two numbers given their product and their sum. The product of the two is given by the constant term of the quadratic, and the sum by the negative of the coefficient of x. We gain further helping hints in our factoring efforts from the signs of the product and the sum. If the product of the two numbers is positive, then the numbers must have the same sign. If the product is negative, then the signs must be different. If the product of the numbers is positive (and hence the numbers are the same sign), the sum will tell us if the numbers are positive or negative.

How would we factor $-4x^2 - 8x - 3$? Our above discussion only deals with quadratics whose leading coefficient is 1. Our first instinct might be to divide the quadratic by -4 to make the leading coefficient 1, but this would introduce fractional coefficients, which usually cause trouble. We will however, factor out a -1, because it is always best to have a positive coefficient of x^2. Now we have $-(4x^2 + 8x + 3)$. We look for a factorization of $4x^2 + 8x + 3$ of the form $(sx + u)(tx + v)$. Expanding this we find

$$(sx + u)(tx + v) = stx^2 + (sv + ut)x + uv = 4x^2 + 8x + 3.$$

We have left the world of simple trial and error and entered the domain of magic and luck. From the above we find $st = 4$, $sv + ut = 8$, and $uv = 3$. Always let s and t be positive, and factoring will be much easier. Now we guess $u = 3$ and $v = 1$.

Thus, $s + 3t = 8$ and $st = 4$. After trying $(s, t) = (1, 4)$; $(4, 1)$; and $(2, 2)$, we note that $(2, 2)$ works, so

$$4x^2 + 8x + 3 = (2x + 1)(2x + 3).$$

Your first choices for u and v will not always work; had we chosen $(u, v) = (-1, -3)$ and maintained that s and t be positive, we would have $-s - 3t = 8$, which has no positive solutions.

Although factoring when the leading coefficient is not $+1$ can be very difficult, the guiding signs noted before can also be used here to determine the signs of u and v. When the coefficient of x^2 is positive, the constant term of the quadratic is the product uv, and thus determines if u and v have the same sign or not. The coefficient of x, if the constant term is positive, determines the common sign of u and v. It is very important to remember in this that the coefficient of x^2 must be positive, as must both s and t in order for these hints to be true. (Why?)

Be patient when learning how to factor. It takes much practice, but in time you'll be able to factor without even writing down the u's and v's.

EXAMPLE 6-2 Solve the quadratic equations $x^2 + 9x + 18 = 0$ and $x^2 - x - 30 = 0$.

Solution: For the first, we seek two numbers whose product is 18 and sum is 9. Since both the product and the sum are positive, both the numbers are positive. Since $18 = 1 \cdot 18 = 2 \cdot 9 = 3 \cdot 6$, we only have 3 possibilities. We find that $x^2 + 9x + 18 = (x + 3)(x + 6)$. Thus, $x^2 + 9x + 18 = 0$ if $x + 3 = 0$ or $x + 6 = 0$. Hence our solutions are $x = \mathbf{-3}$ and $x = \mathbf{-6}$. (Put these solutions back in the original equation to check them.)

For the second, we seek two numbers whose product is -30 and whose sum is -1. Since the product is negative, the two numbers differ in sign. Because the sum of the numbers is -1, the magnitudes of the two numbers differ by 1. Since $5 \cdot 6 = 30$, our only options are 5 and -6, or -5 and 6. The former gives us a sum of -1, and thus is correct. Hence $x^2 - x - 30 = (x - 6)(x + 5) = 0$, and the solutions are $\mathbf{6}$ and $\mathbf{-5}$.

EXAMPLE 6-3 Find all x that satisfy $x^2 + \frac{3}{2}x = 1$.

Solution: Our first step is to get all the terms on one side and make all the coefficients integers by multiplying the whole equation by 2. (This should always be your first step when trying to factor a quadratic equation.) Doing so yields

$$2x^2 + 3x - 2 = 0.$$

Assuming that the factored form is $(sx + u)(tx + v)$, where s and t are positive, we obtain

$$uv = -2 = -st.$$

Since t and u can be at most 2 each and $tu + sv = 3$ (do you see why?), we try $t = u = 2$, $s = 1$, $v = -1$. This works (of course, this isn't always true of your first guess), so the factored form of our quadratic is $(x + 2)(2x - 1)$, and the desired x are -2 and $1/2$.

EXERCISE 6-2 Find the solutions to the following equations:

  i. $x^2 = -5x - 6$.

  ii. $x^2 - 3x - 40 = 0$.

  iii. $2x^2 + \frac{1}{3}x - \frac{2}{3} = 0$.

  iv. $49x^2 - 316x + 132 = 0$. If you can factor this successfully, you have probably mastered the art of factoring.

  v. $x = \dfrac{28}{x - 3}$.

EXERCISE 6-3 When factoring the quadratic $x^2 + bx + c$, where b and c are integers, why do we not consider the case where u and v in the factored form $(x + u)(x + v)$ are fractions?

There are three special factorizations which you should learn and be able to recognize easily.

1. *Equations in which one root is zero.* Because the product of the roots is zero, the constant term is zero. Thus, these equations always look like $ax^2 + bx = 0$. Factoring these is very easy, as we just write $ax^2 + bx = x(ax + b) = 0$.

2. *Equations of the form $x^2 - a^2 = 0$.* These factor as $(x - a)(x + a) = 0$. (Multiply it out yourself and see.) These can also be solved by rearranging the equation and taking the square root: $x^2 = a^2$, so $x = \pm\sqrt{a^2} = \pm a$.

3. *Perfect squares.* The square of $(x + a)$ is $(x + a)^2 = x^2 + 2ax + a^2$. These are usually the hardest to recognize.

EXAMPLE 6-4   Consider the following examples of the above factorizations:

    i. $5x^2 - 3x = x(5x - 3)$.

    ii. $4x^2 - 9 = (2x + 3)(2x - 3)$. This one is a bit tricky. Compare it to the second form above and notice that $4x^2$ is a perfect square of $2x$.

    iii. $x^2 + 6x + 9 = (x + 3)^2$.

    iv. $4x^2 + 12x + 9 = (2x + 3)^2$. Another tricky one. Compare this to the third form above, putting $2x$ in place of x and 3 in place of a.

EXERCISE 6-4   Solve each of the following equations.

    i. $3x^2 + 5x = 0$ ii. $3x^2 + 6x + 3 = 0$

    iii. $5x^2 - 45 = 0$ iv. $\dfrac{x^2}{3} - 2x + 3 = 0$

     v. $4x^2 = 5x$ vi. $36 - 25x^2 = 0$

6.3   The Quadratic Formula

Unfortunately, not all quadratic equations have nice simple roots like 1 or -2. Indeed, not all quadratic equations can be factored easily. For example, try to find all solutions to $x^2 + x - 1 = 0$. It shouldn't take you too long to convince yourself that factoring isn't going to get you far. Hence, we look for a *general* way to find the solutions to quadratic equations, which avoids the limitations of factoring.

     We have already seen that it is pretty easy to solve linear equations, so if we could somehow make the quadratic equation into a linear equation, then we could solve it. Since quadratic equations have a squared term, it seems the easiest way to do this would be to take square roots. Let's try:

$$ax^2 = -bx - c,$$

so

$$\sqrt{a}\,x = \sqrt{-bx - c}.$$

Unfortunately, this is not a linear equation because of the x in the $\sqrt{-bx - c}$. What we really need to do is to manipulate the given quadratic into the form $x^2 + 2xm + m^2$, because we know how to take the square root of that (remember special factorization 3 on page 73). This method is called **completing the square**.

Our first step is to get rid of the coefficient of x^2. Dividing the equation by a gives

$$x^2 + \frac{b}{a}x + \frac{c}{a} = 0.$$

To complete the square, we will need a new constant term. So we first move the old constant term to the other side of the equation, to get

$$x^2 + \frac{b}{a}x = -\frac{c}{a}.$$

We now need to find a constant term which will yield the form $x^2 + 2xm + m^2$. The coefficient of x, or $2m$, needs to be halved, then squared, to get the constant term, m^2. In our quadratic, this x coefficient is b/a, so we add $(b/2a)^2$ to each side, yielding

$$x^2 + \frac{b}{a}x + \frac{b^2}{4a^2} = -\frac{c}{a} + \frac{b^2}{4a^2}.$$

(If you aren't convinced that the left side of this equation is a perfect square, multiply out the expression below and see for yourself.) Now our equation is

$$\left(x + \frac{b}{2a}\right)^2 = \frac{b^2 - 4ac}{4a^2}.$$

Taking the square root of both sides of the equation (remembering that we want both the positive and negative roots), we have

$$x + \frac{b}{2a} = \pm\frac{\sqrt{b^2 - 4ac}}{2a}.$$

As advertised, this is just a linear equation! Solving then yields

$$x = \frac{-b \pm \sqrt{b^2 - 4ac}}{2a}.$$

This is the **quadratic formula**. Don't be confused by the $\pm$ sign; it simply means that there are two solutions to the equation. To get them both, you use the positive sign for one and the negative sign for the other.

To make sure you understand this proof, close the book after reading through the proof a few times and try to re-create the proof. It is important that you understand completing the square as a general solution technique, as it is useful for various other types of problems.

Using the quadratic formula is quite simple. Returning to our introductory example, $x^2 + x - 1 = 0$, the solutions are

$$x = \frac{-1 \pm \sqrt{1+4}}{2} = \frac{-1 \pm \sqrt{5}}{2}.$$

As you can see, you would have a hard time guessing these roots using the trial and error method; the roots are not even rational.

If a quadratic has real coefficients, we can immediately tell whether the roots are real or imaginary by considering the **discriminant** of the equation. Consider the quadratic formula again. If a, b, and c are real, where can imaginary quantities enter? Only through the $\sqrt{b^2 - 4ac}$ term, which is imaginary when $b^2 - 4ac < 0$ and real when $b^2 - 4ac \geq 0$. The quantity $b^2 - 4ac$ is called the discriminant. To reiterate, *if the discriminant is negative, the roots are imaginary, and if it is positive, the roots are real.*

Moreover, if the discriminant is 0, the two roots of the quadratic are the same, and equal to

$$x = \frac{-b \pm \sqrt{b^2 - 4ac}}{2a} = \frac{-b \pm 0}{2a} = \frac{-b}{2a}.$$

EXAMPLE 6-5   Find the roots of $3x^2 + x + 4$.

Solution: Just plug the coefficients into the quadratic formula:

$$x = \frac{-1 \pm \sqrt{1 - 4(3)(4)}}{2(3)} = \frac{-1 \pm i\sqrt{47}}{6}$$

Try using trial and error to arrive at those solutions.

We see that in the above example, the roots are complex conjugates. This is no fluke. How does the quadratic formula suggest this?

 Whenever the roots of a quadratic equation with real coefficients are imaginary, they are conjugates. Furthermore, if the quadratic has rational coefficients and $x + y\sqrt{z}$ is a root, then $x - y\sqrt{z}$ must also be a root.

EXAMPLE 6-6 Prove that if one of the roots of a quadratic with real coefficients is imaginary, then the two roots of the quadratic are complex conjugates.

Proof: As we have seen, one of the roots is imaginary only if $b^2 - 4ac < 0$. From the quadratic formula, the roots of $ax^2 + bx + c = 0$ are

$$-\frac{b}{2a} \pm \frac{\sqrt{b^2 - 4ac}}{2a} = -\frac{b}{2a} \pm \frac{\sqrt{-1}\sqrt{4ac - b^2}}{2a} = -\frac{b}{2a} \pm \frac{\sqrt{4ac - b^2}}{2a}i.$$

This final expression of the roots is a pair of complex conjugates; thus, the roots are complex conjugates if $b^2 - 4ac < 0$.

EXERCISE 6-5 Given that x, y, and z are rational and $\sqrt{z}$ is not, show that if $x + y\sqrt{z}$ is a root of a quadratic with rational coefficients, then $x - y\sqrt{z}$ is also a root.

These two facts are *very* important. If ever we know one of the roots of a quadratic with rational coefficients and it is imaginary or irrational, then we immediately know the other root!

If so many quadratic equations cannot be solved using trial and error, then why should you bother learning how to factor quadratic equations without using the quadratic formula? The answer is simple: speed. It is much faster to factor than to plod through the quadratic formula (as long as the equation is factorable!). With some practice, you will learn to distinguish those quadratics you can factor from those you can't.

Do you actually have to memorize that awful equation? The truth is that after you use the formula enough, you'll memorize it whether you want to or not. More important than the formula itself is how it is derived and why it works. If you know how to derive the equation, you can figure out the formula if you happen to forget it. You can also use the method of completing the square to solve other types of problems.

EXAMPLE 6-7 If one root of $x^2 + bx + c = 0$ is $3 + \sqrt{2}$, find b and c.

Solution: Since $3 + \sqrt{2}$ is a root, $3 - \sqrt{2}$ is also a root. Thus, the quadratic is

$$\left(x - (3 + \sqrt{2})\right)\left(x - (3 - \sqrt{2})\right) = x^2 - 6x + 7.$$

Hence $b = -6$ and $c = 7$. (Can you use the result of the next exercise to avoid performing the above product to answer this problem?)

EXERCISE 6-6   Use the quadratic formula to show that the sum of the roots of $ax^2 + bx + c$ is $-b/a$ and that the product of the roots is c/a.

EXERCISE 6-7   Solve the following equations.

     i. $x^2 + 3x + 1 = 0$ ii. $4x^2 - x + 7 = 0$

    iii. $z^2 - 4/3 = z$ iv. $0.2 - 0.1z^2 = z$

EXERCISE 6-8   Given that $x^3 + 3x^2 + 3x + 1 = (x+1)^3$, find all real x such that $x^3 + 3x^2 + 3x = 1$.

6.4   Variations on a Theme

Not all quadratic equations look like $ax^2 + bx + c = 0$. In this section, we will work a series of examples to show you other forms of quadratic equations and how to solve them. These can generally be divided into two categories, rearrangement problems and substitution problems. The former can be solved by manipulating the equation into quadratic form through multiplications and other operations; the latter can be made into a quadratic with a clever substitution. Although these substitutions are sometimes difficult to see, the problem is usually easy to solve once you've got the substitution.

6.4.1   Rearrangements

These problems generally involve variables in denominators of fractions or as the argument of a square root.

EXAMPLE 6-8   Find all y such that $1 + \dfrac{y+3}{y-2} = \dfrac{3y-3}{6-y}$.

    Solution: Variables in the denominator of fractions are difficult to deal with, so it is usually best to multiply both sides by any expressions which appear in any denominator. We thus obtain

$$(6-y)(y-2)\left(1 + \frac{y+3}{y-2}\right) = (6-y)(y-2)\left(\frac{3y-3}{6-y}\right);$$

then multiplying out yields

$$(6-y)(y-2) + (6-y)(y-2)\frac{y+3}{y-2} = (y-2)(3y-3),$$

or

$$-2y^2 + 11y + 6 = 3y^2 - 9y + 6.$$

Rearranging this last equation yields $5y^2 - 20y = 0$, from which we find that our solutions are $y = 0$ and $y = 4$. We are not quite done yet, though; we must make sure that neither of these solutions causes any denominator to be zero. If one of these does cause the denominator to be zero, that solution must be discarded as an **extraneous root**, which is a solution that does not satisfy the original equation. This is not the case for either of our solutions, so **4** and **0** are our answers.

EXAMPLE 6-9   Find all x such that $\sqrt{x+3} + 4 = \sqrt{8x+1}$.

Solution: We must do something to get rid of the radical signs. Squaring the equation is generally a good way to do this:

$$\begin{aligned}
(\sqrt{x+3}+4)^2 &= (\sqrt{8x+1})^2 \\
(x+3) + 2(4)(\sqrt{x+3}) + 16 &= 8x + 1 \\
x + 19 + 8\sqrt{x+3} &= 8x + 1.
\end{aligned}$$

We still have a radical sign, but if we move all the other terms to the other side, we can square the resulting equation and get rid of the radical. Rearranging gives $8\sqrt{x+3} = 7x - 18$, and squaring this equation gives

$$\begin{aligned}
64(x+3) &= 49x^2 - 2(18)(7x) + 324 \\
64x + 192 &= 49x^2 - 252x + 324.
\end{aligned}$$

Rearranging yields $49x^2 - 316x + 132 = 0$, and factoring this result gives $(x - 6)(49x - 22) = 0$. Thus our solutions are $x = 6$ and $x = 22/49$.

Once again, we are not done; we must check for extraneous solutions. Substituting $x = 6$ in the equation yields $3 + 4 = 7$, which is fine. However, when we plug in the second solution, we reach the erroneous conclusion that $13/7 + 4 = 15/7$. How did this happen?

The problem occurred because $-13/7$ squared is also equal to $x + 3$ when $x = 22/49$. Then the equation reads $-13/7 + 4 = 15/7$, which is fine. However, when working problems in which the radical sign is already present *the positive value of the radical is implied*. Thus $x = 22/49$ is an extraneous solution and the only answer is $x = \mathbf{6}$.

As we see here, the general procedure for solving equations with square roots involved is to manipulate the equation to isolate a radical, then square to get rid of the radical (repeating if there is more than one radical to deal with). We then solve the equation, not forgetting to check that all solutions do indeed 'work'.

EXAMPLE 6-10 Find all pairs (x, y) such that $x + y = xy = 2$.

Solution: Since $x + y = 2$, we have $x = 2 - y$. Since $xy = 2$, we then find

$$xy = (2 - y)y = 2y - y^2 = 2,$$

so $y^2 - 2y + 2 = 0$. Using the quadratic formula, we find

$$y = \frac{2 \pm 2i}{2} = 1 \pm i.$$

Now, we use $x = 2 - y$ to find the x corresponding to each y. Thus, our solutions are $(\mathbf{1 - i}, \mathbf{1 + i})$ and $(\mathbf{1 + i}, \mathbf{1 - i})$.

EXAMPLE 6-11 Note that in the prior exercise, if we let x and y be the roots of the quadratic $z^2 + az + b = 0$, we can determine that $a = -(x + y) = -2$ and $b = xy = 2$. Thus, x and y are the solutions of $z^2 - 2z + 2 = 0$ and hence are $1 + i$ and $1 - i$ as we found above.

EXERCISE 6-9 Find all z such that $\sqrt{5z + 5} - \sqrt{3 - 3z} - 2\sqrt{z} = 0$.

6.4.2 Substitutions

In substitution problems, an expression, like 3^x, and the square of the expression, like 3^{2x}, appear in the same equation. Substituting another variable for the expression, like $y = 3^x$, makes a quadratic in the new variable. We solve for the new variable (y), then find the original unknown (x) from our definition for the new one.

EXAMPLE 6-12   Find all real n such that $1 + 2^n + 2^{2n} = 73$. (MAΘ 1987)

Solution: Here, our expression is 2^n and its square is 2^{2n}. Thus, let $x = 2^n$, so $x^2 = 2^{2n}$. The equation is then $1 + x + x^2 = 73$. Rearranging and factoring gives $(x + 9)(x - 8) = 0$, so $x = -9$ and $x = 8$. Substituting these into our expressions for n yields $-9 = 2^n$, which has no solution, and $8 = 2^n$, for which $n = 3$. Thus $n = \mathbf{3}$ is the only solution.

EXAMPLE 6-13   Find all x such that $x^4 + 3x^2 - 4 = 0$.

Solution: The variable is x^2 and its square is x^4. Letting $z = x^2$, we have $z^2 + 3z - 4 = (z + 4)(z - 1) = 0$. Thus our solutions are $z = 1$ and $z = -4$. Going back to x, we find $x^2 = 1$, which has the solutions $x = \pm\mathbf{1}$, or $x^2 = -4$, which has the solutions $x = \pm\mathbf{2i}$. These are all valid solutions.

What if we were to change the problem to $x^4 + 3x^2 + x - 4 = 0$? The expression x^2 and its square are still present, but there is also a third expression in terms of x which is neither the original expression nor its square. Thus, we cannot rewrite the equation as a quadratic.

EXERCISE 6-10   Find all real values of x which satisfy $\sqrt{x^2 + 1} + x^2 + 1 = 90$. (MAΘ 1991)

6.5   Square Roots of Irrationals and Imaginaries

Recalling the expansion $(x + y)^2 = x^2 + 2xy + y^2$, it should be clear how to square expressions like $1 + \sqrt{3}$ and $1 - 2i$. For example,

$$(1 + \sqrt{3})^2 = 1^2 + 2(1)(\sqrt{3}) + (\sqrt{3})^2 = 4 + 2\sqrt{3}.$$

However, what if we were instead asked to find $\sqrt{4 + 2\sqrt{3}}$? From the above expansion, we know the answer is $1 + \sqrt{3}$, but how would we have determined this starting from scratch? As in solving quadratic equations, there is a guesswork method (like factoring) for simple cases and a rigorous method (like the quadratic formula) for more difficult ones.

When asked to find $\sqrt{a + b\sqrt{c}}$, where a, b, and c are integers, our biggest helping hint is the $b\sqrt{c}$ term. If c is prime, we know one of the terms in our square root has $\sqrt{c}$ and the other is a constant. For example, in determining $\sqrt{4 + 2\sqrt{3}}$, we know the result is of the form $x + y\sqrt{3}$ because 3 is prime.

Thus, if c is prime, $\sqrt{a + b\sqrt{c}}$ will take the form $x + y\sqrt{c}$ for some x and y. How do we find x and y? Squaring, we obtain

$$(x + y\sqrt{c})^2 = x^2 + cy^2 + 2xy\sqrt{c} = a + b\sqrt{c},$$

and matching the terms up yields the system

$$\begin{aligned} 2xy &= b \\ x^2 + cy^2 &= a. \end{aligned}$$

Our task, then, is to solve the system for x and y.

Here is where our two methods diverge. If b has a small number of factors, we can use the first equation to guess at x and y, then substitute the guesses into the second equation to see if the guesses are right. However, if b has a large number of factors, or if x and y are complicated irrational forms rather than nice integers, trial and error could take a very long time. In these cases, we need to solve the equations the hard way.

EXAMPLE 6-14   Find $\sqrt{34 - 24\sqrt{2}}$.

Solution: We know the answer is of the form $x + y\sqrt{2}$. Since $(x + y\sqrt{2})^2 = x^2 + 2xy\sqrt{2} + 2y^2 = 34 - 24\sqrt{2}$, the system we need to solve is

$$\begin{aligned} xy &= -12 \\ x^2 + 2y^2 &= 34. \end{aligned}$$

First let's try trial and error. We write down pairs (x, y) such that $xy = -12$, looking for a pair which satisfies the second equation, $x^2 + 2y^2 = 34$. We try $(1, -12)$, but it fails, as does $(6, -2)$. Finally we try $(4, -3)$, which succeeds, so $(4 - 3\sqrt{2})^2 = 34 - 24\sqrt{2}$.

However, $-(4 - 3\sqrt{2})$ is also a square root of $34 - 24\sqrt{2}$. Which of the two do we want? Recall that the positive square root is implied in the expression $\sqrt{34 - 24\sqrt{2}}$.

Since

$$18 = (3\sqrt{2})^2 > 4^2 = 16,$$

we see that $3\sqrt{2} > 4$, so $-4 + 3\sqrt{2} > 0$ and this is the desired answer. WARNING: When finding the square root of an irrational, always make sure you have a positive answer.

Since 12 has many factors, we may wish to solve the equations for (x, y), rather than resorting to guesswork. We write $y = -12/x$ and substitute this in the second equation, yielding $x^2 + 2(-12/x)^2 = 34$, so $x^2 + 288/x^2 = 34$. Multiplying by x^2 and rearranging, we have

$$x^4 - 34x^2 + 288 = 0.$$

We can factor this as a quadratic (if you don't see this, let $z = x^2$), giving $(x^2 - 16)(x^2 - 18) = 0$. Since we want x to be an integer, $x = \pm 4$. For each of these we find y, generating the same two solutions as before. What would happen if we tried $x = \pm 3\sqrt{2}$, the other solutions to the equation for x?

What if c is not prime, as in $\sqrt{5 + 2\sqrt{6}}$? We first try answers of the form $x + y\sqrt{c}$ ($x + y\sqrt{6}$ in the example), but we are no longer assured that this will work. The answer may be of the form $x\sqrt{w} + y\sqrt{z}$, where $c = zw$. For example, to find $\sqrt{5 + 2\sqrt{6}}$, if we first try expressions of the form $x + y\sqrt{6}$, we won't find the answer. When we consider expressions of the form $x\sqrt{2} + y\sqrt{3}$, we have

$$(x\sqrt{2} + y\sqrt{3})^2 = 2x^2 + 3y^2 + 2xy\sqrt{6}.$$

Now, we're back in common territory, looking for x and y such that $2xy = 2$ and $2x^2 + 3y^2 = 5$. Either by trial and error or direct solution, we find $(x, y) = (1, 1)$, so $\sqrt{5 + 2\sqrt{6}} = \sqrt{2} + \sqrt{3}$.

For imaginary numbers, our search is very similar to that for irrationals. We know the square root of the complex number $a + bi$ is of the form $x + yi$. Thus,

$$(x + yi)^2 = x^2 - y^2 + 2xyi = (\sqrt{a + bi})^2 = a + bi.$$

Equating imaginary parts, $2xy = b$; equating real parts, $x^2 - y^2 = a$. Again we have a system to solve for (x, y).

EXAMPLE 6-15   Find $\sqrt{5 - 12i}$.

Solution: Let $\sqrt{5 - 12i} = a + bi$. Thus

$$(a + bi)^2 = a^2 - b^2 + 2abi = 5 - 12i,$$

so we get the system

$$2ab = -12$$
$$a^2 - b^2 = 5.$$

Solving the equations without trial and error, we write $b = -6/a$ and $a^2 - 36/a^2 = 5$. From the latter equation, we have $a^4 - 5a^2 - 36 = (a^2 - 9)(a^2 + 4)$. Since we want a to be real, $a = \pm 3$. Using this to find b, we get the two solutions $\pm(\mathbf{3} - \mathbf{2i})$. Since there is no distinction between "positive" and "negative" for imaginary numbers, the two solutions are equally valid. (What would happen if we let $a = \pm 2i$? Try it!)

In this particular case, trial and error is just as good an approach as direct solving. From $ab = -6$, we try $(6, -1)$, which fails (because $6^2 - (-1)^2 = 35$, not 5), then $(3, -2)$, which succeeds. Thus $\sqrt{5 - 12i} = 3 - 2i$. As before, $-3 + 2i$ also works.

EXERCISE 6-11   Evaluate the following.

  i. $\sqrt{35 - 10\sqrt{10}}$

 ii. $\sqrt{55 - 10\sqrt{10}}$

iii. $\sqrt{15 + 8i}$

It is important to note that irrational and imaginary numbers don't always have nice neat square roots—for example, try to find $\sqrt{1 + \sqrt{2}}$. However, when we are asked on a test to find a square root of a particular irrational or imaginary number, chances are that the problem will have a simple answer.

6.6   Beyond Quadratics

We have covered linear equations, in which the unknown quantity is raised only to the first power, and quadratics, in which the unknown is raised to the first and second powers. However, these are only the tip of the iceberg. One can consider expressions with any power of the unknown quantity whatsoever, like

$$x^{17} + 38x^{11} + 12x^{10} - 76x^4 + 123.$$

Expressions like this, which are the sum of constants times positive integral powers of x (or any other variable), are called **polynomials**.

We won't examine polynomials in any detail here, because solving them is much harder than solving linear equations and quadratics. However, polynomials *do* have solutions. As with quadratics, the solutions are called **roots**. A polynomial, like a quadratic, can be factored into linear expressions involving its roots, though there will be more such factors. For example, a polynomial with roots 1, 2, 3, ..., 17 could be written in factored form as

$$(x - 1)(x - 2)(x - 3) \cdots (x - 17).$$

A polynomial of degree three is called a **cubic**, and a polynomial of degree four is called a **quartic**.

Problems to Solve for Chapter 6

110. What is the positive difference of the roots of $x^2 - 7x - 9$? (AHSME 1952)

111. Find all the solutions of

$$\sqrt{x + 10} - \frac{6}{\sqrt{x + 10}} = 5.$$

(AHSME 1953)

112. For all values other than $x = -1$ and $x = 2$, what is the value of

$$\frac{2x^2 - x}{(x + 1)(x - 2)} - \frac{4 + x}{(x + 1)(x - 2)}?$$

(AHSME 1954)

113. Find all values of z such that $\dfrac{z}{z - 1} = \dfrac{z + 1}{z} - 2$.

114. Find $\sqrt{-27 + 36i}$.

115. If $9n^2 - 30n + c$ is a perfect square for all integers n, what is the value of c? (MATHCOUNTS 1989)

116. Find all pairs (a, b) such that $2a + b = 12$ and $ab = 3$.

117. When there is no wind, a plane traveling at a constant rate can cover the 1000 kilometer round-trip distance from A to B and back in 10 hours. If the wind blows from A toward B at k km/hr, it adds 25 minutes to the round trip. Find k. (MAΘ 1990)

118. Find $2x + 5$ if x satisfies $\sqrt{40 - 9x} - 2\sqrt{7 - x} = \sqrt{-x}$. (MAΘ 1991)

119. How many roots does $x - \dfrac{7}{x - 3} = 3 - \dfrac{7}{x - 3}$ have? (AHSME 1960)

120. What is the sum of the solutions of $2x^{-2} + x^{-1} - 1 = 0$? (MAΘ 1991)

121. About the equation $ax^2 - 2x\sqrt{2} + c = 0$, with a and c real constants, we are told that the discriminant is zero. Which of the following must the roots be: integral, rational, irrational, imaginary, real? (AHSME 1956)

122. Which of the following statements are *not* true for the equation $ix^2 - x + 2i = 0$?
(A) The sum of the roots is 2.
(B) The discriminant is 9.
(C) The roots are imaginary.
(D) The roots can be found by using the quadratic formula.
(E) The roots can be found by factoring, using imaginary numbers.
(AHSME 1959)

123. Solve for x: $\dfrac{3^{x^2}}{3^{3x}} = \dfrac{1}{9}$. (MATHCOUNTS 1990)

124. For a given value of k the product of the solutions of $x^2 - 3kx + 2k^2 - 1 = 0$ is 7. Are the roots rational, irrational, or imaginary? (AHSME 1960)

125. In a 10 mile race, Janet covered the first 2 miles at a constant rate. She then sped up and rode her bike the last 8 miles at a rate that was 0.5 miles per minute faster. Janet's overall time would have been 2 minutes faster had she ridden her bike the whole race at the faster pace. What was Janet's average speed (in miles per minute) for the whole race? (MAΘ 1990)

126. Solve for x:

$$\sqrt{x + \sqrt{x + 11}} + \sqrt{x - \sqrt{x + 11}} = 4.$$

(MAΘ 1991)

127. Find the sum of the solutions of the equation $8^{x^2+3x+10} = 4^{x^2-x}$. (MAΘ 1992)

128. What is the sum of the roots of the equation $(x^2 - 3x)^2 - (3x^2 - 9x) = 4$? (MAΘ 1991)

129. Two students attempted to solve a quadratic equation, $x^2 + bx + c = 0$. Although both students did the work correctly, the first miscopied the middle term and obtained the solution set $\{-6, 1\}$. The second student miscopied the constant term and obtained the solution set $\{2, 3\}$. What are the correct solutions? (MAΘ 1992)

130. Find all solutions to the equation $x + \sqrt{x - 2} = 4$. (AHSME 1950)

131. Show that if the expression $21x^2 + ax + 21$ can be factored into two linear prime binomial factors with integer coefficients, then a must be even. (AHSME 1951)

132. Find $\sqrt{53 - 8\sqrt{15}}$.

133. Find all z such that $9^{z-1} - 3^{z-1} - 2 = 0$.

134. Without using the quadratic formula, show that the sum of the roots of $ax^2 + bx + c$ is $-b/a$ and that the product of these roots is c/a.

135. What quadratic polynomial with one as the coefficient of x^2 has roots which are the complex conjugates of the solutions of $x^2 - 6x + 11 = 2xi - 10i$? (MAΘ 1990)

136. Evaluate $\sqrt{10 - 4i\sqrt{6}}$.

137. Show that if a and b are such that

$$\frac{a + b}{a} = \frac{b}{a + b},$$

then a and b cannot both be real. (AHSME 1960)

┌─ *the BIG PICTURE* ─

There exists a formula like the quadratic formula for cubic equations! Developed in the mid-1500's by Tartaglia or Cardano (there is still some controversy as to who was first), the derivation is simple, but extremely clever.

Starting with a general cubic equation $x^3 + ax^2 + bx + c = 0$ (where we have already divided out the leading coefficient), we can substitute $y = x + a/3$, which will cause the coefficient of y^2 to become zero, leaving us with

$$y^3 + dy + e = 0$$

for some new d and e. (Can you verify that the y^2 term does indeed vanish?)

The new equation is solved by taking

$$y = \sqrt[3]{u} - \sqrt[3]{v}$$

for properly chosen u and v. If you substitute this y into the equation $y^3 + dy + e = 0$ and manipulate the result a little, you should find that u and v which satisfy the system

$$
\begin{aligned}
v - u &= e \\
uv &= d^3/27
\end{aligned}
$$

will solve the problem; the system can then be solved as an ordinary quadratic. The formula is pretty hideous, and certainly not useful enough to remember, but the derivation is very beautiful, and you are encouraged to fill in the missing steps.

Smart methods also exist to find the solutions of a general quartic (fourth-degree polynomial) by bringing it down to a cubic, but for the fifth and higher degrees there exists none! Such a method was proven not to exist in the 1800's by Galois, using the methods of abstract algebra (see page 276).

Chapter 7

Special Factorizations and Clever Manipulations

7.1 Factorizations

Evaluate $12^2 - 8^2$. This is simple; just do the arithmetic to get $144 - 64 = 80$. How about $102^2 - 98^2$? Considerably more time consuming, but we can find the squares and subtract, $10404 - 9604 = 800$. All right, try $100002^2 - 99998^2$. Squaring and subtracting would take quite a while. Luckily, there is a better way. Recall from page 73 the factorization

$$x^2 - a^2 = (x - a)(x + a).$$

Applying the factorization, we can skip the arithmetic and get

$$100002^2 - 99998^2 = (100002 - 99998)(100002 + 99998) = 4(200000) = 800000.$$

Slick uses of factorizations are not confined to problems involving squares. There are also standard factorizations for sums and differences of cubes as well. Here are a handful of special factorizations that all students should know.

1. Difference of squares:

$$a^2 - b^2 = (a - b)(a + b).$$

2. Sum of squares:
$$a^2 + b^2 = (a + b)^2 - 2ab.$$

3. Difference of cubes:
$$a^3 - b^3 = (a - b)(a^2 + ab + b^2).$$

4. Sum of cubes:
$$a^3 + b^3 = (a + b)(a^2 - ab + b^2).$$

The first two of these we have seen before in our discussion of factoring quadratic equations on page 73. The second isn't exactly a factorization, as we don't express the sum of squares as a product of factors. However, it is an important enough relation that it shouldn't be ignored; it is often useful in solving problems. When asked to factor an expression, however, you may write $x^2 + 2xy + y^2 = (x + y)^2$, but you would not write $x^2 + y^2 = (x + y)^2 - 2xy$ unless this could help you factor the expression further. It may often do just that, as in

$$x^4 + y^4 + x^2y^2 = (x^2 + y^2)^2 - 2x^2y^2 + x^2y^2 = (x^2 + y^2)^2 - (xy)^2,$$

which can then be factored as the difference of squares, yielding $(x^2 + y^2 - xy)(x^2 + y^2 + xy)$.

EXAMPLE 7-1 Show that $a^3 - b^3 = (a - b)(a^2 + ab + b^2)$.

Proof: Expanding the right side above yields:

$$\begin{aligned}
(a - b)(a^2 + ab + b^2) &= a(a^2 + ab + b^2) - b(a^2 + ab + b^2) \\
&= a^3 + a^2b + ab^2 - a^2b - ab^2 - b^3 \\
&= a^3 - b^3.
\end{aligned}$$

It is easy to confuse the factorizations of the sum and difference of cubes. One easy way to remember which is which is that the sign in the expression involving cubes is the same as the sign in the *linear* term of the factored expression.

EXERCISE 7-1 Show that $a^3 + b^3 = (a + b)(a^2 - ab + b^2)$.

Using special factorizations in problems involving sums and differences of squares and cubes is generally quite easy, but how did we ever come up with them? We saw the two involving squares in our discussion of quadratic equations, so let's focus on the two involving cubes.

We discussed in our chapter on quadratics that for every root of an expression, there is a factor of that expression. For example, since $x = 1$ is a root of $x^2 - 1$, $(x - 1)$ is a factor of $x^2 - 1$. Now consider the equation $a^3 - b^3 = 0$. Can you think of any roots? The obvious choice is $a = b$, for when $a = b$, $a^3 - b^3 = a^3 - a^3 = 0$. Since $a = b$ is a root, $a - b$ is a factor. Thus there is some expression, call it $f(a, b)$, such that $a^3 - b^3 = (a - b)[f(a, b)]$. We can determine this expression by noting that the result of the product $(a - b)[f(a, b)]$ must be $a^3 - b^3$. Hence, $f(a, b)$ has a term which is a^2 (since $(a)(a^2) = a^3$) and a term b^2. Let's try $f(a, b) = a^2 + b^2$:

$$(a - b)(a^2 + b^2) = a^3 + ab^2 - ba^2 - b^3.$$

Not quite right; we have two extra terms. How do we get rid of the ab^2 term? We can do this by including ab in our expression for $f(a, b)$, because $(-b)(ab) = -ab^2$, which cancels with ab^2. Let's try it:

$$(a - b)(a^2 + ab + b^2) = a^3 + a^2b + ab^2 - ba^2 - ab^2 - b^3 = a^3 - b^3.$$

Yes! We have found our factorization. Try factoring $a^3 + b^3$ by noting that $a = -b$ is a root of $a^3 + b^3 = 0$.

WARNING: Special factorizations can be cleverly hidden in problems by requiring you to use them *backwards*, where instead of the sum or difference of squares or cubes appearing, one of the factors appears in the problem and you must multiply by the other to obtain the sum or difference and ultimately solve the problem. These are usually pretty obvious when the problem is in terms of variables; expressions like $x^2 + xy + y^2$ are tough to miss. They become less obvious, though, when written in terms of numbers, like $\sqrt{5} - \sqrt{3}$ or $\sqrt[3]{4} + \sqrt[3]{2} + \sqrt[3]{1}$.

EXAMPLE 7-2   If $\dfrac{1}{a + c} = \dfrac{1}{a} + \dfrac{1}{c}$, find $(a/c)^3$. (Mandelbrot #1)

Solution: Variables in denominators are difficult to work with, so we multiply by $ac(a + c)$ first, which leaves

$$ac = c(a + c) + a(a + c).$$

Rearranging this yields $a^2 + ac + c^2 = 0$. Now we seem stuck, unless we note that $a^2 + ac + c^2$ is a factor of $a^3 - c^3$. Since $(a - c)$ is the other factor, we multiply both sides by it:

$$(a^2 + ac + c^2)(a - c) = a^3 - c^3 = 0.$$

Thus $a^3 = c^3$ and $a^3/c^3 = \mathbf{1}$.

EXAMPLE 7-3 Find the sum

$$\frac{1}{3 + 2\sqrt{2}} + \frac{1}{2\sqrt{2} + \sqrt{7}} + \frac{1}{\sqrt{7} + \sqrt{6}} + \frac{1}{\sqrt{6} + \sqrt{5}} + \frac{1}{\sqrt{5} + 2} + \frac{1}{2 + \sqrt{3}}.$$

Solution: We could rationalize each denominator separately, but that would take a while. Instead, let's look at the sum with all numbers under radical signs (for example, writing $\sqrt{9}$ rather than 3):

$$\frac{1}{\sqrt{9} + \sqrt{8}} + \frac{1}{\sqrt{8} + \sqrt{7}} + \frac{1}{\sqrt{7} + \sqrt{6}} + \frac{1}{\sqrt{6} + \sqrt{5}} + \frac{1}{\sqrt{5} + \sqrt{4}} + \frac{1}{\sqrt{4} + \sqrt{3}}.$$

A pretty clear pattern exists. Consider $\sqrt{9} + \sqrt{8}$. If we multiply by $\sqrt{9} - \sqrt{8}$, we have

$$(\sqrt{9} + \sqrt{8})(\sqrt{9} - \sqrt{8}) = (\sqrt{9})^2 - (\sqrt{8})^2 = 9 - 8 = 1.$$

Thus, the reciprocal of $\sqrt{9} + \sqrt{8}$ is $\sqrt{9} - \sqrt{8}$! Writing $1/(\sqrt{9} + \sqrt{8}) = \sqrt{9} - \sqrt{8}$ and doing similarly for the other expressions, we have

$$\frac{1}{\sqrt{9} + \sqrt{8}} + \frac{1}{\sqrt{8} + \sqrt{7}} + \frac{1}{\sqrt{7} + \sqrt{6}} + \frac{1}{\sqrt{6} + \sqrt{5}} + \frac{1}{\sqrt{5} + \sqrt{4}} + \frac{1}{\sqrt{4} + \sqrt{3}}$$

$$= \sqrt{9} - \sqrt{8} + \sqrt{8} - \sqrt{7} + \sqrt{7} - \sqrt{6} + \sqrt{6} - \sqrt{5} + \sqrt{5} - \sqrt{4} + \sqrt{4} - \sqrt{3}.$$

All but the first and last terms cancel and our sum equals $\mathbf{3 - \sqrt{3}}$.

EXERCISE 7-2 Find the sum

$$\frac{1}{\sqrt[3]{1} + \sqrt[3]{2} + \sqrt[3]{4}} + \frac{1}{\sqrt[3]{4} + \sqrt[3]{6} + \sqrt[3]{9}} + \frac{1}{\sqrt[3]{9} + \sqrt[3]{12} + \sqrt[3]{16}}.$$

(MAΘ 1992)

7.2   Manipulations

Consider the problem:

> *Given that the sum of a number and its reciprocal is 1, find the sum of the cube of that number and the cube of its reciprocal.*

This is a fairly harmless–seeming problem, which we could solve by first finding the number then cubing it and evaluating the desired sum. However, if we solve the equation $x + \frac{1}{x} = 1$, we find $x = (1 \pm i\sqrt{3})/2$. Cubing this would be a headache.

Fortunately, clever manipulations provide an easier method; in fact, we can solve the problem without ever finding x. We know that $x + \frac{1}{x} = 1$; we want to find $x^3 + \frac{1}{x^3}$. The simplest way to get an equation involving x^3 is to cube the equation we are given (recall the cube of a binomial expression, page 70). Let's try it:

$$
\begin{aligned}
1^3 &= \left(x + \frac{1}{x}\right)^3 \\
1 &= x^3 + 3x^2\left(\frac{1}{x}\right) + 3x\left(\frac{1}{x}\right)^2 + \left(\frac{1}{x}\right)^3 \\
1 &= x^3 + 3x + \frac{3}{x} + \frac{1}{x^3} \\
1 &= x^3 + 3\left(x + \frac{1}{x}\right) + \frac{1}{x^3}.
\end{aligned}
$$

Since we know that $x + \frac{1}{x} = 1$, we substitute this value in the last equation, getting $x^3 + 3(1) + \frac{1}{x^3} = 1$, so $x^3 + \frac{1}{x^3} = 1 - 3 = -2$. We have never actually determined x!

Both squaring and cubing equations are often helpful in solving systems of equations. Those problems involving the sum of a term and its reciprocal can also often be solved by raising the initial equation to various powers.

Another class of problems which can be solved by raising equations to various powers are those where we are given two of the quantities xy, $x+y$, x^2+y^2, x^3+y^3, etc. and asked for a third. By squaring $x + y$, we get the expression $x^2 + 2xy + y^2$, which involves both xy and x^2+y^2. Similarly, we can cube $x+y$ to get an expression involving $x^3 + y^3$, xy, and $x + y$:

$$(x + y)^3 = x^3 + 3x^2y + 3xy^2 + y^3 = x^3 + y^3 + 3xy(x + y).$$

Thus if we know $x + y$ and xy, we can substitute these values in the above to find $x^3 + y^3$ without ever finding x and y.

The following examples display the various uses of this technique. The two most important tools, both of which you have seen before, are

$$(x + y)^2 = (x^2 + y^2) + (2xy)$$
$$\text{and} \quad (x + y)^3 = (x^3 + y^3) + 3xy(x + y).$$

In each of these, we have 3 quantities: the sum of the variables, the product of the variables, and the sum of either the squares or the cubes of the variables. Usually we are given the values of two of these three, and can then determine the third.

EXAMPLE 7-4   If $a + b = 1$ and $a^2 + b^2 = 2$, find $a^4 + b^4$. (MAΘ 1990)

Solution: First, we square the sum of the variables, yielding

$$(a + b)^2 = a^2 + b^2 + 2ab$$
$$1^2 = 2 + 2ab$$
$$-1/2 = ab.$$

(We have used the given information to determine ab. Generally, we will almost always determine the product of the variables at some point in the problem if it is not given.)

Now, how can we get $a^4 + b^4$? Squaring $a^2 + b^2$ will achieve that:

$$\left(a^2 + b^2\right)^2 = a^4 + 2a^2b^2 + b^4$$
$$2^2 = a^4 + b^4 + 2(ab)^2$$
$$4 = a^4 + b^4 + 2(-1/2)^2.$$

The last equation yields $a^4 + b^4 = \mathbf{7/2}$.

EXAMPLE 7-5   Find $x^6 + \dfrac{1}{x^6}$ if $x + \dfrac{1}{x} = 3$.

Solution: Since our primary tools are squaring and cubing equations, we get to the sixth power by steps, rather than raising the initial equation to the sixth power directly.

First, we square the equation, to obtain

$$x^2 + \frac{1}{x^2} + 2 = \left(x + \frac{1}{x}\right)^2 = 3^2 = 9,$$

so that $x^2 + \frac{1}{x^2} = 7$. Cubing squares gives us sixth powers, so we cube this equation to get

$$
\begin{aligned}
\left(x^2 + \frac{1}{x^2}\right)^3 &= x^6 + 3\left(x^2\right)^2\left(\frac{1}{x^2}\right) + 3\left(x^2\right)\left(\frac{1}{x^2}\right)^2 + \frac{1}{x^6} \\
7^3 &= x^6 + \frac{1}{x^6} + 3\left(x^2 + \frac{1}{x^2}\right) \\
343 &= x^6 + \frac{1}{x^6} + 3(7).
\end{aligned}
$$

Our desired sum is $343 - 21 = \mathbf{322}$.

EXAMPLE 7-6 Find $1/A + 1/B$ if $A + B = 6$ and $AB = 3$.

Solution: Since $1/A + 1/B = (A + B)/AB$, the desired sum is $6/3 = \mathbf{2}$. Remember this simple manipulation; you will see it often.

EXERCISE 7-3 Find $z^5 + \frac{1}{z^5}$, given that $z > 0$ and $z^2 + \frac{1}{z^2} = 14$. (Hint: Square $z + 1/z$ to find $z + 1/z$, then use this to solve the problem.)

EXERCISE 7-4 Find all possible values of $a^3 + b^3$ if $a^2 + b^2 = ab = 4$.

═══

Problems to Solve for Chapter 7

138. Given that $9876^2 = 97535376$, find 9877^2. (Mandelbrot #3)

139. What is the sum of the prime factors of $2^{16} - 1$? (MATHCOUNTS 1992)

140. In the equation $2x^2 - 3x + 4 = 0$, what is the sum of the squares of the roots? (MAΘ 1991)

141. Factor completely: $-a^2b^2 + 2ab^3 - b^4 + a^2c^2 - 2abc^2 + b^2c^2$. (MAΘ 1990)

142. Factor completely: $x^2 + 2mn - m^2 - n^2$. (MAΘ 1992)

143. Factor $x^{12} - y^{12}$ as completely as possible with integral coefficients and integral exponents. (MAΘ 1992)

144. Simplify the following expression as much as possible:

$$\left(\frac{a^3 - 1}{a^2 - 1}\right)\left(\frac{a^2 + 2a + 1}{a^3 + 1}\right)\left(\frac{a^2 - a + 1}{a + 1}\right)$$

(MAΘ 1991)

145. When $x^9 - x$ is factored as completely as possible into polynomials and monomials with integral coefficients, how many factors are there? (MAΘ 1992)

146. If the sum of two numbers is 1 and their product is 1, then what is the sum of their cubes? (AHSME 1966)

147. Find $x^4 + \dfrac{1}{x^4}$ if $x - \dfrac{1}{x} = 5$.

 148. Factor as completely as possible with real coefficients: $x^8 - y^8$. (Hint: There are 5 factors. Note that we say *real* coefficients, not just integers.)

149. Simplify the following expression completely:

$$\frac{bx(a^2x^2 + 2a^2y^2 + b^2y^2) + ay(a^2x^2 + 2b^2x^2 + b^2y^2)}{bx + ay}.$$

(AHSME 1988)

150. Find four nontrivial (not 1) factors in terms of x and y whose product is $8^{2x} - 27^{2y}$.

151. If $x + y = 4$ and $xy = 2$, then find $x^6 + y^6$. (MAΘ 1992)

152. Find all real x such that $\sqrt{x} + 1 = x - \sqrt{x} - 1$. (MAΘ 1990)

153. Evaluate the sum

$$\frac{1}{\sqrt{15} + \sqrt{13}} + \frac{1}{\sqrt{13} + \sqrt{11}} + \frac{1}{\sqrt{11} + 3} + \frac{1}{3 + \sqrt{7}} + \frac{1}{\sqrt{7} + \sqrt{5}}.$$

154. Find all possible values of $x^3 + \dfrac{1}{x^3}$ given that $x^2 + \dfrac{1}{x^2} = 7$.

155. If r and s are the roots of $x^2 + px + q = 0$, then find each of the following in terms of p and q.

    i. $r^2 + s^2$

    ii. $r - s$

    iii. $r^2 s + rs^2$

    iv. $r^4 + s^4$

(MAΘ 1987)

156. Find two four digit numbers whose product is $4^8 + 6^8 + 9^8$.

157. What is the largest number by which the expression $n^3 - n$ is divisible for all possible integral values of n? (AHSME 1951)

158. Find all possible values of ab given that $a + b = 2$ and $a^4 + b^4 = 16$.

159. If $a^3 - b^3 = 24$ and $a - b = 2$, then find all possible values of $a + b$. (MAΘ 1990)

160. Find all prime factors of $3^{18} - 2^{18}$.

161. If q is an integer that can be expressed as the sum of two integer squares, show that both $2q$ and $5q$ can also be expressed as the sum of two integer squares. (Mandelbrot #2)

the BIG PICTURE

One of the most famous special factorizations was discovered by Leonhard Euler en route to a proof that *every positive integer may be written as a sum of four squares.* For example, $23 = 9 + 9 + 4 + 1$ and $24 = 16 + 4 + 4 + 0$.

To prove this theorem, a very typical number theory approach is used. First, show that all *primes* can be written as a sum of four squares. Then, show that if two numbers m and n can be written as a sum of four squares, the product mn can as well. We then use induction (page 339) on the number of primes which divide a number. We know it works for primes, the base case. For the inductive step, assume it works for up to $k - 1$ primes. A number which is a product of k primes can be written as the first prime times the product of the rest, which is a product of $k - 1$ primes and is thus expressible as a sum of four squares. The number with k primes can then be written as a sum of four squares, being the product of two numbers which can be so written.

But how do we prove that if m and n may be written as the sum of four squares, then mn can also? Letting $m = x_1^2 + x_2^2 + x_3^2 + x_4^2$ and $n = y_1^2 + y_2^2 + y_3^2 + y_4^2$, we turn to a very clever manipulation. We have

$$
\begin{aligned}
(x_1^2 + x_2^2 + x_3^2 + x_4^2)(y_1^2 + y_2^2 + y_3^2 + y_4^2) = \ &(x_1y_1 + x_2y_2 + x_3y_3 + x_4y_4)^2 \\
&+ (x_1y_2 - x_2y_1 + x_3y_4 - x_4y_3)^2 \\
&+ (x_1y_3 - x_3y_1 + x_4y_2 - x_2y_4)^2 \\
&+ (x_1y_4 - x_4y_1 + x_2y_3 - x_3y_2)^2.
\end{aligned}
$$

We immediately see that the product of the sums of four squares is itself a sum of four squares! This identity, called **Euler's identity**, supposedly eluded Euler for 12 years. We highly recommend that you multiply it out and watch the beautiful way in which terms cancel, leaving behind exactly what is needed.

Chapter 8

What Numbers Really Are

You think you know all about numbers by now. But could you rigorously define what a rational number *is*? Or worse, an irrational? While seeming petty, questions like these have led to some very significant mathematics. From integers to the rich world of the complex, a continuous chain exists; every type of number must be defined in terms of the next simpler kind, with the integers themselves as the foundation.

8.1   Integers and Rationals

We start with the **natural numbers**: 1, 2, 3, ...   These are the numbers whose meaning is the clearest, corresponding to concrete numbers of objects. Sometime in elementary school we added the **negatives**, $-1, -2, -3, \ldots$, whose meaning takes a little abstraction, but is still simple. Taking all these together and adding 0 we have the **integers**. The integers are

$$\ldots, \ -3, \ -2, \ -1, \ 0, \ 1, \ 2, \ 3, \ \ldots$$

and are extremely important. They are the blocks from which we can build everything else.

EXERCISE 8-1   If a problem refers to a **nonnegative integer**, what set of numbers does it mean? How is this distinguished from a **positive integer**?

Around fifth grade we get the fractions, or, to be more precise, the **rational numbers**. These are defined as ratios p/q, where p and q are both integers and q is positive. Examples of rationals are

$$\frac{3}{4},\ \frac{-17}{34}\ \left(\text{or }-\frac{17}{34}\right),\ \frac{71}{13}.$$

The number p is called the **numerator** and q the **denominator**. Note that every integer n is also a rational with $p = n$, $q = 1$.

Every rational can be written as a decimal, by long dividing the denominator into the numerator. The decimal expansion for a rational either terminates ($3/8 = 0.375$) or repeats ($1/7 = 0.1428571428\ldots = 0.\overline{142857}$). Going backwards, every terminating or repeating decimal can similarly be written as a fraction.

EXAMPLE 8-1   Exactly how can we write a decimal as a fraction? If the decimal terminates, it's easy. For example, suppose we wish to write 7.2451 as a fraction. The decimal is equivalent to 72451/10000, where we add one zero for each digit after the decimal. Sometimes we will have to reduce the fraction: if it were 125/100, for example, we could take a 5 out of the top and the bottom to get 25/20, and another to get 5/4.

EXERCISE 8-2   What can the denominator of a terminating decimal in fraction form be? We have already seen 10000 and 4.

EXAMPLE 8-2   Find the fraction equivalent to $4.\overline{263} = 4.263263263\ldots$

Solution: Call the part after the decimal x, so that

$$x = .263263263\ldots$$

Since the length of the repeating part is 3, we can shift the decimal 3 places to the right by multiplying by 1000 to get

$$1000x = 263.263263263\ldots.$$

Subtracting the first equation from the second, we get

$$999x = 263,$$

so that $x = 263/999$. Thus, the desired fraction is $4 + (263/999) = \mathbf{4259/999}$. (Can this be reduced by taking common factors out of the numerator and denominator?)

EXAMPLE 8-3 Last, how can we go from a fraction to a decimal? The answer is long division. Take 2/7. We long divide:

$$
\begin{array}{r}
0.2\ 8\ 5\ 7\ 1\ 4\ 2\ldots \\
7\overline{)2.0\ 0\ 0\ 0\ 0\ 0\ 0} \\
\underline{1\ 4} \\
6\ 0 \\
\underline{5\ 6} \\
4\ 0 \\
\underline{3\ 5} \\
5\ 0 \\
\underline{4\ 9} \\
1\ 0 \\
\underline{0\ 7} \\
3\ 0 \\
\underline{2\ 8} \\
2\ 0 \\
1\ 4
\end{array}
$$

As soon as the decimal either terminates or repeats, we can stop. In this case, the answer is $0.\overline{285714}$.

EXERCISE 8-3 Convert fraction to decimal or decimal to fraction: 3/11, .345, 4/8, $0.\overline{345}$.

A common task when dealing with rationals is to decide which of two is larger. Unlike with integers, where this is a trivial task (which is larger, 4 or 5?), with fractions this can entail some work. For example, consider 5/56 and 6/67. Which is larger? At a glance it is not obvious.

This dilemma has a fairly simple answer. The easiest approach is to imagine there is either a >, =, or < between the two, proceed in operating, and determine at the end what the symbol must have been. Thus we have

$$5/56\ ?\ 6/67,$$

where the question mark is one of our three symbols. Whatever the symbol is, we can multiply both sides by 56 to get

$$5\ ?\ 56 \cdot 6/67,$$

and then by 67 to get

$$67 \cdot 5 \; ? \; 56 \cdot 6.$$

Doing the multiplications, we have

$$335 \; ? \; 336.$$

Since $335 < 336$, we immediately can tell that the question mark was a $<$ all along, so that $5/56 < 6/67$.

EXERCISE 8-4   Which is larger, $7/17$ or $9/19$?

EXERCISE 8-5   If a and b are both positive integers and $a < b$, which is larger, $1/a$ or $1/b$? What if both are negative?

EXAMPLE 8-4   If a and b are both positive integers and $a < b$, which is larger, $a/(a + x)$ or $b/(b + x)$, where x is any positive integer?

Solution: Using our previous method we write

$$\frac{a}{(a + x)} \; ? \; \frac{b}{(b + x)},$$

so $ab + ax \; ? \; ab + bx$. Subtracting the common term ab from both sides, we have $ax \; ? \; bx$; then dividing through by x, we get $a \; ? \; b$. But we know $a < b$, so the question mark was a $<$ all along, and $\boldsymbol{b/(b + x)}$ is the larger fraction.

EXERCISE 8-6   Show that in general, if a and b are positive and $a < b$, then $a/(ax + y) < b/(bx + y)$, where x and y can be any positive integers.

8.2   Lowest Terms and Irrationals

A rational number, p/q, is said to be in **lowest terms** if p and q have no common factors. For example, $-1/2$ and $4/7$ are in lowest terms, but $-4/16$ and $15/20$ are not. Every rational can be reduced to lowest terms by taking common factors out of the top and bottom simultaneously.

Don't take lowest terms lightly; it is the basis for a surprisingly large number of proofs. For example, at one point it was thought that rational numbers were the only numbers. People really thought that any number could be written as a fraction!

Then a Greek came up with a beautiful proof that $\sqrt{2}$ could not be represented by any fraction. It goes like this:

Proof: Suppose $\sqrt{2}$ *can* be written as the quotient of two integers; we will find a contradiction to this. We can write this fraction in lowest terms, and call the resulting numerator and denominator p and q. We then have $p/q = \sqrt{2}$, so that $p^2/q^2 = 2$, or

$$p^2 = 2q^2.$$

Clearly p is even, since otherwise the right side is divisible by 2 and the left isn't. Thus there is some integer r such that $p = 2r$. For this r we have $4r^2 = 2q^2$, or

$$2r^2 = q^2.$$

But now q must also be even, since otherwise the left is divisible by 2 and the right is not. But if both p and q are even, then the fraction p/q could not have been in lowest terms, because the numerator and denominator have a common factor, 2. This is a contradiction, so the assumption that $p/q = \sqrt{2}$ must have been false.

Isn't that nice? It demonstrated once and for all that not all numbers are rational.

EXERCISE 8-7 Redo the proof above with the following in place of "$\sqrt{2}$":

    i. $\sqrt{3}$.

    ii. $\sqrt{p}$, where p is any prime.

    iii. $\sqrt{m}$, for any integer m which is not a perfect square.

EXERCISE 8-8 If p/q is a fraction in lowest terms, must p^2/q^2 be in lowest terms also? How about $(p + a)/(q + a)$ for some integer a?

EXERCISE 8-9 Show that every fraction whose square root is rational takes the form ap^2/aq^2. (Consider the square root of the fraction in lowest terms.)

You can thus see that the rationals are not everything; we need more numbers. The numbers which are not rational are called **irrational**, though the seemingly derogatory name is not due to any fault of the numbers themselves. As with imaginary and complex numbers (and probably negatives once long ago), there have always been people afraid to extend the number system and the system of thought it entails.

Irrationals can be rigorously constructed from the rationals. We simply write down a sequence of rationals which gets closer and closer to the desired irrational, though it never actually gets there. There are many ways to do this. For example,

$$1, \ 1.4, \ 1.41, \ 1.414, \ 1.4142, \ \ldots$$

is one such sequence for $\sqrt{2}$. A less transparent way is

$$\frac{1}{1}, \ \frac{3}{2}, \ \frac{7}{5}, \ \frac{17}{12}, \ \frac{41}{29}, \ \cdots$$

Though it seems like a joke, the second way is actually better, for it has an elegant structure: the fraction p/q is followed by the fraction $(p+2q)/(p+q)$. (Verify this for the given terms.)

EXERCISE 8-10 Write down the next few terms of the second sequence above, and (calculator in hand) verify that it converges to $\sqrt{2}$.

We will leave it as a mystery for now why this works; feel free to figure it out for yourself. If you like playing with these things, you can also see which of the terms are greater than $\sqrt{2}$ and which are less. There is a pattern.

Other famous irrationals are π and e. These two are particularly interesting, for the following reason: neither one is the solution to *any* polynomial with integer coefficients! This is a highly nontrivial fact, which took mathematicians almost 100 years to prove after they first began to suspect it was true. Such numbers are called **transcendental numbers**.

Combining the rationals and the irrationals, we have the **real numbers**, which have all the familiar properties we are used to. Remember: everything is still built up from the integers.

8.3 Complex and Beyond

We have already dabbled in the **complex numbers**, which are sums of a real and a **pure imaginary**, where pure imaginaries are products of a real and $i = \sqrt{-1}$. (See page 18 for some subtleties in these definitions.)

The most important reason to introduce the complex numbers is not every polynomial has a real root. An example we have seen before is $x^2 + 1$. Over the reals, this has no roots; over the complex, it has the two roots $\pm i$. You might try to find a polynomial which has no roots even over the complex numbers. You wouldn't succeed, because there aren't any. There is a general theorem to this effect with a very pompous name.

The Fundamental Theorem of Algebra. A polynomial of degree n with real or complex coefficients has at least one real or complex root.

What does this mean? With the theorem, we can take a polynomial $f(z)$ of degree n and factor out some root a to get $f(z) = (z - a)g(z)$, where $g(z)$ is a new polynomial of degree $n - 1$. (Factoring works perfectly in complex-land.) We can then factor a root out of g, and so on, until we have n roots of f, and f is completely factored so it can't have any more roots. Why didn't we just say that f had n different roots to begin with? Because they could all be the same, if $f(z) = (z - 1)^n$, for example. To take this into account, we would have to bring in the concepts of multiple roots and so on, so it's better to leave it in the simple form. It still means, though, that every polynomial can be completely factored over the complex numbers. We don't need any more numbers.

EXERCISE 8-11 Having read this chapter, explain why a mathematician once said:

> *"God created the integers; the rest is the work of [humanity]."*

Problems to Solve for Chapter 8

162. Which of the four numbers $\sqrt{\pi^2}$, $\sqrt[3]{0.8}$, $\sqrt[4]{0.00016}$, and $\sqrt[3]{-1}\sqrt{(0.09)^{-1}}$ are rational? (AHSME 1958)

163. Express $0.003\overline{8}$ as a fraction in lowest terms and give the sum of the numerator and denominator. (MAΘ 1991)

164. Given $x = 0.\overline{31}5$, find the value of x, expressed as a fraction in lowest terms. (MAΘ 1990)

165. What is the largest integer x for which $1/x$ is larger than $4/49$? (MATHCOUNTS 1992)

166. Express the absolute value of the difference between $0.\overline{36}$ and 0.36 as a common fraction. (MATHCOUNTS 1986)

Chapter 9

An Introduction to Circles

We'll start our discussion of geometry with one of the simplest geometric figures, the circle. We all know what a circle looks like. Mathematically, a circle is defined as the set of all points which are a fixed distance from a specific point. (Do you see why?) The point in question is called the **center** (point O in the diagram), and the distance is the **radius** (OA). A **chord** 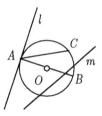 (AC) of a circle is a segment whose endpoints are both on the circle, and a **diameter**, AB, is a chord which passes through the center of the circle. A **tangent** (line l) is a line which touches the circle in only one place, and a **secant**, m, is a line which passes through the circle, intersecting it in two places. Circles are often referred to by their centers, so we can call the circle in the figure circle O. Circles which have the same center are called **concentric**.

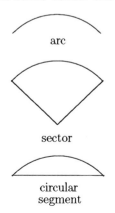

arc

sector

circular segment

A part of the curve of a circle is called an **arc**, and is denoted $\overset{\frown}{AC}$ if A and C are the endpoints. Since $\overset{\frown}{AC}$ can refer to two different arcs, the long way around the circle or the short way, often three points are used to designate the arc, as in $\overset{\frown}{ABC}$. If only two points are used to designate an arc, it is assumed to mean the shorter, or **minor**, arc. As you may have guessed, the larger arc is called the **major** arc. The area inside a circle cut off by two radii is called a **sector**; a **circular segment** is the area between a chord and the arc it intercepts.

In any circle, it should be clear that the diameter d is twice the radius r. The **circumference** of a circle is the distance around it.

For all circles, the ratio of the circumference C to the diameter is the same. This constant ratio is designated by the Greek letter **pi**, which is written π. It is approximately equal to 3.14. (Confirm this approximation with some measuring tape and a compact disc.) Thus, we have

$$C = \pi d = 2\pi r.$$

The area inside a circle or radius r is πr^2.

EXAMPLE 9-1 The area of a circle is 16. What is the circumference of the circle?

Solution: Let the radius of the circle be r, so that $\pi r^2 = 16$. Dividing by π and taking the square root, we find $r = 4/\sqrt{\pi}$. Thus, we have

$$\text{circumference} = 2\pi r = \frac{8\pi}{\sqrt{\pi}} = \mathbf{8\sqrt{\pi}}.$$

EXAMPLE 9-2 What is the maximum area that can be enclosed by 12 feet of fencing? (MAΘ 1992)

Solution: The largest area is enclosed when the fence is circular. (While we encourage that you try to prove all assertions, be satisfied with convincing yourself that this is true. A rigorous proof took some hundred years to emerge.) The circle has circumference 12, and hence has diameter $12/\pi$. Thus, its radius is $6/\pi$ and the area is $(6/\pi)^2\pi = \mathbf{36/\pi}$.

EXERCISE 9-1 What is the circumference of a circle whose area is 8π?

EXERCISE 9-2 In the figure to the right, circle B is tangent to circle A at X, circle C is tangent to circle A at Y, and circles B and C are tangent to each other. If $AB = 6$, $AC = 5$, and $BC = 9$, what is AX? (MAΘ 1987)

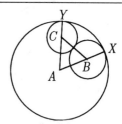

EXERCISE 9-3 A piece of wire 72 cm long is cut into two equal pieces and each is formed into a circle. What is the sum, in square centimeters, of the areas of the circles? (MATHCOUNTS 1991)

EXERCISE 9-4   Circle A, circle B, and circle C are externally tangent. Express the radius of circle A in terms of
BC, AC, and AB, respectively. (MAΘ 1992)

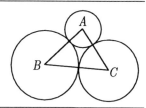

Consider a fly sitting on the edge of a spinning record with radius 10 cm. If the record makes 150 revolutions in one minute, what is the speed of the fly? The velocity we are given is the **angular velocity** of the record, meaning how fast the record is spinning. We are asked to find the speed of the fly. The fly's speed is the distance it moves divided by the time it moves. The fly goes around a circle of radius ten centimeters 150 times in minute. Thus the fly travels around the circumference of the circle 150 times, or $150(20\pi) = 3000\pi$ centimeters. The fly's rate is then 3000π cm/min. Converting angular velocity to linear velocity is very important and is used by every physicist and engineer in the world.

──the *BIG PICTURE*─────

Circles have always been seen as special figures. In particular, they dominated Western astronomical thought for a millennium and a half. Greek astronomy described the motions of all the celestial bodies entirely in terms of circles. Circles were seen as the perfect curves, and it was even imagined that the planets' motion on their crystalline shells made a "music of the spheres."

Many cultures have looked at the positions of the planets in the sky and tried to form geometric models to explain them. Sometimes when a circle was not enough to describe the observed motion, astronomers turned to "epicycles," the curves formed by a circular orbit which is itself moving on a circular orbit, as shown. Imagine a dotted line connecting the various positions of the orbiting object.

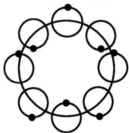

The Copernican theory of 1543 placed the sun at the center of the solar system. This shook the philosophical foundations of astronomy; since Ptolemy in the second century A.D., the Earth had been the center. However, Copernicus still stuck to the basic circular orbit, though his new system was far simpler (meaning it required fewer epicycles). Only with Johann Kepler in the early 1600's was it realized that *ellipses*, not circles, were the fundamental shapes of the planets' orbits. Ellipses will be discussed in Volume 2; an elliptical orbit is shown below.

Chapter 10

Angles

10.1 Lines, Rays, and Segments

A straight path drawn from one point to another is called a **segment**. The two points are called **endpoints**, and the point on the segment which is exactly between the endpoints is the **midpoint**. Segments are sometimes denoted with a bar, as in $\overline{AB}$, but it is easier to just write AB. When written in an equation, AB is the length of the segment, which is the distance from one endpoint to the other. If we continue our straight path past an endpoint and go on forever in that direction, we form a **ray**, which is denoted $\overrightarrow{CD}$. The endpoint from which the path starts, the **origin**, is always written first. If we continue the path in both directions, we form a **line**, which is written $\overleftrightarrow{EF}$.

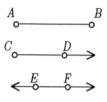

Any two points can be used to determine a line. If three or more points are on the same line, they are **collinear**. Given three points A, B, and X on a segment as shown at left, $AX + XB = AB$. (Why?)

10.2 Classification and Measurement

Two rays which share an origin form an **angle** and the rays are the **sides** of the angle. The common origin is called the **vertex** of the angle. If we consider a circle centered at the vertex, as shown below, we say that the angle **subtends** the arc it cuts off. An angle is denoted by the $\angle$ symbol, as in $\angle AOB$. (The vertex *always* goes in the middle.) When there is only one angle with the given vertex, we can use just the vertex to name the angle, as in ∠O.

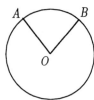 We measure angles as the fraction of a circle, centered at the vertex of the angle, which the angle cuts off. A circle has 360 degrees, so if the angle cuts off one-quarter of the circle, it is 90°. The number of degrees in a circle is rather arbitrary. We could have just as well chosen 100 or 50, but 360 was chosen because it is evenly divisible by many more numbers than 100. For example, we often encounter angles which are one-third or one-sixth of a circle. If a circle were 100 degrees, we'd have to call these 100/3 and 50/3 degree angles rather than 120° and 60°.

Portions of a degree are often measured in "minutes" and "seconds". As you may have guessed, there are 60 minutes in a degree and 60 seconds in a minute. Thus, an angle with measure 0.5° has a measure of 30 minutes. An angle of 20 degrees, 10 minutes, and 5 seconds is written 20°10′5″.

Another more natural way of measuring angles is by **radians**. Just like there are 360° in a circle, there are 2π radians in a circle. Thus

$$\frac{360°}{2\pi} = 1.$$

We can use this as a conversion factor (see page 40) to convert degrees to radians and vice versa.

EXAMPLE 10-1   How many degrees are in $\frac{\pi}{3}$ radians and how many radians are in 135°?

Solution: We can multiply $\pi/3$ by the conversion factor to get

$$\left(\frac{\pi}{3}\right)\left(\frac{360°}{2\pi}\right) = \frac{360°}{6} = \mathbf{60°}.$$

Similarly,

$$(135°)\left(\frac{2\pi}{360°}\right) = 2\pi\left(\frac{135°}{360°}\right) = \mathbf{\frac{3\pi}{4}}.$$

EXAMPLE 10-2   Write $20\frac{5}{9}°$ in terms of minutes and seconds.

Solution: In 5/9 of a degree, there are $(5/9)(60) = 33\frac{1}{3}$ minutes. In 1/3 of a minute, there are $(1/3)(60) = 20$ seconds. Thus, $20\frac{5}{9} = \mathbf{20°33′20″}$.

If we write the measure of an angle in a diagram, we write it by the vertex on the inside of the angle, as in the figure below.

Ninety degree angles are called **right** angles, and any two lines which form a right angle are said to be **perpendicular** or **orthogonal**. If AB and CD are perpendicular, we write $AB \perp CD$. Right angles are usually indicated in diagrams by a little box as shown in the right angle below. Angles which are less than 90° are called **acute** angles. An angle which is greater than 90 degrees but less than 180° is **obtuse**, and any angle of over 180 degrees is a **reflex** angle. A **straight angle** is just a straight line and has 180°.

acute   right   obtuse

Two angles whose sum is 90° are called **complementary angles**, and angles whose sum is 180° are **supplementary angles**. Angles are often named with Greek letters; most often θ, sometimes ϕ, α, β, or γ.

Consider the intersection of lines l and m in the figure. Since a line has 180°, angles α and β, which together form a line, are supplementary. Thus $\alpha + \beta = 180°$. Similarly, $\alpha + \theta = 180°$, so $\theta = \beta$. These angles are called **vertical angles**, and as we see, vertical angles are always equal to each other. In the diagram, ϕ and α are also vertical angles so $\phi = \alpha$.

10.3 Angles and Parallel Lines

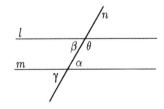

Parallel lines are lines that are in the same plane and never intersect. Thus, two parallel lines are always the same distance apart. In the figure, lines l and m are parallel; this is written $l \parallel m$. Line n is a **transversal**. Angles α and β are called **alternate interior angles**, and they are equal. Since γ and α are vertical angles, they are equal, so $\alpha = \beta = \gamma$. The pair γ and β are called **corresponding angles**. Also, θ and β together form a straight line and thus are supplementary. Since $\beta = \alpha$, we find that θ and α are also supplementary. The angles θ and α are sometimes called **same-side interior**

angles.

Sometimes diagrams get so complex that it would be nice to have a convenient way to mark equal angles. This is done by drawing a small arc inside the angle near the vertex of each of the equal angles. Any angle which has one such arc inside it is equal to all the others which have one such arc inside. Similarly, if we have another set of equal angles which are not equal to the set with one arc, we draw two arcs inside the angles.

Whenever you see a pair of vertical angles, a pair of corresponding angles, or a pair of alternate interior angles, mark them as equal in your diagram. The most important skill in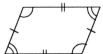
solving geometry problems is making good diagrams. The first step in any problem is to draw the picture as accurately as possible. Then throughout the problem, keep the picture accurate by marking equal angles and equal lengths. Equal lengths are marked somewhat like equal angles; any two segments which have the same length get a tick mark. If another set of segments are all equal, they get two tick marks, and so on.

The following two examples are proofs of *very* important facts which are among the most important tools in solving problems involving angles.

 EXAMPLE 10-3   Prove that the sum of the angles of a triangle is always 180°.

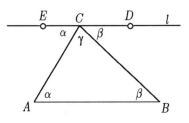

Proof: Read this proof closely—it is not simple. The usefulness of cleverly adding a parallel line to a diagram cannot be overestimated. When standard techniques fail, look for a good place to draw an extra parallel line. Parallel lines form many pairs of equal angles, which can often be used to complete the problem.

In the figure, line l is drawn through C parallel to side AB of triangle ABC. As alternate interior angles, we have $\angle BAC = \angle ACE$ and $\angle ABC = \angle BCD$. Since $\angle ACB$, $\angle ACE$, and $\angle BCD$ together make up a straight line, we get $\angle ACE + \angle ACB + \angle BCD = \alpha + \beta + \gamma = 180°$. Thus, the sum of the angles in a triangle is always 180°.

 EXAMPLE 10-4   **Exterior Angle Theorem**. If we continue a side of a triangle past a vertex as in the diagram, we form an **exterior angle** of the triangle, like θ in the figure below. The interior angles of the triangle which are not adjacent to

the exterior angle are called **remote interior angles**. (In the diagram, α and β are remote interior angles.) Prove that any exterior angle of a triangle is the sum of the remote interior angles.

Proof: From the triangle we find $\alpha + \beta + \gamma = 180°$, and since γ and θ make up a straight line, $\gamma + \theta = 180°$. Combining these gives $\alpha + \beta + \gamma = \gamma + \theta$, so $\alpha + \beta = \theta$. That is, the measure of an exterior angle of a triangle is the sum of the two remote interior angles.

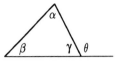

EXERCISE 10-1 Let α, β, and γ be the exterior angles of angles $\angle A$, $\angle B$, and $\angle C$ of $\triangle ABC$. Show that $\alpha + \beta + \gamma = 360°$.

10.4   Arcs, Segments, Sectors, and Angles

We can use our understanding of angles and the circumference and area of a circle to find the areas of sectors and circular segments.

Arcs can be measured by their length or by the measure of the angle from the center of the circle which cuts off the arc, as $\angle AOB$ cuts off arc AB in the figure. As you can see below, the measure of an arc can be denoted by writing the value beside the arc in the figure.

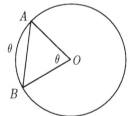

The ratio of the measure of the arc to the measure of the circle, 2π radians, equals the ratio of the length of the arc to the circumference of the circle. Letting r be the radius of the circle, we have

$$\frac{\overarc{AB}}{2\pi r} = \frac{\theta}{2\pi},$$

or $\overarc{AB} = r\theta$, where θ is in radians.

The angle θ which cuts off a sector cuts off an area equal to $\theta/2\pi$ of the area of the entire circle. The area of sector AOB is thus

$$\left(\frac{\theta}{2\pi}\right)(\pi r^2) = \frac{r^2\theta}{2}.$$

The area of circular segment AB is the area of sector ABO minus the area of triangle ABO. (Methods for finding the area of a triangle are presented on page 144.)

10.5   Angles Formed By Lines Intersecting a Circle

We've already seen how angles can be measured by the arcs they cut off of circles centered at the vertex of the angle. Such an angle is called a **central angle**. We will now consider angles formed by chords, tangents, and secants. For now we won't prove these relations, but we'll come back to the proofs later.

1. *Angles formed by two chords with a common endpoint.*

Such an angle is called an **inscribed angle**, and its measure is one-half of the arc it intercepts:

$$\angle ABC = \frac{\widehat{AC}}{2}.$$

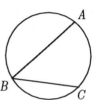

2. *Angles formed by two secants which intersect outside the circle.*

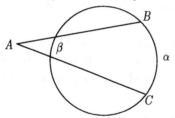

The measure of such an angle is equal to one-half the difference of the arcs intercepted by the secants:

$$\angle BAC = \frac{\alpha - \beta}{2}.$$

The angle between two tangents from a point to a circle, or between a tangent and a secant, can also be found from the arc measures as shown above.

3. *Angles formed by a tangent and a chord.*

This angle is one-half the arc it cuts off:

$$\angle ABC = \frac{\theta}{2}.$$

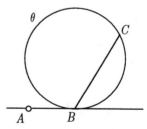

4. *Angles formed by two chords.*

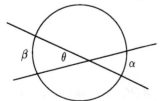

The angle formed by two chords is one-half the sum of the intercepted arcs:

$$\theta = \frac{\alpha + \beta}{2}.$$

The application of these angle properties is in general very straightforward. When you see an angle cutting off arcs in any of the above manners, you can immediately apply the corresponding relation. The following examples and exercises display the use of these principles.

EXAMPLE 10-5 Show that any inscribed angle which subtends a semicircular arc is a right angle.

Proof: Since the angle cuts off a 180° arc, its measure is 180°/2 = 90°. Thus, the angle is right. An angle which cuts off a 180° arc is said to be inscribed in the semicircle formed by the arc.

EXAMPLE 10-6 Show that any diameter drawn from the point of tangency of a tangent line l is perpendicular to the line.

Proof: In the diagram, $\angle CAB$ is formed by a tangent and a chord and hence its measure is half that of the arc it cuts off. Since the chord is a diameter, the arc is half the circle, so $\angle CAB = 180°/2 = 90°$. Thus, $AO \perp l$.

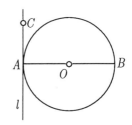

EXERCISE 10-2 Points A, B, Q, D, and C lie on the circle as shown and the measures of arcs $\overset{\frown}{BQ}$ and $\overset{\frown}{QD}$ are 42° and 38° respectively. What is the sum of angles P and Q? (AHSME 1971)

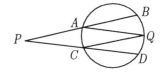

EXERCISE 10-3 Segments PA and PT are tangent to the circle. Find the measure of $\angle TXA$ if $\angle P = 42°$. (MAΘ 1990)

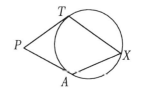

EXAMPLE 10-7 In the figure, if $\overset{\frown}{AB} = 60°$ and $\overset{\frown}{DE} = 40°$, then what is $\angle ACD$?

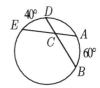

   Solution: Since $\angle ACB$ is one-half the sum of $\overset{\frown}{AB}$ and $\overset{\frown}{DE}$, we have $\angle ACB = 50°$. Since $\angle ACD + \angle ACB = 180°$, we find $\angle ACD = \mathbf{130°}$.

EXAMPLE 10-8 In the figure, given that $\angle ABC = 60°$ and $\angle BCD = 70°$, find $\angle CBD$.

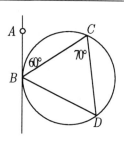

Solution: We know that $\angle CBD$ is one-half $\overarc{CD}$, but we don't know what $\overarc{CD}$ is. We can also find $\angle CBD$ by finding the other two angles of $\triangle CBD$ and subtracting their sum from $180°$. We already have $\angle C$, and $\angle D$ is one-half $\overarc{BC}$. Since $\overarc{BC} = 2\angle ABC = 120°$, we have $\angle D = 60°$, and $\angle CBD = 180° - \angle C - \angle D = \mathbf{50°}$.

In this example we have an instance of the general result that an angle formed by a tangent and a chord ($\angle ABC$ above) is equal to any inscribed angle which cuts off the same arc as the chord ($\angle D$ above).

As you proceed to more advanced problem solving, the most subtle and important result in this section is that any two inscribed angles which subtend the same arc are equal. For example, in the figure we have

$$\angle A = \angle B \quad \text{and} \quad \angle C = \angle D.$$

While the other relations have fairly obvious applications, equal inscribed angles can be cleverly hidden in a problem. This is one of the most common methods of showing that two angles are equal. If you are ever asked to show the equality of two angles whose sides intersect, as angles A and B do at points C and D above, check to see if there is a circle that passes through the vertices of the angles and the two intersection points. If such a circle exists, then the two angles are equal; it's that simple!

If the two angles you are trying to prove equal share a vertex or a side, or if their sides don't intersect, then inscribed angles is not the best immediate method to use, because no such circle will exist. (Why? Draw these cases and see.) We point this out because it is as important to know which methods *not* to try as it is to know which methods to try. Keep in mind, however, that sometimes you will have to get creative; the cut-and-dried methodology won't always work. (And would math be fun if it did?)

EXAMPLE 10-9   The two circles in the figure
are tangent at G. Prove that $\angle E = \angle F$.

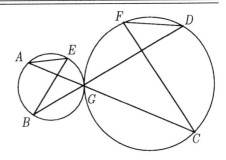

   Proof: The two angles are not related to
each other at all, so it seems we cannot use any
of the above relations. Thus, we start where
we should always start on geometry problems
involving angles: finding angles we know are
equal. Since $\angle AGB$ and $\angle DGC$ are vertical angles, they are equal. Since $\angle F$ and $\angle DGC$ are
inscribed angles which subtend the same arc, they are equal. Finally, $\angle E = \angle AGB$
because they are inscribed angles subtending the same arc. Thus

$$\angle E = \angle AGB = \angle DGC = \angle F.$$

This is an example of a problem where it is very useful to mark equal angles as
discussed on page 114.

10.6   The Burden of Proof

Now that we have demonstrated the many relationships between angles and circles,
we will prove these relations. The importance of this section is not so much the
proofs themselves, but the many valuable techniques which they demonstrate.

   If you do not know anything about isosceles triangles, read about them on page
123 before returning to these proofs.

Proofs of the formulas relating angles and arcs

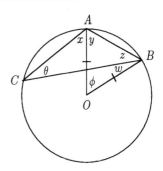

   1. Inscribed angles.

   We must relate the arc measure to something we know,
and the only thing we know about the arc is that it
equals the central angle that subtends it. Thus, to prove
our formula, we must show that $\phi = 2\theta$ in the diagram.
Looking at our diagram, we see that by connecting A

and B we form two triangles, $\triangle ABC$ and $\triangle BOA$. We then label all the angles we form as shown. Since a triangle has $180°$, we have

$$\theta + x + y + z = \phi + z + w + y = 180°.$$

Another important thing to remember in problem solving is to think about what is special about every restriction placed on the problem. In this problem, we are dealing with triangles formed by the center and points on a circle. Any triangle formed by two radii and a chord, such as $\triangle BOA$, is isosceles, and isosceles triangles give us equal angles. For example, from $\triangle AOB$ we have $\angle OAB = \angle OBA$, so $y = z + w$. Just $\triangle BOA$ and $\triangle ABC$ are not enough to finish this problem, because substituting $z + w = y$ in our original equation gives

$$\theta + x + y + z = \phi + 2y = 180.$$

This clearly doesn't quite get us to $\phi = 2\theta$. We must find something else. This brings us to another geometry problem solving technique: cleverly adding lines to the diagram. We've already done this once by drawing AB to complete the two triangles. Looking at the figure, you should see that the line that's begging to be added is OC. Adding that to our diagram gives us the diagram below.

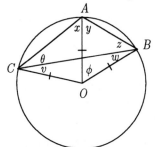

In this picture, we see that the addition of OC gives us more isosceles triangles, and therefore more equal angles. First, from $\triangle AOC$ we have $AO = OC$, so $x = \theta + v$. This makes our equation

$$2\theta + v + z + y = \phi + 2y = 180.$$

We see from this that if we can show that $v + z = y$, then we will be able to show that $\phi = 2\theta$. (Make sure you understand why: substitute $v + z = y$ in the above and get $2\theta + 2y = \phi + 2y$, so $\phi = 2\theta$.)

This shows us yet another powerful tool: working backwards. We look at what we know ($2\theta + v + z + y = \phi + 2y = 180$) and what we want ($\phi = 2\theta$) and see what we must prove to get from one to the other ($v + z = y$).

Working backwards again, we know that $z + w = y$, so if we can show that $w = v$, we are done. From isosceles triangle BOC we get $OC = OB$, so $v = w$. Thus, $z + w = z + v = y$, so $2\theta + v + z + y = 2\theta + 2y$. Hence, our equation is now

$$2\theta + 2y = \phi + 2y = 180.$$

Thus $\phi = 2\theta$, and our proof is complete. Or is it? Whenever you complete a proof, you must make sure that your proof covers all cases and makes no assumptions that are not a part of the problem. If we look at the very first diagram, we see that we made the assumption that the center of the circle lies outside $\angle ACB$. This, of course, is not always true, but our proof is only valid for those cases in which it is. In order for our proof to be **rigorous**, meaning to be complete and make no assumptions, we must prove the formula for the cases where the center of the circle is inside and on a side of the angle. The proofs are almost exactly like the one we've done. Try to do these on your own.

Don't let this proof scare you; it really isn't nearly as long as it looks. It only looks long because we've added a lot of comments. The proof itself is quite short.

2. Angles formed by two secants.

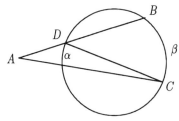

In the figure, we add line DC because not only does this form a triangle, $\triangle ADC$, but also it forms two inscribed angles, $\angle ACD$ and $\angle BDC$, each of which subtends an arc in the formula we wish to prove. Since $\angle A$ is in $\triangle ADC$, we can find its measure by finding the measure of the other two angles in the triangle. (Yes, this is another one of those "proof techniques" we've been telling you about. You've seen this one before, and you'll see it again. And again.)

As inscribed angles, $\angle DCA = \alpha/2$ and $\angle BDC = \beta/2$.

Angles CDB and CDA form a line and thus are supplementary, so

$$\angle CDA = 180° - \angle CDB = 180° - \frac{\beta}{2}.$$

Thus, $\angle A = 180° - \angle CDA - \angle DCA = 180° - \left(180° - \frac{\beta}{2}\right) - \frac{\alpha}{2} = \frac{\beta - \alpha}{2}.$

3. Angle formed by a tangent and a chord.

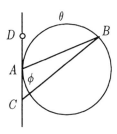

Once again we must add a line. This is a little tricky because it's not so obvious where to add the extra line. We could connect the endpoints of the chord to the center of the circle, but this approach won't get us too far without using what we know about radii being perpendicular to tangents. Since we use what we are trying to prove to show that radii are perpendicular to tangents, we cannot use that fact in this proof or we will be guilty of circular reasoning (see page 343). Do you see why?

We can also connect B to some point on the tangent. Connecting it to D doesn't seem helpful (draw it and see for yourself), but connecting it to C gives us a couple of familiar things. First, we have an angle formed by a secant and a tangent, $\angle ACB$, which subtends an arc in the formula we wish to prove. Second, we have an inscribed angle, $\angle ABC$.

Since $\angle DAB$ is an exterior angle of $\triangle CAB$, it is the sum of $\angle ACB$ and $\angle ABC$. (If you forgot about exterior angles, go back to page 115 and read about them.) Thus,

$$\angle DAB = \angle ABC + \angle ACB = \frac{\phi}{2} + \frac{\theta - \phi}{2} = \frac{\theta}{2}.$$

4. Angles formed by two chords.

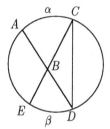

We draw chord DC and use inscribed angles ADC and ECD. Angle ABC is an exterior angle of $\triangle BCD$, so

$$\angle ABC = \angle ECD + \angle ADC = \frac{\alpha + \beta}{2}.$$

Chapter 11

Triangles, a.k.a. Geometry

Nearly all of geometry comes down to the simple three sided figure, the **triangle**. Since triangles are so important, this chapter is long. Take your time; once you master the lessons of this chapter, you will have nearly mastered basic geometry. To keep your morale up (and to remember the material past the time you turn the page!), try some end-of-chapter problems after each section, rather than saving them until you feel you know the whole chapter.

11.1   Classifying Triangles

The points where the sides of a triangle meet are the **vertices**.

Triangles can be classified by their angles or by the lengths of their sides. As proven on page 114, the sum of the measures of the three angles of a triangle is always 180 degrees. Any triangle in which all three angles are acute is called an **acute triangle**. If one of the triangle's angles is right, it is a **right triangle**, and the other two angles are complementary (because the sum of all three must be 180°). The side opposite the right angle is called the **hypotenuse** and the other two sides are called **legs**. Finally, if one of the angles is obtuse, the triangle is called an **obtuse triangle**.

If all three sides of a triangle are equal, the triangle is called an **equilateral triangle**. In an equilateral triangle, all three angles are the same, and therefore equal to 60°. (Why?) If two sides of the triangle are equal, the triangle is **isosceles**

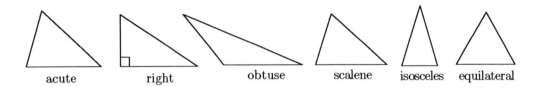

acute　　　　right　　　　obtuse　　　scalene　　isosceles　equilateral

(eye SOS uh leez) and the two angles opposite the equal sides are also equal. The two equal sides are called the **legs** and the other side is the **base**. The angle opposite the base is the **vertex angle** and the equal angles are called the **base angles**. If no two sides of a triangle are the same, the triangle is **scalene**.

11.2　Parts of a Triangle

The sides of $\triangle ABC$ are usually called a, b, and c, with $a = BC$, $b = AC$, and $c = AB$. (Do you see the pattern in this labeling?) The **perimeter** of any polygon is the sum of its sides, so the perimeter p of a $\triangle ABC$ is $a + b + c$. Often we find ourselves working with one-half the perimeter. This is called the **semiperimeter** and is usually denoted s.

There are many special lines and points in a triangle of which you should be aware.

Medians

A segment drawn from a vertex to the midpoint of the opposite side is a **median**. The three medians intersect at the **centroid**, which is usually denoted G. That the three medians are **concurrent**, meaning all three lines meet at one point, is not obvious; it is proven on page 202. The centroid divides each median in a $2 : 1$ ratio, that is:

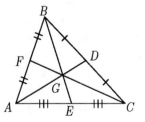

$$\frac{AG}{GD} = \frac{BG}{GE} = \frac{CG}{GF} = \frac{2}{1}.$$

Angle Bisectors

A line which passes through the vertex of an angle and divides the angle into two equal angles is called an **angle bisector**. How do we determine where the angle bisector of an angle is? The measure of an angle is determined by the difference between the directions of the sides of the angle; for example, if the two sides point in nearly the same direction, the angle will be small. An angle bisector therefore must be equally 'far' from both sides of the angle and therefore consist of all the points which are equidistant from the sides of the angle. (The distance from a point to a line is the length of the perpendicular segment from the point to the line.)

Like the medians, the angle bisectors all pass through a single point. How would we prove that all three angle bisectors pass through a single point? If there is a point that is equidistant from all three sides of the triangle, then the angle bisectors all pass through that point because each angle bisector is the set of all points that are equidistant from two of the sides.

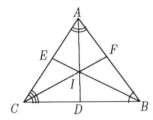
Let I be the intersection of angle bisectors AD and BE. Since I is on AD, it is equidistant from AB and AC. Since I is on BE, it is also equidistant from AB and BC. Since it is equidistant from AC and AB, and from AB and BC, I must also be equidistant from AC and BC. Hence, it must be on the angle bisector of $\angle ACB$. Thus, the angle bisectors are concurrent at the point I.

Let's call the common distance from I to the sides of the triangle r. Suppose we draw a circle with center I and radius r. It will hit the sides of the triangle, but only at exactly one point, because the segment from I to a side with length r is perpendicular to the side. (Remember, I is r from each side.) The diagram at right shows this 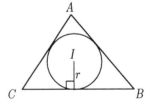 fact. We say that the circle is **inscribed** in the triangle because it is tangent to all three sides of the triangle and we call the circle the **incircle**. Likewise, point I is the **incenter** and r is the **inradius**.

Perpendicular Bisectors

A line which is perpendicular to a segment and passes through the midpoint of the segment is called the **perpendicular bisector** of the segment. Apply the argument we used for angle bisectors to show that the perpendicular bisector of a segment consists of all the points which are equidistant from the two endpoints of a segment.

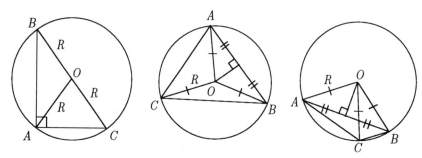

The perpendicular bisectors of the sides of the triangle are concurrent at the **circumcenter**, usually called O. Since O is the same distance, which we'll call R, from the three vertices, if we draw a circle with radius R and center O, it will pass through each of the vertices. Thus we say that the triangle is inscribed in the circle, or the circle is **circumscribed** about the triangle. As you may have guessed, this circle is the **circumcircle**, a circle which passes through all three vertices of the triangle. (Can you convince yourself that such a circle must exist?) The radius of the circumcircle, or **circumradius**, is often called R as above to contrast with the inradius r. As shown in the figure above, the circumcenter of an obtuse triangle is outside the triangle, of an acute triangle is in the triangle, and that of a right triangle is on the triangle.

You should be able to prove for yourself that the perpendicular bisectors are concurrent; the proof is exactly like that for angle bisectors: let O be the intersection of the perpendicular bisectors of AB and AC. Since O is on the perpendicular bisector of AB, it is equidistant from A and B. Continue from here to show that O is equidistant from A, B, and C.

Altitudes

A perpendicular segment from the vertex of a triangle to the side opposite (or the extension of that side, as in the obtuse triangle ABC at right) is called an **altitude**. (Sometimes the altitude of a triangle is also called the **height**.) The length of an altitude is the distance from the vertex to the

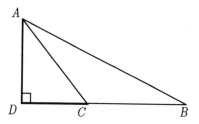

line containing the opposite side. As shown in the figure, to draw the altitudes of an obtuse triangle, we must extend some sides of the triangle, as in the bold extension of BC to D, then we can draw altitude AD to side BC. Remember, any time we say the distance from a point to a line, we mean the length of the perpendicular segment drawn from the point to the line.

The altitudes are usually denoted h_a, h_b, and h_c, where h_a is the altitude from A and so on. The altitudes are concurrent at the **orthocenter**, denoted H. As suggested by the above figure of the altitude of an obtuse triangle, the orthocenter of an obtuse triangle is outside the triangle. (Draw it and see for yourself!) Where is the orthocenter of a right triangle?

EXAMPLE 11-1   Show that the circumcenter of a right triangle is the midpoint of its hypotenuse.

Proof: Since $\angle C$ is an inscribed right angle, we have $\overarc{AB} = 2\angle C = 180°$. Thus $\overarc{AB}$ is a semi-circular arc, and AB is a diameter of the circle. Hence, O, as the midpoint of the diameter, is the center of the circle. Thus the midpoint of the hypotenuse of a right triangle is the circumcenter of the triangle.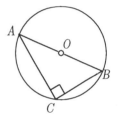

EXERCISE 11-1   Show that the circumradius of a right triangle is equal to half the hypotenuse.

EXERCISE 11-2   Show that the median to the hypotenuse of a right triangle is equal to half the hypotenuse.

EXERCISE 11-3   Show that if a median of a triangle is one-half the side to which it is drawn, then the triangle must be right.

11.3   The Triangle Inequality

Get a ruler and try to draw a triangle with sides 1, 8, and 11 cm. Start from a point A, then pick B so that $AB = 8$ cm. Now we pick point C so that $BC = 1$ cm. What are the possible values of AC? If we start from B and move 1 cm, the closest we can get to A to go directly towards A. Thus, the shortest distance possible from

A to C is 7 cm. How about the longest possible distance? For C to be as far as possible from B, we must move 1 cm from B directly away from A. Now we see that C can be no further than 9 cm from A, and hence we can't create a triangle such that $AB = 8$, $BC = 1$, and $AC = 11$.

This discussion leads us to the **Triangle Inequality**. Given two sides of a triangle the third side must be less than the sum of the first two. For example, above we found that if two sides of a triangle have lengths 1 cm and 8 cm, the third side must be less than $1 + 8 = 9$ cm. If the sum of two sides of a triangle equals the third side, the triangle is **degenerate**, that is, it is a straight line, as discussed on page 129.

(How could we use to Triangle Inequality to support our claim above that if two sides of a triangle are 1 cm and 8 cm, then the third side is greater than 7 cm?)

EXAMPLE 11-2 If two sides of a nondegenerate triangle are 7 and 13, what are the restrictions on the third side?

Solution: Let x be the third side. By the Triangle Inequality, we must have $x + 7 > 13$, so $x > 6$. We must also have $x + 13 > 7$, which is true for all positive x. Finally, we must have $7 + 13 > x$, so $x < 20$. Thus our restriction is $\mathbf{6 < x < 20}$.

EXERCISE 11-4 In how many ways can we form a nondegenerate triangle by choosing three distinct numbers from the set $\{1,2,3,4,5\}$ as the sides?

11.4   The Pythagorean Theorem

By far the most famous theorem in geometry is the **Pythagorean Theorem**, which states that *the sum of the squares of the lengths of the legs of a right triangle equals the square of the length of the hypotenuse.* Thus, for $\triangle ABC$ in the figure, we have

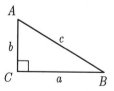

$$(AC)^2 + (BC)^2 = (AB)^2 .$$

The Pythagorean Theorem is proven on page 149.

The application of the Pythagorean Theorem is very simple: whenever we know two of the sides of a right triangle, we can use it to get the third.

EXAMPLE 11-3 Given that the legs of a right triangle are 8 and 4, the hypotenuse is $\sqrt{8^2 + 4^2} = \sqrt{80} = 4\sqrt{5}$.

EXAMPLE 11-4 If in $\triangle ABC$, $\angle A + \angle B = 90°$, $AC = 4$, and $AB = 5$, what is BC?

Solution: Since $\angle A + \angle B = 90°$, we know that $\angle C = 90°$, so we can apply the Pythagorean Theorem: $4^2 + (BC)^2 = 5^2$, so $BC = \mathbf{3}$.

EXAMPLE 11-5 Show that for points B, X, and C, $BX + XC = BC$ if and only if X is on segment BC.

Proof: For the "if" part, it is pretty obvious that X being on segment BC makes $BX + XC = BC$. The "only if" part is subtler: we must show that this equality is *only* true when X is on BC, or to put it another way, that the equality is impossible when X is not on BC. In the diagram, we draw the perpendicular from X, which is not on BC, to BC. We know $BY + YC = BC$. From the Pythagorean Theorem on $\triangle XYB$ we find

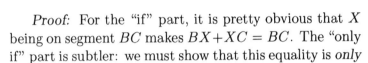

$$XB = \sqrt{XY^2 + BY^2} > \sqrt{BY^2}.$$

Thus we have $XB > BY$, and similarly $XC > YC$. Therefore, we know that $BC = BY + YC < XB + XC$; hence, if X is not on BC, then $BX + XC > BC$. How does this relate to our discussion of degenerate triangles (page 128)?

EXAMPLE 11-6 Show that if a, b, and c are the sides of an obtuse triangle with $a \le b < c$, then $a^2 + b^2 < c^2$.

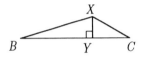

Proof: Because the proposed relation is similar to the Pythagorean Theorem, we are led to draw an altitude to make some right triangles as shown in the diagram. First, from right triangle ACD we have $x^2 + h^2 = b^2$. Then from right triangle ADB we get

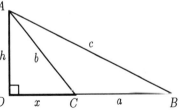

$$c^2 = (a + x)^2 + h^2 = a^2 + (h^2 + x^2) + 2ax = a^2 + b^2 + 2ax.$$

Since $2ax$ is positive, we know that $c^2 > a^2 + b^2$.

EXERCISE 11-5 Find the length of the altitude to the base of an isosceles triangle whose base is 16 and legs are each 10.

EXERCISE 11-6 How many non-congruent obtuse triangles are there with integer side lengths and perimeter 11?

EXERCISE 11-7 Show that if a, b, and c are the sides of an acute triangle, then $a^2 + b^2 > c^2$.

EXERCISE 11-8 A 25-foot ladder is placed against a vertical wall. The foot of the ladder is 7 feet from the base of the wall. If the top of the ladder slips 4 feet, then how far will the foot slide? (MAΘ 1992)

Pythagorean Triples

Any set of integers (a, b, c) which satisfies the Pythagorean Theorem, so that $a^2 + b^2 = c^2$, is called a **Pythagorean triple**. Knowing Pythagorean triples can prevent you from having to use the Pythagorean Theorem in some cases. For cases like the one above where the sides are 3, 4, and 5, going the long way will cost you little; however, what if we are told that the legs are 3636 and 4848? By using Pythagorean triples we could determine that the hypotenuse is 6060 without ever squaring the lengths of the legs. How?

First, if (a, b, c) is a Pythagorean triple, then so is (na, nb, nc) for all integers n. For example, we found above that $(3, 4, 5)$ is a Pythagorean triple, so $(6, 8, 10)$, $(9, 12, 15)$, etc. are all Pythagorean triples. The proof of this assertion is straightforward. If a, b, c are the sides of a right triangle, then $a^2 + b^2 = c^2$ and

$$(na)^2 + (nb)^2 = n^2(a^2 + b^2) = n^2(c^2) = (nc)^2.$$

By this same proof we see that even if any of n, a, b, or c are not integers, (na, nb, nc) satisfies the Pythagorean Theorem if (a, b, c) does.

Some common Pythagorean triples are $(5, 12, 13)$, $(7, 24, 25)$, and $(8, 15, 17)$. (Verify these yourself.) Knowing the common Pythagorean triples can save you a lot of time when problem solving, as shown in some of the following problems. Whenever you are given two sides of a right triangle, write the ratio of the sides as a ratio of integers and see if the ratio fits one of the Pythagorean triples. For example, if the legs are in a ratio of $3 : 4$, they fit the triple $(3,4,5)$. This allows us to conclude that the hypotenuse must fit the triple as well.

EXAMPLE 11-7 The legs of a right triangle have lengths 3/105 and 4/105. What is the length of the hypotenuse?

Solution: The legs are in the ratio 3 : 4. We know from our discussion of Pythagorean triples that if the legs are in a ratio of 3 : 4, then the ratio of the legs and the hypotenuse is 3 : 4 : 5. Thus, since the legs are 3(1/105) and 4(1/105), the hypotenuse is 5(1/105) = 5/105 = **1/21**.

EXAMPLE 11-8 If the hypotenuse of a right triangle is 4.25 and one of the legs is 2, what is the length of the other leg?

Solution: The ratio of the leg to the hypotenuse is 2 : 4.25, or 8 : 17. (Always write the ratios as integers because it makes it much easier to see Pythagorean triples.) Since (8,15,17) is a Pythagorean triple and the hypotenuse is 17(1/4) while a leg is 8(1/4), the other leg must be 15(1/4) = **3.75**.

EXERCISE 11-9 Find the hypotenuse of a right triangle whose legs are $9\sqrt{2}$ and $12\sqrt{2}$.

EXERCISE 11-10 Find the second leg of a right triangle whose hypotenuse has length 175 and which has one leg of length 49.

Any time you see a right triangle, the three sides can be related by the Pythagorean Theorem. If you can determine two sides of the triangle, you know the third by the Pythagorean Theorem. If it is not obvious that the Pythagorean Theorem can answer your problem, however, you probably need to find some other method to use instead of, or along with, the Pythagorean Theorem.

11.5   Congruent Triangles

Two figures are **congruent** if they are exactly alike. Thus, all that is true in one of the figures is also true of the other. A simple example of two congruent figures is two circles of the same radius. The circles are exactly alike, and therefore they are congruent.

In this section we discuss how to prove that two triangles are congruent. Triangle congruency is one of the most effective ways to show that segments or angles are equal.

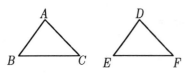

Two triangles are congruent if all their corresponding sides and corresponding angles are equal. When two triangles ABC and DEF are congruent, as in the diagram, we write $\triangle ABC \cong \triangle DEF$.

We always order the vertices the same way for each triangle, that is, $\angle A = \angle D$, $\angle B = \angle E$, and $\angle C = \angle F$, so we write $\triangle ABC \cong \triangle DEF$ rather than $\triangle ACB \cong \triangle DEF$.

Although we said that in two congruent triangles, all three sides and all three angles are equal, we don't in general need to show all six of these equalities just to prove the congruency of two triangles. Each of the seven criteria described below is sufficient to show that two triangles are congruent. The first four work for any triangles, while the last three work only for right triangles.

Congruency Theorems

1. Side-Side-Side (SSS)

If we show that the three sides of a triangle are equal to the sides of another triangle, then it follows that the corresponding angles are equal and hence the triangles are congruent. In a proof, we would write "the two triangles are congruent by SSS."

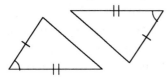

2. Side-Angle-Side (SAS)

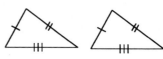

If two sides and the angle *between* them of one triangle are equal to two sides and the angle between them of another triangle, then the triangles are congruent.

WARNING: The angles which are equal in the triangles must be the ones between the sides you are using. This is very important, because as you can see at right,

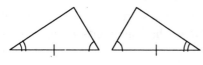

if the equal angles are not between the equal corresponding sides, the triangles are not necessarily congruent. There is no such thing as SSA congruency.

3. Angle-Side-Angle (ASA)

If a side in one triangle equals a side of another, and the angles formed by that side and each of the other two sides are equal to the corresponding angles in the other triangle, then the triangles are congruent.

WARNING: The *corresponding* angles in each triangle must be equal. At right, we have equal sides and a pair of equal angles, but the angles are not corresponding, for in one triangle they share the equal side and in the other they do not.

4. Angle-Angle-Side (AAS)

If two angles and a side other than the side between the two angles are equal to the corresponding parts of another triangle, then the triangles are congruent.

AAS is actually just the same as ASA, because if two angles of a triangle equal two angles of another triangle, then the third angles must be equal as well. (Do you see why?) Thus, all we need are two angles and a side in one triangle equal to their corresponding parts in another triangle to show that the triangles are congruent. As we showed above, however, this is not true of two sides and an angle.

5. Hypotenuse-Leg (HL)

If the hypotenuse and one leg of a right triangle equal that of another, the triangles are congruent.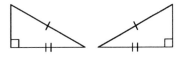

6. Leg-Leg (LL)

If the legs of a right triangle equal those of another, then by LL, the right triangles are congruent. (This is just SAS applied to right triangles. Can you see why?)

7. Side-Angle (SA)

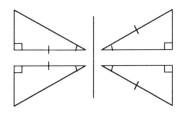 If one of the acute angles of a *right triangle* equals that of another right triangle, and one of its sides equals a corresponding side of the other triangle, then the right triangles are congruent. These corresponding sides may be hypotenuses or corresponding legs, as the diagram to the left suggests.

The most difficult part of using congruent triangles is recognizing that two triangles are indeed congruent. As you will see in the first two problems, using triangles you know are congruent is very easy. The tough part is determining that two triangles are congruent; however, if you are diligent about finding and marking equal angles and equal segments, you will become quite proficient at finding congruent triangles.

What good is finding congruent triangles? The most useful tool is that if two figures are congruent, all parts of one figure are the same as the other. Thus, if we can prove that a side of triangle ABC has length 50, then any triangle congruent to $\triangle ABC$ has a side of length 50. In the problems that follow, you will see how useful this seemingly simple principle is.

EXAMPLE 11-9 If, in the figure, $\triangle ABC \cong \triangle BAD$, then find $\angle D$.

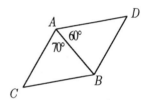

Solution: From the given triangle congruence we have $\angle ABC = \angle BAD = 60°$. Thus we find

$$\angle D = \angle C = 180° - \angle BAC - \angle ABC = \mathbf{50°}.$$

EXAMPLE 11-10 Prove that if two angles of a triangle are equal, then the sides opposite those angles are equal.

Proof: We first draw altitude AX from the vertex which does not contain one of the equal angles. Thus, in right triangles AXB and AXC we have $AX = AX$ and $\angle B = \angle C$. By SA for right triangles we find $\triangle AXB \cong \triangle AXC$; hence, $AB = AC$.

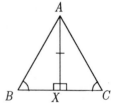

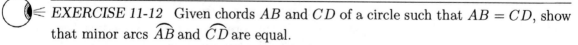

EXERCISE 11-11 Prove that a chord and a radius of a circle are perpendicular if and only if the chord is bisected by the radius.

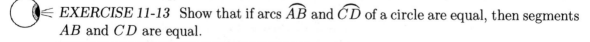

EXERCISE 11-12 Given chords AB and CD of a circle such that $AB = CD$, show that minor arcs $\overset{\frown}{AB}$ and $\overset{\frown}{CD}$ are equal.

EXERCISE 11-13 Show that if arcs $\overset{\frown}{AB}$ and $\overset{\frown}{CD}$ of a circle are equal, then segments AB and CD are equal.

EXERCISE 11-14   Prove that if two sides of a triangle are equal, then the angles opposite those sides are also equal.

EXERCISE 11-15   Show that in an isosceles triangle the centroid, incenter, orthocenter, and circumcenter all lie on the same line, and that in an equilateral triangle they are all the same point.

Triangle congruency is one of the most effective ways to show that angles or segments are equal. Sometimes you may have to introduce extra segments, as in the isosceles triangle proofs above, in order to use congruent triangles. Mark the sides and angles of congruent triangles as you go, because it's very easy to get confused as to which angles or sides in the diagram are equal.

11.6   Similar Triangles

Two triangles are **similar** if one is a magnified version of the other. If two triangles are similar, their corresponding sides have a constant ratio. For example, in the similar triangles below we have

$$\frac{c}{f} = \frac{b}{e} = \frac{a}{d}.$$

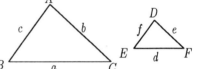

In addition to the sides, all other corresponding lengths, such as medians, altitudes, etc., have the same ratio as the common ratio of the sides. Furthermore, if the ratio of the sides is k, the ratio of the areas is k^2.

To show that two triangles ABC and DEF are similar, we write $\triangle ABC \sim \triangle DEF$. As with congruent triangles, we always make sure to write the vertices in the same order for each triangle. (For example, we wouldn't write $\triangle ABC \sim \triangle DFE$ for the above triangles.)

There are three general ways to prove that triangles are similar.

Similarity Theorems

1. Angle-Angle (AA)

AA is the most useful method of proving that two triangles are similar. If the three angles of one triangle are equal to those of another, the two triangles are similar. (Does this make sense? Why does AA not imply congruence?) In working a problem, it is sufficient to show that just two pairs of corresponding angles are equal, because the third will follow from the constant sum of the angles in a triangle. Conversely, if two triangles are similar, their corresponding angles are equal.

2. Side-Angle-Side (SAS)

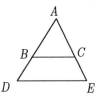

If triangles RST and XYZ are such that $RS/XY = RT/XZ$ and $\angle R = \angle X$, then $\triangle RST \sim \triangle XYZ$. This similarity theorem has very limited usefulness. In fact, it is generally used only in situations like the one on the right. If we are given that $AB/AD = AC/AE$, then $\triangle ABC \sim \triangle ADE$.

3. Side-Side-Side (SSS)

As we noted above, two triangles are similar if all the ratios of corresponding sides are equal. This is the most rarely used method of showing that two triangles are similar.

Similar triangles are useful because of what they tell us about the ratios of the sides of the triangles and about the equality of angles. From these ratios and equalities, many other facts usually follow.

EXAMPLE 11-11   On sides AB and AC of $\triangle ABC$, we pick points D and E, respectively, so that $DE \parallel BC$. If $AB = 3AD$ and $DE = 6$, find BC.

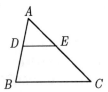

Solution: Since $DE \parallel BC$, we have $\angle ADE = \angle ABC$ and $\angle AED = \angle ACB$; thus, triangles ABC and ADE are similar. Hence we have $AB/AD = BC/DE$. We are given that $AB/AD = 3$, so $BC = 3DE = \mathbf{18}$.

EXAMPLE 11-12   Given that the altitude to the hypotenuse of a right triangle divides the hypotenuse into segments of lengths 4 and 8, find the length of the altitude.

Solution: First we draw the altitude CD. Since $\angle CDA = \angle ACB$ and $\angle DAC = \angle BAC$, we have $\triangle ACD \sim \triangle ABC$ by AA similarity. Similarly we find $\triangle CBD \sim \triangle ABC$. (The equal angles are all marked in

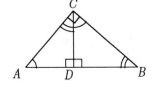

the diagram.) Combining these, we have $\triangle ACD \sim \triangle ABC \sim \triangle CBD$. Whenever you see an altitude to the hypotenuse of a right triangle, think of these key similarity relations.

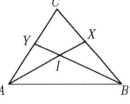

From similar triangles ADC and CDB we have $AD/CD = CD/BD$. Thus $CD^2 = (AD)(BD) = 4(8) = 32$, and the altitude has length $\sqrt{32} = \mathbf{4\sqrt{2}}$.

EXAMPLE 11-13 Prove the **Angle Bisector Theorem**, which states that if AX bisects $\angle A$ of $\triangle ABC$, then $AC/CX = AB/BX$.

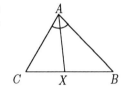

Proof: Seeing the ratio of sides, we think to look for similar triangles—most facts involving ratios of lengths can be proven using similar triangles. As the figure is drawn, however, no similar triangles stand out. We thus look for extra lines to draw. Parallel lines usually make equal angles, and equal angles mean similar triangles. Thus, we extend AX to E as shown so that $BE \parallel AC$. Since $\angle CAE$ and $\angle AEB$ are alternate interior angles, they are equal. Since AX is an angle bisector, we have $\angle CAX = \angle XAB$. Thus $\angle EAB = \angle AEB$, which implies $AB = BE$. Since $\angle CAX = \angle XEB$ and $\angle AXC = \angle BXE$, we find $\triangle BXE \sim \triangle CXA$ by AA. Thus $AC/CX = BE/BX = AB/BX$.

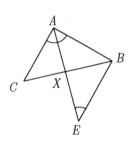

EXAMPLE 11-14 If AX and BY are angle bisectors which intersect at I, show that

$$\frac{AI}{IX} = \frac{AC}{CX}.$$

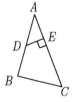

Proof: Remember that the angle bisectors of a triangle are concurrent. Hence, CI bisects $\angle C$. Applying the Angle Bisector Theorem to $\angle C$ of $\triangle ACX$, we have $AC/AI = CX/XI$. Rearranging this slightly gives the desired relation.

EXAMPLE 11-15 In the diagram, $AD = DB = 5$, $EC = 2AE = 8$, and $\angle AED$ is a right angle. Find the length of BC. (MAΘ 1987)

Solution: As the problem appears, there are no similar triangles in sight; however, we can introduce similar triangles by drawing BH, as shown below, such that $BH \parallel DE$.

From the new triangles we see that $\triangle DAE \sim \triangle BAH$ and $AE/AH = AD/AB = 5/(5+5) = 1/2$. Hence, we have $AH = 8$ and $EH = AH - AE = 4$, so $HC = 4$. From the Pythagorean Theorem we find $DE = 3$, and since $DE/BH = 1/2$, we have $BH = 2(3) = 6$. Finally, using the Pythagorean Theorem on $\triangle BHC$ we find $BC = \sqrt{36 + 16} = 2\sqrt{13}$.

EXERCISE 11-16   Chord EF is the perpendicular bisector of chord BC, intersecting it at M. Between B and M point U is taken, and EU extended meets the circle again at A. Then for any selection of U, which triangle is always similar to $\triangle EUM$: $\triangle EFA$, $\triangle EFC$, $\triangle ABM$, $\triangle ABU$, or $\triangle FMC$? (AHSME 1963)

EXERCISE 11-17   In $\triangle ABC$, M and N are the midpoints of AB and AC respectively. If $AB = 5$, $BC = 6$, and $AC = 7$, find MN.

EXERCISE 11-18   In the figure, $TAPZ$ has $TZ \parallel AP \parallel ER$, and R and E are the midpoints of AT and PZ respectively. If $AP = 64$, $TZ = 28$, and $AZ = 46$, find OI. (MAΘ 1990)

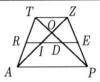

EXERCISE 11-19   Show that if $AB \parallel CD \parallel EF$, then $1/x + 1/y = 1/z$ in the diagram. (This relation is commonly used by test writers, so don't overlook it.)

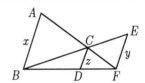

Any time a problem involves finding the length of a segment or the ratio of two segment lengths, consider looking for similar triangles. This is especially true when the problem involves triangles and/or parallel lines. As you saw in the examples above, parallel lines often lead to similar triangles, so whenever you must determine a length in a problem involving parallel lines, look for similar triangles. Also, drawing parallel lines in a diagram often leads to similar triangles, as in our proof of the angle bisector theorem.

WARNING: Other polygons besides triangles can be similar; however, it is important to remember that equal corresponding angles implies similarity *only* for triangles. This method does not work for any other type of polygon.

11.7   Introduction to Trigonometry

Right triangles are of paramount importance in geometry. Thus, mathematicians have developed a shorthand for writing the ratios of the sides of right triangles. Instead of writing "the ratio of the leg adjacent to an 18° angle to the hypotenuse of the triangle," we write "cos 18°". Because expressions of this type frequently come up in physics, engineering, and many other branches of science, you can see why such a shorthand was developed. We'll start off with a few definitions.

With respect to $\angle A$ in right $\triangle ABC$ with $\angle C = 90°$, BC is considered the **opposite** leg and AC the **adjacent** leg. These labels are reversed when working with $\angle B$: AC is opposite and BC adjacent. The six basic trigonometric relations are as defined and abbreviated below:

$$
\begin{aligned}
\textbf{sine}: \quad \sin A &= \frac{\text{opposite}}{\text{hypotenuse}} = \frac{a}{c} \\[4pt]
\textbf{cosine}: \quad \cos A &= \frac{\text{adjacent}}{\text{hypotenuse}} = \frac{b}{c} \\[4pt]
\textbf{tangent}: \quad \tan A &= \frac{\sin A}{\cos A} = \frac{\text{opposite}}{\text{adjacent}} = \frac{a}{b} \\[4pt]
\textbf{secant}: \quad \sec A &= \frac{1}{\cos A} = \frac{\text{hypotenuse}}{\text{adjacent}} = \frac{c}{b} \\[4pt]
\textbf{cosecant}: \quad \csc A &= \frac{1}{\sin A} = \frac{\text{hypotenuse}}{\text{opposite}} = \frac{c}{a} \\[4pt]
\textbf{cotangent}: \quad \cot A &= \frac{\cos A}{\sin A} = \frac{\text{adjacent}}{\text{opposite}} = \frac{b}{a}
\end{aligned}
$$

The most important are the first three: sine, cosine, and tangent.

Thinking about the trigonometric definitions, we can come up with a few important identities. First, because $\angle B = 90° - \angle A$ and $\cos B = a/c$, we have

$$\sin A = \frac{a}{c} = \cos B = \cos\left(90° - A\right).$$

The identity $\sin A = \cos(90° - A)$ is true for all angles A. In the same way, we can show $\tan A = \cot\left(90° - A\right)$ and $\sec A = \csc\left(90° - A\right)$.

Second, we can show the most common and useful trigonometric identity,

$$\sin^2 A + \cos^2 A = 1. \tag{11.1}$$

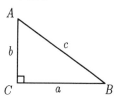

This follows directly from the Pythagorean Theorem:

$$\sin^2 A + \cos^2 A = \frac{a^2}{c^2} + \frac{b^2}{c^2} = \frac{a^2 + b^2}{c^2} = \frac{c^2}{c^2} = 1.$$

Dividing (11.1) by $\cos^2 A$, we have a new relation,

$$\tan^2 A + 1 = \sec^2 A,$$

and dividing (11.1) by $\sin^2 A$ yields

$$\cot^2 A + 1 = \csc^2 A.$$

Values of the Trigonometric Functions

The three most important angles in geometry are the 30°, 45°, and 60° angles. Whenever you bisect a right angle, you get a 45° angle; the angles of an equilateral triangle are 60°; whenever you draw an angle bisector (which is also a median and an altitude) in an equilateral triangle, you form a 30° angle. Since these angles are so common, it is of particular interest to find the values of the trigonometric functions for these angles.

To do this, we will discuss two special cases of right triangles: the **45°-45°-90° triangle** and the **30°-60°-90° triangle**.

At right is an isosceles right triangle. From the Pythagorean Theorem, we can see that if both legs have length a, the hypotenuse has length $\sqrt{a^2 + a^2} = a\sqrt{2}$. Thus we have

$$\sin 45° = \cos 45° = \frac{a}{a\sqrt{2}} = \frac{\sqrt{2}}{2}.$$

We similarly see that $\tan 45° = 1$. Remember these values; you will see them often. Remember also that the ratio of the hypotenuse to the side lengths in 45°-45°-90° triangles is always $\sqrt{2}$.

In the triangle at right, one of the acute angles is twice the other one. The relationship among the sides is not as obvious as in the isosceles case. Perhaps adding a few extra lines will help us with this problem.

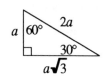

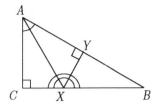

First we draw AX, the angle bisector of the 60° angle. This creates two more 30° angles. Drawing the perpendicular from X to AB divides $\triangle ABX$ into two congruent triangles (by Angle-Side-Angle; make sure you see this). Furthermore, by ASA we find $\triangle ACX \cong \triangle AYX$, so we have

$$\triangle ACX \cong \triangle AYX \cong \triangle BYX.$$

From this we can see that

$$AB = AY + YB = AC + AC = 2AC.$$

Hence, in a 30°-60°-90° triangle, the hypotenuse (AB) is twice the length of the leg opposite the 30° angle (AC). Now, using the Pythagorean Theorem and writing $AB = 2AC$, we get

$$BC = \sqrt{AB^2 - AC^2} = \sqrt{4AC^2 - AC^2} = AC\sqrt{3}.$$

To sum this all up, in 30°-60°-90° triangle BAC we have

$$AC : BC : AB = 1 : \sqrt{3} : 2.$$

Once you know one side of a 30°-60°-90° triangle, you can use it to determine the other two sides. Also, whenever you see a right triangle whose hypotenuse is twice the length of a side, you know you have found a 30°-60°-90° triangle. Any time a 30° or a 60° angle appears in a problem, you should think of these relations; for example, when you draw an altitude of an equilateral triangle, you divide the triangle into two 30°-60°-90° triangles. (Challenge: Let the midpoint of the hypotenuse of 30°-60°-90° triangle ABC be M, where $\angle C = 90°$. Can you prove the relationship among the sides of the 30°-60°-90° triangle using the diagram resulting from drawing CM without adding any more lines?)

Finally, with all this newfound wisdom, we apply our trigonometric relations to $\triangle ABC$.

$$\sin 30° = \cos 60° = \frac{AC}{AB} = \frac{AC}{2AC} = \frac{1}{2}$$

$$\cos 30° = \sin 60° = \frac{BC}{AB} = \frac{AC\sqrt{3}}{2AC} = \frac{\sqrt{3}}{2}$$

$$\tan 30° = \frac{\sin 30°}{\cos 30°} = \frac{\sqrt{3}}{3}$$

$$\tan 60° = \frac{\sin 60°}{\cos 60°} = \sqrt{3}$$

Keep in mind before memorizing these tables that it is not really necessary to memorize the tangent values, because as long as you know the sine and cosine, you know the tangent.

Students often forget whether it is the sine or the cosine of a 30° angle which is 1/2. If you ever forget, draw a 30°-60°-90° triangle. The leg opposite the 30° angle is the shorter leg, so $\sin 30° = 1/2$. Similarly, the leg adjacent to the 30° angle is the longer leg, so $\cos 30° = \sqrt{3}/2$. You can do the same to remind yourself of the trigonometric values for 60° angles.

Two other angles which are common in trigonometry problems are 0° and 90°. If we consider right triangle ABC with hypotenuse AB, when $\angle A = 0°$, B and C are the same point and $BC = 0$! (Try drawing triangles with smaller and smaller measures of $\angle A$.) Also, $AB = AC$. Thus we have the following trigonometric values:

$$\sin 0° = \cos 90° = \frac{BC}{AB} = 0$$

$$\cos 0° = \sin 90° = \frac{AC}{AB} = 1$$

$$\tan 0° = \frac{BC}{AC} = 0$$

$$\tan 90° = \frac{AC}{BC} = \text{undefined}$$

The value $\tan 90°$ is undefined because it involves a division by zero, which we cannot do.

The following table summarizes all we have discussed about trigonometric relations in this section.

Function	In terms of sin and cos	In a right triangle	0°	30°	45°	60°	90°
sin	sin	$\dfrac{\text{opposite}}{\text{hypotenuse}}$	0	$\dfrac{1}{2}$	$\dfrac{\sqrt{2}}{2}$	$\dfrac{\sqrt{3}}{2}$	1
cos	cos	$\dfrac{\text{adjacent}}{\text{hypotenuse}}$	1	$\dfrac{\sqrt{3}}{2}$	$\dfrac{\sqrt{2}}{2}$	$\dfrac{1}{2}$	0
tan	$\dfrac{\sin}{\cos}$	$\dfrac{\text{opposite}}{\text{adjacent}}$	0	$\dfrac{\sqrt{3}}{3}$	1	$\sqrt{3}$	undef.
sec	$\dfrac{1}{\cos}$	$\dfrac{\text{hypotenuse}}{\text{adjacent}}$	1	$\dfrac{2\sqrt{3}}{3}$	$\sqrt{2}$	2	undef.
csc	$\dfrac{1}{\sin}$	$\dfrac{\text{hypotenuse}}{\text{opposite}}$	undef.	2	$\sqrt{2}$	$\dfrac{2\sqrt{3}}{3}$	1
cot	$\dfrac{\cos}{\sin}$	$\dfrac{\text{adjacent}}{\text{opposite}}$	undef.	$\sqrt{3}$	1	$\dfrac{\sqrt{3}}{3}$	0

$$\sin^2\theta + \cos^2\theta = 1$$
$$\tan^2\theta + 1 = \sec^2\theta$$
$$\cot^2\theta + 1 = \csc^2\theta$$
$$\sin(90° - \phi) = \cos\phi$$
$$\csc(90° - \phi) = \sec\phi$$
$$\tan(90° - \phi) = \cot\phi$$

 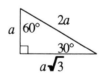

What use is trigonometry? In a word, it's a shortcut. Using the trigonometric functions and our knowledge about special right triangles, we can quickly find various side lengths and angle measures. Examples are included among the problems below. Trigonometry also gives us yet another method to prove that two angles are equal. If we know that two acute angles have the same value for some trigonometric function (e.g. $\sin\alpha = \sin\beta$), then we know the angles are equal ($\alpha = \beta$). (Can you prove this?)

EXAMPLE 11-16   Given that $\angle B = 90°$ and $\cot C = 5/6$ in $\triangle ABC$, find side BC if $AC = 5\sqrt{61}$.

Solution: We have $\cot C = BC/AB = 5/6$. Thus, letting $BC = x$, we know $AB = 6x/5$. Using the Pythagorean Theorem we get $AB^2 + BC^2 = 61x^2/25 = AC^2 = 25(61)$. Thus $x^2 = 25(25)(61)/61 = 25^2$, and $x = \mathbf{25}$.

EXAMPLE 11-17   Find side BC of $\triangle ABC$ if $AB = 8$, $AC = 8\sqrt{2}$, $\angle ABC = 45°$, and $\angle ACB = 30°$.

Solution: By drawing altitude AD we form the two special right triangles discussed in this section. First, since $\angle ABD = 45°$, $\triangle ABD$ is an isosceles right triangle. Thus $BD = AB/\sqrt{2} = 8/\sqrt{2} = 4\sqrt{2}$. Since $\angle ACD = 30°$ and $\triangle ACD$ is a right triangle, we know that $AD = AC/2 = 4\sqrt{2}$ and $CD = AD\sqrt{3} = 4\sqrt{6}$. Thus, $BC = BD + DC = \mathbf{4\sqrt{2} + 4\sqrt{6}}$.

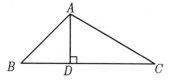

EXERCISE 11-20   In circle O with radius 6, $\overset{\frown}{AB} = 60°$ and $\overset{\frown}{CD} = 90°$. Find the difference in the lengths of segments CD and AB.

EXERCISE 11-21   Find, in degrees, the smallest positive angle x such that $\sin 3x = \cos 7x$. (Mandelbrot #3)

EXERCISE 11-22   Find side AC of $\triangle ABC$ if $\angle A = 90°$, $\sec B = 4$, and $AB = 6$.

11.8   Area of a Triangle

In this section we will prove three general methods to determine the area of a triangle. Namely,

$$[ABC] = \frac{ah_a}{2} = \frac{ab\sin C}{2} = rs.$$

Recall that h_a is the altitude to side a, s the semiperimeter (half the sum of the sides), and r the inradius of the triangle.

The following examples display the use of these three formulas.

EXAMPLE 11-18 Find the area of $\triangle ABC$ if $AB = AC = 50$ and $BC = 80$.

Solution: Since the triangle is isosceles, the altitude AX to side BC bisects BC. Thus, from the Pythagorean Theorem on right triangle ABX, we find $AX = 30$, so $[ABC] = (BC)(AX)/2 = (80)(30)/2 = \mathbf{1200}$.

EXAMPLE 11-19 Find the radius of the circle which is inscribed in a triangle whose perimeter is 40 and area is 120.

Solution: Call the triangle $\triangle ABC$. Since $[ABC] = rs = 120$ and $s = 40/2 = 20$, we find that $r = \mathbf{6}$.

EXAMPLE 11-20 In isosceles triangle ABC, we are given $AB = AC = 4$ and $\angle C = 75°$. Find the area of $\triangle ABC$.

Solution: Since $AB = AC$, we have $\angle B = \angle C = 75°$, so $\angle A = 30°$ (because $\angle A + \angle B + \angle C = 180°$). The area of ABC is then

$$[ABC] = \frac{(AB)(AC)}{2} \sin A = 8 \sin 30° = \mathbf{4}.$$

EXAMPLE 11-21 Prove that if $\triangle ABC \sim \triangle DEF$ then the ratio of corresponding altitudes equals the ratio of corresponding sides and the ratio of the areas of the triangles equals the square of the ratio of the sides.

Proof: In the triangles shown, let $AX = h_a$ and $DY = h_d$, where a and d are BC and EF, respectively. First we wish to show that $h_a/h_d = a/d$. Since this is a problem involving ratios of sides, we look for similar triangles. Indeed, $\triangle AXC \sim \triangle DYF$ because $\angle C = \angle F$ and $\angle AXC = \angle DYF$. Thus $h_u/h_d = b/e = a/d = c/f$ and the proof is complete. We can use this same method on any other significant lengths in a triangle; however, unless specifically told to prove it, you can assume that this relationship holds for all other lengths, such as inradii or medians.

Now for the ratio of areas. Since we know $[ABC] = ah_a/2$ and $[DEF] = dh_d/2$, we have

$$\frac{[ABC]}{[DEF]} = \frac{ah_a}{dh_d} = \left(\frac{a}{d}\right)\left(\frac{h_a}{h_d}\right) = \left(\frac{a}{d}\right)\left(\frac{a}{d}\right) = \left(\frac{a}{d}\right)^2.$$

(We have used what we just proved about the ratio of altitude lengths.)

The proofs of these area formulas will give the reader important tips on how to attack area problems in general.

Proofs of Triangle Area Formulas

1. $[ABC] = ah_a/2$

We'll start our proof with right triangles. Consider the figure at the right. Congruent triangles ABC and CDA together form a rectangle as shown. Thus the areas of the two are equal, so the area of one is half the area of the rectangle they form together. The area of the rectangle is its length times its width, so

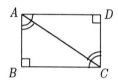

$$[ABC] = \frac{[ABCD]}{2} = \frac{(AB)(BC)}{2}.$$

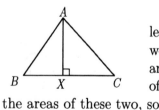

We will prove our area formula for acute triangles and leave the proof for obtuse triangles as an exercise. Because we know the area of a right triangle, we draw altitude AX and form two right triangles. The area of ABC is the sum of the areas of ABX and ACX, and we know how to find the areas of these two, so

$$[ABC] = [ABX] + [ACX] = \frac{(AX)(BX)}{2} + \frac{(AX)(CX)}{2} = \frac{(AX)(BC)}{2}.$$

2. $[ABC] = \dfrac{ab\sin C}{2}.$

Seeing sines involved, we think of right triangles, so we draw the altitude from A. (We don't draw the altitude from C because the expression $\sin C$ leads us to look for a right triangle in which $\angle C$ is one of the acute angles.) Now we find

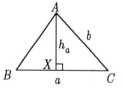

$$\sin C = \frac{AX}{AC} = \frac{h_a}{b}.$$

Using this value for $\sin C$ in $\frac{1}{2}ab\sin C$ yields

$$\frac{1}{2}ab\sin C = \left(\frac{ab}{2}\right)\left(\frac{h_a}{b}\right) = \frac{ah_a}{2} = [ABC].$$

Proving this formula for an obtuse triangle is a little trickier, as we haven't yet defined trigonometric relationships for anything but acute and right angles.

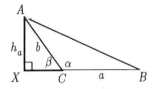

For any angle θ, $\sin(180° - \theta) = \sin\theta$. (Take this on faith for now.) Using this we can deal with two sides and the included angle when the angle is obtuse. As before, we draw altitude AX. Thus, since $\sin\beta = h_a/b$, we have

$$\frac{1}{2}ab\sin\alpha = \frac{1}{2}ab\sin(180° - \alpha) = \frac{1}{2}ab\sin\beta = \left(\frac{ab}{2}\right)\left(\frac{h_a}{b}\right) = \frac{ah_a}{2} = [ABC].$$

For an obtuse triangle given two sides and an included acute angle, the proof is the same as the acute triangle case.

3. $[ABC] = rs$.

In proving this formula, we learn an important method in solving area problems: chopping up a desired area into pieces and finding the sum of the areas of the pieces. Since the formula involves the inradius, let's draw some inradii. But where? The only choices that make sense are the radii to where the circle is tangent to the sides of the triangle.

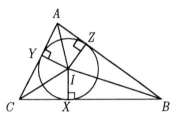

These are perpendicular to the sides. Connecting the incenter to the vertices of the triangle, we form the three triangles AIB, BIC, and CIA. For each of these triangles, an inradius forms an altitude, so

$$\begin{aligned}
[ABC] &= [AIB] + [BIC] + [CIA] \\
&= \frac{(IZ)(AB)}{2} + \frac{(IX)(BC)}{2} + \frac{(IY)(AC)}{2} \\
&= \frac{rc}{2} + \frac{ra}{2} + \frac{rb}{2} \\
&= r(a+b+c)/2 = rs,
\end{aligned}$$

and we are done.

Knowing when to use the area formulas is generally quite straightforward. If you need to find the area of a triangle and it is not readily obvious which of these three to use, look for one of the following hints. The most common method is to draw an altitude to a side whose length you know and try to determine the altitude's length. If this fails, you have other options. Given an angle of the triangle, try to find the two sides adjacent to it. If you know two sides of the triangle, you can find the area if you find the angle between them. Finally, the relationship between the area and the inradius is generally only useful in problems involving the incircle or inradius.

The area formulas can also be used together to determine other things about a triangle. For example, if we are given that $h_a = 3$ and $b = 4$ in $\triangle ABC$, we can find $\sin C$ from our area relations. We write

$$[ABC] = \frac{ah_a}{2} = \frac{1}{2}ab \sin C,$$

and solving the second equality for $\sin C$, we have

$$\sin C = \frac{h_a}{b} = \frac{3}{4}.$$

This application of triangle areas is limited now, because you only know three ways to find triangle areas. However, as you learn more ways to find the area of a triangle, this method will become considerably more useful.

EXAMPLE 11-22 Given an equilateral triangle with side length s, find the area of the triangle in terms of s.

Solution: Since each angle of an equilateral triangle is 60°, we have

$$[ABC] = \frac{ab \sin C}{2} = \frac{s^2 \sin 60°}{2} = \frac{s^2\sqrt{3}}{4}.$$

EXAMPLE 11-23 What is the radius of the circle inscribed in a triangle whose sides have lengths 8, 15, and 17?

Solution: Since $8^2 + 15^2 = 17^2$, the triangle is right. (Always check for this when given the side lengths of a triangle in a problem.) Thus the area is $8(15)/2 = 60$. The perimeter is $8 + 15 + 17 = 40$, so the semiperimeter is 20. Solving $[ABC] = rs$ for r, we find $r = 60/20 = \mathbf{3}$.

EXAMPLE 11-24   Use the shown diagram to prove the Pythagorean Theorem.

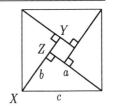

Proof: We can find the area of the large square in two ways. First, as the square of the length of its sides (c^2); second, as the sum of the area of the smaller square and the areas of the four triangles. Since $XY = a$ and $XZ = b$, the sides of the smaller square have length $a - b$. Thus we have

$$c^2 = (a - b)^2 + 4(ab/2) = (a^2 - 2ab + b^2) + 2ab = a^2 + b^2.$$

EXERCISE 11-23   What is the area of an equilateral triangle which has altitude length 12?

EXERCISE 11-24   Prove that the area of an obtuse triangle is one-half the product of a side and the length of the altitude to that side.

EXERCISE 11-25   Tangents from point C to circle O are extended to A and B such that AB is tangent to O at X. If the perimeter of $\triangle ABC$ is 50 and $[ABC] = 100$, find the area of circle O.

EXERCISE 11-26   Eight points are equally spaced on the circumference of a circle of radius 1. Find the area of the region enclosed by connecting the points in order. (Hint: Draw radii of the circle to the vertices.)

11.9   A Handful of Helpful Hints

Congruent triangles, similar triangles, parallel lines, perpendicular lines; these will be your closest friends when working on geometry problems. Much of this section is repeated from earlier sections in this chapter, but it is so important that it is worth repeating.

Let's first discuss parallel and perpendicular lines. Their importance must not be underestimated. In problems, these lines occur in three ways: some we are given, some we draw, and some we discover.

The first case is pretty clear. When given parallel lines, mark the angles you know are equal and proceed. For perpendicular lines, mark the right angles and keep an eye open for chances to use all the special facts we have learned about right triangles.

The second case, the lines we draw, is the most difficult to master. Often geometry problems can be solved by adding an extra parallel or perpendicular line to a diagram; there are examples of this scattered throughout the problems in this chapter. While it may seem that we pulled some of the lines we drew out of thin air, there actually are signs to look for. This takes practice, but any good geometrician is expert at adding a line or two to a diagram to make the problem easier.

Finally come those lines that we discover, which brings us to the question of how we know that two lines are parallel or perpendicular.

Given two lines and a transversal as shown, the following are ways to determine that the two lines are parallel.

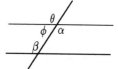

1. Show that a pair of alternate interior angles are equal:

$$\alpha = \beta.$$

2. Show that a pair of corresponding angles are equal:

$$\beta = \theta.$$

3. Show that a pair of same-side interior angles are supplementary:

$$\beta + \phi = 180°.$$

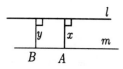

Each of the preceding conditions is sufficient to prove that two lines are parallel. Another very useful way is to show that two points on one of the lines are equidistant from the other line. For example, in the diagram, points A and B on m are distances x and y from l. If $x = y$, then $l \parallel m$.

There are many, many ways to show that two lines are perpendicular. The simplest is to prove that they form a right angle. The methods of proving two lines are perpendicular can be divided in the following categories: using angle relations to show that the angle formed by the lines is 90°, proving that the angle is the largest angle of a right triangle, and showing that the lines are perpendicular without using angle measures.

Ways to show an angle is 90°

1. Show that the angle is inscribed in a semicircle.

2. Given two intersecting lines, show that a pair of adjacent angles are equal. Adjacent angles are angles which share a side. Intersecting lines form adjacent lines which are supplementary, and two angles which are equal and supplementary are right.

Ways to show a triangle is a right triangle

1. Show that two of the angles in the triangle are complementary.
If two angles add to 90°, the third must be 90°.

2. Show that the sides satisfy the Pythagorean Theorem.
We showed on page 129 that if the sum of the squares of two sides of an acute or obtuse triangle cannot equal the square of the third side. Thus, any triangle whose sides satisfy the Pythagorean Theorem must be right.

3. Show that the triangle is similar or congruent to some other triangle which is right.

4. Show that a median of the triangle is equal to half the side to which it is drawn.
This is discussed on page 127.

Ways to show two lines or segments are perpendicular without using angles

1. Show that one line passes through the center of a circle which is tangent to the other line where the two lines intersect.

Since a diameter drawn from the point of tangency of a line is perpendicular to the line, this shows that the two lines are perpendicular.

2. If the segments are a radius (or diameter) and a chord of a circle, show that the radius bisects the chord.

This is given as an exercise on page 134. Look for this in problems involving chords of circles.

3. Show that one segment is an altitude in a triangle and the other segment is the side to which the altitude is drawn.

This occurs quite rarely, but sometimes we come across a problem in which we are given two altitudes of a triangle and their intersection. It pays to remember that this intersection is the orthocenter and that any line through this point and a vertex is perpendicular to the side opposite the vertex.

We mentioned above that there are sometimes signs as to when and how we can draw extra lines. Perpendicular lines are useful in problems involving areas, while adding parallel lines is helpful in any problem which calls for similar or congruent triangles. As discussed in the relevant sections, congruent triangles are most useful for showing that segments and angles are equal, while problems involving determining segment lengths or ratios thereof are often solved with similar triangles.

The following example shows the importance of cleverly adding parallel lines to a diagram and using congruent and similar triangles. Various problems at the end of the chapter will also give you experience using these tools.

EXAMPLE 11-25 Point E is selected on side AB of $\triangle ABC$ in such a way that $AE : EB = 1 : 3$, and point D is selected on side BC so that $CD : DB = 1 : 2$. The point of intersection of AD and CE is F. Find $EF/FC + AF/FD$. (AHSME 1965)

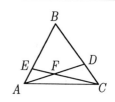

Solution: Seeing ratios, we look for similar triangles involving the segments. Seeing no such triangles, we endeavor to make some. Drawing $DH \parallel EA$ achieves this. Since $\angle EBC = \angle GDC$ and $\angle BEC = \angle DGC$ (corresponding angles), we have $\triangle EBC \sim \triangle GDC$. Thus $DG/EB = DC/BC = 1/3$. Since $EA/EB = 1/3$ also, we conclude that $EA = DG$. From ASA we have $\triangle EAF \cong \triangle GDF$ (the equal angles are alternate interior angles). Thus, $AF = FD$ and $AF/FD = 1$. That takes care of one of the ratios.

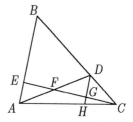

Returning to similar triangles EBC and GDC, we know $GC/EC = 1/3$. Since $EF = FG$ and $EF + FG = EC - GC = 2EC/3$, we have $EF = FG = GC = EC/3$.

Thus, $EF/FC = (EC/3)/(2EC/3) = 1/2$. Putting this together with AF/FD, we find $EF/FC + AF/FD = \mathbf{3/2}$.

This is a very difficult problem, but it shows the amazing amount of information that can be found from cleverly adding a single segment to a diagram.

Problems to Solve for Chapter 11

167. In $\triangle ADC$, segment DM is drawn such that $\angle ADM = \angle ACD$. Prove that $AD^2 = (AM)(AC)$.

168. How many scalene triangles have all sides of integral lengths and perimeter less than 13? (AHSME 1956)

169. The sides of $\triangle BAC$ are in the ratio $2:3:4$. BD is the angle bisector drawn to the shortest side AC, dividing it into segments AD and CD. If the length of AC is 10, then find the length of the longer segment of AC. (AHSME 1966)

170. What is the number of distinct lines representing the altitudes, medians, and interior angle bisectors of a triangle that is isosceles, but not equilateral? (AHSME 1957)

171. Triangle ABD is right-angled at B. On AD there is a point C for which $AC = CD$ and $AB = BC$. Find $\angle DAB$. (AHSME 1963)

172. Triangle PYT is a right triangle in which $PY = 66$ and $YT = 77$. If PT is more than 50 and is expressed in the simplified form $x\sqrt{y}$, then find $x + y$. (MAΘ 1990)

173. If triangle PQR has sides 40, 60, and 80, then the shortest altitude is K times the longest altitude. Find the value of K. (MATHCOUNTS 1990)

174. In this figure, $\angle ACD$ is a right angle, A, B, and C are collinear, $\angle A = 30°$, and $\angle DBC = 45°$. If $AB = 3 - \sqrt{3}$, find the area of $\triangle BCD$. (MAΘ 1992)

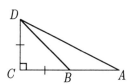

175. The perpendicular bisectors of two of the sides of triangle ABC intersect the third side at the same point. Prove that the triangle is right-angled. (M&IQ 1992)

176. Show that if h_a, h_b, and h_c are the altitudes of a triangle, then

$$\frac{1}{h_a} < \frac{1}{h_b} + \frac{1}{h_c}.$$

177. In right triangle ABC, $\angle C = 90°$ and $\sin A = 7/25$. Find $\sin B$, $\cos A$, $\cot A$, and $\csc B$.

178. The angle between the median CM and the hypotenuse AB of right triangle ABC is equal to $30°$. Find the area of ABC if the altitude CH is equal to 4. (M&IQ 1992)

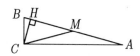

179. The base of a triangle is 15 inches. Two lines are drawn parallel to the base, terminating in the other two sides and dividing the triangle into three equal areas. What is the length of the parallel closer to the base? (AHSME 1953)

180. The straight line AB is divided at C so that $AC = 3CB$. Circles are drawn with AC and CB as diameters and a common tangent to these meets AB extended at D. Show that BD equals the radius of the smaller circle. (AHSME 1954)

181. Segments AD and BE are medians of right triangle ABC, and AB is its hypotenuse. If a right triangle is constructed with legs AD and BE, what will be the length of its hypotenuse in terms of AB? (Mandelbrot #2)

182. Let CM be the median in equilateral triangle ABC. Point N is on BC such that $MN \perp BC$. Prove that $4BN = BC$. (M&IQ 1992)

183. In right triangle ACD with right angle at D, B is a point on side AD between A and D. The length of segment AB is 1. If $\angle DAC = \alpha$ and $\angle DBC = \beta$, then find the length of side DC in terms of α and β. (MAΘ 1991)

184. Angle B of $\triangle ABC$ is trisected by BD and BE which meet AC at D and E respectively. Prove that

$$\frac{AD}{EC} = \frac{(AB)(BD)}{(BE)(BC)}.$$

(AHSME 1952)

185. Given that I is the incenter of $\triangle ABC$, $AB = AC = 5$, and $BC = 8$, find the distance AI. (Mandelbrot #3)

186. Let ABC be an equilateral triangle and points F, Q, and N be such that $AF = QB = NC = 2AB/3$. Prove that the angles AFQ, NQB, and FNC are right and that FQN is an equilateral triangle. (M&IQ 1992)

187. The area of a given triangle is equal to the product of the length of an altitude and the median toward the same side. Prove that the triangle is right-angled. (M&IQ 1992)

188. In $\triangle ABC$, $\angle A = 100°$, $\angle B = 50°$, $\angle C = 30°$, AH is an altitude, and BM is a median. Find $\angle MHC$. (AHSME 1989)

189. Two altitudes of scalene triangle ABC have length 4 and 12. If the length of the third altitude is also an integer, what is the biggest it can be? (AHSME 1986)

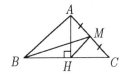

190. The medians of a right triangle which are drawn from the vertices of the acute angles are 5 and $\sqrt{40}$. What is the length of the hypotenuse? (AHSME 1951)

191. If $\tan x = \dfrac{2ab}{a^2 - b^2}$, where $a > b > 0$ and $0° < x < 90°$, then find $\sin x$ in terms of a and b. (AHSME 1972)

192. A right-angled triangle ABC is given in which F is the midpoint of the hypotenuse AB and $BC = 3AC$. Let the points D and E divide the side BC in three equal segments. Prove that the triangle DFE is isosceles and right-angled. (M&IQ 1992)

193. The median to a 10 cm side of a triangle has length 9 cm and is perpendicular to a second median of the triangle. Find the exact value in centimeters of the length of the third median. (MAΘ 1990)

194. A point is selected inside an equilateral triangle. From this point perpendiculars are dropped to each side. Show that the sum of the lengths of these perpendiculars is equal to the altitude length. (AHSME 1950)

195. Let M be the midpoint of side AB of equilateral triangle ABC, and let points N, S, and K divide side BC into four equal segments. Given that P is the midpoint of CM, prove that $\angle MNB = \angle KPN = 90°$. (M&IQ 1992)

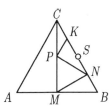

196. Prove that in $\triangle ABC$, if $\angle A > \angle B$, then $BC > AC$.

the BIG PICTURE

Geometry was already in full swing when Euclid came along in around 300 B.C., but it was never the same once he was through with it. In the *Elements*, Euclid started with a set of five simple laws, or **axioms**, from which all the theorems of geometry could be derived. Loosely, they are:

1. Every two points determine exactly one straight line.

2. A segment may be extended arbitrarily far in a straight line.

3. A circle may be drawn with any center and any radius.

4. All right angles are the same.

5. Given any line and any point not on that line, there is exactly one line through the point which is parallel to the original line.

And that's it! Everything else in plane geometry results from these five. Why did Euclid use these particular five? Apparently, he considered them the most aesthetically simple set which still covered everything.

In much of the rest of the *Elements*, Euclid builds geometry up from his postulates in a fully rigorous (and fully beautiful) way. Even 2000 years later, many great mathematicians have first become fascinated with math after reading Euclid's work.

Chapter 12

Quadrilaterals

12.1   The Fundamentals

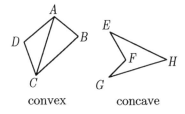

convex   concave

A **quadrilateral** is a four-sided figure. A **convex quadrilateral** is one in which all angles are less than 180°, while one of the interior angles of a **concave quadrilateral** is a reflex angle (an angle greater than 180°). Problems involving concave quadrilaterals are quite rare, so we will generally just be working with convex quadrilaterals.

A **diagonal** of a quadrilateral is a segment from any vertex to the vertex which is not adjacent to it. For example, in the diagram above, AC is a diagonal but AB is not. All quadrilaterals have two diagonals. A quadrilateral is **orthodiagonal** if its diagonals are perpendicular.

Looking at $ABCD$ above, we can see that the sum of the interior angles of a quadrilateral is 360°, because the sum of the angles in $ABCD$ is the sum of the angles in triangles ABC and ACD. As with triangles, the perimeter of a quadrilateral is the sum of the sides of the quadrilateral.

The vertices are always in order when we name a quadrilateral. Thus, we would never call the convex quadrilateral above $ACBD$, but we might call it $BCDA$.

In the following sections, we will discuss several special types of quadrilaterals.

12.2 Trapezoids

A **trapezoid** is a quadrilateral in which two of the sides are parallel. These parallel sides are the **bases** of the trapezoid, while the other sides are the **legs**.

In the figure, $AB \parallel CD$, so

$$\angle ABC + \angle BCD = \angle BAD + \angle ADC = 180°.$$

Segment EF, the distance between the parallel sides of the trapezoid, is the **altitude**, or height, and XY, the segment which connects the midpoints of the legs is called the **median**. The median is most useful in determining the area of the trapezoid. Let's figure out how.

It should be clear that the median is parallel to the bases of the trapezoid. Try to prove this rigorously by showing that X and Y are equidistant from CD. Before moving on to area, we'll discover how to find the length of the median.

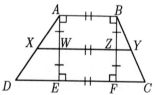

We first draw altitudes AE and BF forming rectangles $EFZW$ and $WZBA$. Make sure you see why these are rectangles. Thus, $AB = WZ = EF$. Since $XY \parallel DC$, by AA we have

$$\triangle AXW \sim \triangle ADE \qquad \text{and} \qquad \triangle BZY \sim \triangle BFC.$$

Since XY is exactly between the bases, we have $BZ = ZF = AW = WE$. Thus,

$$\frac{AW}{AE} = \frac{XW}{DE} = \frac{ZY}{FC} = \frac{1}{2}.$$

Now we determine the median length:

$$
\begin{aligned}
AB + DC &= AB + EF + DE + FC = AB + AB + 2XW + 2ZY \\
&= 2WZ + 2XW + 2ZY = 2(XW + WZ + ZY) \\
&= 2XY,
\end{aligned}
$$

so $XY = (AB + CD)/2$. Hence the length of the median is the average of the lengths of the bases.

We find the area of the trapezoid as the sum of the areas of triangles BFC and AED and rectangle $EFBA$. Thus,

$$[ABCD] = [BFC] + [AED] + [EFBA] = \frac{1}{2}(BF)(FC) + \frac{1}{2}(DE)(EA) + (EF)(EA).$$

Using similar triangles as before and the equal lengths of the opposite sides of a rectangle ($EA = BF$ and $WZ = EF$) we have

$$\begin{aligned}
[ABCD] &= \frac{1}{2}(EA)(2ZY) + \frac{1}{2}(EA)(2XW) + \frac{1}{2}(EA)(2WZ) \\
&= (EA)(ZY + XW + WZ) = (EA)(XY)
\end{aligned}$$

Thus, the area is the product of the median and the height.

If a trapezoid's legs are equal in length, the trapezoid is called **isosceles**. However, equal legs are not the only way we can tell a trapezoid is isosceles. Below we have dissected a trapezoid by drawing altitudes and diagonals. In doing so, we form a number of congruent triangles.

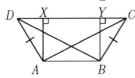 By HL congruency, we have $\triangle AXD \cong \triangle BYC$. Thus $DX = YC$ and $\angle ADC = \angle BCD$. From this angle equality, $\angle ABC = \angle BAD$ follows. (Remember the supplementary relationship between angles in a trapezoid.) Hence, the base angles of an isosceles trapezoid are congruent.

Now look at right triangles AXC and BYD. These are congruent by LL because $AX = BY$ and $XC = XY + YC = XY + XD = DY$. Thus, the diagonals of the trapezoid, as the hypotenuses of these congruent triangles, are equal.

The proof of the converse (that equal diagonals imply equal legs) is the same as above, but in reverse. Start by showing that $\triangle AXC \cong \triangle BYD$, then $YC = DX$, so $\triangle AXD \cong \triangle BYC$, and finally $AD = BC$. Can you show that if $\angle ADC = \angle DCB$, then the trapezoid must be isosceles?

EXAMPLE 12-1   An isosceles trapezoid has altitude 4 and leg length 8. If the smaller base has length 5, find the area of the trapezoid.

Solution: Given the altitude and one base, we can find the area by finding the length of the other base. We first draw altitudes AX and BY. Since $XY = AB$ (why?), we have $XY = 5$. To find CY, we use the Pythagorean

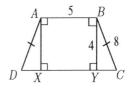

Theorem on $\triangle BYC$ to find $CY = 4\sqrt{3}$. Since $AD = BC$, we can use the same method to show $DX = 4\sqrt{3}$. Thus, $CD = DX + XY + YC = 5 + 8\sqrt{3}$. Finally, we find

$$[ABCD] = \frac{(AB + CD)}{2}(AX) = \frac{(10 + 8\sqrt{3})}{2}(4) = \mathbf{20 + 16\sqrt{3}}.$$

EXERCISE 12-1   Find the area of a trapezoid which has height 3 and bases whose average length is 6.

EXERCISE 12-2   One angle of a trapezoid is 20°. Find x such that another angle of the trapezoid must be $x°$.

12.3   Parallelograms

If both pairs of opposite sides of $ABCD$ are parallel, then $ABCD$ is a **parallelogram**. By drawing the diagonals of a parallelogram, we learn a lot more.

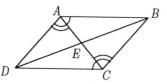

Because the opposite sides of $ABCD$ are parallel, we have $\angle CAB = \angle ACD$ and $\angle BCA = \angle DAC$. By ASA, we have $\triangle ABC \cong \triangle CDA$, so $BC = DA$ and $AB = CD$. Also we find $\angle ABC = \angle CDA$. Similarly we can show that $\angle BCD = \angle DAB$. Thus, we have shown that the opposite angles of parallelograms are equal, as are the opposite sides. Try to show that the diagonals bisect each other by proving that $BE = ED$ and $AE = EC$.

We have marked the equal opposite sides and opposite angles below. Any pairs of angles which are not equal are supplementary:

$$\angle A + \angle B = \angle B + \angle C = \angle C + \angle D = \angle D + \angle A = 180°.$$

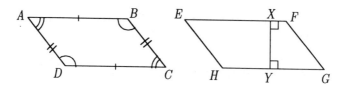

The distance between a pair of opposite sides in a parallelogram is the **height**, and the area is the product of the height and the length of the sides it is drawn between. For example, for $EFGH$ above, $[EFGH] = (EF)(XY)$. (Prove this formula by noting that $EFGH$ is a trapezoid whose bases are equal.)

Another formula for the area of a parallelogram is the product of any two adjacent sides and the sine of the angle between them:

$$[ABCD] = (AB)(BC)\sin B.$$

(Can you prove this relationship by drawing a diagonal to divide the parallelogram into 2 congruent triangles?)

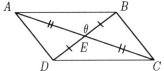

As shown at left, the diagonals of a parallelogram bisect each other. (Did you prove this fact like we suggested? If not, try to now.) Letting the lengths of these diagonals be d_1 and d_2 and the angle between them be θ, we have yet another area formula:

$$[ABCD] = \frac{1}{2}d_1 d_2 \sin \theta.$$

Note that for θ we can use either $\angle AEB$ or $\angle BEC$ because $\angle AEB = 180° - \angle BEC$ and $\sin \theta = \sin(180° - \theta)$.

How do you think you would prove that formula? Notice that it closely resembles one of the triangle area formulas. Now try to prove it.

EXAMPLE 12-2   The opposite angles of a parallelogram are $3x + 20°$ and $40 - x°$. Find one of the other two angles of the parallelogram.

Solution: The opposite angles of a parallelogram are equal, so $3x + 20 = 40 - x$. Thus, $x = 5$, and each of these angles has measure $35°$. The other angles of the parallelogram are supplementary to these, so they have measure $180° - 35° = \mathbf{145°}$.

EXERCISE 12-3   A parallelogram has two sides of length 3 and 6. The angle opposite the angle included between these sides is $30°$. Find the area of the parallelogram.

EXERCISE 12-4   The diagonals of parallelogram $EFGH$ meet at X. Find the distance from X to EF if $EF = 8$ and $[EFGH] = 56$.

12.4   Rhombuses (Rhombi?)

If all four sides of a quadrilateral are equal then the quadrilateral is a **rhombus**. By drawing the diagonals of a rhombus as shown, we can quickly show that any rhombus is also a parallelogram. By SSS congruency, we have $\triangle ABD \cong \triangle CDB$, so $\angle ABD = \angle CDB$ and $\angle ADB = \angle CBD$. Thus $AB \parallel CD$ and $BC \parallel DA$, so $ABCD$ is a parallelogram.

Now that we know the rhombus is a parallelogram, we can easily show that $\triangle ABE \cong \triangle CBE$ by SSS. (Remember, $AE = EC$ because the diagonals of a parallelogram bisect each other.) Hence, we find $\angle AEB = \angle CEB$. How can we now use this fact to show that $AC \perp BD$?

Finally, we have a nice expression for the area of a rhombus. If we let the diagonals have lengths d_1 and d_2, we can use the four congruent right triangles formed by drawing the diagonals to prove that

$$[ABCD] = d_1 d_2/2.$$

EXAMPLE 12-3 Find the length of the side of a rhombus which has area 40 and diagonals with lengths $2x$ and $3x - 2$.

Solution: Since the area of a rhombus is one-half the product of the diagonals, we have

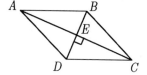

$$40 = \frac{(2x)(3x - 2)}{2} = 3x^2 - 2x.$$

Solving this quadratic yields $x = 4$ and $x = -10/3$. Since x must be positive, $x = 4$ and the diagonals have lengths 8 and 10. Since a rhombus is a parallelogram, the diagonals bisect each other and are perpendicular. Thus, $\triangle AEB$ is a right triangle whose legs are half the lengths of the diagonals. From the Pythagorean Theorem, we find $AB = \sqrt{5^2 + 4^2} = \sqrt{41}$.

EXERCISE 12-5 Two sides of a rhombus are $3x + 2$ and $x + 7$. Find the perimeter of the rhombus.

EXERCISE 12-6 One diagonal of a rhombus is 10. Find the other diagonal if a side of the rhombus has length 17.

12.5 Rectangles and Squares

A **rectangle** is a quadrilateral with four equal angles.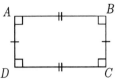
Since the sum of the angles in a quadrilateral is 360°, the
four angles of a rectangle are right angles. Since $\angle A + \angle B =$
$\angle B + \angle C = 180°$, we find $AB \parallel CD$ and $BC \parallel AD$. Thus
all rectangles are parallelograms, so all that is true of parallelograms is also true of
rectangles. The two side lengths of rectangles are commonly called the **length**, l,
and the **width**, w, where the length is usually the longer side and the width the
shorter. The perimeter of a rectangle is $2l + 2w$ and the area is the product of these,
$[ABCD] = lw$.

Furthermore, the diagonals not only bisect each other, but as a result of the
Pythagorean Theorem they are equal, with length $\sqrt{l^2 + w^2}$. (Prove it!)

EXAMPLE 12-4 Find the perimeter of a rectangle with area 40 and diagonal
length 10.

Solution: Let the length be l and the width be w. From our given information we have $lw = 40$ and $\sqrt{l^2 + w^2} = 10$. The perimeter is $2w + 2l$, so if we find
$l + w$, we can solve the problem. Squaring the second equality above and using
$l^2 + w^2 = (l + w)^2 - 2lw$, we have

$$
\begin{aligned}
l^2 + w^2 &= 100 \\
(l + w)^2 - 2lw &= 100 \\
(l + w)^2 &= 100 + 2(40) = 180 \\
l + w &= 6\sqrt{5}.
\end{aligned}
$$

Thus, the perimeter is $2(l + w) = 12\sqrt{5}$.

EXERCISE 12-7 The diagonals of a rectangle intersect at a point which is 5 units
from one side and 3 units from another. Find the area of the rectangle.

EXERCISE 12-8 A diagonal forms an angle of 30° with one of the sides of a
rectangle. Find the perimeter of the rectangle if the diagonal has length 8.

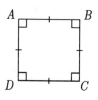

A quadrilateral in which all the sides and all the angles are equal is a **square**. As you see from this definition, a square is also a rectangle and a rhombus. All that is true of rectangles, rhombuses, and parallelograms is also true of squares. From the Pythagorean Theorem, if the side length of the square is s, the diagonals have length $s\sqrt{2}$.

As a rectangle with length and width equal to s, the area is s^2 and the perimeter is $4s$.

In problems involving rectangles and squares, since the sides are all perpendicular or parallel, drawing additional perpendicular lines is often useful to solving problems, as you will find in the final exercise below.

EXAMPLE 12-5 Prove that by connecting the midpoints of the sides of a square in order, we form another square.

Proof: To prove a quadrilateral is a square, we must show that its sides are all equal and so are its angles. First, we'll do the angles. Since E, F, G, and H are the midpoints of the sides, the triangles in the diagram are isosceles right triangles as shown. Thus $\angle AEH = \angle BEF = 45°$. Since these two along with $\angle HEF$ form a straight line, we have

$$\angle HEF = 180° - \angle HEA - \angle FEB = 90°.$$

Similarly, we can show that the other three angles of $EFGH$ are also right. As for showing that the sides of $EFGH$ are equal, from Leg-Leg, the four right triangles are congruent, so their hypotenuses, the sides of $EFGH$, are equal. Since $EFGH$ has equal sides and equal angles, it is a square.

EXERCISE 12-9 One of the diagonals of a square has length 8. Find the area of the square.

EXERCISE 12-10 Given square $ABCD$ with side length 6, point E is on AB such that it is twice as far from A as from B. Similarly, F is on CD and is twice as far from C as from D. Find EF.

12.6 Hints and Problems

Many of these problems are converses of facts we have proven above. It is important to note that the converse of a true statement is not necessarily true unless proven separately (see page 339). Thus, although the diagonals of a rhombus are perpendicular, a quadrilateral with perpendicular diagonals isn't necessarily a rhombus. Can you draw a quadrilateral with perpendicular diagonals that isn't a rhombus?

EXAMPLE 12-6 Prove that a quadrilateral whose diagonals are perpendicular and bisect each other is a rhombus.

Proof: To prove that a quadrilateral is a rhombus, we must show that its sides are equal. By LL we have

$$\triangle ABE \cong \triangle ADE \cong \triangle CDE \cong \triangle CBE.$$

Thus, the hypotenuses of these triangles, which are the sides of the quadrilateral, are all equal. Hence $ABCD$ is a rhombus.

EXAMPLE 12-7 Prove that if the opposite angles of a quadrilateral are equal then the quadrilateral is a parallelogram.

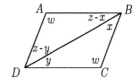

Proof: To show that a quadrilateral is a parallelogram, we must show that its opposite sides are parallel. First, we draw diagonal BD of $ABCD$ and label the angles as shown, where z is the measure of angles ABC and ADC. Thus, as shown, $\angle ABD = z - \angle DBC = z - x$ and $\angle ADB = z - \angle BDC = z - y$. Looking at our diagram we see that we can show that $AB \parallel CD$ if we show that $\angle ABD = \angle BDC$, or $z - x = y$.

From $\triangle BCD$ and $\triangle ABD$, we have $w + x + y = w + z - y + z - x = 180°$. Thus, $x + y = 2z - x - y$, or $z = x + y$.

From this we see that $z - x = y$, so $\angle ABD = \angle BDC$, which means $AB \parallel CD$. Similarly, we can show that $\angle ADB = \angle CBD$, so $AD \parallel BC$ and $ABCD$ is a parallelogram.

EXERCISE 12-11 Show that $ABCD$ is a parallelogram if $AB = CD$ and $AD = BC$.

EXAMPLE 12-8   Let E, F, G, and H be the midpoints of the sides of parallelogram $ABCD$. Prove that $EFGH$ is also a parallelogram.

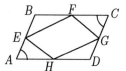

    Proof: Since $AB = CD$, we find $AE = CG$ since E and G are midpoints of equal sides. Similarly, $FC = AH$. Since $\angle A$ and $\angle C$ are opposite angles of a parallelogram, they are equal. Thus, $\triangle FCG \cong \triangle HAE$ by SAS congruence, so $FG = EH$. In a similar manner, we can show $\triangle EBF \cong \triangle GDH$, so $GH = EF$. As you should have shown in the previous exercise, since the opposite sides of $EFGH$ are equal, $EFGH$ is a parallelogram.

EXERCISE 12-12 $ABCD$ is a trapezoid with $AB \parallel CD$. Prove that if $\angle A = \angle B$, then $ABCD$ is isosceles.

EXERCISE 12-13   Prove that if the diagonals of a quadrilateral are equal and bisect each other, then the quadrilateral is a rectangle.

EXERCISE 12-14   Prove that the sum of the squares of the sides of a parallelogram equals the sum of the squares of its diagonals.

EXERCISE 12-15   Use the previous exercise to find the length of median BM in $\triangle ABC$, where $AB = 5$, $BC = 6$, and $AC = 7$.

Problems to Solve for Chapter 12

197. Prove that if a quadrilateral is orthodiagonal, then its area equals half the product of its diagonals. (M&IQ 1991)

198. A rhombus is inscribed in a circle. The length of one diagonal of the rhombus is $8x$. What is the length of the other diagonal? (MAΘ 1990)

199. Find the area of trapezoid $DUCK$. (MATHCOUNTS 1992)

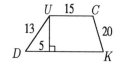

200. Find the area of a rhombus with a side of length 13 and one diagonal of length 24. (MAΘ 1990)

201. The diagonal of a rectangular lot is measured at 37. The length is 1 less than 3 times the width. What length of fence is needed to enclose the lot? (MAΘ 1987)

202. Figure $ABCD$ is a trapezoid with $AB \parallel DC$, $AB = 5$, $BC = 3\sqrt{2}$, $\angle BCD = 45°$, and $\angle CDA = 60°$. Find DC. (AHSME 1984)

203. Prove that if a quadrilateral is orthodiagonal, then the midpoints of its sides are the vertices of a rectangle. (M&IQ 1991)

204. The length of a rectangular picture is three times its width. The picture is surrounded by a frame which is 4 inches wide. If the perimeter of the outside of the frame is 96 inches, what is the length of the picture in inches? (MATHCOUNTS 1985)

205. Given rectangle $ABCD$ such that $AM = MB$, $AB = 24$, $BC = 18$, and $x = DE$, find the value of x such that the area of region $AMED$ is exactly twice that of region $MBCE$. (MATHCOUNTS 1984)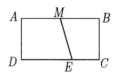

206. What is the length of the common external tangent segment of two externally tangent circles whose radii are 8 and 11? (MAΘ 1990)

207. The line joining the midpoints of the diagonals of a trapezoid has length 3. If the longer base is 97, what is the shorter base? (AHSME 1959)

208. Let $ABCD$ be a trapezoid with the measure of AB twice that of base DC, and let E be the point of intersection of the diagonals. If the measure of diagonal AC is 11, then find that of segment EC. (AHSME 1972)

209. Prove that connecting, in order, the midpoints of the sides of any quadrilateral, a parallelogram is formed.

210. If $ABCD$ and $EFGH$ are squares and $AB = 1$, find the area of square $EFGH$. (Mandelbrot #1)

211. Prove that if quadrilateral $ABCD$ is orthodiagonal, then $AB^2 + CD^2 = BC^2 + DA^2$. (M&IQ 1992)

212. Prove that if trapezoid $ABCD$ ($AB \parallel CD$) is orthodiagonal, then $AC^2 + BD^2 - (AB + CD)^2$. (M&IQ 1991)

213. In the accompanying figure, segments AB and CD are parallel, the measure of angle B is twice that of angle D, and the measures of segments CB and AB are a and b respectively. Find CD in terms of a and b. (AHSME 1970)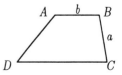

214. $ABCD$ is a rectangle (see the accompanying diagram) with P any point on AB. Also, $PS \perp BD$, $PR \perp AC$, $AF \perp BD$, and $PQ \perp AF$. Which must always equal $PR + PS$: PQ, AE, $PT + AT$, AF, or EF? (AHSME 1958)

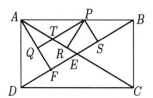

 215. Let $ABCD$ be a parallelogram of area 10 with $AB = 3$ and $BC = 5$. Locate E, F, and G on segments AB, BC, and AD, respectively, with $AE = BF = AG = 2$. Let the line through G parallel to EF intersect CD at H. Find the area of the quadrilateral $EFHG$. (AHSME 1992)

216. Prove that if isosceles trapezoid $ABCD$ $(AB \parallel CD)$ is orthodiagonal, then its altitude is equal to $(AB + CD)/2$. (M&IQ 1991)

 217. Let E be the point of intersection of the diagonals of convex quadrilateral $ABCD$, and let P, Q, R, and S be the centers of the circles circumscribing triangles ABE, BCE, CDE, and ADE, respectively. Prove that $PQRS$ is a parallelogram. (AHSME 1977)

Chapter 13

Polygons

13.1   Types of Polygons

A **polygon** is a simple closed planar figure formed by line segments. Polygons are classified by the number of sides they have; we have already discussed triangles, which have three sides, and quadrilaterals, which have four sides. A polygon with n sides is generically called an n-gon, but many types of polygons have special names as well. The most common ones are shown in the table below.

# sides	Name	# sides	Name
3	triangle	8	octagon
4	quadrilateral	9	nonagon
5	pentagon	10	decagon
6	hexagon	12	dodecagon
7	heptagon		

A polygon is called a **regular polygon** if all of its sides are equal and all of its angles are equal. Remember, as we saw with quadrilaterals, just because all the sides of a polygon are equal doesn't mean the polygon is regular. The same is true of the angles of a polygon. (Can you draw a polygon whose interior angles are equal but which is still not regular?)

As with quadrilaterals, any segment drawn from one vertex to a non-adjacent vertex is called a diagonal.

To count the number of diagonals in an n-gon, we can count the number of diagonals from each vertex. Each vertex can be connected to $n - 1$ other vertices. Two of these segments form sides, while the other $n - 3$ form diagonals. Since there are n vertices, there are a total of $n(n - 3)$ diagonals. To test this formula, consider a quadrilateral, for which $n = 4$. Our formula gives $4(4 - 3) = 4$ diagonals, not 2! Obviously we have overlooked something. In our counting method we have actually counted every diagonal twice, once for each endpoint. Thus, to get an accurate count of the diagonals, we must divide by 2, leaving $n(n - 3)/2$ diagonals in an n-gon.

13.2 Angles in a Polygon

To determine the sum of the angles in a polygon, we divide the polygon into triangles just as we did for the quadrilateral. Draw the $n - 3$ diagonals from one vertex. This divides the polygon into $n - 2$ triangles as shown. Adding up all the angles in these triangles gives the sum of the angles of a polygon with n sides: $180(n - 2)$ degrees.

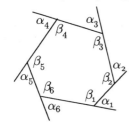

Now, if we consider the exterior angles of a polygon as shown at left, we see that if we let the interior angle at vertex i equal β_i and the exterior angle be α_i, then at each vertex we have $\alpha_i + \beta_i = 180°$. If we add these equations together for all n vertices and group the interior and exterior angles together, we get

$$(\alpha_1 + \beta_1) + \cdots + (\alpha_n + \beta_n) = (\alpha_1 + \cdots + \alpha_n) + (\beta_1 + \cdots + \beta_n) = 180n.$$

Using what we know about the sum of the interior angles, we have

$$(\alpha_1 + \cdots + \alpha_n) + (\beta_1 + \cdots + \beta_n) = (\alpha_1 + \cdots + \alpha_n) + 180(n - 2) = 180n.$$

Thus,

$$(\alpha_1 + \cdots + \alpha_n) = 180n - 180(n - 2) = 360,$$

and the sum of the exterior angles of any polygon is $360°$.

13.3   Regular Polygons

Most polygons you will encounter in geometry problems which have more than four sides will be regular polygons. As we stated before, the angles of a regular polygon are all equal, so knowing the sum of the interior angles and the sum of the exterior angles, we can determine the measure of each angle in a regular polygon.

$$\text{Interior angle} = \frac{180(n-2)}{n} = 180 - \frac{360}{n}$$

$$\text{Exterior angle} = \frac{360}{n}$$

Below is a table of the interior angle measures of some common regular polygons.

# Sides	Angle	# Sides	Angle
3	60°	8	135°
4	90°	9	140°
5	108°	10	144°
6	120°	12	150°

It's not necessary to memorize these; just be familiar with them.

EXAMPLE 13-1   Prove that by connecting every other vertex of a regular hexagon, we form an equilateral triangle.

Proof: To show this, we must merely show that the three sides AC, CE, and AE, are equal. By SAS we have

$$\triangle ABC \cong \triangle CDE \cong \triangle EFA.$$

The sides in question are corresponding sides of these triangles, so we have $AC = CE = AE$ and thus $\triangle ACE$ is equilateral.

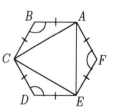

EXAMPLE 13-2   Find the number of sides in a polygon whose interior angles have sum 2340°.

Solution: A polygon with n sides has interior angle sum $180(n-2)$. Solving $180(n-2) = 2340$, we find that $n = \mathbf{15}$.

EXAMPLE 13-3   Given that $ABCD\cdots L$ is a regular dodecagon, find the length
of AD if $AB = 4$.

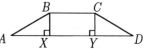

Solution: We attack this problem as we do most
geometry problems: cut the problem into quadrilaterals
and triangles. The diagram only shows the relevant
portion of the dodecagon. Since a dodecagon has 12 sides, each interior angle has
measure $150°$. Since $ABCD$ is an isosceles trapezoid (why?), we have $\angle BAX =$
$\angle CDY = 180° - \angle BCD = 30°$. Drawing BX and CY perpendicular to AD,
we find that $BCYX$ is a rectangle because $\angle YCD = 90° - \angle CDY = 60°$, so
$\angle BCY = 150° - 60° = 90°$. Thus, $XY = BC = 4$. Since $\angle BAX = 30°$ in right
triangle ABX, we have $BX = AB/2 = 2$ and $AX = BX\sqrt{3} = 2\sqrt{3}$. Similarly
$YD = 2\sqrt{3}$. Thus $AD = AX + XY + YD = \mathbf{4 + 4\sqrt{3}}$.

EXERCISE 13-1   Find the number of sides in a regular polygon which has interior
angle measure $162°$.

EXERCISE 13-2   Prove that we form a square if we connect every other vertex of
a regular octagon. (Remember: just showing the sides are equal does not mean the
quadrilateral is a square.)

Just as with triangles, the perpendicular bisectors of the sides of a regular polygon all pass through a single point. (Can you use triangle congruence to prove
this fact?) Furthermore, the angle bisectors of the interior angles also meet at this
point. Thus, we can construct both a circle which passes through the vertices of
the polygon and a circle which is tangent to all the sides of the polygon. We have
drawn these circles below with radii R and r, respectively.

As shown in the figure, these two circles are concentric. If the polygon has side length l and n sides,
then we can determine the inradius (sometimes called
the **apothem**), r, the circumradius, R, and the area of
the polygon by breaking the polygon into right triangles like $\triangle AXO$ at right. Remember that the radius
of the circle is perpendicular to a tangent at the point
of tangency, so $\angle OXA = 90°$. In this triangle, the hy-

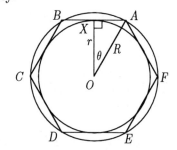

potenuse is R, while the legs have length r and $l/2$. If we can determine θ, we can find R and r using our basic trigonometric relations. If we draw a radius like OX to all the sides of the polygon, we will form $2n$ congruent triangles like OXA. All the angles at O together make up $360°$, so $\theta = 360°/2n = 180°/n$.

Thus, we find r and R from the following trigonometric relations:

$$\tan \theta = \tan (180°/n) = \frac{l/2}{r}$$

$$\sin \theta = \sin (180°/n) = \frac{l/2}{R}.$$

The area of the polygon is just $2n$ times the area of the OXA, or

$$\text{Area} = 2n[(l/2)(r)/2] = nlr/2.$$

13.4 Regular Hexagons

Regular hexagons appear enough in problems that they merit their own short section. As with many other things which come up often in problems, the main reason hexagons appear so often is that the numbers which pop up in hexagon problems are relatively simple.

Drawing the lines from the center, O, of the hexagon to the vertices forms six equilateral triangles. (Why?) Chopping regular hexagons into 6 equilateral triangles is in general a good way to attack regular hexagons. For example, it immediately tells us that the area of a regular hexagon with side length s is 6 times the area of an equilateral triangle with side length s, or

$$[ABCDEF] = 6\left(\frac{s^2\sqrt{3}}{4}\right) = \frac{3s^2\sqrt{3}}{2}.$$

We also see that the longest diagonals, like AD, are twice the length of a side.

EXAMPLE 13-4 Six points are equally spaced around a circle with radius 1. What is the sum of the lengths of all possible segments formed by connecting two of the points?

Solution: As shown, six of the possible segments form sides of a regular hexagon. The center of the circle is the center of the hexagon, so as we saw earlier, the hexagon has side length 1. Three of the segments form main diagonals of the hexagon, and these have length 2.

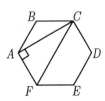

The other 6 segments are diagonals congruent to AC in the figure at the left. Since $\triangle ABC$ is isosceles and $\angle ABC = 120°$, we have $\angle BAC = 30°$. Since $\angle FAB = 120°$, $\angle FAC$ is a right angle, so $\triangle CAF$ is a 30°-60°-90° triangle. (Make sure you see why this is so.) Thus, $AC = AF\sqrt{3} = \sqrt{3}$. Since there are six such diagonals, six sides, and 3 diagonals like CF, the total of all possible lengths is $6(\sqrt{3}) + 6(1) + 3(2) = \mathbf{12 + 6\sqrt{3}}$.

EXERCISE 13-3 The shortest diagonal of a regular hexagon has length $8\sqrt{3}$. What is the radius of the circle inscribed in the hexagon? (MAΘ 1990)

Problems to Solve for Chapter 13

218. Find the number of diagonals that can be drawn in a polygon of 100 sides. (AHSME 1950)

219. Given that $ABCDEF$ is a regular hexagon with side length 6, find the area of triangle BCE. (MATHCOUNTS 1986)

220. Two angles of a convex octagon are congruent. Each of the other angles has a degree measure triple that of each of the first two angles. Find the degree measure of the larger angles. (MAΘ 1990)

221. Two congruent regular 20-sided polygons share a side as shown. Find the degree measure of $\angle ACB$. (MATHCOUNTS 1992)

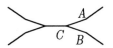

222. An equilateral triangle and a regular hexagon have equal perimeters. If the area of the triangle is 2, find the area of the hexagon. (AHSME 1970)

223. The coplanar regular hexagons shown share the side EF. Given that the perimeter of quadrilateral $ABCD$ is $44 + 22\sqrt{3}$, find EF. (MATHCOUNTS 1992)

224. Find the area of a regular dodecagon if its circumscribed circle has a circumference of 12π. (MAΘ 1990)

225. Find the ratio of the area of a circle inscribed in a regular hexagon to the area of the circle circumscribed about the same hexagon.

226. Let S be the sum of the interior angles of a polygon P for which each interior angle is 7.5 times the exterior angle at the same vertex. Find S. Is P necessarily regular? (AHSME 1960)

227. A regular polygon with exactly 20 diagonals is inscribed in a circle. The area of the polygon is $144\sqrt{2}$. Find the area of the circle. (MAΘ 1990)

228. Twelve points are equally spaced on the circumference of a circle. How many chords can be drawn that connect pairs of these points and which are longer than the radius of the circle but shorter than its diameter? (MATHCOUNTS 1989)

229. In regular polygon $ABCDE\cdots$, we have $\angle ACD = 120°$. How many sides does the polygon have? (MAΘ 1992)

230. The numbers 1, 2, 3, $\ldots$, n are evenly spaced on the rim of a circle. If 15 is directly opposite 49, then find n. (MAΘ 1987)

231. Suppose a goat is tethered to a corner of a building which is in the shape of a regular n-gon. The length of a side of the building and length of the tether are each r. Find the area of the region over which the goat can graze as a function of r and n. (MAΘ 1992)

232. Exactly three of the interior angles of a convex polygon are obtuse. What is the maximum number of sides of such a polygon? (AHSME 1985)

233. A park is in the shape of a regular hexagon 2 km on a side. Starting at a corner, Alice walks along the perimeter of the park for a distance of 5 km. How many kilometers is she from her starting point? (AHSME 1986)

234. If the sum of all the angles except one of a convex polygon is $2190°$, then how many sides does the polygon have? (AHSME 1973)

235. Find the sum of angles 1, 2, 3, 4, and 5 in the star-shaped figure shown. (MAΘ 1987)

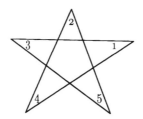

Chapter 14

Angle Chasing

The problems that follow will help you learn the art of "angle chasing." These are problems in which you are asked to find the measure of angles. You have many tools at your disposal with which to attack these problems; these are listed below. Whenever you are stuck on a problem which follows, come back to this list and see if there's anything on it which applies to the problem.

sum of angles in a triangle   isosceles triangles
sum of angles in a quadrilateral   equilateral triangles
angles intercepting arcs   vertical angles
angles which together form a line   similar triangles
angles around a point   congruent triangles
angles in a right triangle   parallel lines and angles
inscribed angles subtending the same arc   exterior angles
angle bisectors   perpendicular lines

Problems to Solve for Chapter 14

236. ABC is an isosceles triangle such that $AC = BC$. CBD is an isosceles triangle such that $CB = DB$. BD meets AC at a right angle. If $\angle A = 57°$, what is $\angle D$? (MATHCOUNTS 1986)

237. In $\triangle ABC$ shown, D is some interior point, and x, y, z, w are the measures of angles in degrees. Solve for x in terms of y, z, and w. (AHSME 1987)

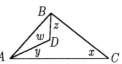

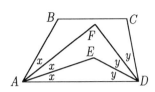

238. In quadrilateral $ABCD$, $\angle ABC = 110°$, $\angle BCD = 100°$, and angles BAD and CDA are trisected as shown. What is the degree measure of $\angle AFD$? (MATHCOUNTS 1991)

239. In the adjoining figure, $ABCD$ is a square, ABE is an equilateral triangle and point E is outside square $ABCD$. What is the measure of $\angle AED$? (AHSME 1979)

240. In the figure, triangles RTS and UTV are congruent, $\angle R = 36°$, and $\angle T = 42°$. Find $\angle RQV$. (MATHCOUNTS 1989)

241. In $\triangle ACD$ in the figure, $\angle A = 50°$ and $\angle CFD = 110°$. If CE bisects $\angle ACD$ and DB is the altitude to AC, then find $\angle CDF$. (MAΘ 1987)

242. Triangle ABC is isosceles with base AC. Points P and Q are respectively on CB and AB such that $AC = AP = PQ = QB$. Find $\angle B$. (AHSME 1961)

243. In a circle with center O, AD is a diameter, ABC is a chord, $BO = 5$ and $\angle ABO = \overset{\frown}{CD} = 60°$. Find BC. (AHSME 1985)

244. In the drawing, EBC is an equilateral triangle and $ABCD$ is a square. Find the measure of $\angle BED$. (MAΘ 1987)

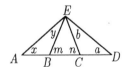

245. In a general triangle ADE (as shown) lines EB and EC are drawn. Show that $x + y + n = a + b + m$. (AHSME 1958)

246. Prove that if the midpoints of the sides of a quadrilateral are vertices of a rectangle, then this quadrilateral is orthodiagonal. (M&IQ 1991)

247. Triangle PAB is formed by PR, PT, and AB, all tangent to circle O. If $\angle APB = 40°$, find $\angle AOB$. (AHSME 1956)

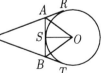

248. In the figure to the right, O is the center of the circle, $\angle EAD = 40°$ and $\overset{\frown}{ED} = 40°$. Find $\angle DAB$. (MAΘ 1987)

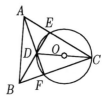

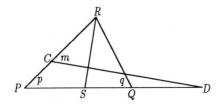

249. Given triangle PQR with RS bisecting $\angle R$, PQ extended to D, and $CD \perp RS$, show that $m = (p+q)/2$. (AHSME 1954)

250. Quadrilaterals $ABCG$ and $FGDE$ are parallelograms. Points A, B, C, D, E, and F are points on the circle. Determine $\overset{\frown}{AB} + \overset{\frown}{ED}$. (MAΘ 1990)

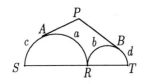

251. In the figure PA is tangent to semicircle SAR; PB is tangent to semicircle RBT; SRT is a straight line; the arc measures (not lengths!) are indicated in the figure. Show that $\angle APB = c + d$. (AHSME 1955)

Chapter 15

Areas

In earlier chapters we discussed how to find the areas of simple figures like circles and triangles. In this chapter, we learn how to find the area of more complex figures and of simple figures in complex problems.

15.1 Similar Figures

On page 145, we showed that if two triangles are similar and their sides have common ratio k, the ratio of their areas is k^2. This is true of any two similar figures. For example, since all circles are similar, if one has a radius which is twice as large as another, its area is 4 times as large as the second. Thus, when working on a problem in which you are able to prove that two figures are similar, you can easily relate the areas of the figures.

EXAMPLE 15-1 The area of a triangle is 36. Find the area of the triangle formed by connecting the midpoints of its sides.

Solution: We first prove that any triangle is similar to the triangle formed by connecting the midpoints of its sides. In the figure, since E and F are midpoints, we have $AE/AC = AF/AB = 1/2$. Since $\angle EAF = \angle CAB$, we have $\triangle CAB \sim \triangle EAF$ from SAS Similarity. Hence $EF/CB = 1/2$. Similarly, we can show $FD/AC = 1/2$ and $ED/AB = 1/2$. Thus, by SSS Similarity, we have $\triangle ABC \sim \triangle DEF$.

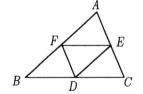

Thus,

$$\frac{[DEF]}{[ABC]} = \left(\frac{1}{2}\right)^2 = \frac{1}{4}.$$

Hence $[DEF] = [ABC]/4 = \mathbf{9}$.

EXAMPLE 15-2   The ratio of the areas of two squares is 6. Find the ratio of the lengths of the diagonals of the two squares.

Solution: Like circles, all squares are similar. Thus, the ratio of the areas is the square of the ratio of *any* corresponding lengths of the figures. Hence, the ratio of the lengths of the diagonals is the square root of the ratios of the areas, or $\sqrt{6}$.

EXAMPLE 15-3   In trapezoid $ABCD$, $AB \parallel CD$ and the diagonals meet at E. If $AB = 4$ and $CD = 12$, show that the area of $\triangle CDE$ is 9 times the area of $\triangle ABE$.

Proof: First, since $AB \parallel CD$, we have $\angle BAE = \angle DCE$ and $\angle ABE = \angle CDE$ as shown. Thus, by AA Similarity we get $\triangle ABE \sim \triangle CDE$. Since $CD/AB = 3$, we find $[CDE]/[ABE] = (CD/AB)^2 = 9$.

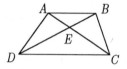

15.2   Same Base/Same Altitude

If two triangles with the same altitude have different bases, the ratio of their areas is just the ratio of their bases. The proof of this is quite straightforward. Given $\triangle ABC$ and $\triangle DEF$ where the altitudes h_a and h_d to BC and EF, respectively, of the triangles are equal, we have

$$[ABC] = \frac{(BC)h_a}{2} \quad \text{and} \quad [DEF] = \frac{(EF)h_d}{2}.$$

Thus

$$\frac{[ABC]}{[DEF]} = \frac{(BC)h_a/2}{(EF)h_d/2} = \frac{BC}{EF}\frac{h_a}{h_d} = \frac{BC}{EF}.$$

Similarly, we can show that if two triangles have the same base, the ratio of their areas is the ratio of their altitudes. (Try it.) As you will see in the examples, these facts are often used when the equal bases in question are actually the same segment, not just the same length. This approach is also often used to show that two triangles have the same area. If the triangles have the same base (or altitude), we can show they have the same area by showing that their altitudes (or bases) have the same length.

EXAMPLE 15-4 Show that by drawing the three medians of a triangle, we divide the triangle into six regions of equal area.

Proof: First, we will show that $[ACD] =$ $[ABC]/2$. These two triangles have the same altitude from A, so the ratio of their areas is the ratio of the bases CD and CB. Since D is the midpoint of BC, we have $CD/CB = 1/2$. Thus, $[ACD]/[ABC] = 1/2$.

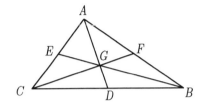

Now, we show that $[GCD] = [ACD]/3$. Since GD and AD are on the same line, triangles GCD and ACD have the same altitude from C. Thus the ratio of their areas is GD/AD. Since G is the centroid, we have from page 124 that $GD/AD = 1/3$. Thus

$$[GCD] = \frac{[ACD]}{3} = \frac{[ABC]/2}{3} = \frac{[ABC]}{6}.$$

Similarly, we can show that each of the other 5 smaller triangles formed by drawing all the medians have area $[ABC]/6$. Thus, the three medians divide a triangle into 6 sections of equal area.

EXAMPLE 15-5 In $\triangle ABC$, D is the midpoint of AB, E is the midpoint of DB, and F is the midpoint of BC. If the area of $\triangle ABC$ is 96, then find the area of $\triangle AEF$. (AHSME 1976)

Solution: Since $\triangle ABF$ has the same altitude as $\triangle ABC$ and $\frac{1}{2}$ the base, it has $\frac{1}{2}$ the area of $\triangle ABC$. Thus, $[ABF] = [ABC]/2 = 48$. Now, $\triangle AEF$ has the same altitude (from F) as $\triangle ABF$. The base of $\triangle AEF$ is $\frac{3}{4}$ that of $\triangle ABF$ ($AE = \frac{3}{4}AB$), so $[AEF] = \frac{3}{4}[ABF] = \mathbf{36}$.

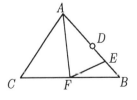

EXAMPLE 15-6 Line l is parallel to segment AB. Show that for all points X on l, $[ABX]$ is the same.

Proof: No matter where X is on l, the altitude from X to AB is the same. Since AB is obviously always constant, the area of $\triangle ABX$ is constant.

EXAMPLE 15-7 If the diagonal AC of quadrilateral $ABCD$ divides the diagonal BD into two equal segments, prove that $[ACD] = [ACB]$. (M&IQ 1992)

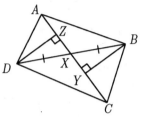

Proof: As described in the problem, X, the intersection of the diagonals, is the midpoint of BD. Since $\triangle ACD$ and $\triangle ABC$ share base AC, we can prove the areas of the triangles are equal if we show that the altitudes of the triangles to this segment are equal. Thus, we draw altitudes BY and DZ. Since $DX = BX$ and $\angle DXZ = \angle BXY$, we have $\triangle DZX \cong \triangle BYX$ by SA for right triangles, so $DZ = BY$. Hence, $[ABC] = (AC)(BY)/2 = (AC)(DZ)/2 = [ABD]$.

15.3 Complicated Figures

Sometimes it is easiest to find the area of a figure by breaking it up into smaller pieces, like triangles or sectors, of which the area can easily be found. Problems involving parts of circles together with other geometric shapes can often be solved this way. Areas of complex polygons can often be found by breaking the polygon into rectangles and triangles. A few tips will help solve these problems.

▷ Draw radii to separate sectors and circular segments from the rest of the diagram. Find the area of these regions, then the area of the rest of the figure.

▷ Look out for right and equilateral triangles. Draw additional sides to separate these triangles from the remainder of the problem. This often makes the method of finding the area of the rest of the figure clear.

▷ Draw diagonals of quadrilaterals to split the quadrilaterals into two triangles whose areas can be easily found.

EXAMPLE 15-8 Find the area between the two concentric circles shown if the circles have radii 2 and 3.

Solution: None of the simple formulas we have learned so far can give us the area of this figure; however, we do know how to find the area of a circle. The larger circle has area 9π and is the sum of the smaller circle and the shaded area. The smaller circle has area 4π, and the sum of the small circle and the shaded area is the area of the larger circle. Thus, the shaded region has area $9\pi - 4\pi = \mathbf{5\pi}$. The shaded region is called an **annulus**.

EXAMPLE 15-9   Find the area of a regular octagon with side length 2.

Solution: We can form a regular octagon by cutting the corners out of a square, like $\triangle ABC$ shown. (Prove this yourself.) Since $BC = 2$, we have $AB = 2/\sqrt{2} = \sqrt{2}$. Thus, the length of one side of the square is $2 + 2\sqrt{2}$ and the square has area $(2 + 2\sqrt{2})^2 = 12 + 8\sqrt{2}$. Each of the corners has area $(\sqrt{2})^2/2 = 1$, so the octagon has area $(12 + 8\sqrt{2}) - 4(1) = \mathbf{8 + 8\sqrt{2}}$.

EXAMPLE 15-10   Find the shaded area, given that $\triangle ABC$ is an isosceles right triangle. The midpoint of AB is the center of semicircle $\overset{\frown}{AB}$, point C is the center of quarter circle $\overset{\frown}{AB}$, and $AB = 2\sqrt{2}$. (MAΘ 1990)

Solution: What simple areas can we find in this figure? Since $AB = 2\sqrt{2}$ and ABC is an isosceles right triangle, we have $AC = CB = 2$ and $[ABC] = (2)(2)/2 = 2$. We can also find the area of sector ABC and the semicircle with diameter AB. The area of quarter circle ABC is $1/4$ that of the circle with radius BC. Thus, it has area $(2^2)\pi/4 = \pi$. The semicircle is half the area of the circle with diameter AB, or $(\sqrt{2})^2\pi/2 = \pi$. How can we combine these pieces to get the shaded area? This is where these problems become like puzzles. We are given three pieces, the triangle, the semicircle, and the quarter circle, which we must add or subtract to form the shaded region. This requires some intuition and practice. Here, we add together the triangle and the semicircle, then subtract the quarter circle to leave the shaded region. Make sure you see this. Thus, the desired area is $\pi + 2 - \pi = \mathbf{2}$. This is how we do all problems of this sort. We find the area of the simple figures in the diagram and determine how these figures can be added together or subtracted from each other to find the desired (usually 'shaded') region.

EXAMPLE 15-11   Given the square in the figure with side length 4 and four semicircles which have the sides of the square as their diameters as shown, find the area of the 'leaves' which are marked by X's in the diagram.

Solution: The simple figures we have here are 4 semicircles and a square. The desired area is the region where semicircles overlap. Hence, we note that by adding together the areas of the four semicircles, we exceed the area of the square by the total area of the desired region. (Make sure you see this; it is because each 'leaf' is in two of the semicircles.) This is somewhat similar to our discussion of over-counting on page 301. We are 'overcounting' the area covered by the semicircles by twice counting the amount of area in the Xed regions. Hence, the area of the desired region is the total area of the four semicircles minus the area of the square, or $4(2^2\pi/2) - 4^2 = \mathbf{8\pi - 16}$.

EXAMPLE 15-12 Each of the circles shown has a radius of 6 cm. The three outer circles have centers that are equally spaced on the original circle. Find the area, in square centimeters, of the sum of the three regions which are common to three of the four circles. (MATH-COUNTS 1992)

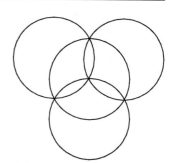

Solution: Our pieces in this problem are four circles which we unfortunately cannot puzzle together to make the desired region as we have done in prior examples. Thus, we must add lines to the diagram to give us more pieces. In problems involving intersecting circles, the best lines to add are radii and lines which divide the regions of intersection in half, forming segments and sectors as mentioned in our tips.

In the diagram, we have drawn AC to divide one of the 'leaves' in half and we have drawn radii AB and BC of the lowest circle. Since AC is also a radius of the circle A, which has the same radius as the circle B, we have $AB = BC = AC$, and $\triangle ABC$ is equilateral. Now we can find the area of circular segment AC, since it is the area of sector ABC minus the area of $\triangle ABC$. Since this triangle is equilateral, the sector is $60°/360° = 1/6$ of the circle. Thus, the sector has area $(6^2\pi/6) = 6\pi$.

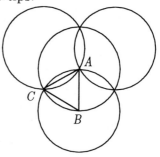

The area of the segment then is $6\pi - (6^2\sqrt{3}/4) = 6\pi - 9\sqrt{3}$. Since the three leaves together consist of 6 such segments, the total area is $\mathbf{36\pi - 54\sqrt{3}}$.

Through these examples and the numerous similar problems at the end of this chapter, you should become quite adept at manipulating simple figures to find seemingly difficult areas.

Problems to Solve for Chapter 15

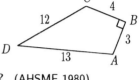

252. Sides AB, BC, CD, and DA of convex quadrilateral $ABCD$ have lengths 3, 4, 12, and 13, respectively; and $\angle CBA$ is a right angle. What is the area of the quadrilateral? (AHSME 1980)

253. Find the total area of the figure with right angles and segment measures as shown. (MAΘ 1990)

254. Find the ratio of the area of an equilateral triangle inscribed in a circle to the area of a square circumscribed about the same circle. (MAΘ 1987)

255. If a square is inscribed in a semicircle of radius r and the square has an area of 8 square units, then find the area of a square inscribed in a circle of radius r. (MAΘ 1987)

256. Points D, E, and F are midpoints of the sides of equilateral triangle ABC. The shaded central triangle is formed by connecting the midpoints of the sides of $\triangle DEF$. What fraction of the total area of ABC is shaded? (MATHCOUNTS 1992)

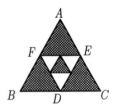

257. A cow is tied to the corner of a 20 foot by 15 foot shed with a 30 foot rope. Find her total grazing area. (MAΘ 1992)

258. Find the ratio of the area of $\triangle ACE$ to the area of rectangle $ABCD$. (MATHCOUNTS 1986)

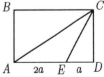

259. Find the area of the largest triangle that can be inscribed in a semicircle whose radius is r. By inscribed in a semicircle, we mean that the vertices are either on the semicircle or the diameter cutting off the semicircle. (AHSME 1950)

260. Given hexagon $ABCDEF$ with sides of length 6, six congruent 30°-60°-90° triangles are drawn as in the figure. Find the ratio of the area of the smaller hexagon formed to the area of the original hexagon. (MATHCOUNTS 1988)

261. In the figure, $\triangle ABC$ and $\triangle ADE$ are both equilateral with side length 4. Segment AD is perpendicular to BC. Find the area of the region common to both triangles. (MAΘ 1992)

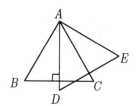

262. A rhombus is formed by two radii and two chords of a circle whose radius is 16 feet. What is the area of the rhombus in square feet? (AHSME 1956)

263. The square in the figure has sides length 9 centimeters. The radius of the circle is 2 centimeters. What is the area of the shaded region? (MATHCOUNTS 1992)

264. In the diagram, $ABCD$ and $DEFG$ are squares of area 16. If H is the midpoint of BC and EF, then find the total area of $ABHFGD$. (MAΘ 1987)

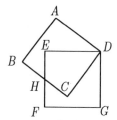

265. Let M, N, P be the midpoints of the sides BC, CA, AB of triangle ABC respectively. Prove that the segments MN, NP, PM divide triangle ABC into four triangles of equal area. (M&IQ 1992)

266. In rectangle $ABCD$, interior point E is chosen at random. Prove that the sum of the areas of triangles AEB and EDC is the same regardless of where in $ABCD$ point E is chosen. (MAΘ 1990)

267. Find the number of square units in the area of the inscribed pentagon with right angle and dimensions as shown. (MATHCOUNTS 1988)

268. Let N be an arbitrary point on the median CM of $\triangle ABC$. Prove that $[AMN] = [NMB]$ and $[ANC] = [BNC]$. (M&IQ 1992)

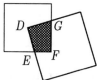

269. A 3-meter square and a 4-meter square overlap as shown in the diagram. D is the center of the 3-meter square. Find the area of the shaded region $DGFE$. (MAΘ 1987)

270. Square $ABCD$ is inscribed in a circle. Point X lies on minor arc AB such that $[XCD] = 993$ and $[XAB] = 1$. Find $[XAD] + [XBC]$. (Mandelbrot #3)

271. The convex pentagon $ABCDE$ has $\angle A = \angle B = 120°$, $EA = AB = BC = 2$ and $CD = DE = 4$. What is the area of $ABCDE$? (AHSME 1993)

272. A triangle is inscribed in a circle. The vertices of the triangle divide the circle into three arcs of lengths 3, 4, and 5. What is the area of the triangle? (AHSME 1989)

273. In the figure, point A is the center of a 100 cm by 100 cm square. Find x, in centimeters, such that the shaded region has an area that is one-fifth of the area of the square. (MATHCOUNTS 1992)

274. Let M be any point on diagonal AC of rectangle $ABCD$. Show that $[ADM] = [AMB]$. (M&IQ 1992)

275. $ABCD$ is a square and $AE = AF = CG = CH$. Given $AB = 5$ and the shaded region is five-ninths the area of $ABCD$, find AF. (MATHCOUNTS 1992)

276. The medians to the legs of an isosceles triangle are perpendicular to each other. If the base of the triangle is 4, find its area. (MAΘ 1990)

277. In the diagram, the curved paths are arcs of circles centered at vertices A and B of a square of side 6. Find the area of the shaded section. (Mandelbrot #3)

──the *BIG PICTURE*──

We have seen here how to calculate the areas of many kinds of plane figures, but without fail they are made up only of straight lines and circular arcs. One of the great accomplishments of **calculus** (which you will get to in a few years) is enabling us to find the areas of a great many other figures.

For example, consider a river in which the amount of water flowing past a given point at time t is given by, say, $f(t) = t(1 - t)$. How could we find the total amount of water which flowed by between times $t = 0$ and $t = 1$?

If we plot the graph of the function $x(1-x)$ on a set of coordinate axes, then the total flow will equal the area between the curve and the x-axis. Do you see why? Think about the same problem, but with a constant flow $f(t) = 17$ or a linearly increasing flow $f(t) = t$. Then the areas we are concerned with are just areas of a rectangle or triangle. In the real problem, however, the area is more complicated.

So how does calculus endeavor to find this area (which, incidentally, was called by Isaac Newton the "Flowing Quantity" of a "fluxion" and is today called the **integral** of a function)? By breaking it up into little rectangles! Unable to find anything better for such a complicated figure, in calculus we just let the rectangles get smaller and smaller, and put together more and more of them, until we approximate the true curve very well. Calculus is extremely interesting in the ways it builds up complex ideas from simple rectangles and straight lines. (And it's not as hard as people make it out to be.)

Chapter 16

The Power of Coordinates

16.1   Labeling the Plane

Already in this book we have discussed extensively the methods of solving geometric problems using nothing more than the relationships in the figures themselves. However, there exists a whole different approach to geometry which, though less creative, is incredibly powerful. The idea is that of **coordinates**; it allows many complex geometric relationships to be rephrased as simple formulas. The idea was first rigorously used in the 1600's by Descartes (day-CART), though it is so simple that it's hard to believe that it wasn't used earlier by others.

-7 -6 -5 -4 -3 -2 -1 0 1 2 3 4 5 6 7   The easiest way to explain coordinates is to recall the number line, as we were taught in elementary school. Each point on a line is labeled by a number, the distance from a fixed origin. The resulting picture is above. (Of course, the line extends forever in both directions; for this reason, many people put an arrow on both ends.) This is an interesting way to look at the real numbers, but is certainly not very useful for geometry, since there isn't much geometry in one dimension.

However, with a little modification we can extend the same idea to cover the entire plane: we add another axis, perpendicular to the first and crossing it at the point 0. Then we can label each point in the plane by its distance to *each* axis. (It makes sense to label points with two numbers each because the plane is two dimensional.) The new picture is at right.

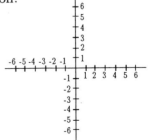

To be precise, each point is labeled by an **ordered pair** like $(3, -2)$ or $(17, 17)$. The first number is the distance *right* (negative for left) and the second is the distance *up* (negative for down). The horizontal axis is called the **x-axis**, and the corresponding number the **x-coordinate** (or sometimes **abscissa**); the vertical axis is called the **y-axis**, and the corresponding number the **y-coordinate** (or sometimes **ordinate**). The coordinates (x, y) of a point are called its **Cartesian (car TEA zhun) coordinates**, after Descartes.

Keep in mind that the Cartesian way of labeling the points of the plane is an entirely arbitrary choice. For example, we could just as well have one axis be slanted with respect to the other, and form the coordinates by the distances in the new grid. This particular choice would in virtually all cases be more complicated than straight Cartesian coordinates. However, there are choices of coordinates which may have a simplifying effect (which is the sole purpose of coordinates to begin with).

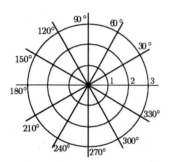

By far the most important such coordinate system is that of **polar coordinates**. In this setup, a point is labeled by the ordered pair (r, θ), where r is the distance from the origin and θ is the angle with respect to a chosen axis, usually taken to be the positive Cartesian x-axis. The "grid" of polar coordinates is shown in the figure. The circles represent increasing r, the lines increasing θ. Do you see why each set of coordinates (r, θ) identifies one and only one point?

There exist other ways to put coordinates on the plane, but polar and Cartesian are plenty for most purposes. Because Cartesian coordinates are the most generally useful, any coordinates in which the coordinate system is not specified may be assumed to be Cartesian.

EXERCISE 16-1 Plot the Cartesian points $(4.5, 3)$, $(1, -7/2)$, and $(-6, -4)$ and the polar points $(2, 3\pi/4)$, $(3/2, 270°)$, and $(1, 0°)$.

In both polar and Cartesian systems, the plane is sometimes thought of as being composed of four **quadrants**. The upper right (positive x, positive y) is called the first quadrant (labeled with a Roman numeral I), and they go counterclockwise from there.

EXERCISE 16-2 In which quadrant is x positive and y negative?

16.2   What's it Good For?

The beauty of a coordinate approach to geometry
is that we can often convert geometric pictures into
easily understood equations. The simplest examples
in Cartesian coordinates are equations like $x = 1$ or
$y = -5$. What do these equations mean? Take $x = 1$,
for instance. This is understood to mean the set of all
points in the plane whose coordinates (x, y) satisfy the
equation $x = 1$. Thus y can be anything, but x must
stay equal to 1. The result is a vertical line, as shown
above. Similarly, an equation like $y = -5$ represents a horizontal line, as x can have
any value while y must equal -5.

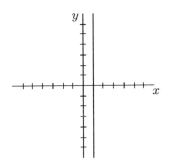

The simplest equations in polar coordinates produce different results. First,
consider an equation like $r = 3$. As with the Cartesian case, this means that θ can
be anything, while r, the distance to the origin, is restricted to 3. The result is a
circle of radius 3 centered at the origin. (Draw it and see.)

EXERCISE 16-3   What curve does the equation $\theta = 47°$ represent?

The dramatic difference between the simplest curves in Cartesian and polar coordinates is a clue as to what the different coordinate systems are good for. Cartesian
coordinates are much better than polar for describing straight lines and line segments, while polar coordinates are often better for circles (and, to a lesser extent,
lines through the origin). Other curves may go either way, or be equally well described by both.

Perhaps more important than the basic curves, however, is how the two coordinate systems handle transformations (more on these in Chapter 19). Let's consider
a point in the plane with polar coordinates (r, θ) and Cartesian coordinates (x, y).
Three basic transformations are translations, rotations, and reflections. Under a
translation (page 228), it is the Cartesian coordinates that change in a simple way:
(x, y) becomes $(x + a, y + b)$ for some constants a and b which describe the direction and amount of translation. The picture is shown on the left side below. On
the other hand, describing the change under translation with polar coordinates is
considerably more complicated.

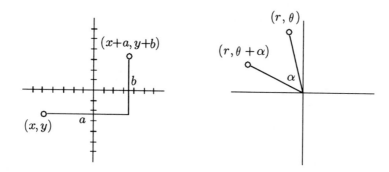

Under rotations (page 229), however, the situation is different. Assuming that we set up our polar coordinates with the origin at the center of rotation, the transformation just adds some fixed angle α to the angle of the point: (r, θ) becomes $(r, \theta + \alpha)$, as in the right side above. Here, Cartesian coordinates is the weaker system.

EXERCISE 16-4 What happens to the coordinates (x, y) and (r, θ) under a reflection across the x-axis? The y-axis?

16.3 Straight and Narrow

Now that we have a fairly good handle on coordinates, let's begin to apply them to what they were invented for: describing curves. The straight line is the simplest curve that there is, so it is a good starting point. For most lines, Cartesian coordinates provide the simplest description.

What do we need to plot a line? Geometry tells us that two points are enough. However, in a coordinate approach it is usually simpler to specify one point and the "steepness" of the line.

Any line which is not vertical must intersect the y-axis at some point. Does this make sense? The point will have coordinates $(0, b)$ for some b, and is called the **y-intercept**. (In the same way, the place where a line intersects the x-axis is called the **x-intercept**.)

EXAMPLE 16-1   Find the x- and y-intercepts of the line $2x + 7y = 14$.

Solution: The x-intercept is the point where we cross the x-axis; that is, where $y = 0$. Setting $y = 0$ in the equation and solving for x yields the $x = 7$, so the x-intercept is $(7, 0)$. Similarly, we find the y-intercept by setting $x = 0$ and solving for y. This yields $y = 2$, and the y-intercept is $(0, 2)$.

EXERCISE 16-5   Find the area of the region enclosed between the line $3x + 4y = 12$ and the two coordinate axes. (Hint: you don't need to draw a picture.)

In developing an equation for a line, we will start with the y-intercept $(0, b)$. Since $(x, y) = (0, b)$ is on the line, the equation must be of the form

$$y = mx + b \qquad\qquad (16.1)$$

for some m.

What does m signify? Consider starting at the y-intercept $(0, b)$ and moving over by 4. Moving over by 4 increases x from 0 to 4, so (16.1) becomes

$$y = 4m + b.$$

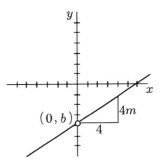

As x increases by 4, y increases by $4m$ from b to $4m + b$! In general, if we move to the right by some amount, we must move up by m times that amount to stay on the line. As you can see in the diagram, this m determines the "steepness" of the line. The larger m is, the higher the we have to climb. The form (16.1) is called the **slope-intercept form** of a line, because it specifies the line once we have the slope and the y-intercept.

EXERCISE 16-6   Think about it.

EXERCISE 16-7   What should the steepness of a horizontal line be? What is m for a horizontal line? What should the steepness of a vertical line be? What is m for a vertical line? Does m properly account for negative "steepness"?

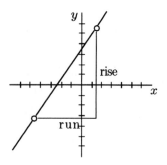

Since m corresponds to a steepness, we call it the **slope** of the line. Some people like to remember the slope as "rise over run," where "run" is the horizontal travel and "rise" the vertical, as shown below. These quantities can be computed between any two points on the line; the same slope will emerge. Both rise and run can be negative; if the ratio is negative, the line is sloped downward.

EXAMPLE 16-2 Let's find the slope of a line which contains the points $(15, 16)$ and $(-2, -18)$. From the first point to the second, the line must go over by $(-2) - 15 = -17$ and up by $(-18) - 16 = -34$. The slope is the amount up divided by the amount over, which is $(-34)/(-17) = \mathbf{2}$.

EXAMPLE 16-3 Find the slope of the line which contains (x_1, y_1) and (x_2, y_2).

Solution: From the first point to the second, the line goes over $(x_2 - x_1)$ and goes up $(y_2 - y_1)$; therefore, the slope is $m = (y_2 - y_1)/(x_2 - x_1)$.

EXAMPLE 16-4 Find the equation of a line which passes through the points $(-1, -1)$ and $(3, 7)$.

Solution: We can easily find the slope of the line: between the two points we go over 4 and up 8, so the slope is $8/4 = 2$. Substituting this into the slope-intercept form yields $y = 2x + b$. Putting the point $(-1, -1)$ in this equation will give us b; we have $-1 = -2 + b$, so $b = 1$. Thus the line equation is $y = 2x + 1$; every point (x, y) on the line should satisfy this equation.

EXERCISE 16-8 Find the equation of a line if its x-intercept is at $(-4, 0)$ and its y-intercept at $(0, 3)$.

EXERCISE 16-9 Find the equation of a line whose x- and y-intercepts are $(2, 0)$ and $(0, -6)$ respectively.

The slope-intercept form is a universal method for finding the equation of a line. Just use the given information with the equation $y = mx + b$ to find both m and b.

EXAMPLE 16-5 Suppose we are given two points on the line; what is the equation which describes the line? Let the points be (p_1, q_1) and (p_2, q_2). We can plug these points into the slope-intercept form and solve the resulting equations,

$$q_1 = mp_1 + b$$
$$\text{and} \quad q_2 = mp_2 + b,$$

for m and b. The results will be

$$m = \frac{q_1 - q_2}{p_1 - p_2} \quad \text{and} \quad b = \frac{-q_1 p_2 + q_2 p_1}{p_1 - p_2}.$$

(Verify these results.) The final equation will thus be

$$y = \frac{q_1 - q_2}{p_1 - p_2} x + \frac{-q_1 p_2 + q_2 p_1}{p_1 - p_2},$$

or the more symmetric-looking

$$(q_1 - q_2)x - (p_1 - p_2)y = p_2 q_1 - p_1 q_2.$$

EXERCISE 16-10 Verify that the original points (p_1, q_1) and (p_2, q_2) satisfy the equation above.

EXERCISE 16-11 Find the equation for a line with slope m containing the point (p, q).

If you can do generalized examples like those above, you should have no problem with numerical problems.

The slope-intercept form is the most practical way to write a line equation. For presentation purposes, however, a more general form is often preferred. This is the so-called **standard form**, $Ax + By = C$ (or sometimes $Ax + By + C = 0$). Here A, B, and C are simplified (integers if possible) and A is nonnegative.

EXAMPLE 16-6   What are the slope, x-intercept, and y-intercept of $2x + 3y = 6$?

Solution: The intercepts are pretty simple to determine. Since the x-intercept is the point where the line crosses the x-axis, we let $y = 0$ and solve $2x = 6$. Thus the x-intercept is $(3, 0)$. Similarly, we let $x = 0$ and find that the y-intercept is $(0, 2)$.

To find the slope, we put the line in slope-intercept form by solving for y, or $y = -2x/3 + 2$. The slope is the coefficient of x, or $-2/3$. (In general, the slope of a line in the form $Ax + By + C = 0$ is $-A/B$. Make sure you see why this is true.)

It is often important to determine whether two lines are parallel or perpendicular. You should be able to convince yourself rather easily that two lines are parallel if and only if they have the same slope. So how do we know if they are perpendicular? If one slope is the negative of the other?

EXERCISE 16-12   Find an example showing that two lines whose slopes are negatives of one another are in general not perpendicular.

Figuring out if two lines are perpendicular is a little tougher, but the idea is that if one line goes over a while it goes up b, a perpendicular one will go up $-a$ while it goes *over* b, as in the figure. Make sure you see why perpendicular lines have this property. After your study of rotations (page 229), come back to this and try to apply the principles of rotation.

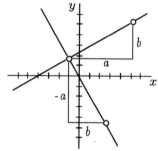

The slopes of the lines shown are a/b and $-b/a$, which multiply to -1; thus, two lines are perpendicular if and only if their slopes multiply to -1! (Note that this can't be used for horizontal or vertical lines.)

EXERCISE 16-13   Draw the lines $y = \dfrac{x}{2} + 1$ and $y = -2x + 3$, whose slopes do multiply to -1, to confirm.

16.4 Plotting a Line

An old adage says that a picture is worth a thousand words. Surprisingly, this is often true in working with equations. Effectively graphing an equation often helps in understanding it.

We have shown how to construct the equation of a line given certain information, like the slope and a point, or two points. Once we have that equation, how can we see what the line actually looks like? Plotting a curve given an equation is often harder than it seems, but the line is not one of those cases. Just plug in various values for x and solve the equation to get the corresponding y's. Once you've got two or three points on the line, it is easy to draw the line itself, which just connects the points.

This method is useful for all sorts of plotting: plug in x values, find the y values, draw the points, and connect them. If you know certain things about the shape of the graph, you may only need one or two points; if you have little or no information, and can't figure it out, you may need to draw many points. Often such plotting is the best way to figure out, given some strange equation, what sort of thing you're dealing with, and hence how to approach the equation.

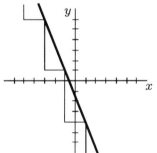

Of course, with lines, you don't always have to follow such a step-by-step procedure. If the equation is in slope-intercept form, with slope m and y-intercept b, for example, you can just start at the y-intercept $(0, b)$ and begin following the slope, using the "rise over run" idea. That is, say $m = -5/2$: just go right 2, down 5, right 2, down 5, and so on, then left 2, up 5, etc., as shown at left.

All you need is two points to draw a line. If you get stuck or confused, you can always revert to the plug-in method.

EXAMPLE 16-7 Plot the line $3x + 4y = 5$.

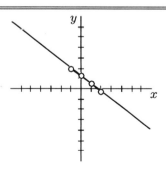

Solution: We just plug in some x values, find the corresponding y's, plot the points, and connect the dots. Plugging in $x = -1$, 0, 1, and 2, we get the corresponding y's: 2, $\frac{5}{4}$, $\frac{1}{2}$, and $-\frac{1}{4}$. Plotting these four points gives a line as shown. Note that while only two points are really required to plot a line, sometimes more may help plot the line more accurately, especially if, as here, fractional coordinates are involved.

EXERCISE 16-14 Plot the lines $y = -12x + 2$ and $(x - 2) = 3(y + 4)$.

16.5   The Distance Formula and Circles

Given the coordinates (x_1, y_1) and (x_2, y_2) of two points in the plane, how far apart are they? The answer is a simple application of the Pythagorean Theorem. To get from the first to the second, we go right a distance $(x_2 - x_1)$ and up a distance $(y_2 - y_1)$. These two distances form the legs of a right triangle as shown.

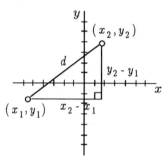

The hypotenuse of that triangle is the distance we want, which we'll call d. Thus, by the Pythagorean Theorem, we have

$$d^2 = (x_2 - x_1)^2 + (y_2 - y_1)^2,$$

so that

$$d = \sqrt{(x_2 - x_1)^2 + (y_2 - y_1)^2}.$$

This formula is called the **distance formula**.

EXAMPLE 16-8 Find all x such that the point $(x, 3)$ is 5 units away from $(-1, 7)$.

Solution: From the distance formula, we have $5 = \sqrt{(-1 - x)^2 + 16}$. Squaring and rearranging the equation yields $x^2 + 2x - 8 = 0$, which has solutions $x = \mathbf{2}$ and $x = \mathbf{-4}$.

The distance formula provides an easy way to figure out the equation for a circle in any coordinates. If the center of a circle is called O and the radius R, the circle is just all points whose distance to O is equal to R. Let the coordinates of O be (p, q). Then all points (x, y) on the circle are R away from (p, q), so the distance formula yields

$$\sqrt{(x - p)^2 + (y - q)^2} = R,$$

or the more preferred

$$(x - p)^2 + (y - q)^2 = R^2. \tag{16.2}$$

EXAMPLE 16-9 Circles are easy to plot. Take the circle

$$(x + 1)^2 + (y - 2)^2 = 9.$$

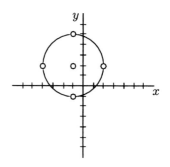

By comparison with equation (16.2), we see that the center of the circle is $(-1, 2)$ and the radius 3. (Make sure you see this.) To find the first four points on the circle we go 3 in the four main directions (left, right, up, down) from the center, to the points $(2, 2)$, $(-4, 2)$, $(-1, -1)$, and $(-1, 5)$. From there we can draw the circle, as in the figure.

A more general form of the circle equation is

$$x^2 + y^2 + Ax + By + C = 0. \tag{16.3}$$

This is not a form we would willingly put a circle in, because the relevant information (center, radius) is hard to see. However, sometimes we will be given this form and asked to find the center or radius or even to plot the circle. How can we go back to the nice form of (16.2)?

The answer: completing the square. As in Chapter 6, we can convert a general quadratic to a square plus some constant. Here we need to do it twice, once on x and once on y.

EXAMPLE 16-10 Find the center and radius of the circle described by

$$2x^2 + 2y^2 + 8x - 12y + 3 = 0.$$

The first thing to do is to divide by 2, to make the coefficients of x^2 and y^2 both 1. We then collect x and y terms to obtain

$$(x^2 + 4x) + (y^2 - 6y) + \frac{3}{2} = 0.$$

Completing both squares by adding $(4/2)^2 = 4$ to $(x^2 + 4x)$ and $(-6/2)^2 = 9$ to $(y^2 - 6y)$, this equation becomes

$$(x^2 + 4x + 4) - 4 + (y^2 - 6y + 9) - 9 + \frac{3}{2} = 0,$$

or

$$(x + 2)^2 + (y - 3)^2 = \frac{23}{2}.$$

Thus the center is $(-2, 3)$ and the radius is $\sqrt{23/2} = \sqrt{46}/2$.

EXERCISE 16-15   What if the number we had gotten on the right side in the last equation above had been 0? Negative?

Note that we only get a circle if the coefficients of x^2 and y^2 in Equation (16.3) are the same. Do you have a guess about what happens if they aren't?

16.6   Went Down to the Crossroads...

One thing coordinate geometry is very good at is finding the intersection points of figures. All that's necessary is to find the equations of the two figures, then solve those equations simultaneously. If solving is too hard, you can find approximate intersections by plotting both figures accurately, and then locating the intersection points on the graph.

EXERCISE 16-16   Find the intersection of the lines

$$\begin{aligned} x + y &= -3 \\ -2x + 3y &= 2 \end{aligned}$$

by solving the equations simultaneously, then plot the lines and find the intersection graphically.

EXAMPLE 16-11   Find the intersections of the line $x + y = -2$ and the circle $(x + 3)^2 + (y - 8)^2 = 25$.

Solution: First we can use the line equation to write $y = -2 - x$. Plugging this into the circle equation, we have

$$(x + 3)^2 + (-10 - x)^2 = 25.$$

This equation can be solved easily: just square out the squares, collect terms, and solve the resulting quadratic in x. Then plug these x values back into the linear equation to get the corresponding y's. You should find the solutions $(-6, 4)$ and $(-7, 5)$.

EXERCISE 16-17   In what numbers of points can two distinct lines intersect? Two circles? A line and a circle? Justify your answers based on the equations of the figures in question.

16.7   ...Fell Down on My Knees

Geometry that is done in a coordinate system is called **analytic geometry**. ("Analytic" means using equations rather than pictures.) Most geometry can best be done with basic geometric principles rather than resorting to describing the figures by equations. When in doubt about whether or not to use an analytic approach to a problem, always try a geometric approach first. What types of problems can be solved with analytic geometry? One easy example is finding the midpoint of a segment.

EXAMPLE 16-12   Prove that the midpoint of the segment whose endpoints are (x_1, y_1) and (x_2, y_2) is given by $\left(\dfrac{x_1 + x_2}{2}, \dfrac{y_1 + y_2}{2} \right)$.

Solution: Consider the figure at right. Since the two dotted right triangles have equal hypotenuses (since M is the midpoint) and equal angles (from the parallel dotted lines), they are congruent by SA for right triangles. Thus each pair of corresponding legs is equal. Since the distance covered by the two horizontal legs is $x_2 - x_1$, each must thus be of length $(x_2 - x_1)/2$. The x-coordinate of the midpoint is obtained by adding this to the x-coordinate x_1 of the starting point, to get $(x_1 + x_2)/2$, as desired. The y-coordinate is found in exactly the same way.

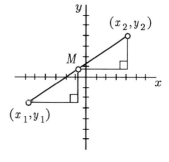

Another important example is the most crucial figure in geometry: the triangle. Since we can choose our coordinates any way we please, we should think about how to place the coordinate axes to make analysis simple. The best choice is to place two of the vertices, A and B, on the x-axis, and the other, C, on the y-axis. Then the coordinates of the triangle are $(a, 0)$, $(b, 0)$, and $(0, c)$ for some a, b, and c. We can thus reduce the six variables to only three without making any limiting assumptions. (Convince yourself that every triangle can be represented in this way.)

EXAMPLE 16-13   Using this system, we can prove that the centroid of a triangle exists. Recall that the centroid is supposed to be the intersection of all three medians of the triangle. However, there is no real guarantee that the medians come together at a single point. Let's show that they do.

The midpoints opposite $A = (a, 0)$, $B = (b, 0)$, and $C = (0, c)$ are given by $(b/2, c/2)$, $(a/2, c/2)$, and $((a + b)/2, 0)$, respectively. Using the formulas we developed in Section 16.3, the equations of the lines connecting these midpoints to the vertices are

$$
\begin{aligned}
cx + (2a - b)y &= ac \\
cx + (2b - a)y &= bc \\
2cx + (a + b)y &= c(a + b).
\end{aligned}
$$

Verify all these equations. Solving the first two simultaneously, we find that the intersection is given by $\left(\dfrac{a + b}{3}, \dfrac{c}{3}\right)$. Trying this in the third equation, we find that it is indeed on this line. (Again, verify this.) Thus the single point given by

$$
\left(\frac{a + b}{3}, \frac{c}{3}\right) \tag{16.4}
$$

is the centroid of the triangle, as it is on all three medians.

You might argue that we have only proven that the centroid exists for one choice of the coordinate system. However, we can choose the coordinate system in any way we want! We choose the simplest system and prove the general result there. As long as only geometric relationships are involved in the result we want to prove, as in this example and Exercise 16-18, this is entirely permissible. However, if we are asked to prove something about specific coordinates themselves, as in Exercise 16-19 below, we are *not* free to choose our coordinates.

EXERCISE 16-18   Prove that if G is the centroid of $\triangle ABC$ and AM is a median, then $AG = 2GM$.

EXERCISE 16-19   The point (16.4) is the average of the three coordinates of the triangle! Show that this is true regardless of how the triangle is oriented in the coordinate plane. (For example, if the triangle doesn't have one vertex on the y-axis and the others on the x-axis.)

One thing to remember about analytic geometry: as Example 16-13 shows, even simple problems can get heavily algebraic. Don't get into the habit of trying analytic techniques on every geometry problem you see, for you will get caught in a mass of equations and miss the simple geometric solution. It is for this reason that analytic geometry can never be a complete substitute for the techniques of pure Euclidean geometry. That's a good thing, because Euclidean geometry is one of the most beautiful subjects there is. Experience will teach which types of problems work nicely in analytic geometry, and in which problems analytic techniques are an uncreative dead end.

Problems to Solve for Chapter 16

278. Find the distance between the points $(2, 12)$ and $(-4, 10)$.

279. A right triangle is drawn with legs of lengths 3 on the x-axis and 4 on the y-axis lying along the positive coordinate axes. Find the coordinates of the midpoint of the hypotenuse.

280. How many points with integer coordinates are exactly 5 units away from $(0, 0)$?

281. Find the equation of a line which passes through $(5, 7)$ and cuts the area of the circle $(x + 12)^2 + (y + 3)^2 = 4$ in half.

282. Find the centroid of a triangle with vertices $(10, 66)$, $(19, 72)$, and $(17, 56)$.

283. Find the distance from the point $(5, 7)$ to the center of the circle $4x^2 + 8x + 4y^2 - 16y - 16 = 0$.

284. If $a, b > 0$ and the triangle in the first quadrant bounded by the coordinate axes and the graph of $ax + by = 6$ has area 6, then find ab. (AHSME 1989)

285. Parallelogram $ABCD$ has vertices $A(0, 0)$, $B(2, 4)$, and $D(5, 1)$. If the remaining vertex, C, is in the first quadrant, what are its coordinates? (MATHCOUNTS 1992)

286. The graphs of the equations $x + 3y = 6$ and $kx + 2y = 12$ are perpendicular. What is the value of k? (MATHCOUNTS 1989)

287. What are the coordinates of the point that is two-thirds of the way from $(2, 4)$ to $(-1, 1)$? (MATHCOUNTS 1990)

288. We are given the line $3x + 5y = 15$ and a point on this line equidistant from the coordinate axes. In which quadrants can such a point exist? (AHSME 1960)

289. Prove analytically that the diagonals of a rectangle bisect each other.

290. Find y if $(3, y)$ lies on the line joining $(0, 3/2)$ and $(9/4, 0)$. (MAΘ 1987)

291. Describe analytically all the lines which bisect the area of the square with vertices $(0, 0)$, $(s, 0)$, (s, s), and $(0, s)$.

292. Find the vertices of a square which is centered at $(-17, 23)$, has side length 4, and whose diagonals are parallel to the coordinate axes.

293. A circle is drawn with center at the origin and radius 3. Find the coordinates of all intersections of the circle with an origin-centered square of side length 4 whose sides are parallel to the coordinate axes.

Chapter 17

Power of a Point

17.1 Introduction

The Power of a Point Theorem is a very simple yet very powerful theorem.

> **Power of a Point Theorem.** Given a point P and a line through P which intersects some circle in two points A and B, the product $(PA)(PB)$ is the same for any choice of the line.

We will show several important cases of the basic theorem. As with our discussion of angles and circles, we will present the relationships now and prove them in a later section. Do you see why we need to consider various cases?

===

Power of a Point Formulas

1. Two tangents from a point.

Two tangents from the same point to a circle are always equal.
$$AB = AC.$$

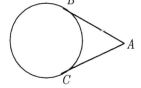

2. A tangent and a secant from a point.

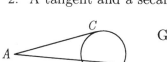

Given tangent AC and secant AD at left, we have
$$AC^2 = AB(AD).$$

3. Two secants from a point.

Given secants AC and AE at right, we have

$$(AB)(AC) = (AD)(AE).$$

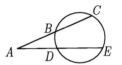

4. Two chords through a point.

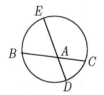

Given two chords BC and DE which intersect at A, we have

$$(BA)(AC) = (DA)(AE).$$

When just given a circle and intersecting chords, or lines to a circle from a common exterior point, you can use Power of a Point. Whenever you see two tangents to the same circle from the same point, mark the tangents as equal. Like similar triangles, Power of a Point is most useful in proofs when working with ratios of segments. You will see examples of all these in the following problems.

Unlike similar and congruent triangles, which are sometimes difficult to see, Power of a Point is generally very easy to notice. If you have a couple of chords in a circle, or a tangent and a secant, you have Power of a Point; it's pretty hard to hide. As you move to more advanced problem solving, you will find fewer and fewer problems which can be solved completely by Power of a Point; at the same time, though, there will be more and more in which it is an important step.

EXAMPLE 17-1   Given tangent AC and secant AB with $AC = 6$, $AD = 4$, and $BD = x$, find the value of x.

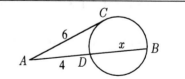

Solution: From the power of point A, we have $(AB)(AD) = AC^2$. Thus $4(4 + x) = 36$; solving this equation yields $x = \mathbf{5}$.

EXAMPLE 17-2   Two diagonals AX and BY of a regular polygon intersect at W. Prove that $(AW)(WX) = (BW)(WY)$.

Proof: Seeing the suggestive equation $(AW)(WX) = (BW)(WY)$, we think of Power of a Point. Since the polygon is a regular polygon, there exists a circle which passes through all of its vertices.

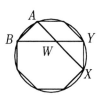

Since AX and BY are chords of the circle which intersect at W, the power of point W gives us $(AW)(WX) = (BW)(WY)$.

EXAMPLE 17-3 In $\triangle ABC$, points X, Y, and Z are where the incircle is tangent to the sides, X opposite A, Y opposite B, and Z opposite C. Prove that $AZ = s-a$, $BX = s - b$, and $CY = s - c$.

Proof: Since tangents from a point to a circle are equal, we let $AZ = AY = x$, $BZ = BX = y$, and $CY = CX = z$ as shown in the diagram. The perimeter of the triangle is

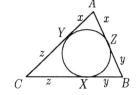

$$p = 2s = (x + y) + (y + z) + (x + z) = 2(x + y + z),$$

so that $s = x + y + z$. Since $x + z = b$, we have $y = BX = s - (x + z) = s - b$, and the other equalities are proven likewise.

EXAMPLE 17-4 Prove that if $ABCD$ can be circumscribed about a circle, then $AB + CD = BC + AD$.

Proof: Since $ABCD$ can be circumscribed about a circle, we can draw a circle which is tangent to all four sides of the quadrilateral. (Such a circle cannot be drawn for every quadrilateral.) Since tangents to a circle from a point are equal, we label the tangent lengths as shown. We then have

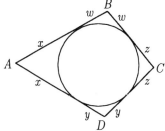

$$AB + CD = (x + w) + (y + z) = w + x + y + z = (w + z) + (x + y) = AD + BC,$$

so we are done.

EXERCISE 17-1 Prove that the inradius of a right triangle with leg lengths a and b and hypotenuse c is $(a + b - c)/2$.

EXERCISE 17-2 Show that if AB is a diameter of a circle and CD a chord perpendicular to AB intersecting AB at X, then $CX^2 = (AX)(BX)$.

It is also important to note that Power of a Point can be used to prove that a segment is tangent to a circle. For example, if a line through point A outside circle O intersects the circle at B and C, and another line through A meets the circle at X such that $AX^2 = (AB)(AC)$, then AX is tangent to the circle. Remember this if other methods of proving that AX is a tangent, such as showing that $\angle AXO = 90°$, fail.

17.2   Power of a Point Proofs

The proofs of the various Power of a Point configurations are excellent exercises in elementary geometry. How we came to our methods is easy to understand: since the Power of a Point formulas involve ratios of sides, we look for similar triangles, and since the Power of a Point Theorem also involves circles, we use circular arcs to relate angles.

Power of a Point Proofs

1. Point outside the circle.

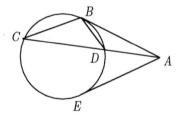

We can knock off all of these configurations with a single proof. Once we establish the case with one secant and one tangent, the cases of two secants and two tangents will soon follow. Thus, in the diagram, we wish to show that $(AD)(AC) = AB^2$. Rearranging this yields

$$\frac{AD}{AB} = \frac{AB}{AC},$$

which will be true if $\triangle ADB \sim \triangle ABC$. Since $\angle DAB = \angle CAB$ because they are the same angle, we need only to prove that one of the other two pairs of corresponding angles are equal to prove the similarity.

As an inscribed angle, $\angle BCD = \overset{\frown}{BD}/2$. Similarly, as the angle between a tangent and a chord, we have $\angle ABD = \overset{\frown}{BD}/2$; thus, $\triangle ADB \sim \triangle ABC$, and we have the desired

$$\frac{AD}{AB} = \frac{AB}{AC}.$$

From this we find $(AD)(AC) = AB^2$, proving the Power of a Point for a secant and a tangent.

As advertised, we can quickly use the secant-tangent case to prove the secant-secant and tangent-tangent cases. Since the above relation must hold for any secant, we have $(AD)(AC) = AB^2$ for all secants. Thus $(AD)(AC)$ is constant for all secants passing through A. Finally, in the same way we showed that $(AD)(AC) = AB^2$, we can show that $(AD)(AC) = AE^2$, where E is the point of tangency of the other tangent from point A. Putting this together with the original expression gives

$$AB^2 = (AD)(AC) = AE^2.$$

Thus $AB = AE$, showing that two tangents to a circle from the same point are equal.

2. Point inside the circle.

Just like before, we use similar triangles. First, $\angle AEC = \angle DEB$ as these are vertical angles. Since $\angle CAB$ and $\angle CDB$ are inscribed angles which subtend the same arc $(\overset{\frown}{BC})$, they are equal. Thus we have shown that triangles EAC and EDB are similar, so

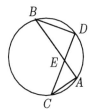

$$\frac{AE}{DE} = \frac{CE}{BE}.$$

Rearranging this yields the desired $(AE)(BE) = (CE)(DE)$.

If you haven't already, think carefully about the tools we have used in these proofs; they will guide you in your own. Seeing ratios of sides, we look for similar triangles. To show that triangles are similar, we show that their angles are equal. Since there are circles involved, we do this by using the relationships between arcs and angles, as well as the sum of the angles in both a straight line and a triangle.

Problems to Solve for Chapter 17

294. A point P is outside a circle and is 13 inches from the center. A secant from P cuts the circle at Q and R so that the external segment of the secant PQ is 9 inches and QR is 7 inches. Find the radius of the circle. (AHSME 1954)

295. The points A, B, and C are on circle O. The tangent line at A and the secant BC intersect at P, B lying between C and P. If $BC = 20$ and $PA = 10\sqrt{3}$, then find PB. (AHSME 1956)

296. In the diagram, EB bisects CD and C is the midpoint of AD. Find GB if $AB = 16$, $EF = 2$, and $FB = 3$. (MAΘ 1990)

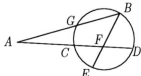

297. Two tangents are drawn to a circle from an exterior point A; they touch the circle at points B and C, respectively. A third tangent intersects segment AB at P and AC at R, and touches the circle at Q. If $AB = 20$, then find the perimeter of $\triangle APR$. (AHSME 1961)

298. A circle is inscribed in a triangle with sides of lengths 8, 13, and 17. Let the segments of the side of length 8 made by a point of tangency be r and s, with $r < s$. Find the ratio $r : s$. (AHSME 1964)

299. In this figure the center of the circle is O. $AB \perp BC$, $ADOE$ is a straight line, $AP = AD$, and AB has length twice the radius. Show that $AP^2 = (PB)(AB)$. (AHSME 1960)

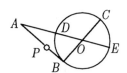

300. Find the area of the inscribed circle of a triangle with sides of length 20, 21, and 29. (MAΘ 1990)

301. In the adjoining figure, AB is tangent at A to the circle with center O; point D is interior to the circle; and DB intersects the circle at C. If $BC = DC = 3$, $OD = 2$ and $AB = 6$, then find the radius of the circle. (AHSME 1976)

302. Prove that if quadrilateral $ABCD$ is orthodiagonal and circumscribed around a circle, then $(AB)(CD) = (BC)(AD)$. (M&IQ 1991)

Chapter 18

Three Dimensional Geometry

18.1   Planes, Surface Area, and Volume

Consider two lines in space. If these two lines have exactly the same orientation, they are parallel. If they don't have the same orientation, but still never intersect, they are called **skew** lines. To understand skew lines, hold two pens so that they are not touching. If they aren't pointing the same direction, chances are they are skew.

Consider a flat sheet of paper which continues forever in every direction. This is a **plane**. Just as a line is a one-dimensional figure, a plane is a two-dimensional figure. In three dimensions, an area which extends forever in every direction is called a **space**. Given a plane, any line is either in the plane, intersects the plane at one point, or never intersects the plane. The three possibilities are displayed at right. If the line does not intersect the plane, it is parallel to the plane. A line l is perpendicular to a plane if every line in the plane through the intersection point of l and the plane is perpendicular to l. As you may have guessed, the distance from a point to a plane is the length of the perpendicular segment from the point to the plane.

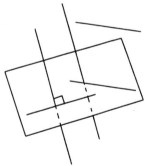

How many points must we have to determine a plane? Given any three non-collinear points, we can form a triangle. A triangle is a planar figure, so our three points have determined a plane. We cannot always form a plane through four given points. To see this, draw a triangle and then lift your pen from the paper. Try to form a plane that goes through the vertices of the triangle and the point of your pen. If your pen is above the paper, you'll find that this is impossible. If you do have a set of four or more points which lie in a single plane, the points are **coplanar**.

Suppose we have a three dimensional figure, like a box or a ball, made of cloth which encloses a region. The area of the cloth needed to make the figure is called the **total surface area** of the figure. For example, if the figure is a box, the total surface area is the sum of the areas of the sides of the box.

Some shapes have a well-defined top and bottom. In this case, we may be interested in only the surface area which is *not* on the top or bottom. This area is often called the **lateral surface area** of the figure. Whenever a problem asks for just the surface area of a figure, the total surface area is implied.

Finally, the amount of space enclosed within a figure is the **volume** of the figure. To add something concrete to all these general definitions, let's look at the most common three-dimensional figures.

18.2 Spheres

A **sphere** is just a ball. Just as a circle is the set of all points in a plane which are a fixed distance from a given point, a sphere is the set of all points in *space* which are a fixed distance from a given point. As with the circle, the fixed point is the center, and the distance is the radius of the sphere.

The surface area of a sphere with radius r is $4\pi r^2$ and the volume is $4\pi r^3/3$.

If a plane intersects a sphere, the intersection is either a point (if the plane is tangent to the sphere) or a circle. The intersection of a sphere and a plane passing through its center is called a **great circle** of the sphere.

EXAMPLE 18-1 A plane intersects a sphere, forming a circle. Find the radius of the circle if the radius of the sphere is 8 and the center of the sphere is 5 units from the plane.

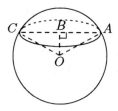

Solution: Draw diameter AC of the circle, where B is its the center. Drawing segment OB and radii OA and OC, we form two triangles OBC and OBA. Since $AB = BC$ (as radii of the circle), $OB = OB$, and $OC = OA$ (radii of the sphere), we have $\triangle OBC \cong \triangle OBA$ by SSS. Thus $\angle OBC = \angle OBA$. Since these two angles are equal and together form a line, they are right angles. Thus OB is the distance from the center to the plane, so $OB = 5$. From the Pythagorean Theorem we find $AB = \sqrt{8^2 - 5^2} = \sqrt{39}$. Remember this method of relating the radius of the sphere to the radii of circles of the sphere.

EXAMPLE 18-2 Find the diameter of a sphere whose volume is 288π.

Solution: First we find the radius, then the diameter. Solving

$$\frac{4\pi r^3}{3} = 288\pi,$$

we find $r^3 = 216$ and $r = 6$. Thus the diameter has length $2r = \mathbf{12}$.

EXERCISE 18-1 A ball was floating in a lake when the lake froze. The ball was removed (without breaking the ice), leaving a hole 24 cm across at the top and 8 cm deep. What was the radius of the ball in centimeters? (AHSME 1987)

EXERCISE 18-2 Find the volume of a sphere which has surface area 100.

18.3 Cubes and Boxes

A simple six-sided die is a **cube**. All the sides, or **faces**, are squares and each face is perpendicular to the faces which are adjacent to it. The segments which form the faces are called **edges**, and the edges meet at the **vertices**. Since all the faces are congruent squares, all the edges have the same 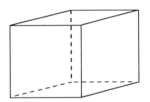 length; let this length be s. Since the faces are squares, each face has area s^2, and since there are six such faces, the surface area of the cube is $6s^2$. To find the volume of the cube, we multiply the area of a face by the altitude to the face. This altitude is the same length as an edge of the cube, so the volume is s^3.

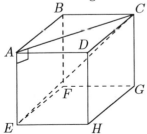 A diagonal of a cube is a segment drawn from a vertex of the cube to the vertex opposite it, as EC at left. To find the length of EC, first draw diagonal AC of face $ABCD$. Since $ABCD$ is a square, we know that $AC = s\sqrt{2}$. Moreover, since AE is perpendicular to the plane $ABCD$, we have $AE \perp AC$. Thus, using the Pythagorean Theorem on right triangle CAE, we find $EC = \sqrt{s^2 + 2s^2} = s\sqrt{3}$, so the diagonal of a cube is $\sqrt{3}$ times the length of a side.

EXAMPLE 18-3 In cube $ABCDEFGH$, $ABCD$ is a face and M is the midpoint of edge DE. Find BM if $AB = 4$.

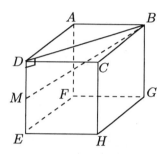

Solution: The first step is draw the picture as accurately as possible. Nearly all three dimensional problems which do not involve volume are solved by chopping the problem into a series of two-dimensional problems, as we did in determining the length of a diagonal. Here, by drawing face diagonal BD, we form right triangle BDM. (There are lots of right triangles in cube problems.) Since BD is a face diagonal, it has length $4\sqrt{2}$. Segment DM is half an edge, so it has length 2. From the Pythagorean Theorem we have $BM = \sqrt{4 + 32} = \mathbf{6}$.

EXAMPLE 18-4 A cube with edge length 6 units is made from blocks which are unit cubes (cubes with edge length 1), and then all faces are painted. How many of the blocks have no faces painted? One face painted? Two faces painted? Three faces painted?

Solution: Counting those cubes with three faces painted is easy. Those are just the corners, so there are **8** of them.

For two faces to be painted, the block must be on an edge but not a corner. Since each of the 12 edges contains 4 such cubes, there are $12(4) = \mathbf{48}$ cubes with two faces painted.

For a cube to have only one face painted, it must be in the interior of a face, not on an edge or a corner. Taking away the outside blocks of a 6 by 6 square leaves a 4 by 4 square (try it), so there are $4(4) = 16$ blocks with one face painted on each of the six faces of the cube. Hence, there are $6(16) = \mathbf{96}$ blocks with only one face painted.

Now we have counted all the cubes that have some face painted. We could get the number of cubes with no faces painted by subtracting from the total number of blocks ($6^3 = 216$), but there is a slicker way. Just as we removed the edge blocks to count blocks with one face painted, we can remove the outside blocks from the cube to count to number of blocks with no faces painted. Removing the outer layer of blocks from a 6 by 6 by 6 cube leaves a 4 by 4 by 4 cube, which contains $4^3 = 64$ blocks. There are **64** blocks with no faces painted.

EXAMPLE 18-5 Find the area of △*BDE*, where *ABCDEFGH* is a cube as shown and *AB* = 6.

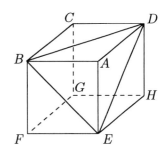

Solution: Drawing the sides of the triangle as shown, we see that they are face diagonals and hence have length $6\sqrt{2}$. Since these sides are all equal, △*BDE* is equilateral. Hence, we find

$$[BDE] = \frac{(BD)(BE)\sin 60°}{2} = \frac{(6\sqrt{2})^2\sqrt{3}}{4} = \mathbf{18\sqrt{3}}.$$

EXERCISE 18-3 Find the volume of a cube which has diagonal length 6.

EXERCISE 18-4 Given that *AB*, *AD*, and *AE* are all edges of a cube, find ∠*LMN* if *L*, *M*, and *N* are the midpoints of these three edges.

In mathematical terms, the figure at right is a **right parallelepiped**, which in English reads 'box.' A **parallelepiped** is a six sided solid in which the opposite faces are congruent parallelograms. A box is a special case of a parallelepiped in which all the faces are rectangles. Opposite faces are congruent and perpendicular to each other as shown at vertex *A*. Since the faces are rectangles, we have

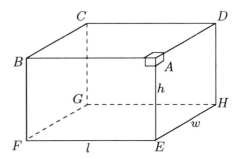

$$AE = DH = CG = BF, \quad EF = HG = DC = AB, \quad \& \quad AD = BC = FG = EH.$$

These three lengths are called the height, length, and width, respectively, and are commonly labelled h, l, and w. We only need these three dimensions to completely describe any box.

Since the faces are rectangles, we can easily find the surface area as the sum of the face areas:

$$\text{Surface Area} = 2(lw + hl + hw).$$

The volume of the box is the area of one face times the altitude to the other, or

$$\text{Volume} = lwh.$$

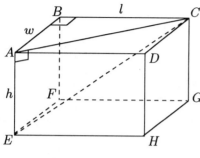

As with a cube, a diagonal of a box is a segment from a vertex of the box to the opposite vertex. Segment EC is a diagonal of the box. We find the length of this diagonal just as we found the length of a diagonal of a cube. By drawing face diagonal AC, we form right triangles ABC and EAC. The Pythagorean Theorem then yields

$$AC = \sqrt{BC^2 + AB^2} = \sqrt{l^2 + w^2}$$
$$\text{and} \quad EC = \sqrt{AC^2 + AE^2} = \sqrt{l^2 + w^2 + h^2}.$$

EXAMPLE 18-6 Find the volume of a box which has diagonal length $\sqrt{35}$ and two dimensions 1 and 5.

Solution: Since the length of a diagonal is given by $\sqrt{l^2 + w^2 + h^2}$, we have $35 = 1 + 25 + h^2$. Solving for h, we find $h = 3$, so the volume is $lwh = \mathbf{15}$. There are two things to note in this example. First, we neglect $h = -3$ as a solution of the equation, as negative lengths are impossible. Second, we tacitly assumed the given dimensions were the length and width. They could in fact have been any two of the dimensions. The names length, width, and height really have no meaning, and are only used to differentiate the three dimensions, so we can use the letters l, w and h to name the dimensions in any order.

EXAMPLE 18-7 Given that the areas of three faces of a rectangular solid (another name sometimes used for a box) are 24, 32, and 48, find the volume of the solid.

Solution: Let the dimensions be x, y, and z. Since the faces are rectangles, the areas are the products of pairs of these lengths. We thus have the equations

$$xy = 24, \quad xz = 32, \quad yz = 48.$$

We could use trial and error to solve these and find $(x, y, z) = (4, 6, 8)$, but there is a better method to find the volume. Since the volume is xyz, we need only find this product. Consider the product of the three area equations.

$$(xy)(xz)(yz) = (24)(32)(48)$$
$$x^2 y^2 z^2 = 2^{12} \cdot 3^2$$
$$(xyz)^2 = 2^{12} \cdot 3^2$$

Taking the square root of this equation, we find $xyz = 2^6 \cdot 3 = 192$. Thus the volume is **192**, and we never had to find the side lengths.

Why is this method better for finding the volume? What if the areas of the faces had been $9\sqrt{6}$, $36\sqrt{3}$, and $54\sqrt{2}$? Using trial and error to find the dimensions of that solid could take a long time. Our method will still solve this problem quickly.

EXERCISE 18-5   Find the number of 2 inch cubes required to fill a 4 inch by 8 inch by 10 inch box.

EXERCISE 18-6   In the rectangular parallelepiped $ABCDEFGH$ at the right, $AB = 4$, $BC = 3$, $CG = 9$, $BY = 3$, and $DX = 5$. Find XY.

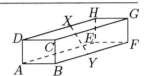

18.4   Prisms and Cylinders

A **prism** is a figure in which the **bases** are two parallel and congruent faces, and the **lateral faces** are parallelograms formed by connecting corresponding vertices of the bases. As shown at the right, the bases can be any geometric figure. A **regular prism** is one in which the bases are regular polygons. For example, a regular hexagonal prism is one in which the bases are regular hexagons. The **height** is the distance between the bases, where the distance is the length of a perpendicular segment from one base to the other. The total surface area is found by summing the areas of the faces, while the lateral surface area is the sum of the areas of the lateral faces. As with boxes and cubes, the volume of a prism is the product of the area of a base and the height of the prism.

A **right prism** is a prism in which the lateral edges are perpendicular to the bases. Cubes and boxes are right prisms.

A **cylinder** is a prism whose bases are curved surfaces rather than polygons. A **circular cylinder** has bases which are circles, and a **right circular cylinder** is a right prism whose bases are circles. A typical can is a right circular cylinder. The line joining the centers of the bases is called the **axis** of the cylinder. Generally, in problems which refer to a cylinder, a right circular cylinder is implied.

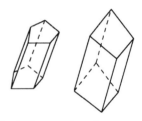

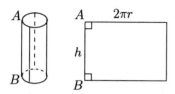

Given a cylinder with height h and radius r, the base area is πr^2, so

$$\text{Volume} = \pi r^2 h.$$

To find the surface area we add the area of the bases to the area of the curved surface. As circles of radius r, the bases each have area πr^2. To find the area of the curved surface, consider cutting the curved surface along the vertical line AB shown and 'unrolling' the surface. We form a rectangle as shown in the diagram. One side of the rectangle is the altitude, h, of the cylinder, and the other is the circumference, $2\pi r$, of the bases. If you don't follow this, get a can and wrap a piece of paper around it. This should make it clear that the curved surface of a cylinder is actually a rectangle. Thus, the lateral surface area of a cylinder is $2\pi h r$, and as the sum of the area of the curved surface and the two circular ends, we get

$$\text{Total Surface Area} = 2\pi h r + 2\pi r^2.$$

EXAMPLE 18-8 Show that the lateral surface area of a right prism is given by the product of the perimeter of one of the bases and the altitude of the prism.

Proof: Each face of a right prism is a rectangle. Two sides of each rectangle are lateral edges and are equal to the altitude, h, of the prism. The other two sides are corresponding sides of the bases. The area of each face is the product of these lengths. If we let the lengths of the sides of the base be x_1, $x_2, \ldots$, x_i, then the sum of the areas is

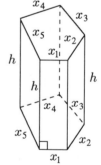

$$x_1 h + x_2 h + \cdots + x_i h = (x_1 + x_2 + \cdots + x_i)h = ph,$$

where p is the perimeter of the base.

EXERCISE 18-7 Find the total surface area of a cylinder whose height is 5 and volume is 45π.

EXAMPLE 18-9 An ant is on the edge of the top of a cylinder. The ant wishes to crawl to a point diagonally across from his current position at the base of the cylinder. If the cylinder is 8 inches high with a diameter of 4 inches, what is the shortest distance the ant may crawl to get to the desired point? (MAΘ 1992)

Solution: The ant must crawl along the outside surface of the cylinder from A to B, so we are not just looking for the length AB inside the cylinder. Instead we must 'unroll' the surface of the cylinder and find AB on this rectangle. Since B is directly opposite A, it is the midpoint of one side of the

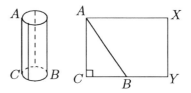

unrolled rectangle. (The distance from C to B along the circle is half the circumference of the circle.) Thus, $CB = CY/2 = 2\pi r/2 = \pi r = 2\pi$. Since AC equals the height of the cylinder, we know $AC = 8$. The Pythagorean Theorem then gives

$$AB = \sqrt{AC^2 + BC^2} = \sqrt{64 + 4\pi^2} = \mathbf{2\sqrt{16 + \pi^2}}.$$

Note how we have turned a three dimensional problem into a two dimensional one by unrolling the cylinder's surface.

EXERCISE 18-8 What is the greatest possible distance in space between two points on a right circular cylindrical can with radius 4 and height 6?

18.5 Pyramids and Cones

A solid figure with one polygonal face and all other faces triangles with a common vertex is called a **pyramid**. The common vertex is the **vertex** of the pyramid, the polygonal face (which may also be a triangle) is the **base**, the triangles with the common vertex are the **lateral faces**, and the **altitude**, h, of a pyramid is the

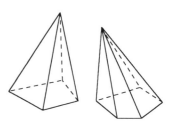

perpendicular distance from the vertex of the pyramid to the base. If A is the area of the base, the volume of any pyramid is given by $Ah/3$. As you may have guessed, the lateral surface area is the sum of the areas of the faces.

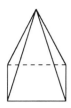

A **regular pyramid** is a pyramid which has a regular polygon as its base and vertex such that all lateral faces make the same angle with the base. The foot of the altitude is the center of the base, so the vertex is directly above the base's center. Thus the lateral faces are all congruent triangles. We sometimes call the common altitude of the faces from the vertex of the pyramid the **slant height**. The lateral surface area of a regular pyramid is $pl/2$, where l is the slant height and p is the perimeter of the base.

EXAMPLE 18-10   Show that the lateral surface area of a regular pyramid with base perimeter p and slant height l is $pl/2$.

Proof: The slant height is the altitude to the sides of the lateral faces which are also sides of the base. Letting the side length of the base be s and the number of sides of the base be n, the area of each lateral face is then $sl/2$ and the total lateral surface area is $nsl/2$. Since ns represents the perimeter of the base, the lateral surface area is $pl/2$.

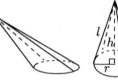

As with prisms, there is a special name for a pyramid with a curve as a base. Such a pyramid is called a **cone**. A **circular cone** has a circle as a base, and a **right circular cone** is a regular pyramid with a circular base. Thus the foot of the altitude of a right circular cone is the center of the circular base. If we let r be the radius and h the altitude, the volume is $\pi r^2 h/3$. The lateral surface area is the area of the curved surface. We define the slant height, l, of a right circular cone as the distance from the vertex, which is sometimes called the **apex**, to the boundary of the circular base. We see in the diagram that the height, radius, and slant height of a cone are related by the Pythagorean Theorem, $h^2 + r^2 = l^2$. (Problems which just read 'cone' usually refer to a right circular cone.)

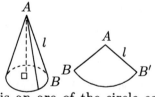

As we did with the right circular cylinder, we can 'unroll' the curved surface of the cone. We do this by cutting along a slant height, like AB. Since the distance from A to any point on the boundary of the circular base is constant (equal to the slant height, l), the curve BB' is an arc of the circle centered at A with radius l. The length of this arc is the circumference of the base of the cone, or $2\pi r$. Make sure you understand this. If you don't, go to an ice cream store, get an ice cream cone, and instead of ripping off the paper around the cone, cut it along a slant height and unroll it.

Using this "unrolling" approach, we can prove that the lateral surface area of a cone is $\pi r l$.

EXAMPLE 18-11   Find the total surface area of a right circular cone with radius 5 and altitude 12.

Solution: The area of the base is $5^2\pi = 25\pi$. To get the area of the curved surface, we must find the slant height of the cone. Drawing an altitude and radius of a cone, we form a right triangle whose hypotenuse is the slant height. Thus the slant height has length $\sqrt{5^2 + 12^2} = 13$, and the total surface area is $25\pi + \pi(5)(13) = \mathbf{90\pi}$.

EXERCISE 18-9   Prove that the lateral surface area of a cone with radius r and slant height l is πrl. (Hint: 'Unroll' the curved surface and find the area of the resulting sector.)

EXERCISE 18-10   Find the volume of a cone whose vertex is the center of a sphere of radius 5 and whose base is the intersection of this sphere with a plane 3 units away from the sphere's center.

18.6   Polyhedra

A **polyhedron** is a solid figure whose faces are planar polygons. Parallelepipeds, prisms, and pyramids are all examples of polyhedra. A **regular polyhedron** is a polyhedron whose faces are all congruent regular polygons. The table provides information about the only five regular polyhedra. We will prove in Volume 2 that these are the only regular polyhedra.

Name	Shape of Faces	Number of Faces	Number of Vertices	Number of Edges
Tetrahedron	triangles	4	4	6
Hexahedron	squares	6	8	12
Octahedron	triangles	8	6	12
Dodecahedron	pentagons	12	20	30
Icosahedron	triangles	20	12	30

Looking over these numbers of faces, vertices, and edges, we note that for each of these special polyhedra, the number of edges is 2 less than the sum of the number of faces and the number of vertices. This is no accident. In fact, for *any* polyhedron, regular or not, it is true that

$$(\# \text{ vertices}) + (\# \text{ faces}) - (\# \text{ edges}) = 2.$$

Although the five polyhedra shown above are the only regular polyhedra, they are certainly not the only polyhedra whose faces are regular polygons. Look at a soccer ball; the hexagons and pentagons which make up the surface are all regular polygons.

EXAMPLE 18-12 Find the volume of a regular tetrahedron with side length 1.

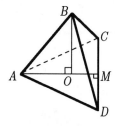

Solution: Note that a tetrahedron is just a special regular pyramid with a triangular base. Thus, to find the volume of the tetrahedron, we must find the area of its base and find its altitude. Its base is an equilateral triangle with side length 1, so it has area $1^2\sqrt{3}/4 = \sqrt{3}/4$. We know that the foot of the altitude is the center of the base (why?), and by connecting this point to a vertex of the base, we form a right triangle as in $\triangle ABO$. Since $\triangle ACD$ is equilateral, AM is a median and an altitude, and O, the center of the triangle, is the centroid; thus $AO = \frac{2}{3}AM$. Since $\triangle AMD$ is a 30°-60°-90° triangle, we have $AM = \frac{\sqrt{3}}{2}AD = \sqrt{3}/2$, and

$$AO = \frac{2}{3}AM = \frac{\sqrt{3}}{3}.$$

From the Pythagorean Theorem, we can then find BO:

$$BO = \sqrt{AB^2 - AO^2} = \sqrt{1 - \frac{1}{3}} = \sqrt{\frac{2}{3}} = \frac{\sqrt{6}}{3}.$$

Thus the volume of a regular tetrahedron with side length 1 is

$$V = \frac{([ACD])(BO)}{3} = \frac{1}{3}\left(\frac{\sqrt{3}}{4}\right)\left(\frac{\sqrt{6}}{3}\right) = \frac{\sqrt{2}}{12}.$$

EXAMPLE 18-13 Find the volume of a regular octahedron with side length 1.

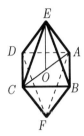

Solution: We can split an octahedron into two pyramids with base *ABCD* as shown. We then find the volume of one of the pyramids and multiply by 2 to get the desired volume. The base of the pyramid is square *ABCD*, which has area 1. To find the height, we once again form a right triangle, namely $\triangle EOA$. The segment *OA* is one-half a diagonal of *ABCD* and hence has length $\sqrt{2}/2$. From the Pythagorean Theorem we find that

$$EO = \sqrt{1^2 - \left(\frac{\sqrt{2}}{2}\right)^2} = \sqrt{\frac{1}{2}} = \frac{\sqrt{2}}{2}.$$

Note that *EO* has the same length as half the diagonal of the base. This suggests that there may be an easier way to find *EO*. Indeed, *EO* is half the diagonal of square *EAFC*, and as such, has length $\sqrt{2}/2$. As we've said before, solving three dimensional problems is best done by splitting the problem into two dimensional problems. Cleverly choosing the two dimensional figure to use (like square *EAFC* rather than triangle *EAO*) can save you a lot of work.

Finally, the volume of the octahedron is twice the volume of the pyramid, or

$$V = 2\left(\frac{([ABCD])(EO)}{3}\right) = \frac{2}{3}(1)\left(\frac{\sqrt{2}}{2}\right) = \frac{\sqrt{2}}{3}.$$

Challenge: *EAFC* is clearly a rhombus, but how would you prove it is a square?

18.7   How to Solve 3D Problems

Problems involving the volume and surface area of simple figures are quickly solved by the methods discussed in the previous section. To find the volume or surface area of more complicated figures, try to dissect the figure into pieces whose area or volume you can find. This is how we found the volume of an octahedron, and how we in general solve all surface area problems. In very extreme cases, we can find the volume of an object by finding a larger object of which it is a part and subtracting those parts of the larger object which are not parts of the desired object. These problems are usually fairly obvious, and we are almost always given the 'larger object' as part of the problem.

To solve other problems in three dimensions, such as finding specific lengths, areas, or angles, we will repeat what we have said many, many times. Three dimensional problems of this nature are disguised two-dimensional problems. If looking for a length, consider a particular plane (or triangle) containing that length. The same goes for angles and areas. Since three dimensional problems are very much like two dimensional ones, the same rules apply to adding extra lines. Perpendicular lines are very useful, because right triangles are at the heart of many solutions.

By working on the problems at the end of this chapter, you will come to master the technique of applying the principles of two dimensional geometry to three dimensional problems.

Problems to Solve for Chapter 18

303. The sum of the lengths of all the edges of a cube is 144 inches. What is the number of inches in the length of a diagonal of the cube? (MATHCOUNTS 1989)

304. A 5 inch by 8 inch rectangular sheet of paper can be rolled up to form either of two right circular cylinders, a cylinder with a height of 8 inches or a cylinder with a height of 5 inches. What is the ratio of the volume of the 8 inch tall cylinder to the volume of the 5 inch tall cylinder? (MATHCOUNTS 1989)

305. How many triangular faces does a pyramid with 10 edges have? (MATHCOUNTS 1992)

306. Regular hexagon $JKLMNO$ intersects the edges of a cube at the midpoints of the cube's edges. What is the ratio of the area of the hexagon to the total surface area of the cube? (MAΘ 1990)

307. The surface area of a cube is numerically equal to twice its volume. Find the length of a diagonal of the cube. (MATHCOUNTS 1988)

308. Find the radius of a right circular cone if its volume is 1.5 times its lateral surface area and its radius is half its slant height. (MAΘ 1990)

309. A cube is inscribed in a sphere. Find the ratio of the surface area of the sphere to the surface area of the cube. (MAΘ 1992)

310. If h is the height of a rectangular solid room and the areas of two adjacent walls are a and b, what is the area of the floor in terms of a, b, and h? (MATHCOUNTS 1990)

311. Liquid X does not mix with water. Unless obstructed, it spreads out on the surface of water to form a circular film 0.1 cm thick. A rectangular box measuring 6 cm by 3 cm by 12 cm is filled with liquid X. Its contents are poured onto a large body of water. What will be the radius, in centimeters, of the resulting circular film? (AHSME 1991)

312. The radius of a cylindrical box is 8 inches and the height is 3 inches. Find the number of inches that may be added to either the radius or the height to give the same non-zero increase in volume. (AHSME 1951)

313. A paper cone, when cut along its slant height and opened out forms a semicircle of radius 10. What is the altitude of the original cone? (MAΘ 1987)

314. Four of the eight vertices of a cube are vertices of a regular tetrahedron. Find the ratio of the surface area of the cube to the surface area of the tetrahedron. (AHSME 1980)

315. Consider the unit cube (a cube with unit side length) $ABCDEFGH$. Let X be the center of the face $ABCD$. Find FX. (MAΘ 1992)

316. A wooden cube with edge length n units (where n is an integer > 2) is painted black all over. By slices parallel to its faces, the cube is cut into n^3 smaller cubes each of unit edge length. If the number of smaller cubes with just one face painted black is equal to the number of smaller cubes completely free of paint, what is n? (AHSME 1985)

 317. In the adjoining figure, a wooden cube has edges of length 3 meters. Square holes of side one meter, centered in each face, are cut through to the opposite face. The edges of the holes are parallel to the edges of the cube. Find the entire surface area, including the inside. (AHSME 1982)

318. A cube of side 3 inches has a cube of side 1 inch cut from each corner. A cube of side 2 inches is then inserted in each corner. What is the number of square inches in the surface area of the resulting solid? (MATHCOUNTS 1991)

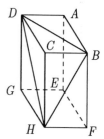

319. In the adjoining figure of a rectangular solid, $\angle DHG = 45°$ and $\angle FHB = 60°$. Find the cosine of $\angle BHD$. (AHSME 1982)

320. A truncated octahedron is a geometric solid with 14 faces (6 congruent squares and 8 congruent hexagons). In this particular solid, 2 hexagons and 1 square meet to form each corner. How many corners does the solid have? (MATHCOUNTS 1984)

321. What is the volume of a regular octahedron whose vertices are the centers of the faces of a cube whose edge has length 6? (MATHCOUNTS 1985)

322. A ball of radius R is tangent to the floor and one wall of the room. Find, in terms of R, the radius of the largest sphere that can be rolled through the space between the ball, the wall, and the floor. (MAΘ 1992)

323. The water tank in the diagram is in the shape of an inverted right circular cone. The radius of its base is 16 feet, and its height is 96 feet. What is the height, in feet, of the water in the tank if the amount of water is 25% of the tank's capacity? (MATHCOUNTS 1992)

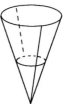

324. A truncated icosahedron is a polyhedron which has 32 faces, 60 vertices, and 90 edges. Some of the faces are pentagons and the others are hexagons. Exactly two hexagons and a pentagon meet to form each vertex of the polyhedron. How many of the faces of this solid are hexagons? (MATHCOUNTS 1988)

325. Find the distance from vertex B to face ACD if $ABCD$ is a regular tetrahedron with side length 6.

326. Nine congruent spheres are packed inside a unit cube in such a way that one of them has its center at the center of the cube and each of the others is tangent to the center sphere and to three faces of the cube. What is the radius of each sphere? (AHSME 1990)

327. A right circular cone with radius 6 and height 6 is cut by a plane parallel to base and 2 units away from the base. What is the volume of the cone contained between the plane and the base?

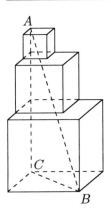

328. Three cubes are stacked as shown. If the cubes have edge lengths 1, 2, and 3, what is the length of the portion of segment AB that is contained in the center cube? (MATHCOUNTS 1991)

Chapter 19

Shifts, Turns, Flips, Stretches, and Squeezes

When we perform a **geometric transformation** of a figure, we use some set of rules to move each point to a new point. There are many ways to do this, from simply shifting or turning the figure as if it were a rigid frame to distorting it crazily. The figure you get out is called the **image** of the original figure, and we say that we **map** the original figure to its image via the transformation. Thus, transformations are sometimes called **mappings**.

Transformational geometry is a very beautiful and elegant subject which has many applications in other fields of science such as physics and optics.

19.1 Translation

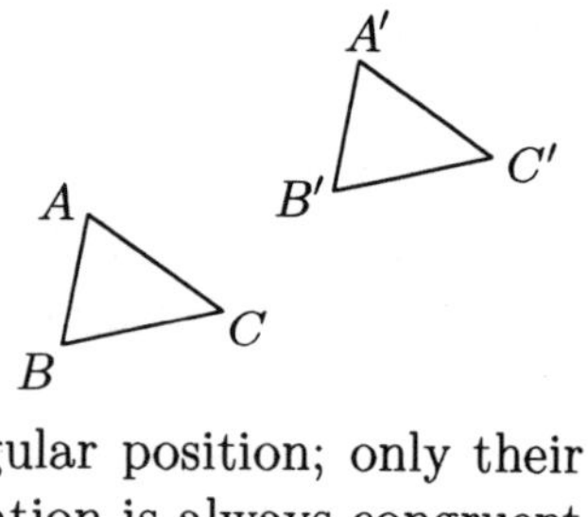

Slide a pen a small distance without changing the direction the pen is pointing. The pen has just undergone a **translation**. When a figure is translated, it is just slid from one position to another without any distortion or rotation. In the figure, the triangle ABC is translated upwards and to the right to form $\triangle A'B'C'$. Notice that the two triangles are exactly the same in size and in angular position; only their locations differ. This is always true: the image of a translation is always congruent to the original figure.

How would we describe a translation using coordinates? Sliding a figure to the right or left corresponds to increasing or decreasing its x-coordinate. Similarly, moving up or down is increasing or decreasing the y-coordinate. Thus, to translate a figure a units to the right and b units up, we would apply the mapping $x' = x + a$ and $y' = y + b$, where (x', y') are the coordinates of the new figure, the image. We could also 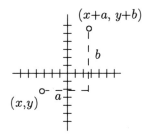 write this as $(x', y') = (x+a, y+b)$ or $(x, y) \to (x+a, y+b)$; in Cartesian coordinates, all are equivalent to the desired translation.

EXAMPLE 19-1   What translation would move a point 3 units left and 5 units down?

Solution: To move 3 units left, we subtract 3 from the x-coordinate, and to move 5 units down, subtract 5 from the y-coordinate. Thus, the mapping is $(x', y') = (x - 3, y - 5)$.

EXERCISE 19-1   What translation maps the point $(3, 4)$ to the point $(5, -3)$?

EXERCISE 19-2   A **fixed point** of a transformation is a point whose image is the same as itself. Which translations have fixed points?

19.2   Rotation

Stand up and turn 180°. You can look at this as you turning or as you standing still and the universe turning around you! The strange-seeming second interpretation brings us to **rotations**. In a rotation, one point, the **center of rotation**, is fixed and everything else rotates about it. Since we can turn in two directions, we generally have to specify a direction, clockwise or counterclockwise, as well as an angle.

Since a rotation just spins everything about a point, the distance of any point from the center of rotation is the same as the distance from the point's image to the center. The **angle of rotation** is the angle formed by any point (as B at right), the center of rotation (O), and the point's image (B'). Thus, the image of B upon rotation by angle θ about point O is found by locating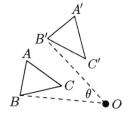

the point B' such that $OB = OB'$ and $\angle BOB' = \theta$. In doing any rotation, make sure you are rotating in the proper direction if a direction is specified.

Like translations, rotations map figures to congruent figures; however, unlike translations, a rotation changes the orientation of the figure in the plane. In particular, we know that $AB = A'B'$ and $OA = OA'$. Many rotation problems are solved by using these distance preserving qualities of rotation and the definition of angle of rotation (the angle formed by connecting the center to any point and its image).

EXAMPLE 19-2   Which of the following points could possibly be the rotation of $(5, 3)$ about $(2, 7)$: $(2, 5)$, $(5, 8)$, or $(7, 7)$?

Solution: Since a rotation preserves the distance from a point to the center and $(5, 3)$ is 5 units from $(2, 7)$, we look for a point in our list which is 5 units from the center $(2, 7)$. The point $(\mathbf{7, 7})$ is the only point for which this is true.

EXAMPLE 19-3   How many nonnegative clockwise rotations of less than 360° about the center of a regular pentagon map the pentagon to itself? (MATHCOUNTS 1984)

Solution: By "maps the pentagon to itself" we mean that after the rotation, the pentagon is unchanged. A rotation of 0° always leaves everything unchanged, so this is one answer. To find the others, we note that if the pentagon $ABCDE$ is rotated onto itself, the vertex A must be rotated onto one of the vertices. To rotate A onto B, the angle of rotation must be $\angle BOA$. To find $\angle BOA$, just observe that the five angles formed by connecting O to the vertices are all congruent and sum to 360°. Thus, each is $360/5 = 72°$. Hence, a rotation of 72° rotates A onto B. A rotation of 144° rotates A onto C. (Why?) Finally, rotations of 216° and 288° map A to D and E respectively. Thus there are **5** rotations of the type desired.

EXERCISE 19-3   Show that if a line l is rotated about any point O through an angle with measure α to a new line l', then lines l and l' intersect in an angle with measure α. (Remember to use the facts that rotations preserve distances and map lines to lines!) (Mandelbrot #3)

EXERCISE 19-4   If $ABCDEF$ is a regular hexagon, what rotation about D maps B to F?

Rotations, like translations, can be easily represented in coordinates. All we have to do is adopt a polar coordinate system centered at the center of rotation; then a point (r, θ) can be rotated by α by just adding the new angle to the old, to get $(r, \theta + \alpha)$.

19.3   Reflection

Look in a mirror. You see a **reflection**. Everything you see in the mirror is exactly like what exists in reality; if you could be that person in the mirror, you would find that everything in your mirrored realm is exactly congruent in size and shape to its image in the real world. Here, we will concentrate on the simpler reflections of planar figures rather than solid figures as in the mirror example.

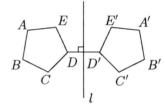

When working in two dimensions, a line is the equivalent of a mirror. A reflection of a planar figure in a line is equivalent to flipping the figure over the line. When we reflect a figure in a line, we map every point on that figure to a point which is symmetric to the original point with respect to the line. By **symmetric**, we mean that if we folded the plane over using the line as a fold, the point and its image would coincide. Thus, any point and its image are the same distance from the line in which the point is reflected, and this line is perpendicular to the segment connecting a point and its image. All of this is exhibited in the figure, where the pentagon $ABCDE$ is reflected in line l to form congruent pentagon $A'B'C'D'E'$. Drawing DD', we see that this segment is perpendicular to l and that l splits DD' into two equal segments. If you were to fold this page over along line l, you would find that each point would coincide with its image. These pentagons are said to be symmetric with respect to l. If the image of reflection of a figure in a line is the figure itself, the line is a **line of symmetry** of that figure. For example, the diameter of a circle is a line of symmetry of the circle.

We've seen reflection in a plane (the introductory mirror example) and in a line. We can also have reflection in a point. To reflect a point A in another point O, we draw the line through E and O. The image, E', of E upon reflection through O is the point on line EO on the opposite side of O such that $EO = E'O$. As with reflections in a line, E' is said to be symmetric to E with respect to O. If the image of the reflection of a figure about a point is that figure itself, then the point is a **point of symmetry** of the figure.

EXERCISE 19-5 Show that reflection through a point in the plane is the same as a 180° rotation about the same point. Draw some pictures to back up your claim.

EXERCISE 19-6 Draw a figure with a line of symmetry but no point of symmetry. Draw a figure with a point of symmetry. Can a figure have a point of symmetry, but no line of symmetry?

   Useful properties for solving problems involving reflection are the facts that a point and its image are equidistant from the line of reflection, and that this line is perpendicular to the segment connecting any point and its reflection. Also, any segment upon reflection is equal in length to its image. The proof of this fact is left as an exercise.

EXAMPLE 19-4 Find the image of reflecting the point $(4, 3)$ in the point $(2, 0)$.

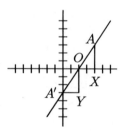

   Solution: In the diagram, we draw the line through $A(4, 3)$ and $O(2, 0)$. Using horizontal and vertical lines, we form right triangles AXO and OYA'. Thus, $XO \parallel YA'$, and $\angle YA'O = \angle XOA$. Since $A'O = OA$, we have $\triangle AXO \cong \triangle OYA'$. Thus, since O is 2 units to the left of and 3 units below point A, point A' is 2 units to the left of and 3 units below point O. (Make sure you see this.) Hence, $A' = (2 - 2, 0 - 3) = (\mathbf{0}, \mathbf{-3})$.

EXAMPLE 19-5   If line l intersects line m at an angle α, show that line l', the reflection of l in m, also intersects m at an angle α.

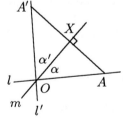

   Proof: First, we show that the intersection point of l and l' is on m. Consider the intersection point, O, of l and m. The reflection of O in m is itself (why?), so O is also on l'. To show that the angles between l and m and l' and m are the same, we consider point A on l and its image A' on l'. Connecting these points and denoting the intersection of AA' and m as X, we form right triangles $A'XO$ and AXO. Since A' is the image of A in m, we have $A'X = AX$, and by Leg-Leg the two right triangles are congruent. Thus, $\angle A'OX = \angle AOX = \alpha$.

EXERCISE 19-7   How many lines of symmetry does a regular hexagon have?

19.4   Distortion

Draw a picture with a marker on a piece of cellophane. Now pull on the cellophane from either side, stretching the picture. You'll notice that while the figure gets wider, it does not get shorter or taller. This is a **distortion**. In a distortion, one dimension of a figure is multiplied by some factor, while the other dimension(s) remain the same. Distortions are equivalent to squishing or stretching figures.

As an example of distortion, consider isosceles triangle ABC. By distorting the vertical scale of the diagram (i.e. by squishing down or stretching up), we can make the triangle taller or shorter. Thus, we can distort $\triangle ABC$ into $\triangle ABC'$ or $\triangle ABC''$. Most notably, there is some distortion that maps the isosceles triangle into an equilateral triangle.

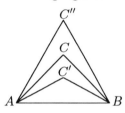

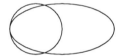
In Volume 2 of this series, we will have to tangle with a type of curve called an **ellipse**. As shown in the figure, an ellipse is really just a circle distorted along some direction.

Distortions are different from all the other transformations in this chapter in that they do not "preserve angles." With translations, rotations, reflections, and dilations (next section), if three points form an angle θ before the transformation, their images will form the same angle! With distortions this is not the case, as is shown by the fact that an isosceles triangle, with only two equal angles, can be distorted into an equilateral triangle, with three. Angles are not preserved, and a figure is not similar to its image. That's why we call them *distortions*; the shape of a figure is not the same after the transformation.

19.5   Dilation

When we look at an object in a magnifying glass, we perform a **dilation**. This is also sometimes called a **similitude**, which means that the figure is made bigger or smaller by some factor. To perform a dilation, we must have a fixed point, or **center**. Letting the center be O, the image of a point A upon dilation with factor

k about point O is the point A' on the ray $\overrightarrow{OA}$ such that $OA' = k(OA)$. For example, in the figure quadrilateral $ABCD$ is dilated with center O and the image is $A'B'C'D'$.

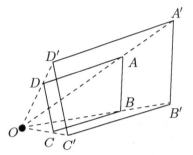

A figure is similar (though not congruent unless the dilation factor is 1!) to its image upon dilation, and is oriented the same way in the plane. Thus, $ABCD \sim A'B'C'D'$, and the distances from any two corresponding points of the quadrilaterals to O have a fixed ratio. For example, $OA/OA' = OB/OB' = OC/OC' = OD/OD'$. Conversely, given any two similar figures which are oriented in the same way in the plane, one is the image of the other under some dilation. Such figures are called **homothetic**. These figures are special because if we draw lines through corresponding parts of the two figures, *all these lines will pass through the center of dilation.* This is also demonstrated in the figure. (Food for thought: where do congruent figures oriented in the same direction fit in here? Where is the proposed center of dilation?)

Most problems involving dilation and homothecy can be solved by using the principles of similarity. The ratio of corresponding sides of a figure and its image have ratio equal to the ratio of dilation. Because a figure is similar to its image under dilation, the ratio of the areas of the figure and its image is the square of the dilation ratio. As you will see, these are the principles that, together with basic similarity relations, are used to solve dilation problems.

EXAMPLE 19-6 Square $ABCD$ with $AB = 4$ is dilated about its center with ratio 2 to form $A'B'C'D'$. Find $A'C$.

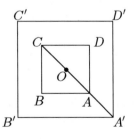

Solution: The diagonal AC of the square passes through the center of dilation, O. Thus, if we extend AC past A, it will pass through A', since O, A, and A' are collinear. Hence, $A'C$ passes through O, so $A'C = A'O + OC$. Since $A'B'C'D'$ is the image of $ABCD$ under a dilation with center O and ratio 2, we have $OA' = 2OA$. Thus,

$$A'C = 2OA + OC = 2\left(\frac{4\sqrt{2}}{2}\right) + \frac{4\sqrt{2}}{2} = \mathbf{6\sqrt{2}}.$$

EXAMPLE 19-7 Show that if segment AB is dilated about any center with ratio 2, then the image is twice as long as AB.

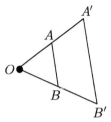

Proof: Let $A'B'$ be the image and O be the center. It is important to note that by ratio of dilation, we refer by definition to the ratio OA'/OA, not $A'B'/AB$. While in general we assume these ratios are equal, we are asked in this problem to prove that they're equal. In the figure we have $OA/OA' = OB/OB'$ and $\angle AOB = \angle A'OB'$. Thus by SAS Similarity we have $\triangle AOB \sim \triangle A'OB'$, so $A'B' = 2AB$. (Note that by using this we can show that $\angle OAB = \angle OA'B'$, and hence $A'B' \parallel AB$.)

19.6   The More Things Change...

Although transformations are defined in terms of what they change, some of their most important features are the things they leave the same. For example, a translation preserves collinearity (if three points lie on a line before, they will lie on a line after), area (area after equals area before), shape (figure similar to its image), angles, and so on. Rotations and reflections preserve almost as much—the only change is the way the figure is oriented on the plane.

Distortions and dilations, however, preserve different things. Both do preserve lines and collinearity, but neither preserves area; the area of a figure after the transformation is not the same as it was before. Dilations preserve angles, and thus shape, but distortions don't; a figure is actually distorted by the transformation. Under a distortion, circles don't stay circles, equilateral triangles don't stay equilateral (though they do stay triangles, since lines go to lines), and so on.

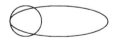

Although distortions do not preserve area, they do have simple behavior with respect to area. Any area is multiplied by the same factor k with which the figure is distorted. For example, suppose the circle in the figure has area 2, and is stretched by a factor of 3 to get the thin ellipse. The area of the ellipse must then be $2(3) = 6$. This proportionality means that distortions preserve *ratios of areas*: if two figures have areas a and b before the transformation, they will have areas ka and kb after, and the ratio of their areas, a/b before and $ka/kb = a/b$ after, stays the same.

EXAMPLE 19-8   Prove that any area is multiplied by the stretching factor k under a distortion.

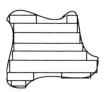

   Solution: We can think of the area of a figure as the sum of the areas of tiny parallel rectangles which cover it, as in the figure. If we line these rectangles up with the distortion, each will be stretched by a factor k in one direction, and stay the same in the other, so the area of each will be multiplied by k. Thus the area of the entire figure should be multiplied by k.

EXERCISE 19-8   Because it calls on these imaginary rectangles, the prior proof is not completely rigorous. For triangles and rectangles, you should be able to come up with a more sturdy proof which rests only on basic geometry. Do so.

19.7   Transformation Proofs

Throughout this chapter, we have asserted countless properties of transformations which, while seemingly obvious, should be rigorously proven. For example, we should prove that the image of a segment upon rotation, reflection, or translation is an equal-length segment. In the examples below, we show how to approach these proofs. After reading these, try your newly learned techniques on the exercises.

EXAMPLE 19-9   Show that if any three points are collinear, then the images of these points when rotated about any point are also collinear.

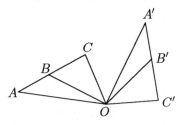

   Proof: To show that the image points A', B', and C' are collinear, all we have to show is that $\angle OB'A' + \angle OB'C' = \pi$. (Why?) Since rotations preserve angles, $\angle A'OB' = \angle AOB$. Since rotations preserve distances, we have $A'O = AO$ and $B'O = BO$. Thus by SAS we have $\triangle A'B'O \cong \triangle ABO$. In exactly the same way, we have $\triangle C'B'O \cong \triangle CBO$. Using corresponding angles from these congruent triangles we then have $\angle OB'A' + \angle OB'C' = \angle OBA + \angle OBC = \pi$, and the image points are collinear.

EXAMPLE 19-10 Assuming that the reflection of a segment is a segment of equal length, show that the reflection of a circle is a circle of the same radius.

Proof: Let the original center be O, the radius of the circle be r, and the reflection of O be O'. First we will show that the image of every point on the original circle is a distance r from O'. If the point P is on the original circle, then $OP = r$. The image of OP is $O'P'$, where P' is the image of P, so $O'P' = r$ because lengths are preserved. Thus the image P' of a point P on the original circle is on a circle of radius r with center O'.

Are we done? No. For all we know at this point, the image of a circle could be a *semicircle*. (Do you see why?) We still need to show that each point which is r from O' is, in fact, on the image. For any point P' such that $O'P' = r$, we can form the image P of P' under the reflection. Since P is the image of P', P' is the image of P (why?), and moreover $OP = r = O'P'$, since distances are preserved. Thus any point which is on the desired circle is the image of a point on the original circle. Since we have every point which is r away from O', and have no other points, the image is a circle of radius r.

Go through these logical contortions again to make sure you follow all the ins and outs. To make transformation proofs rigorous, we need to be pretty careful.

EXERCISE 19-9 Show that any segment is equal in length to its image upon reflection (that "reflections preserve distances").

Problems to Solve for Chapter 19

329. Prove that given any two points A and A', there is a point O such that A' is the image of A under reflection through O.

330. Let $y = mx + b$ be the image when the line $x + 3y + 11 = 0$ is reflected across the x-axis. Find the value of $m + b$. (AHSME 1992)

331. Given points $P_0(0,0)$ and $P_1(3,4)$ in the coordinate plane, reflect P_1 into P_0 to get P_2, reflect P_2 into P_1 to get P_3, etc. If $P_4 = (a, b)$, find $a + b$. (MAΘ 1991)

332. Two successive clockwise rotations about the origin of angles x and y ($0 \leq x, y \leq \pi$) result in a reflection through the origin. Find $x + y$. (MAΘ 1992)

333. Prove that if a rotation maps A to C and B to D, then it maps segment AB to segment CD. (Mandelbrot #3)

334. Let $\triangle ABC$ be an isosceles triangle with $AB = AC$, $\angle BAC = \alpha$, and circumcenter O. Prove that there exist rotations about both A and O which carry segment AB to segment AC. (Mandelbrot #3)

335. Let $\triangle ABC$ be as in the prior problem, and suppose points M and N on AB and AC respectively are such that $BM = AN$. Compute the angle of rotation (in terms of α) needed to map segment AB to AC with center O. Show that $\angle MON$ equals this angle. (Mandelbrot #3)

336. Find the reflection of the point $(2, 2)$ in the line $x + 2y = 4$.

337. The center of a circle has coordinates $(6, -5)$. The circle is reflected about the line $y = x$. What are the x-y coordinates of the center of the image circle? (MATHCOUNTS 1992)

338. Which figure does not have point symmetry: equilateral triangle, square, or regular hexagon? (MATHCOUNTS 1984)

339. If $ABCDE$ is a regular pentagon, find the smallest rotation about E which maps A to D. (MATHCOUNTS 1984)

340. The image of quadrilateral $ABCD$ when reflected over line l is $A'B'C'D'$. E is the point of intersection of the lines $\overleftrightarrow{AB}$ and $\overleftrightarrow{A'B'}$. If $AA' = 10$ and $A'E = 13$, find the number of square units in the area of $\triangle AEA'$. (MATHCOUNTS 1984)

341. If the graph of the equation $y = 3x + 2$ is reflected with respect to the y-axis, what is the equation of the resulting graph? (MATHCOUNTS 1989)

342. The points $Q(9, 14)$ and $R(a, b)$ are symmetric with respect to the point $P(5, 3)$. What are the coordinates of point R? (MATHCOUNTS 1989)

Chapter 20

A Potpourri of Geometry

Problems to Solve for Chapter 20

343. Congruent circles O and P are tangent, and AP is tangent to circle O as shown. If $AP = 15$, what is the radius of circle P? (MATHCOUNTS 1989)

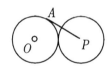

344. In the diagram, a square is built on side AC of right triangle ABC. If $AB = 4$ and $BC = 6$, find the area of the square. (Mandelbrot #3)

345. Triangle ABC is inscribed in a circle. The measure of the non-overlapping minor arcs AB, BC, and CA are, respectively, $x + 40°$, $2x + 20°$, and $2x - 20°$. Find x.

346. The diagram shows a triangle inscribed in a circle of radius 4. Given that $BA \perp AC$ and $\angle ABC = 30°$, find the area of $\triangle ABC$. (MAΘ 1991)

347. A triangle has vertices with coordinates $A(0, 15)$, $B(0, 0)$, and $C(10, 0)$. Find the coordinates of point D on AC so that the area of triangle ABD is equal to the area of triangle DBC. (MATHCOUNTS 1990)

348. Find the area of $BCDE$ if $AC = 20$, $CD = 12$, and $BE = 3$. (MATHCOUNTS 1986)

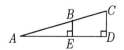

349. What are the possible numbers of common external tangents two congruent non-concentric circles in the same plane can have? (AHSME 1952)

350. Quadrilateral $BDEF$ is a rhombus with vertices on $\triangle ABC$. Given $AB = 10$ and $BC = 15$, find DE. (MATHCOUNTS 1992)

351. Let $ABCD$ be an isosceles trapezoid such that $AB \parallel CD$, $AB = 8$, $CD = 4$, and $AC \perp BD$. Find the area of $ABCD$. (M&IQ 1992)

352. Find the area of a semicircle inscribed in $\triangle ABC$ as in the diagram, where $AB = AC = 25$ and $BC = 40$. (Mandelbrot #1)

353. A band is wrapped tightly around two pulleys whose centers are 6 feet apart. The radii of the pulleys are 4 feet and 1 foot. How many feet long is the band? (MAΘ 1992)

354. A triangle and a trapezoid are equal in area. They also have the same altitude. If the base of the triangle is 18 inches, then find the median of the trapezoid. (AHSME 1953)

355. $\triangle ABC$ is inscribed in circle O with $AB = 4$, $BC = 8$, and $AC = 9$. Segment BY bisects arc AC. Find DC. (MAΘ 1990)

356. In pentagon $ABCDE$, the perpendicular bisector of AB passes through the vertex D and point P on AB. The pentagon is symmetric with respect to DP and $BC \parallel AE$. If $BC = 4$, $AB = 16$, and $DP = 7$, find the area of pentagon $ABCDE$. (MATHCOUNTS 1984)

357. In the adjoining figure TP and RQ are parallel tangents to a circle of radius r, with T and R the points of tangency. PSQ is a third tangent with S as point of tangency. If $TP = 4$ and $RQ = 9$ then find r. (AHSME 1974)

358. A square $ABCD$ has line segments drawn from vertex B to the midpoints N and M of sides AD and DC respectively. Find the ratio of the perimeter of quadrilateral $BMDN$ to the perimeter of square $ABCD$. (MATHCOUNTS 1989)

359. $ABCD$ is a rectangle and $DE = DC$. Given $AD = 5$ and $BE = 3$, find DE. (MATHCOUNTS 1992)

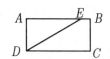

360. Find the ratio of the perimeter of an equilateral triangle having an altitude equal to the radius of a circle to the perimeter of an equilateral triangle inscribed in the circle. (AHSME 1952)

361. In $\triangle ABC$, $\angle ACB$ is a right angle and $DE \parallel CB$. If $AE = 3$ and $EB = 7$, find the ratio of the area of $\triangle ADE$ to the area of the trapezoid $BCDE$. (MAΘ 1990)

362. An equilateral triangle is circumscribed about a circle with radius 9. Find the area of the triangle.

363. A corner of a rectangular piece of paper of width 8 inches is folded over so that it coincides with point C on the opposite side. If $BC = 5$ inches, find the length in inches of fold l. (MATHCOUNTS 1991)

364. In a right triangle with sides a and b, and hypotenuse c, the altitude drawn to the hypotenuse is x. Prove that

$$\frac{1}{x^2} = \frac{1}{a^2} + \frac{1}{b^2}.$$

(AHSME 1956)

365. A square with side 6 inches is shown. If P is a point such that the segments PA, PB, and PC are equal in length, and segment PC is perpendicular to segment ED, what is the area in square inches of triangle APB? (MATHCOUNTS 1991)

366. Show that the segment from a point, P, outside circle O to the center of the circle bisects the angle formed by the two tangents from P to circle O.

367. $ABCD$ is a square and $\triangle DCE$ is an equilateral triangle. Given $FE = 1$ and $FE \parallel AD$, find DC. (MATHCOUNTS 1992)

368. In a 5 by 12 rectangle, one of the diagonals is drawn and then circles are inscribed in both right triangles formed. Find the distance between the centers of the two circles. (MAΘ 1987)

369. In $\triangle ABC$, $DE \parallel BC$, $\angle B = 60°$, $AG \perp BC$, $\angle AED = 45°$, $AD = 6$, and $AB = 10$. What is the area of $FECG$? (MAΘ 1990)

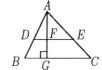

370. Find the length of the longest diagonal of a regular dodecagon of side length 1. (Mandelbrot #3)

371. The segments from AB to F, from BC to D, and from CA to E are perpendicular bisectors of AB, BC, and AC. If the perimeter of $\triangle ABC$ is 35 and the radius of the circle is 8, find the area of the hexagon $AECDBF$. (Mandelbrot #1)

372. Three sides of a quadrilateral have lengths 1, 2, and 5. The fourth side is an integer, x. What is the sum of all the possible values of x?

373. In the figure, AB, BC, DC, and AD are tangent to the circle. If $AR = 3$, $\angle D = 90°$, and arc RST measures $210°$, find the area of the circle. (MAΘ 1990)

374. Two circles with equal radii are drawn such that each circle passes through the center of the other. If the distance between the centers of the two circles is 6, find the area of the region which is common to both circles.

375. Given a circle O whose diameter is 12 inches long, another circle is inscribed in a quarter circle of circle O as shown in the diagram. Find the radius of the smaller circle. (MATHCOUNTS 1988)

376. A man is 6 miles east and 5 miles south of his home. He is also 3 miles north of a river which is 8 miles south of his home. What is the least number of miles he may travel if he must fetch water from the river, then return home? (MAΘ 1992)

377. In $\triangle ABC$, CD is the altitude to AB and AE is the altitude to BC. If the lengths of AB, CD, and AE are known, determine DB in terms of these lengths in each of the following cases. (AHSME 1962)

     i. Both angles A and B are acute.

     ii. Angle A or angle B is obtuse.

     iii. Angle A is right.

     iv. Angle B is right.

378. In the diagram, chords AB and CD intersect at point E within the circle. If $CE = 12$, $AE = 8$, $AB = 14$, and $AD = 10$, find AX. (MAΘ 1990)

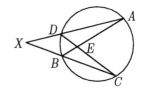

379. The six edges of tetrahedron $ABCD$ measure 7, 13, 18, 27, 36, and 41 units. If the length of edge AB is 41, then find the length of edge CD. (AHSME 1988)

380. Circle O of radius 20 is inscribed in equilateral triangle ABC. Circle P is tangent to circle O and segments AB and AC. Find the radius of circle P. (MATHCOUNTS 1986)

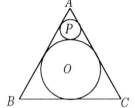

381. A hexagon is inscribed in a circle of radius r. Find r if two sides of the hexagon are 7 units long, while the other four sides are 20 units long. (USAMTS #1)

382. Circle O has diameters AB and CD perpendicular to each other. AM is any chord intersecting CD at P. Which of the following equals $AP \cdot AM$: $AO \cdot OB$, $AO \cdot AB$, $CP \cdot CD$, $CP \cdot PD$, or $CO \cdot OP$? (AHSME 1957)

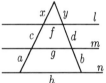

383. In triangle ABC, point D is the midpoint of BC and point E is the midpoint of AC. If $AD = 6$, $BE = 9$, and $AC = 10$ then find the area of triangle ABC. (Mandelbrot #2)

384. Given that $l \parallel m \parallel n$, show that $x/y = c/d = a/b$ and $(g - f)/d = (h - g)/b$, where f, g, and h are the lengths of the parallel segments cut off by the two transversals as shown.

385. Let $ABCD$ be a right-angled trapezoid where $AB \parallel CD$ and $AD \perp AB$, and let M be the midpoint of AD. Let $BC = AB + CD$ and let S be a point on BC, such that $CS = CD$. Prove first that $\angle ASD$ is a right angle then use this to show that $\angle MDS = \angle MSD$. (M&IQ 1992)

386. Let BC of right triangle ABC be the diameter of a circle intersecting hypotenuse AB at D. At D a tangent is drawn cutting leg CA at F. Prove each of the following. (AHSME 1965)

    i. DF bisects CA.

    ii. $DF = FA$.

    iii. $\angle A = \angle BCD$.

    iv. $\angle CFD = 2\angle A$.

387. In the diagram, the semicircles centered at P and Q are tangent to each other and to the large semicircle, and their radii are 6 and 4 respectively. Line LM is tangent to semicircles P and Q. Find

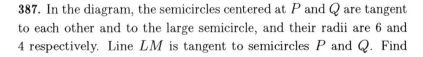

LM. (Mandelbrot #3)

388. In a narrow alley of width w a ladder of length a is placed with its foot
at a point P between the walls. Resting against one wall at Q, a distance k
above the ground, the ladder makes a 45° angle with the ground. Resting
against the other wall at R, a distance h above the ground, the ladder
makes a 75° angle with the ground. Find w in terms of h and k. (AHSME 1982)

389. In the diagram points C and B are centers of the
circles which are tangent to each other. Points E and F
are points of tangency, $BF = 4$, and $DB = 20$. Lines DB
and EF intersect at point A. Find AE. (MAΘ 1990)

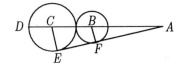

390. Triangle ABC is inscribed in a circle with center O. A circle with center I is inscribed
in $\triangle ABC$. AI is drawn, and extended to intersect the larger circle at D. Prove that D is
the circumcenter of $\triangle CIB$. (AHSME 1966)

391. Inside square $ABCD$, with sides of length 12 inches, segment AE
is drawn, where E is the point on DC which is 5 inches from D. The
perpendicular bisector of AE is drawn and intersects AE, AD, and BC
at points M, P, and Q respectively. Find the ratio of segment PM to
MQ. (AHSME 1972)

392. Suppose we form a triangle by connecting all the points of contact of the sides of a
triangle and its incircle. Prove that the new triangle is acute. (AHSME 1954)

393. The two circles in the diagram are incircles of $\triangle ADB$
and $\triangle ADC$. These incircles are tangent to AD and each to
other at G. (Mandelbrot #1)

    i. If $AB = c$, $AC = b$, and $BC = a$, find the length
of BD in terms of a, b, and c.

    ii. Let the radii of the two circles in the diagram be r
and s. Show that the length of DE is $\sqrt{rs}$.

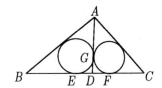

394. In triangle ABC with medians AE, BF, and CD, FH
is parallel and equal in length to AE, and FE extended meets
BH in G. Prove each of the following. (AHSME 1955)

    i. $AEHF$ is a parallelogram.

    ii. $BH = DC$.

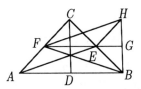

iii. FG is a median of $\triangle BFH$.

iv. $FG = 3AB/4$.

395. A square with side length one is rotated about one vertex by an angle α, where $0° < \alpha < 90°$. If $\cos\alpha = 4/5$ find the area common to both the original square and its rotated image. (Mandelbrot #2)

396. Let $ABCD$ be an isosceles trapezoid with $AB \parallel CD$ and $AD = BC$; let O be the intersection of AC and BD; let $\angle AOB = 60°$; and let M, N, P be the midpoints of AO, DO, BC respectively. Prove that the triangle MNP is equilateral. (M&IQ 1992)

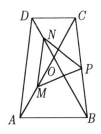

397. A large sphere is on a horizontal field on a sunny day. At a certain time the shadow of the sphere reaches out a distance of 10 m from the point where the sphere touches the ground. At the same instant a meter stick (held vertically with one end on the ground) casts a shadow of length 2 m. What is the radius of the sphere in meters? Assume the sun's rays are parallel and the meter stick is a line segment. (The answer is *not* 5/2!) (AHSME 1983)

398. Given $\triangle ABC$ with $AB \perp BC$, BD is the altitude to AC, AF bisects $\angle BAC$, $AP = 12$, and $PF = 8$. Find $\tan\angle BAF$ and find PD. (MAΘ 1990)

399. Find the length of the median of a trapezoid whose diagonals are perpendicular segments of lengths 7 and 9. (Mandelbrot #3)

400. Triangle ABC in the figure has area 10. Points D, E, and F, all distinct from A, B, and C, are on sides AB, BC, and CA respectively, and $AD = 2$, $DB = 3$. If triangle ABE and quadrilateral $DBEF$ have equal areas, then what is that area? (AHSME 1983)

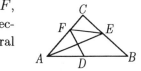

401. In $\triangle ABC$, M is the midpoint of side BC, AN bisects $\angle BAC$, and $BN \perp AN$. If sides AB and AC have lengths 14 and 19, respectively, then find MN. (AHSME 1981)

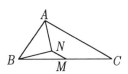

Chapter 21

Functions

21.1   Welcome to the Machine

Consider the line given by the standard form equation

$$-3x + 4y = 12.$$

In our discussion of analytic geometry, we treated this line solely as a geometric figure, defined by the points (x, y) satisfying the equation. However, there is another very productive way to look at such a line. Change the equation into slope-intercept form:

$$y = \tfrac{3}{4}x + 3.$$

Now for each x we put in, running it through the procedure $\tfrac{3}{4}x + 3$ automatically gives back the corresponding y. We can thus think of the line equation as a machine which, for each x we put in, gives us back one, and only one, y.

EXERCISE 21-1   Do all line equations give back one, and only one, y for each x?

The "machine," given by $\tfrac{3}{4}x + 3$, is called a **function**. A function always has one, and only one, output for each input; for this reason, not every expression is a function. For example, $\sqrt{x}$ is not a valid function, since most numbers have two square roots—if we tried to take $\sqrt{1}$, we would not know whether the machine should produce 1 or -1. We can make the square root a function, however, by specifying that we will take only the positive answer.

When we wish to treat an equation as a function, we no longer write it using x and y, which seems to imply a parallelism between the two variables. Instead, we give the machine part a name of its own, like f. To show that f is a function of the variable x, we usually write it as $f(x)$, which is pronounced "f of x." We would thus rewrite our line equation as

$$f(x) = \tfrac{3}{4}x + 3. \tag{21.1}$$

EXERCISE 21-2 Which of the following are functions?

  i. $\sqrt[3]{x}$

  ii. $\sqrt[4]{x}$

  iii. $x/(x+1)$

EXAMPLE 21-1 If $r(x) = x/(x^2 + 1)$, find $r(-1)$, $r(0)$, and $r(2)$.

Solution: We just substitute the input into the machine and turn the crank, so that $r(-1) = (-1)/[(-1)^2 + 1] = -1/2$, $r(0) = 0/1 = 0$, and $r(2) = 2/(2^2 + 1) = 2/5$.

EXERCISE 21-3 For each of the functions $f(x)$ in Exercise 21-2, find $f(64)$.

EXERCISE 21-4 If $f(x) = 2^x$, find $f(4)/f(3)$.

EXERCISE 21-5 Given that $f(x + 1) = x^3 + 6x^2 + x + 3$, find $f(4)$. (MAΘ 1987)

21.2 Graphing Functions

A function is graphed in the same way as a normal equation is. On the horizontal axis we place the **independent variable** (x in this case), which can vary freely. On the vertical is the value of the function. The graph of Equation 21.1 is thus the same as if we were graphing the line equation $y = \tfrac{3}{4}x + 3$, with the difference that the vertical axis is called $f(x)$, rather than y.

A common test to check if a graph represents a function is that if any vertical line passes through more than one point of the curve, the curve does not represent a function. Compare this to the statement that a function gives only one output for every x.

EXAMPLE 21-2   Graph the function $f(x) = x^2$.

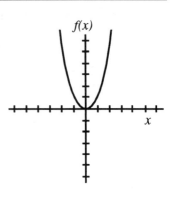

    Solution: The simplest way to do this is simply to plug in values of x. For each, we find the value of the function and plot the point $(x, f(x))$. If $x = 0$, $f(x) = 0$. If $x = 1$ or $x = -1$, then $f(x) = 1$. (Note that two different x values can go to a single $f(x)$; a single x just cannot go to two values of $f(x)$.) If $x = 2$ or $x = -2$, $f(x) = 4$. If $x = 3$ or $x = -3$, $f(x) = 9$. If we plot these few points, we can see what the basic shape of the curve must be, and fill it in. The result is at right.

EXERCISE 21-6   Graph the functions $f(x) = x^3$ and $h(x) = x^3 + 3$.

EXERCISE 21-7   Graph the function $f(x) = \dfrac{1}{1 + x^2}$. (You will have to use some non-integral values for x to get an idea of the shape near $x = 0$.)

21.3   Inputs and Outputs

In examples above, we've examined how to graph several different functions. Consider graphing the function $f(x) = 1/(1 - x^2)$. When we plug in $x = 1$, we find that $f(x)$ is undefined, because it is a fraction with denominator 0. Thus the point $x = 1$ is not allowed as an input to the function, and neither is $x = -1$.

    The set of allowable inputs to a function is called the **domain**; the domain of $f(x)$ in this case is *all real numbers except $x = \pm 1$*. The domains of all the functions from the previous section are *all reals*. Unless specified otherwise, you can almost always assume that the domain is restricted to the reals, rather than allowing complex inputs. You can also generally assume that complex *outputs* are forbidden, so that -1 is *not* in the domain of $\sqrt{x}$.

EXAMPLE 21-3   What is the domain of $\log x$?

    Solution: The logarithm of x is the number y such that $10^y = x$. If $x > 0$, there will always be such a number y, but for $x \leq 0$ there can be no such power. Thus the domain is **the positive real numbers.**

EXERCISE 21-8   Plot $f(x) = \log_2 x$.

EXERCISE 21-9   Find the domains of:

   i. $f(x) = \dfrac{x^2 + 3x - 2}{x^2 - 3x + 2}$.

   ii. $h(y) = 2^y$. (Note that the input variable does not have to be called x.)

   iii. $g(t) = \sqrt{t}$, where the positive square root is the one taken.

Just as the domain of a function is the set of allowed inputs, the **range** is defined as the set of all outputs of the function. For example, the range of $x^2 - 1$ is all numbers greater than or equal to -1, the range of $1/x$ is all real numbers except zero, and the range of the line function of Section 21.1 is all reals. (Make sure you understand all of these.) As was noted above, the outputs are almost always restricted to the reals, rather than allowing complex outputs. You can usually find the range of a function with pure common sense through thinking about what the outputs can be.

EXAMPLE 21-4   Find the range of 2^x.

Solution: A power of a positive number is always positive, but can be any positive number, as you should have observed in the previous set of examples. Thus the range is **the positive real numbers.**

EXERCISE 21-10   Find the ranges of $\log x$, $x^2 + 1$, and $1/(x - 1)$.

EXERCISE 21-11   Find the range of $x/(x + 1)$. You will probably need to draw a graph.

Given a function $f(x)$, one thing that can be done is to create a new function in which you put an input x into f, then take the output, $f(x)$, and put it through again, if it can go through. (That is, if it is in the domain of f.) The result is $f(f(x))$. We can play this game as many times as we wish, as long as each output is still in the domain of f. The function $f(f(\cdots f(x) \cdots))$, with n f's, is often written $f^n(x)$.

EXAMPLE 21-5   If $f(x) = x + 2$, then $f^6(x) = (((((x+2)+2)+2)+2)+2)+2 = x + 12$.

EXERCISE 21-12   Find $f^2(x)$ if $f(x)$ is

    i. $x/(x+1)$.

    ii. $1/x$.

    iii. x.

WARNING: The function $f^n(x)$ is NOT the same as the function $[f(x)]^n$, which is the nth power of f. Do not confuse the two. This is easier said than done, because some very confusing notation has become popular, in which, for example, $\sin^2 x$ is meant to mean $(\sin x)^2$. By what we have just said, $\sin^2 x$ should mean $\sin(\sin x)$. The reason that $\sin^2 x = (\sin x)^2$ is that constructions like $\sin(\sin x)$ are very rare, while expressions like $(\sin x)^2$ are very common. Thus the simple notation $\sin^2 x$ is used for the latter rather than the former. Be careful.

EXAMPLE 21-6   If $f(x) = x^2$, then the function $f^3(x)$ is $((x^2)^2)^2 = (x^4)^2 = x^8$, while the function $[f(x)]^3$ is $(x^2)^3 = x^6$.

Still another thing we can do with the output of a function is to put it through a *different* function. If f is the first function and g the second, the outcome looks like $g(f(x))$. Of course, we again must make sure that $f(x)$ is in the domain of g, and so on. One notation to watch for is writing $g(f(x))$ as $g \circ f$.

EXAMPLE 21-7   Suppose $f(x) = 6x^2$ and $g(x) = x/(\sqrt{x}+1)$. Then $(g \circ f)(x) = 6x^2/(\sqrt{6}\,x + 1)$.

EXERCISE 21-13   Find a counterexample to the "identity" $f \circ g = g \circ f$.

21.4   Even and Odd

Some functions have certain kinds of symmetry which make them easier to work with. One function we looked at earlier was $f(x) = x^2$, graphed in Example 21-2. If you look back at that graph, you will see that it is symmetric about the y-axis.

EXERCISE 21-14   Show that symmetry of the graph of a function $f(x)$ about the y-axis is equivalent to $f(x)$ satisfying the identity

$$f(x) = f(-x).$$ (21.2)

EXERCISE 21-15   What type of symmetry has the graph of a function $f(x)$ which satisfies the identity

$$f(x) = -f(-x)?$$ (21.3)

Functions with symmetry about the y-axis, or, equivalently, which satisfy (21.2), are called **even**. Similarly, functions which map to themselves when rotated $180°$ about the origin (those which satisfy (21.3)) are called **odd**.

EXAMPLE 21-8   Consider a function which for $x > 0$ looks like the first picture below. If the function is even, the continuation to $x < 0$ looks like the second picture. If the function is odd, the continuation to $x < 0$ looks like the third picture.

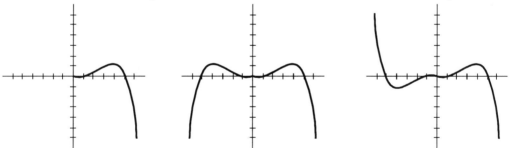

EXERCISE 21-16   Draw some functions which are even, odd, and neither even nor odd.

EXERCISE 21-17   Write down some functions which are even, odd, and neither.

EXERCISE 21-18   Find which of the following are odd or even: x, x^2, x^3, x^4, $x^6 + 27x^4 + x^2$, $x^5 + 1$, $x^6 + x^5$?

EXERCISE 21-19   A function of the form $a_n x^n + a_{n-1} x^{n-1} + \cdots + a_0$, where n is a positive integer and the a_i's are constants, is called a **polynomial**. When is a polynomial even? Odd?

EXAMPLE 21-9   What are the possible values at $x = 0$ of even or odd functions?

    Solution: If f is odd, then we have $f(-x) = -f(x)$. Substituting in $x = 0$, we then have $f(0) = -f(0)$, so $2f(0) = 0$ and $f(0) = 0$! On the other hand, if f is even, we merely get $f(0) = f(0)$, and $f(0)$ can be anything at all. Hence an odd function must pass through the origin, but an even function has no similar restriction.

21.5   Some Special Functions

There are certain functions which, while useful, don't fit in nicely with anything else. The only way to study such functions is on a case-by-case basis.

21.5.1   Absolute Values

One very important such function is the **absolute value function**, denoted by $f(x) = |x|$. The function returns the distance from x to 0, which is just the positive version of x: x itself if x is positive, $-x$ if x is negative. For example, $|4| = 4$, $|17| = 17$, $|-3| = 3$, $|-9| = 9$, and $|0| = 0$. Absolute value can also be used to denote the distance between two numbers; for example, $|x - y| < 2$ means that x and y are less than 2 units apart.

EXERCISE 21-20   Make sure you understand why $|x - y| < 2$ means that x and y are less than 2 apart. Why do we need an absolute value here?

EXERCISE 21-21   Graph the absolute value function $f(x) = |x|$. What are its domain and range?

    When confronted with the absolute value sign in a problem, the easiest thing to do is usually to replace the absolute value problem by a new problem without the absolute value. We use the fact that if $|M| = N$ for any expressions M and N, then either $M = N$ or $M = -N$.

EXAMPLE 21-10 Find all solutions to the equation $|x^2 - 3x| = 4$.

Solution: We can split the problem into two cases: either $x^2 - 3x = 4$ or $x^2 - 3x = -4$. The first case yields the solutions **4** and **−1**; the second yields $(3 \pm i\sqrt{7})/2$. If we restrict ourselves to real solutions, only 4 and −1 are acceptable.

EXERCISE 21-22 Solve the equation $|(x+2)/(3x-1)| = 5$.

21.5.2 Floored

Another important special function is the **greatest integer function** or **floor function**, denoted by $f(x) = \lfloor x \rfloor$ or $f(x) = [x]$. The value of the function is just x itself if x is an integer, or the integer directly below x if not. Thus $[3] = 3$, $\lfloor 4.3 \rfloor = 4$, $[-\pi] = -4$, and $\lfloor \sqrt{2}/2 \rfloor = 0$. Because they nicely suggest what the function does and are more distinctive, we prefer the $\lfloor \rfloor$ notation and the name "floor function."

EXERCISE 21-23 Find $\lfloor -\sqrt{17} \rfloor$, $\lfloor \sqrt[3]{17} \rfloor$, $\lfloor -\sqrt[4]{17} \rfloor$, and $\lfloor \sqrt[5]{17} \rfloor$.

To plot the floor function is difficult, because it is the first function we have tried to plot which is not **continuous** . A continuous function is one which can be drawn in one curve without picking up the pen.

Suppose we try to draw the floor function in this way. Start from 0, where the value is 0. Moving to the right, we *stay at 0*, since $\lfloor 0.1 \rfloor = 0$, $\lfloor 0.2 \rfloor = 0$, etc. Thus the line will stay at $f(x) = 0$ through $x = 0.9$, 0.99, 0.999, closer and closer to 1. But as soon as we cross $x = 1$, the function value jumps up to $f(x) = 1$; we have to pick up the pen.

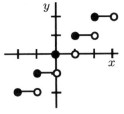

The graph ends up looking like the figure at right. The open circles are to emphasize that the points circled are *not* part of the graph; the closed circles emphasize that the points circled are part of the graph.

EXERCISE 21-24 The function $x - \lfloor x \rfloor$ is called the **fractional part** of x, and is usually denoted with curly braces: $\{x\}$. Find $\{17\}$, $\{-17/2\}$, $\{17/3\}$, $\{-17/4\}$, and $\{17/5\}$. Plot the function $f(x) = \{x\}$.

EXERCISE 21-25   The **ceiling function** $\lceil x \rceil$ is defined as the smallest integer which is greater than or equal to the input. Plot the floor and ceiling functions on the same set of axes. Where do the two coincide?

EXERCISE 21-26   If $f(x) = \lfloor x \rfloor$ and $g(x) = \lceil x \rceil$, express $g(x)$ in terms of $f(x)$ and x. Check that your expression works by substituting in some numbers.

EXERCISE 21-27   Are the absolute value and floor functions even, odd, or neither?

EXERCISE 21-28   Prove the following for all real x.

    i. $\lfloor x \rfloor + \lfloor -x \rfloor$ is equal to either 0 or -1.

    ii. $\lfloor x + \frac{1}{2} \rfloor$ is the integer nearest x.

    iii. $\lfloor x \rfloor - 2\lfloor x/2 \rfloor$ is equal to either 0 or 1. (Hint: consider the decomposition $\lfloor x \rfloor = x - \{x\}$.)

21.5.3   Split Up

Not all functions can be simply described by a single expression. Sometimes a function will behave one way in one region and another way in another. For example, consider the absolute value function $f(x) = |x|$. The function is really *two* functions: $f(x) = x$ for positive x and $f(x) = -x$ for negative x. So instead of writing $|x|$, which would be confusing to someone who had not seen this special shorthand, we could be explicit and write

$$ f(x) = \left\{ \begin{array}{ll} x, & \text{if } x \geq 0 \\ -x, & \text{if } x < 0 \end{array} \right. $$

This structure clearly acknowledges that there are two **cases** involved, and that the function takes a simple form for each case.

For the absolute value function this is a bit formal—most people know what the function is. For other functions, however, this type of construction might be necessary. We might wish, for some reason, to construct a function $g(x)$ which is x^2 in the region $x \geq 3$, x^3 for $-2 \leq x < 3$, and x^4 for $x < -2$. (Note the way the entire real line is covered by our cases.) Since there is no ready-made notation for this function as there is for the absolute value, we could use the general case structure to write

$$g(x) = \begin{cases} x^2, & x \geq 3 \\ x^3, & 3 > x \geq -2 \\ x^4, & -2 > x \end{cases}$$

EXERCISE 21-29 How many times does the function

$$g(x) = \begin{cases} x^2 - 8, & x \geq 3 \\ x^3 + 9, & 3 > x \geq -2 \\ x^4 - 15, & -2 > x \end{cases}$$

intersect the x-axis?

21.6 Transforming a Function

Once you have a basic understanding of functions, you can begin to construct new functions from functions you already have. There are four basic transformations which can be done.

EXAMPLE 21-11 The first basic transformation is to replace the old function $f(x)$ with $f(x + a)$, for some number a. What does this do to the function? Let's try it for a simple function, like $|x|$, and take $a = 2$. We can plug in some values of x to see what is going on. The values of $f(x)$ and $f(x + 2)$ for various x values can be easily arranged in a table, as below. Using these values, we can draw the two graphs on one pair of axes.

x	$|x|$	$|x + 2|$
-4	4	2
-3	3	1
-2	2	0
-1	1	1
0	0	2
1	1	3
2	2	4
3	3	5
4	4	6

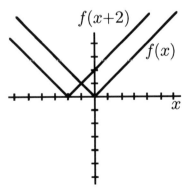

In the table and the corresponding graph, we can clearly see that the graph of $|x+2|$ is just the graph of $|x|$ shifted toward the left by 2! Why is this? For each x, the value of $f(x+2)$ will equal the value of $f(x)$ for $x+2$, which is the point 2 to the right of x. Hence $f(x)$ is 2 units to the right of $f(x+2)$. Thus the entire graph of $|x+2|$ must be a shifted version of the graph of $|x|$.

EXERCISE 21-30   Understand why $f(x+2)$ must be a shift of $f(x)$, using the table for $|x|$ if necessary. Why should the shift be to the negative, even though 2 is added to x?

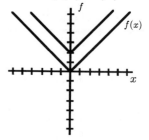

EXAMPLE 21-12   A second basic functional transformation is to add some number a *outside* the function, taking $f(x)$ to $f(x)+a$. Let's try this with $f(x) = |x|$.

Taking $a = 2$, we can quickly plot $|x|$ and $|x|+2$ on the same graph, as at right. Put in a few points yourself to confirm that these are the correct graphs; for example, for $x = -4$, $|x| = 4$ and $|x|+2 = 6$. From the graphs we can immediately see that adding 2 to the function shifts the graph *up* by 2. Can you see why this must be true?

EXAMPLE 21-13   Yet another transformation we can apply is multiplying the function $f(x)$ by a constant a, to get $af(x)$.

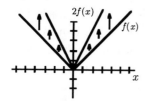

As before, we take $f(x) = |x|$ and $a = 2$. Let's draw the graphs again. The transformed graph this time is a vertical *stretch* by a factor of 2, as shown. The distance from each point on $f(x)$ to the x-axis is doubled when we draw $2f(x)$, so $2f(x)$ is the result of the aforementioned stretch.

EXAMPLE 21-14   The last transformation we will consider is going from $f(x)$ to $f(ax)$.

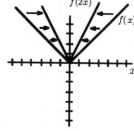

At the right, we plot $f(x) = |x|$ and $f(2x) = |2x|$; it is clear in this graph that multiplying by 2 corresponds to a horizontal *shrink* by a factor of 2. For example, let $g(x) = f(2x)$, then note that $g(1) = f(2)$, $g(2) = f(4)$, etc. Now do you see why $f(2x)$ is a horizontal shrink of $f(x)$?

WARNING: Though the pictures resulting from $2|x|$ and $|2x|$ are the same, a vertical stretch by 2 and a horizontal shrink by 2 are not generally the same thing. For example, take $g(x) = 2\sqrt{x}$ and $h(x) = \sqrt{2x}$; we have $g(8) = 4\sqrt{2}$, but $h(8) = 16$.

EXERCISE 21-31 What relationship does the function $f(x/2)$ have to the function $f(x)$?

EXERCISE 21-32 Shift and stretch some more functions to get comfortable with these techniques. If necessary, you can always resort to plotting the functions on a point-by-point basis, though you should soon be able to plot the transformed function without this. Always plot both the original function and the transformed function, to make sure you understand what the transformation does.

Problems to Solve for Chapter 21

402. Which values of x must be excluded from the domain of

$$g(x) = \frac{\frac{2}{2+x}}{2 - \frac{2}{2+x}}?$$

(MAΘ 1990)

403. If $f(x) = 2x^2 - 3x + 1$, then find $f(4x)$. (MAΘ 1990)

404. If $f(x + 1) = x^2 + 3x + 5$, then find $f(x)$. (MAΘ 1991)

405. If $f(4x + 3) = 2x + 1$, then find $f(-9)$. (MAΘ 1987)

406. How many solutions are there to the equation $|x^2 - 6x| = 9$? (MAΘ 1991)

407. Let $[x]$ denote the greatest integer function, and $\{x\} = x - [x]$ the fractional part of x. If

$$z = \frac{\{\sqrt{3}\}^2 - 2\{\sqrt{2}\}^2}{\{\sqrt{3}\} - 2\{\sqrt{2}\}},$$

find $[z]$. (MAΘ 1992)

408. Let f be the function from real numbers to real numbers defined by:

$$f(x) = \begin{cases} x + 2, & \text{if 3 is a divisor of } [x] \\ x - 1, & \text{otherwise} \end{cases}$$

As usual, $[x]$ stands for the greatest integer function. Compute $f(f(f(f(f(\pi)))))$. (MAΘ 1992)

409. Solve for all real values of y: $|3y + 7| = |2y - 1|$. (MATHCOUNTS 1990)

410. Find the area of the region determined by the system

$$
\begin{aligned}
y &\geq |x| \\
y &\leq -|x + 1| + 4.
\end{aligned}
$$

(MATHCOUNTS 1992)

411. Find the coordinates of the points of intersection of the graphs of the equations $y = |2x| - 2$ and $y = -|2x| + 2$. (MATHCOUNTS 1989)

412. Find the equation whose graph is as shown at the right. (MATHCOUNTS 1989)

413. Prove that $\lfloor 2x \rfloor + \lfloor 2y \rfloor \geq \lfloor x \rfloor + \lfloor y \rfloor + \lfloor x + y \rfloor$ for all real x and y.

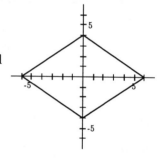

Chapter 22

Inequalities

When we go from considering only expressions in which two sides are equal to those in which they are not necessarily equal, we enter a new and surprisingly different realm of mathematics. There are as many types of inequalities as there are of equations; the only thing they all have in common is the use of $>$, $<$, $\geq$, or $\leq$.

22.1   What They Do

There are two types of inequality signs: **strict** and **nonstrict**. Strict inequalities have either the $>$ or $<$ sign in them, and mean that the expression on the larger (open) side of the inequality sign is *definitely larger* than the expression on the smaller (pointy) side. For instance, $3 < 4$, $-1000 < -100$, or $1.01 > 1$.

A special notation is often used when several different variables satisfy the same inequality. Suppose x, y, and z are all greater than -17, for example. Rather than write $x > -17$ and $y > -17$ and $z > -17$, we can just write $x, y, z > -17$. Be warned, however, that this does *not* specify any relationship between x, y, and z, only that each independently satisfies the constraint.

In nonstrict inequalities, the inequality sign has a little bar under it, as in $\leq$ and $\geq$. This bar means that the expressions on the two sides can also be equal. Just because an inequality is nonstrict does not mean the two quantities must necessarily be equal. For example, $1 \geq 0$ is a true statement, but 1 does not equal 0. The statement $x \leq y$ is usually pronounced "x is less than or equal to y"; $x > y$ is just "x is greater than y." To emphasize strictness, that the two sides absolutely *may not be equal*, you can also say $x < y$ as "x is strictly less than y."

In some ways, inequalities work just like equations. For example, we can add or subtract the same thing on both sides, so that $x - 2 < y - 2$ and $x + 2 < y + 2$ both follow from $x < y$. We can also do manipulations like "$a \leq c$ and $b \leq d$, so $a + b \leq c + d$."

EXERCISE 22-1   Convince yourself that these assertions are true by trying some examples.

In other ways, inequalities and equations work differently. Consider multiplication. Obviously $2 > 1$, but if we multiply both sides by -1, we get $-2 > -1$, which is false. If you multiply by a negative on both sides, you have to *reverse* the sign in the middle, so that $x \leq y$ implies $-x \geq -y$. The same is true with dividing by a negative number. As usual, multiplying both sides by 0 is illegal, since it will always yield 0 on both sides; dividing by 0 is also forbidden, for obvious reasons.

Multiplication does work fine as long as we stay with positive quantities. For example, if $a > c$ and $b > d$, we *can* write $ab > cd$ so long as all the numbers are positive. In particular, $x > y$ implies $x^2 > y^2$, $x^3 > y^3$, and so on, if $x, y > 0$. Also, $x > y$ implies $\sqrt{x} > \sqrt{y}$.

EXERCISE 22-2   For what restrictions on x and y is it true that $x > y$ implies $-x < y$?

EXAMPLE 22-1   One thing we have not considered, which we *can* do with an =, is take reciprocals of both sides. With inequalities, this gets tricky. If one side is negative and the other positive, they will maintain their signs after the reciprocal is taken, so the negative must still be less than the positive:

$$-2 \leq 3 \quad \Rightarrow \quad -1/2 \leq 1/3.$$

However, if both are positive, it's a different story. For example, we can start with $2 \leq 3$, divide by 2 to get $1 \leq 3/2$, and divide by 3 to get $1/3 \leq 1/2$. Thus, $2 \leq 3$ implies $1/2 \geq 1/3$; the inequality sign is *reversed* when we take the reciprocals.

EXERCISE 22-3   Finish the previous example by figuring out what happens if both sides of the inequality are negative.

The rule built up in Example 22-1 and Exercise 22-3 is a good one to remember. The inequality sign must be reversed when reciprocals are taken if the two sides are both positive or both negative.

22.2   Linear Inequalities

The simplest types of inequalities are linear inequalities. In exact analogy to linear equations, they contain only first powers of the variables involved; for example, $x > 4y + 3$ is linear, while $x^2 > 1/y$ is not.

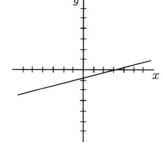

The tools for dealing with linear inequalities are similar to those for dealing with linear equations. For example, we can graph them. Let's consider the one cited above, $x > 4y + 3$. Using the standard techniques we learned in Chapter 16, we graph the line which comes from the equality, $x = 4y + 3$.

Now what is the relation of this line to the solutions of the inequality? The line itself contains points which are *not* solutions, since the inequality is strict and for points on this line, x and $4y + 3$ are equal. However, the line still serves an important purpose.

Let's rewrite our original inequality as $x - 4y - 3 > 0$. Consider all possible things that $x - 4y - 3$ could equal. The points satisfying $x - 4y - 3 = k$, for any constant k, will always form a straight line which is *parallel* to the line we have already drawn. (Why parallel?) If we consider *all* the lines $x - 4y - 3 = k$, then all the ones where $k > 0$ should be on one side of the original line, and those with $k < 0$ on the other.

EXERCISE 22-4 To verify this and see how it works, draw the lines $x - 4y - 3 = -4$, $x - 4y - 3 = -2$, $x - 4y - 3 = 0$, $x - 4y - 3 = 2$, and $x - 4y - 3 = 4$ on one graph.

So how does all this help with the original problem? It actually solves the problem completely! The solutions of the inequality $x - 4y - 3 > 0$ are all points (x, y) such that $x - 4y - 3 = k$ where $k > 0$. Thus the solution of the inequality consists of all the lines on *one side* of our original line, where k is 0. The solution is an entire half-plane, as at right. The original line has to be drawn

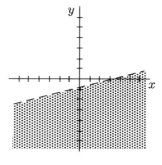

in dashes, since it is not part of the solution, even though it forms the boundary between the solution and the rest of the plane. If we went back to the start and changed the $>$ to a $\geq$, this line *would* be part of the solution, and we would draw it as a solid line.

Notice that we can determine which side of the initial line to shade by selecting a point in the plane on one side of the line. For example, in the case of $x > 4y + 3$, we try $(0,0)$ and find that the statement $0 > 4 \cdot 0 + 3$ is false. Therefore, we shade the side of the line which does not contain $(0,0)$, since we know that $(0,0)$ is not a solution.

EXERCISE 22-5   Draw the solution of the inequality $x + y > 0$.

EXERCISE 22-6   Draw the solution of the inequality $x - y < 0$ on the same graph as that of the previous exercise.

EXERCISE 22-7   Draw the solution to the simultaneous inequalities

$$\begin{aligned} x + y &> 0 \\ x - y &< 0. \end{aligned}$$

EXERCISE 22-8   Show the various ways this simultaneous solution would change if either or both of the strict inequalities were made nonstrict.

EXAMPLE 22-2   The linear inequalities we have looked at so far have all been in two variables; however, there can also be linear inequalities in only one variable. These are fairly trivial: for example, $x < -3$. The plotting of such an inequality is done on a number line; the inequality $x < -3$ is shown below. Note that the open circle at -3 emphasizes that -3 is *not* included; if we used a $\leq$ instead, this would be a filled circle, to show that it is included.

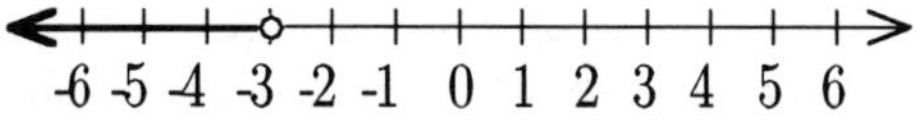

22.3   Quadratic Inequalities

Passing from linear to quadratic inequalities is a big step. While linear inequalities in two variables are fairly simple to deal with, quadratic inequalities in only one variable are plenty to keep us busy. We consider inequalities like

$$x^2 - x - 6 \geq 0,$$

with one variable in a quadratic expression.

What is the first step in approaching such an inequality? With a quadratic *equation*, we begin by finding the zeros of the expression; we can then factor the equation. The strategy here is the same, though what we *do* with the factorization is much different.

Consider the inequality above. It factors into

$$(x - 3)(x + 2) \geq 0.$$

We thus have a product which must be greater than 0. The product of two positive numbers or two negative numbers is positive, but the product of a negative and a positive is negative. We can thus conclude that $(x - 3)$ and $(x + 2)$ must have the same sign.

But what are the signs of $(x - 3)$ and $(x + 2)$? Consider $x - 3$. The inequality $x - 3 \geq 0$ is equivalent to $x \geq 3$ by adding 3 to both sides. As explained in Example 22-2, the graph of this inequality looks like

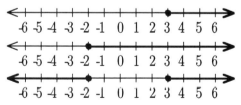

Similarly, the graph of $x + 2 \geq 0$, or equivalently $x \geq -2$, looks like

The graph of the full inequality, $(x - 3)(x + 2) \geq 0$, should consist of all points which are either in either plot (both factors positive) or not in both plots (both factors negative). We also should include all points where either term is 0, since at those points the product equals 0, which is compatible with our $\geq$ sign. We thus draw the two plots next to each other and read the final plot directly off. Watch:

The bottom plot, the solution to $(x - 3)(x + 2) \geq 0$, consists of those points which are either in both or in neither of the first two graphs. Had the inequality been $(x - 3)(x + 2) \leq 0$, we would look for points which are on one of the first two graphs but not the other. (Why?)

EXERCISE 22-9 Plot the solution to the inequality $x^2 + 5x + 6 < 0$.

EXERCISE 22-10   Plot the solutions to the inequalities $x^2 - 6x + 9 > 0$ and $x^2 - 6x + 9 < 0$.

While finding the graph of the inequality is enough to understand it, there are other ways to present the answer. One is to write it as simple inequalities. Thus the answer to the first example we did would be

$$x \leq -2 \text{ or } x \geq 3,$$

and that of Exercise 22-9 would be

$$-3 < x < -2.$$

Another way to present these same answers uses **interval notation**. An interval of the real line is represented as an ordered pair of the starting and ending points; square braces [or] mean that the endpoint is included in the interval, while parentheses (or) mean that it is not.

EXAMPLE 22-3   The interval which is drawn as

is represented in interval notation as $[-3, 6]$, while $(-3, 6)$ denotes the interval

---

EXERCISE 22-11   What should the interval notation $[-3, 6)$ mean? Draw it.

EXAMPLE 22-4   We can now convert the answers to our quadratic inequalities above to interval notation. The solution to $x^2 + 5x + 6 \leq 0$ is just $[-3, -2]$. The solution to $x^2 - x - 6 \geq 0$ is more complicated, because of the "or" which we are forced to include. The interval notation looks like

$$(-\infty, -2] \cup [3, \infty).$$

There are several points to note here. First, the $\cup$ is a set symbol meaning all elements in either set (see Chapter 27 for more information); it replaces the "or."

Second, since the intervals have no ends, going out to infinity, we symbolically make the ends of the intervals be ∞, the symbol for infinity. We use a parenthesis on ∞ rather than a square bracket, because it is not included in the interval, not being a real number. This may all seem kind of contrived, but it is an efficient way to write the solutions.

EXERCISE 22-12 Solve the inequality

$$x^4 - 5x^2 + 6 \geq 0$$

by factoring (let $y = x^2$ first) and considering the signs of the factors, just as we did for quadratics.

WARNING: When an inequality contains proportions, we should be extra careful. Let's look at the inequality $2/(x+1) \geq 3/(x-3)$. Our immediate instinct is to cross-multiply and get rid of the fractions; however, it's not that simple. If we tried to multiply through by $x - 3$, we would have to worry about its sign (negative or positive), and thus whether to reverse the $\geq$.

Thus, instead of removing the fractions, we write our inequality as

$$\frac{2}{x+1} - \frac{3}{x-3} \geq 0$$

and combine the fractions to get

$$\frac{-x - 9}{(x+1)(x-3)} \geq 0.$$

Since we have something which we want to be greater than 0, we have the same problem as with quadratic inequalities. We factor all the expressions involved and consider the signs of the factors as before—it doesn't matter whether the terms are in the numerator or the denominator. We look for where the three linear terms are all positive or where two are negative and the other positive. See if you can find that the solution to the above is $(-\infty, -9] \cup (-1, 3)$. Can you see why $x = -9$ is included in the solution while $x = -1$ and $x = 3$ are not?

22.4   Absolute Value Inequalities

Another important type of inequality contains absolute values. These are really no more complicated than quadratics. Suppose we have

$$4|x + 3| + 3 > 9.$$

The key to solving this is being able to remove the absolute value signs. So we first isolate the absolute value, subtracting 3 from both sides and then dividing by 4 to get

$$|x + 3| > 3/2.$$

Using the techniques of Chapter 21, this is now equivalent to

$$x + 3 > 3/2 \qquad \text{or} \qquad x + 3 < -3/2.$$

Make sure you see why the second inequality above is $<$ rather than $>$. The answer then is

$$x > -3/2 \qquad \text{or} \qquad x < -9/2.$$

EXERCISE 22-13   Plot this answer and express it in interval notation.

All absolute value inequalities come down to this basic notion of removing the absolute value signs. If we have the absolute value on the small side of the inequality, the result upon removing the absolute value signs will be between two numbers; for example

$$|x + 3| < 3/2$$

becomes

$$-3/2 < x + 3 < 3/2,$$

from which adding -3 to all three components yields

$$-9/2 < x < -3/2.$$

22.5   A Trivial Inequality

All the inequality types we have discussed so far have been applicable only in particular types of problems. The true art of inequalities lies in manipulating a few basic inequalities. The two most useful ones, the Arithmetic-Geometric Mean Inequality and the Cauchy Inequality, won't be approached until Volume 2. There remains, however, a very useful general inequality to discuss here.

The inequality itself seems absolutely trivial. It is merely the statement that for any real number x, we have

$$x^2 \geq 0.$$

EXAMPLE 22-5   As a first demonstration that this content-free inequality can be of use, we will prove this statement: for all real x and y,

$$\frac{x^2 + y^2}{2} \geq xy.$$

We can multiply through by 2 to get

$$x^2 + y^2 \geq 2xy,$$

then rearrange to find

$$x^2 - 2xy + y^2 \geq 0.$$

We can factor the left side into a square, to get

$$(x - y)^2 \geq 0,$$

which is true because of the Trivial Inequality.

EXERCISE 22-14   In the previous example, we worked from our result *backwards* to a true statement. This is an extremely useful method, but it only proves the result we want if we can reverse our steps, showing that the true statement at the end necessarily implies the result at the start. Show that this is so, that each equation in the argument forces the previous one to be true.

A crucial use of the Trivial Inequality is finding the minimum of quadratic expressions like $x^2 + 5x + 1$. Just complete the square to get

$$x^2 + 5x + 1 = \left(x + \frac{5}{2}\right)^2 - \frac{21}{4}.$$

Since the square term is greater than or equal to 0, the entire expression must be greater than or equal to $-21/4$. At what value of x is this minimum, $-21/4$, attained?

Problems to Solve for Chapter 22

414. Describe all y such that $3y \geq 4 - y$ and $-2y \geq 1 + y$.

415. Find all z such that $2/z \geq 1$.

416. Find all x such that $x^2 + x - 30 \geq 0$ and $6/x > 0$.

417. A ball is thrown upward from the top of a tower. If its height is described by $-t^2 + 60t + 700$, what is the greatest height the ball attains?

418. Find all x which satisfy the inequality $\sqrt{x} < 2x$. (AHSME 1980)

419. If $1.2 \leq a \leq 5.1$ and $3 \leq b \leq 6$, then find the highest possible value for the quotient a/b. Give your answer as a decimal. (MATHCOUNTS 1988)

420. How many integers satisfy $|x| + 1 \geq 3$ and $|x - 1| < 3$? (MATHCOUNTS 1987)

421. For how many integers n is $\left| \dfrac{n}{3} - 2 \right| \leq 3$? (MATHCOUNTS 1992)

422. If $x < a < 0$, prove that $x^2 > ax > a^2$. (AHSME 1956)

423. Show that if $x - y > x$ and $x + y < y$, then both x and y must be negative. (AHSME 1966)

424. Given that the positive integers a, b, c, and d satisfy $\dfrac{a}{b} < \dfrac{c}{d} < 1$, arrange the following in order of increasing magnitude:

$$\frac{b}{a}, \frac{d}{c}, \frac{bd}{ac}, \frac{b+d}{a+c}, \ 1.$$

(MAΘ 1987)

425. Solve for x: $x + 1/x \leq -2$. (MAΘ 1990)

426. If the smallest value of y satisfying the equation $y = 3x^2 + 6x + k$ is 4, find the value of k. (MATHCOUNTS 1989)

427. If $r > 0$, then for all p and q such that $pq \neq 0$ and $pr > qr$, we have

A. $-p > -q$ B. $-p > q$ C. $1 > -q/p$ D. $1 < q/p$ E. none of these

428. Find the greatest integer x for which $3^{20} > 32^x$. (MAΘ 1991)

—*the BIG PICTURE*—

One very famous inequality comes from the strange world of quantum mechanics. **Bell's Inequality** was proven by J.S. Bell in the mid-1960's to answer some nagging doubts about the theory.

Quantum mechanics does not describe the exact motions and interactions of physical particles, but only the *probabilities* of those motions and interactions. In fact, this is assured by another inequality, the so-called Uncertainty Principle, which places a rigid upper bound on the extent to which quantum mechanics can determine a particle's position and speed.

Many have had doubts about this restriction and other weird properties of the quantum description; Einstein himself had grave difficulties. Along with Podolsky and Rosen, he developed a thought experiment which showed that quantum mechanics violated the common-sense notion that nothing can take effect instantaneously, showing, he felt, that there must be a more fundamental set of variables than quantum mechanics evaluates.

Bell's inequality provided a rigid bound on the possibilities of a theory of the type Einstein was hoping for, however. Experiment soon confirmed that the bound is broken by the real world, meaning that Einstein's hopes of a more satisfying theory were in vain.

The interpretation of quantum mechanics was thus shown to be a very tricky business. (This has been confirmed by a flood of popular books asserting that quantum mechanics proves various religious or philosophical assertions. Be skeptical.)

Chapter 23

Operations and Relations

23.1 What is an Operation?

An **operation** is any action performed on some set of quantities. For example, the operation $+$ on a pair of numbers, as in $2 + 4$, is addition. Multiplication, subtraction, and division are also operations.

The most important types of operations are those which, like $+$ or $-$, take two inputs. Such operations are called **binary operations**.

Most operations have symbols associated with them, like $-$, $\times$, $*$, $\circ$, $/$, or $\div$. However, not all operations have symbols; some are denoted in other ways. Exponentiation, for example, is denoted by a superscript, as in 2^4.

An operation can be defined in any way whatsoever. For example, we could define a new operation with the symbol $\#$ such that $a \# b = a + b - ab$. To evaluate $4 \# 3$, just write $4 \# 3 = 4 + 3 - 4(3) = -5$. Using operations is that simple. Once you have defined an operation, just put the numbers in the operation formula where they belong.

EXAMPLE 23-1 If $a \# b = a + b - 3a/b$, find $(1 \# 2) \# 3$.

Solution: When parentheses appear, the rule is to evaluate the innermost parentheses first and work outward. Thus we get

$$(1 \# 2) \# 3 = (1 + 2 - 3(1/2)) \# 3 = \frac{3}{2} \# 3 = \frac{3}{2} + 3 - 3 \left(\frac{3/2}{3} \right) = \mathbf{3}.$$

Since addition, multiplication, division, subtraction, and exponentiation are so common, a series of conventions has been adopted regarding the order in which these operations are executed when more than one is present. First, as noted in the example above, when parentheses appear, work from the inside out. Second, in an expression with no parentheses, perform all exponentiations first. After this, perform all multiplications and divisions, starting from the left of the expression, then finally do all additions and subtractions, once again starting from the left. These rules should be familiar, so we won't dwell on them.

23.2   Properties of Operations

Various properties can be used to classify, describe, and manipulate operations. After defining and giving examples of these properties, we will demonstrate how they are useful.

1. **Commutativity**

If an operation # is **commutative**, then for any pair of numbers a and b,

$$a\#b = b\#a.$$

In other words, the order of the numbers in the operation doesn't matter. For example, addition is commutative, since $a + b = b + a$ for any a and b. Similarly, multiplication is commutative, but division and subtraction are not.

To show that an operation is *not* commutative, we need only show that it fails for one set of numbers. For example, subtraction is not commutative because $1 - 2 \neq 2 - 1$. (Find a similar example to show that division is not commutative.)

2. **Associativity**

An operation # is **associative** if for all a, b, and c we have

$$a\#(b\#c) = (a\#b)\#c.$$

Thus the placement of the parentheses is irrelevant, so we don't need them at all; we can just write $a\#b\#c$ for an associative operation. Addition and multiplication are both associative, but neither division nor subtraction are.

3. Distributivity

If the operation # is **distributive** over another operation @, then for all a, b, and c, we have

$$a\#(b@c) = (a\#b)@(a\#c).$$

The most useful distributive law is that of multiplication over addition: for example, $2(3 + 1) = 2(3) + 2(1) = 6 + 2 = 8$.

Distributivity can also be used in reverse, to compact an expression instead of expanding it. Using the distributive law in reverse is called **factoring**.

Since a, b, and c can be negative in the multiplicative distributive law, we can use distributivity on expressions like $4(5 - 1) = 4(5) - 4(1) = 20 - 4 = 16$.

In addition to these properties, an operation # is said to have an **identity** if there is some number e such that $b\#e = e\#b = b$ for all b. For example, the identity of addition is 0, because for all x, $x + 0 = 0 + x = x$.

EXAMPLE 23-2 Evaluate $45(33333)+45(66667)$.

Solution: Using the distributive property in reverse, we have

$$45(33333) + 45(66667) = 45(33333 + 66667) = 45(100000) = \mathbf{4500000}.$$

(You'll agree that this is easier than performing the multiplications before the addition.)

EXAMPLE 23-3 Use the distributive property to evaluate the product $(x-1)(x-2)$.

Solution: We use the distributive property once to expand the product as

$$(x - 1)(x - 2) = x(x - 2) - 1(x - 2).$$

We then use the distributive property a second time to expand each of these products, so

$$(x - 1)(x - 2) = x^2 - 2x - x + 2 = \mathbf{x^2 - 3x + 2}.$$

EXAMPLE 23-4 Is there an identity element of the relation $a\#b = 2ab + a + b$? If so, what is it?

Solution: To find the identity, we solve $a\#b = b$. The resulting equation, $a\#b = 2ab + a + b = b$, is true for all b if and only if $a = 0$. Similarly, $b\#0 = b$ for all b. Thus, **0** is an identity of this operation.

If the operation were $a\#b = 2ab - a - b$, then there would be no a for which $a\#b = b\#a = b$ is always true. (Make sure you see why.)

EXERCISE 23-1 Is division distributive over addition?

EXERCISE 23-2 What is the identity element of multiplication?

EXAMPLE 23-5 Prove that an operation $\#$ can have only one identity.

Proof: Suppose we want the two identities to be e_1 and e_2. For e_1 to be an identity, we must have $e_1\#e_2 = e_2$. But for e_2 to be an identity, we must have $e_1\#e_2 = e_1$. This is a contradiction unless the two identities are the same.

If an operation has an identity, then we can also define **inverses**. The inverse of a, if it exists, is some b such that $a\#b = b\#a = e$, the identity. (From this definition, we can immediately see that if b is the inverse of a, then a is the inverse of b.)

EXERCISE 23-3 If the operation is addition, then what is the inverse of 2? What if the operation is multiplication?

EXAMPLE 23-6 Prove that an element a can have at most one inverse if $\#$ is an associative operation.

Solution: Suppose instead that a has two inverses, b and c. We have $a\#b = e$, since b is an inverse of a. Applying c on both sides, we have

$$c\#(a\#b) = c\#e = c.$$

We can use the associative property to change $c\#(a\#b)$ to $(c\#a)\#b = e\#b = b$, which means that $b = c$. Thus b and c are the same, so a can have only one inverse if the operation is associative.

23.3 Relations

A **relation** is exactly what it sounds like: a way of specifying the relationship between two or more objects. The most basic relation is equality. However, the objects being related by a relation need not be numbers. For example, when we say two lines are parallel, we form a relation between them. Thus, ∥ is a relation just as = is. Similarly, perpendicularity and congruence are relations, as are greater than (>) and less than (<). We can even take humans as the objects being related; then possible relations might be love and friendship.

There are many properties which a relation may have. We examine the three most important below. Equality, as one of the "nicest" relations, has all three properties; other relations may satisfy only some subset of the properties.

1. Reflexivity
Equality is **reflexive** because for all a, we have $a = a$. Triangle congruence is also reflexive, while greater than, less than, and perpendicularity all are not. (A number is not greater than itself; nor is a line perpendicular to itself.) Love is reflexive in most well-adjusted people (I love myself).

2. Symmetry
Equality is **symmetric** because for all a and b, $a = b$ implies $b = a$. Once again, triangle congruence is also symmetric, but greater than (>) is not symmetric, because if $x > y$, then $y > x$ is not true. Friendship is usually symmetric. (I am her friend, so she is my friend.) On the other hand, love isn't, a fact which has broken many hearts.

3. Transitivity
Equality is **transitive** because for all a, b, and c, $a = b$ and $b = c$ imply $a = c$. Greater than is also transitive, because if $a > b$ and $b > c$, then we can write $a > b > c$, so $a > c$. Parallelism is also transitive, for if one line is parallel to two others, then the other two lines are parallel to each other.

If all three of the above properties are true for a relation, the relation is called an **equivalence relation**. An equivalence relation works in most ways just like an =, because it shares many of the same properties.

EXERCISE 23-4   Is love transitive? How about friendship?

EXERCISE 23-5   Which of the following are equivalence relations: equality, congruence, perpendicularity, greater than or equal to ($\geq$), similarity, less than?

Problems to Solve for Chapter 23

429. If $a \star b$ is defined as $2a - b^a$, what value is associated with $3 \star 2$? (MATHCOUNTS 1990)

430. Find $(3\#5)/(5\#7)$ if $A\#B = \dfrac{1/A + 1/B}{A + B}$. (Mandelbrot #1)

431. Define a binary operation @, with $x@y = (x + y)/(x - y)$. If $3@a = 3$, find a. (Mandelbrot #3)

432. Consider a binary operation $\star$, defined by $a \star b = a^b$ for all positive numbers a and b. Then which of the following is true for all positive a, b, c, and n: $a \star b = b \star a$, $a \star (b \star c) = (a \star b) \star c$, $(a \star b^n) = (a \star n) \star b$, or $(a \star b)^n = a \star (bn)$? (AHSME 1970)

433. Suppose the operation $\#$ is defined on the set of real numbers as $a\#b = a + ab$. What is the identity for this operation? (MAΘ 1992)

─ the *BIG PICTURE* ─

The methods of abstract operators and relations which we have introduced here are not as useless as they might seem. At the college level (and beyond), this type of consideration becomes the subject of **abstract algebra**, one of the most important areas of mathematics.

Abstract algebra gets its name because it is a generalization of what you learn in ordinary algebra. Instead of dealing with numbers, the abstract version of algebra uses operations and relations on general sets which, however, still satisfy some of the properties of ordinary numbers. As a simple example, we could imagine such a set with only two members a and b. The set could have some operation $*$, such that $a * b = b * a = a$ and $b * b = a * a = b$.

If an operation is associative, has an identity, and every element has an inverse, such a set is called a **group** under the operation. (Can you verify that the set $\{a, b\}$ is a group under $*$?) The study of groups, or **group theory**, is one important aspect of abstract algebra. Group theory is crucial, for example, to modern views of particle physics; on the mathematical side, it is used to prove that there is no general solution to fifth-degree equations! (See page 88.)

Chapter 24

Sequences and Series

24.1 Arithmetic Series

A child's mother gives her 10 cents one day. Every day thereafter her mother gives her 3 more cents than the previous day. After 20 days, how much does she have?

This simple problem exhibits what is called an **arithmetic series**. After 1 day, she has 10 cents. On the second day she gets 13 cents, so after two days, she has 23; after three, $23 + 16 = 39$. The list of amounts she gets each day,

$$10, \ 13, \ 16, \ 19, \ 22, \ 25, \ 28, \ldots,$$

is called a **sequence**. When we add up the terms to get the total amount she has at some point,

$$10 + 13 + 16 + 19 + 22 + 25 + 28 + \cdots,$$

the result is a **series**. In this particular case, where each term is separated by a fixed amount from the previous one, both series and sequence are called **arithmetic** (air ith MET ic). So the problem we need to solve is adding up an **arithmetic series**.

EXERCISE 24-1   Which of the following are arithmetic sequences?

   i. 1, 2, 3, 4, 5,...

   ii. 1, 3, 6, 10, 15,...

   iii. 34, 41, 48, 55, 62,...

In general, an arithmetic sequence is defined by the first term, which we call a, and the difference between successive terms, d. The sequence is thus

$$a, \ a + d, \ a + 2d, \ a + 3d, \ \ldots$$

The nth term is $a + (n - 1)d$, since it is $(n - 1)$ d's away from the first. The sum of the first n terms is thus

$$a + (a + d) + (a + 2d) + \ldots + (a + (n - 1)d).$$

Such a series may be summed by a relatively simple method. We write the series down, calling the sum S, and write it again backwards underneath.

$$
\begin{array}{ccccccc}
S & = & a & + & a + d & + \cdots + & a + (n - 1)d \\
S & = & a + (n - 1)d & + & a + (n - 2)d & + \cdots + & a
\end{array}
$$

Summing the pairs which are vertically aligned, we get

$$2S = (2a + (n - 1)d) + (2a + (n - 1)d) + \ldots + (2a + (n - 1)d),$$

where the sum has n identical terms. Thus we have $2S = n(2a + (n - 1)d)$, or $S = \frac{n}{2}(2a + (n - 1)d)$. This is one formula which is probably worth remembering, but don't let that distract you from the elegance of the method.

EXAMPLE 24-1   The problem we started the section with can easily be solved. We have $a = 10$, $d = 3$, $n = 20$. The sum is $\frac{20}{2}\left(2(10) + 19(3)\right) = 10(77) = \mathbf{770}$.

EXERCISE 24-2   Show that our formula is equivalent to

$$\text{Sum} = \frac{\#\text{ terms}}{2}(\text{first term} + \text{last term}).$$

When we are presented with the first and last terms, this formula quickly gives results.

EXERCISE 24-3   Find the sum of $8 + 5 + 2 + \cdots + (-10)$.

EXERCISE 24-4   Find the sum of the first 100 terms of $(-101) + (-99) + (-97) + \ldots$.

EXERCISE 24-5   Find the sum of the first k integers: $1 + 2 + \cdots + k$.

EXAMPLE 24-2 Often, complicated problems are formed from the basic idea of the arithmetic series. These are usually pretty easy to untangle. Here's one: If the sum of the first ten terms of an arithmetic progression is four times the sum of the first five terms, find the ratio of the first term to the common difference. (AHSME 1952)

Solution: Just remember that our formula, together with the parameters a, d, and n, contains all the information you need. We know that the sums of the first five and first ten terms are $5(2a+4d)/2$ and $10(2a+9d)/2$, respectively. Setting the second equal to four times the first and simplifying a little, we get a linear equation:

$$4(5)(2a + 4d) = 10(2a + 9d).$$

Expanding and pulling the variables to different sides, we then have $20a = 10d$, so that $a/d = \mathbf{1/2}$.

Calm application of the sum formula will easily solve all problems of this last type. There are many to practice on at the end of the chapter.

24.2 Geometric Series

A geometric series is like an arithmetic series, except instead of having a constant difference, successive terms have a constant *ratio* r. For example, a fable says that a wise woman solved a king's dire problem, and the king said she could have anything she wanted in return. She demurely asked only for a chessboard with 1 grain of wheat on the first square, 2 on the second, 4 on the third, 8 on the fourth, and so on up to the sixty-fourth square.

EXERCISE 24-6 How many grains would she have if she had asked for 1, 2, 3, 4, ..., rather than 1, 2, 4, 8, ...?

Since each term is equal to r times the previous one, the general form of a geometric sequence is a, ar, ar^2, and so on. The nth term is clearly ar^{n-1}. (Compare this to the nth term of an arithmetic series.) We can sum the series with a method similar to the one from the arithmetic series. Watch:

$$\begin{aligned} S &= a + ar + \cdots + ar^{n-1} \\ Sr &= \quad\quad ar + \cdots + ar^{n-1} + ar^n \end{aligned}$$

If we now *subtract* the second row from the first, all the terms in the sum but two will cancel. We are left with

$$S - Sr = a - ar^n,$$

or, as long as $r \neq 1$,

$$S = \frac{a - ar^n}{1 - r}. \tag{24.1}$$

Make sure you understand the method used to find this sum. It is a very useful one in many circumstances.

EXAMPLE 24-3   Let's find the sum $2 - \frac{2}{3} + \frac{2}{9} - \frac{2}{27} + \frac{2}{81}$. We see that $a = 2$, $r = -\frac{1}{3}$, and $n = 5$, and applying the formula we get

$$S = \frac{2 + \frac{2}{243}}{1 + \frac{1}{3}} = \frac{488/243}{4/3} = \frac{\mathbf{122}}{\mathbf{81}}.$$

If you're not yet convinced of the correctness of our formula, verify this by adding the terms up in the normal way.

 EXERCISE 24-7   What is the sum of the series $1 + 2 + 4 + \cdots + 2^k$? How many grains of wheat did the wise woman ask for? If a loaf of bread requires a million grains of wheat, how many loaves could she make? Could the king pay her?

EXERCISE 24-8   Show how equation (24.1) yields the polynomial factorization

$$x^k - 1 = (x - 1)(x^{k-1} + x^{k-2} + \cdots + x + 1).$$

24.3   Infinite Series

We have up to now assumed that our series terminated after some finite number of terms; however, this need not be so. Consider the geometric series with $a = 1$, $r = \frac{1}{2}$:

$$1 + \frac{1}{2} + \frac{1}{4} + \frac{1}{8} + \frac{1}{16} + \cdots.$$

If we add the first two terms only, the sum is 3/2. If we add the first three, it is 7/4, if we add the first four, it is 15/8. The sums of the first n terms of the series are approaching a set value, 2. An infinite series is called **convergent** if its sums tend to a fixed value like this.

When can a series converge? First of all, *the terms must tend to zero.* Thus series like

$$1 + 1 + 1 + 1 + 1 + \cdots$$

or

$$1 - 2 + 3 - 4 + 5 - \cdots$$

don't converge. The sums of the first n terms, or **partial sums**, do not tend to anything. Series for which this is the case are called **divergent**.

EXAMPLE 24-4 WARNING: Just because the terms tend to zero, the sum need not converge! The standard example is

$$1 + \frac{1}{2} + \frac{1}{3} + \frac{1}{4} + \cdots.$$

If we group the terms like $1 + \frac{1}{2} + (\frac{1}{3} + \frac{1}{4}) + (\frac{1}{5} + \frac{1}{6} + \frac{1}{7} + \frac{1}{8}) + \cdots$, we can see that $(\frac{1}{3} + \frac{1}{4}) > (\frac{1}{4} + \frac{1}{4}) = \frac{1}{2}$, $(\frac{1}{5} + \frac{1}{6} + \frac{1}{7} + \frac{1}{8}) > 4(\frac{1}{8}) = \frac{1}{2}$, and so on. Thus the given series is greater than the obviously divergent series

$$1 + \frac{1}{2} + \frac{1}{2} + \frac{1}{2} + \frac{1}{2} + \cdots,$$

and thus must itself be divergent, *even though the terms tend to 0.* (This is one example of the **comparison test** in which we show that each term or group of terms in a series is greater than corresponding terms in a divergent series, such as $1 + \frac{1}{2} + \frac{1}{2} + \cdots$.)

EXERCISE 24-9 Write an arithmetic series which is convergent.

When is a geometric series convergent? Consider the infinite geometric series

$$a + ar + ar^2 + ar^3 + \cdots.$$

Rearranging Equation (24.1), we can see that the sum of the first n terms is

$$S = \left(\frac{a}{1 - r}\right)(1 - r^n).$$

As n gets bigger, the first term in the product on the right stays the same, so we can ignore it for now. The second term gets bigger and bigger if the absolute value of r is greater than 1, because then each power of r is even bigger in magnitude.

If the absolute value of r is less than 1, each power of r gets smaller in absolute value, and the term r^n tends to zero. For example, the powers of 0.5 are 0.25, 0.125, 0.0625, etc. Thus the sum is divergent if $|r| > 1$, and convergent if $|r| < 1$. For the second case we can even write the formula for the sum. Since r^n tends to zero as n gets large (as for 0.5 above), the second factor $(1 - r^n)$ becomes 1 in the product, and the sum tends to

$$a + ar + ar^2 + ar^3 + \cdots = \frac{a}{1 - r}.$$

Try using the method we used to sum a terminating geometric series to prove this formula.

EXERCISE 24-10   What happens in the above discussion if $|r| = 1$, that is, for $r = 1$ or -1?

24.4 $\displaystyle\sum_{i=1}^{n}$

There is a very useful shorthand for summation. The large symbol $\sum$ is used, since it is the letter S, for *sum*, in Greek. Let's look at an example:

$$\sum_{k=1}^{5} k = 1 + 2 + 3 + 4 + 5.$$

The expression on the bottom specifies that k is a **dummy variable**. That is, it will be substituted in for, but will not appear in the final expression. Common dummy variables are i, j, and k. The bottom specifies that k will start as 1; the top specifies that k will stop when it equals 5. The dummy variable is incremented by 1's, and the values of the expression in front of the $\sum$ are added up for all the different values of k.

EXAMPLE 24-5 Let's do the sum

$$\sum_{k=3}^{7} 2^k.$$

We have

$$
\begin{aligned}
k = 3 : &\quad 2^k = 8 \\
k = 4 : &\quad 2^k = 16 \\
k = 5 : &\quad 2^k = 32 \\
k = 6 : &\quad 2^k = 64 \\
k = 7 : &\quad 2^k = 128
\end{aligned}
\quad \Rightarrow \quad
\sum_{k=3}^{7} 2^k = 8 + 16 + 32 + 64 + 128 = \mathbf{248}.
$$

EXERCISE 24-11 Write the following in $\sum$ notation.

   i. $1 + 1 + 1 + 1 + 1 + 1 + 1 + 1$

   ii. $13 + 12\frac{1}{2} + 12 + \cdots + \frac{1}{2}$

   iii. $1 - 4 + 9 - 16 + \cdots - 64$

EXERCISE 24-12 Can you figure out what

$$\sum_{k=1}^{4} \left(\sum_{j=1}^{4} kj \right)$$

must mean? What is its value?

EXERCISE 24-13 Or worse: what if we made it

$$\sum_{k=1}^{4} \left(\sum_{j=1}^{k} kj \right)?$$

To write down an infinite sum, we just let the dummy variable go off to ∞, so that we can write

$$a + ar + ar^2 + ar^3 + \cdots = \sum_{i=0}^{\infty} ar^i.$$

Besides being an efficient code for writing down sums, the $\sum$ notation may be manipulated in some useful ways.

1. $\sum(a_n + b_n) = \sum a_n + \sum b_n$. This is just the associative property of addition.

2. $\sum k a_n = k \sum a_n$. This is just the distributive property of multiplication over addition.

Related to $\sum$ notation for sums is $\prod$ notation for products, which works in exactly the same way.

EXAMPLE 24-6   The expression $(x-1)(x-2)(x-3)(x-4)$ can be written

$$\prod_{k=1}^{4} (x-k).$$

     Any time you encounter an unfamiliar series or product, try to write it in $\sum$ or $\prod$ form. Feeling comfortable with these symbols and being able to manipulate them will be very useful later on; moreover, unless you can write the formula for the ith term you may not really understand the sum. (Though being able to do so does not ensure understanding!)

24.5   Sequences

We have spent most of the chapter dealing with series. **Sequences** are even simpler, though: a sequence is just a list of terms. For example, 1, 1, 1, 1, 1; or 2, 4, 6, 8; or $1, -\frac{1}{2}, \frac{1}{3}, -\frac{1}{4}$. Just like a series, a sequence can stop after a while or go on forever.

Like the $\sum$ notation for series, there is a shorthand for sequences: write the nth term in curly braces, where n is a dummy variable. Thus the three sequences above can be written $\{1\}$, $\{2n\}$, and $\{(-1)^{n+1}\frac{1}{n}\}$. The dummy variable is assumed to start at 1 and increase by 1's.

EXERCISE 24-14 Write the following sequences in shorthand.

  i. 10, 9, 8, 7, ...

  ii. 1, 0.5, 0.25, 0.125, ...

EXERCISE 24-15 Write the first five terms of the following sequences.

  i. $\{n(n+1)\}$

  ii. $\{\frac{1}{n!}\}$

  iii. $\{n^3\}$

In some sequences, each term may be defined as a function of previous terms. The standard example of such a **recursion** is one in which each term is equal to the sum of the previous two terms. We arbitrarily set the first two terms, F_0 and F_1, to 1, since they don't have two "previous terms." The rest of the terms are then determined; we have $F_2 = F_1 + F_0 = 2$, $F_3 = F_2 + F_1 = 3$, $F_4 = F_3 + F_2 = 5$, $F_4 = F_3 + F_2 = 8$, and so on. This sequence, called the **Fibonacci sequence**, is only one of infinitely many possible recursions.

EXERCISE 24-16 Find the next few terms of a sequence whose first three terms are 1, and whose succeeding terms each equal the sum of the three previous terms.

EXERCISE 24-17 Find recursive representations for arithmetic and geometric sequences. What is the first term? What is the rule which gives each term from those preceding?

EXAMPLE 24-7 Prove that $F_{n+2} = \sum_{i=0}^{n} F_i + 1$, where F_n is the Fibonacci sequence described above.

Solution: Let's try induction. Read the section on page 339 if you aren't familiar with induction. As a base case, we have $F_2 = 2 = 1 + 1 = F_0 + 1$; so far so good. Then, assuming the theorem holds for $n = k - 1$, we show that it holds for $n = k$:

$$\begin{aligned} F_{k+2} &= F_k + F_{k+1} \\ &= F_k + \sum_{i=0}^{k-1} F_i + 1 \\ &= \sum_{i=0}^{k} F_i + 1, \end{aligned}$$

where we use the inductive assumption in the second line. The theorem holds for $n = 0$, and if the theorem holds for $n = k - 1$, it must also hold for $n = k$. Therefore it holds for all positive integers.

24.6   Sequences and Means

We have already discussed arithmetic and geometric sequences. An interesting point in relation to these two sequences is why they are named as they are. There is a simple reason.

Consider some terms in a general arithmetic sequence $\{x_n\}$:

$$\ldots, x_{n-1} = a + (n-2)d, x_n = a + (n-1)d, x_{n+1} = a + nd, \ldots$$

If we add the terms directly before and after x_n, we get

$$x_{n-1} + x_{n+1} = 2a + 2(n-1)d = 2x_n,$$

which means that

$$x_n = \frac{x_{n-1} + x_{n+1}}{2}.$$

Each term is the arithmetic mean, or average (page 311), of its nearest neighbors! This allows some strange language in which, for example, "insert three arithmetic means between 3 and 4" means to find numbers x, y, and z so that

$$3, x, y, z, 4$$

is an arithmetic sequence.

EXERCISE 24-18   Insert three arithmetic means between 3 and 4.

EXERCISE 24-19   Given that the geometric mean of two numbers x and y is $\sqrt{xy}$, prove that each term in a geometric sequence is the geometric mean of its nearest neighbors.

EXAMPLE 24-8   Insert two geometric means between 2 and 16.

Solution: We wish to find x and y such that $2, x, y, 16$ is a geometric sequence. Thus, $x = 2r$, $y = xr$, and $16 = yr$ for some r, so $16 = yr = xr^2 = 2r^3$ and $r = 2$. Thus, the two numbers are $x = 2(2) = \mathbf{4}$ and $y = 2x = \mathbf{8}$.

EXERCISE 24-20   Insert three geometric means between 3 and 4.

Problems to Solve for Chapter 24

434. What is the sixth term of the arithmetic sequence whose 31st and 73rd terms are 18 and 46, respectively? (MAⲐ 1991)

435. The second term of a geometric sequence is 4 and the sixth term is 16. Find the fourth term if the ratio of consecutive terms is a real number. (MAⲐ 1992)

436. Evaluate $\sum_{n=0}^{\infty} \left(\dfrac{3^n + 5^n}{8^n} \right)$. (Mandelbrot #1)

437. For what value of x does

$$1 + x + x^2 + x^3 + x^4 + \cdots = 4?$$

(Mandelbrot #1)

438. Find the sum of the first forty terms of the series $(-59) + (-56) + (-53) + \cdots$. (Mandelbrot #3)

439. If five geometric means are inserted between 8 and 5832, find the fifth term in the geometric sequence thus formed by the seven numbers. (AHSME 1950)

440. Find the sum to infinity of

$$\frac{1}{7} + \frac{2}{7^2} + \frac{1}{7^3} + \frac{2}{7^4} + \cdots$$

(AHSME 1950)

441. A man writes 1 on the first line of his paper, then writes 2 and 3 on the second line, then 4, 5, and 6 on the third, and continues so that on any line n he writes the first n integers following the last integer on line $n - 1$. What is the sum of the first and last integers on line 17? (Mandelbrot #1)

442. The sum of the first three terms of a geometric sequence of positive integers is equal to seven times the first term, and the sum of the first four terms is 45. What is the first term of the sequence? (MATHCOUNTS 1992)

443. A wall has been built in such a way that the top row contains one block, the next lower row contains 3 blocks, the next lower row contains 5 blocks, and so on, increasing by two blocks in each row. How many rows high is the wall if the total number of blocks used was 900? (MATHCOUNTS 1992)

444. Given a geometric sequence with first term and common ratio both not 0, and an arithmetic sequence with first term 0, a third sequence 1, 1, 2, ... is formed by adding corresponding terms of the two given sequences. Find the sum of the first ten terms of the third sequence. (AHSME 1955)

445. Find the sum of the infinite series $1 - \frac{1}{2} - \frac{1}{4} + \frac{1}{8} - \frac{1}{16} - \frac{1}{32} + \frac{1}{64} - \frac{1}{128} - \cdots$ (AHSME 1959)

446. Thirty-one books are arranged from left to right in order of increasing prices. The price of each book differs by \$2 from that of each adjacent book. For the price of the book at the extreme right a customer can buy the middle book and an adjacent one. Is the adjacent book to the right or left of the middle book? (AHSME 1961)

447. Consider the sets of consecutive integers $\{1\}$, $\{2, 3\}$, $\{4, 5, 6\}$, $\{7, 8, 9, 10\}$, $\cdots$, where each set contains one more element than the preceding one, and where the first element of each set is one more than the last element of the preceding set. Let S_n be the sum of the elements in the nth set. Find S_{21}. (AHSME 1967)

448. For every n the sum of n terms of an arithmetic progression is $2n + 3n^2$. What is the rth term of the sequence in terms of r? (MAΘ 1987)

449. Simplify $\dfrac{1 + 3 + 5 + \cdots + 199}{2 + 4 + 6 + \cdots + 200}$. (MAΘ 1991)

450. Write the following sum in summation notation :

$$32 - 16 + 8 - 4 + 2 - 1.$$

(MAΘ 1991)

451. Find the sum of the odd integers between 10 and 50. (MAΘ 1990)

452. Find x so that the sequence $4x - 1$, $2x + 2$, and $2x - 3$ is an arithmetic progression. (MAΘ 1990)

453. 852 digits are used to number the pages of a book consecutively from page 1. How many pages are there in the book? (MAΘ 1990)

454. Three numbers a, b, and c, none zero, form an arithmetic progression. Increasing a by 1 or increasing c by 2 results in a geometric progression. Find b. (AHSME 1963)

455. Prove that any two consecutive Fibonacci numbers F_k and F_{k+1} are relatively prime.

456. Ashley, Bob, Carol, and Doug are rescued from a desert island by a pirate who forces them to play a game. Each of the four, in alphabetical order by first names, is forced to roll two dice. If the total on the two dice is either 8 or 9, the person rolling the dice is forced to walk the plank. The players go in order until one player loses: A, B, C, D, A, B, ... What is the probability that Doug survives? (MAΘ 1990)

the BIG PICTURE

By learning mathematics in the modern era, you are getting instant access to concepts which took an immense amount of time to develop. We think of them as "intuitively obvious," but that description is far from the truth; only by slow development were the ideas first understood, and they once seemed revolutionary.

One such idea is that of an infinite series. The Greeks, despite their remarkable geometric insights, had no notion that an infinite number of terms could have a finite sum. You may have heard of **Zeno's paradoxes**; the simplest one goes something like this:

> *Motion cannot exist. To move a certain distance, you must first move half the distance, then half of the remaining distance, then half the remaining distance, and so on. Thus you cannot move, and all motion is an illusion.*

Think about this one a second, and explain it.

Believe it or not, the Greeks were stumped! The idea of an infinite sum just hadn't occurred to anyone yet. The resolution is to say that the distance travelled is given by the infinite sum $\frac{d}{2} + \frac{d}{4} + \frac{d}{8} \cdots = d$ units, where d is the distance we wish to travel. We can accomplish this distance, moreover, in $\frac{d}{2r} + \frac{d}{4r} + \frac{d}{8r} \cdots = d/r$ seconds, where r is the rate of travel. Thus, though the motion seems to entail an infinite set of activities, they can all be performed in a finite time. Speed, motion, and reality are saved by something which seems very straightforward to us who have inherited the idea of infinity.

Other of Zeno's "paradoxes" were much subtler:

> *If an arrow in flight is observed at any given moment, it is merely standing still. But if it is always standing still, how can it fly?*

Don't decide the question is trivial until you've thought about it.

Chapter 25

Learning to Count

25.1 What's to Learn?

Suppose someone gives you a pile of seventeen things and asks how many there are. Chances are you count them in the normal way: $1, 2, 3, \ldots, 17$. Or maybe you group them somehow: 3, 6, 9, 12, 15, and two is 17, or 5, 10, 15, and 17. But suppose the pile has seventeen hundred seventeen things: the first method is now entirely impractical. Only by intelligent grouping can the counting be done efficiently.

Similarly, suppose you are asked to count in how many ways two coins can come up when flipped. Head-head, head-tail, tail-head, tail-tail, you say, so 4. But what if there are six coins? Let's see: head-head-head-head-head-head, tail-head-head... so much for that idea. To count sets like this, we need some smart, and sometimes slick, methods.

EXAMPLE 25-1   Suppose we want to know the number of integers between 45 and 317 exclusive. (**Exclusive** means not including 45 and 317 in the total. The opposite, or **inclusive**, includes those numbers.) The naïve way to count them would be one by one: 46, 47, 48, ... The smart way is to simply subtract the two numbers and subtract 1, to get $317 - 45 - 1 = 271$. Why does this work? The number of integers between 0 and n, exclusive, is $n - 1$, since the numbers are 1, 2, ..., $n - 1$. By subtracting 45 from our range, we change the range from "45 to 317" to "0 to $(317 - 45) = 272$" without affecting the number of integers inside. We then have $n = 272$, and thus our total is $n - 1 = 271$. By the same argument, the number of integers between the integers a and b ($b > a$) exclusive is $b - a - 1$.

EXERCISE 25-1   Find the number of integers between 45 and 317 inclusive and between a and b inclusive.

25.2   Multiplication

Let's again consider the second coin problem addressed above.

> *In how many ways can six coins come up when flipped?*

We will group cases so that the answer is clear.

Consider the first coin. No matter how the other coins come up, it has two possibilities, heads and tails. Thus we can immediately do some grouping:

$$\text{total \# of ways for all six} \quad = \quad (\text{\# ways for last 5 when first is heads})$$
$$+ \ (\text{\# ways for last 5 when first is tails}).$$

But whether the first is heads or tails, the other five flips can still occur the same number of ways. We can thus reduce the above to

$$\text{total \# of ways for all six} = 2(\text{\# ways for last 5}).$$

We then look at the second coin. Again, its two possibilities do not affect the rest of the coins, so we have

$$\text{total \# of ways for all six} \quad = \quad 2(\text{\# ways for last 4; second is heads})$$
$$+ \ 2(\text{\# ways for last 4; second is tails})$$
$$= \quad 2 \cdot 2(\text{\# ways for last 4}).$$

We continue like this for all six coins; each coin has two independent choices, so the total number of ways is $2 \cdot 2 \cdot 2 \cdot 2 \cdot 2 \cdot 2 = 2^6 = 64$. By independent, we mean that the coins have no effect on each other.

The solution to the coin problem is a simple application of the most fundamental principle of counting: each independent contributor adds a factor of its number of possibilities to the overall product. This is an example of using grouping to count; instead of counting all possibilities, we just count the possibilities of each contributor separately, then multiply them all.

EXAMPLE 25-2 How many four-letter "words" are there (ignoring spelling, etc.)?

Solution: The choices of the first, second, third, and fourth letters are independent. Since each has 26 possibilities, the total number is 26^4.

EXAMPLE 25-3 How many four-letter "words" are there with vowels (not 'y') in the middle two places and a consonant at the end?

Solution: For the first, unspecified letter, there are still 26 choices. For the middle two letters, there are 5 choices each. For the last letter, there are 21 choices. The total is thus $26 \cdot 5 \cdot 5 \cdot 21$.

EXERCISE 25-2 In how many ways can Horatio give M&M's to three kids? (M&M's come in red, yellow, green, brown, and tan.)

EXERCISE 25-3 How many odd numbers with third digit 5 are there between 20000 and 69999 inclusive?

25.3   Example: The Number of Divisors

A very important application of the multiplicative principle lies in the realm of number theory. Given a number n, the **divisors** of n are the numbers which divide n. The counting problem is to find out how many there are.

Let's tackle the problem with a specific number, say 540. The first step is to find the prime factorization of the number. Using our standard methods, we obtain $540 = 2^2 3^3 5$. Given this, how can we find the number of divisors? Any number which divides 540 could only have 2, 3, and 5 as prime factors. Thus, all divisors of 540 are of the form $2^a 3^b 5^c$. A divisor of 540 cannot have more factors of 2 than 540 has. (For example, $2^3 = 8$ does not divide 540.) Thus, $a \le 2$, so a can be 0, 1, or 2. Similarly, b can be 0, 1, 2, or 3, and c can be 0 or 1. Putting this together, we have 3 choices for a, 4 choices for b, and 2 for c. Since our choices for a, b, and c are independent, there are $(3)(4)(2) = 24$ factors of 540.

Thus we see that counting the number of divisors is a simple application of the multiplication rule. For each prime-power p^d which divides our number, there is an *independent* contribution of 0, 1, 2, ..., or d powers of p, for a total of $d + 1$ possibilities. This independence is exactly the condition for the application of the multiplication principle.

EXERCISE 25-4 Use our arguments to find the general formula: how many divisors does the number $n = p_1^{e_1} p_2^{e_2} \cdots p_k^{e_k}$ have?

EXERCISE 25-5 Find the number of divisors of 12 both using the multiplication concept and by direct counting.

EXERCISE 25-6 How many divisors does 1,000,000 have?

The number of divisors of a positive integer n is often denoted $d(n)$.

25.4 Restrictions on Multiplication

Simple multiplication only works when all contributors are completely independent. This fails for a problem like:

> *In how many ways can Michaelangelo give five differently-colored M&M's to five kids?*

The answer is not $5 \cdot 5 \cdot 5 \cdot 5 \cdot 5$. The reason that independence breaks down here is that there are a limited number of M&M's. If Michaelangelo gives a red M&M to the first kid, the option no longer exists of giving a red to any of the others.

In such a situation, we can still use multiplication, but incorporating the restriction that there is only one of each color. So we line the kids up (in our head), and start giving out candy. There are 5 ways to give the first kid a piece, then only 4 for the second, since one is gone (doesn't matter which), then 3 for the third, and so on.

EXERCISE 25-7   Make sure that the process described above does give all the possible ways. Check also that it does not **overcount**, or count the same possibility twice.

You should do Exercise 25-7 to make sure you understand why the method counts each possible distribution of candy exactly one time. Once this is clear, the answer is clear also; the total number of ways is $5 \cdot 4 \cdot 3 \cdot 2 \cdot 1 = \mathbf{120}$.

Using the multiplication rule with restrictions like this is somewhat trickier, but as long as you repeat the considerations of Exercise 25-7 each time you use the method, it is really no harder than multiplication. One way to keep things sorted out is to write down a series of "blanks," one for each item which has an independent choice, and fill them in as you go. Let's consider some easy extensions of the exercises from the previous section.

EXAMPLE 25-4 How many four-letter "words" are there with vowels in the middle two places and consonants in the other two, and with no letter repeated?

Solution: For the first and last letters, there are 21 and 20 choices. (Again, for the second of the two, 1 of the 21 possible choices is already off-limits.) For the middle two letters, there are 5 and 4 choices. The total is thus **21 · 5 · 4 · 20**. If we were doing this by filling in the blanks, we would write

$$- \ - \ - \ - ,$$

then place a 21 in the first space, a 20 in the last, and a 5 and a 4 in the middle two.

EXERCISE 25-8 How many four-letter "words" can be made without repeating the same letter twice? (You can leave your answer as a product of integers.)

EXERCISE 25-9 How many odd numbers with middle digit 5 are there between 40000 and 69999 inclusive, with no digits repeated?

Sometimes the order in which we treat the contributors matters in restricted problems. For example, take

> *How many five-digit numbers ending with 1, 2, or 4 are there with no digit repeated?*

If we naïvely take the digits in order, we will get to the last digit and break down. Let's try it: there are 9 choices for the first digit (we can't have 0), 9 for the second, 8 for the third, and 7 for the fourth. How many possibilities are there for the last digit? We might think there are 3, since it has to be 1, 2, or 4. However, some of those possibilities might be used up in the preceding digits! We have no way to know whether there are 0, 1, 2, or 3 possibilities left.

We thus take care of the last digit first; it has 3 possibilities. Now the first digit cannot be 0, since the number is a five digit one, so excluding 0 and the number picked for the last slot, there are 8 possibilities. The three middle digits now have, respectively, 8, 7, and 6 possibilities, so the total is $3 \cdot 8 \cdot 8 \cdot 7 \cdot 6$.

This method is usually necessary when the number of choices (numbers above) for some of the 'blanks' (digits above), are restricted in more ways than for other 'blanks'.

EXERCISE 25-10   In how many ways can a five letter "word" be written using only the first half of the alphabet with no repetitions such that the third and fifth letters are vowels and the first a consonant?

These problems can get really out of hand. Let's move on.

25.5   Permutations, Arrangements, and !

Here are two fairly important examples, which are really just rehashes of what we've already done.

EXAMPLE 25-5   In how many ways can n people be seated in a row of n chairs?

Solution: We can choose a person to go in the first seat in n ways, to go in the second in $n - 1$ ways, the third $n - 2$ ways, and so on. The total is $(n)(n - 1)(n - 2) \cdots (2)(1)$.

EXERCISE 25-11   In how many ways can a row of k seats be filled from a set of n people?

The number $(n)(n - 1) \cdots (2)(1)$ is called n **factorial**, and is written $n!$. Note that $0!$ is defined to be 1, because there is exactly 1 way to lay out zero things in order—do nothing!

The answer to Exercise 25-11 is

$$n(n - 1)(n - 2) \cdots (n - k + 1), \text{ or } \frac{n!}{(n - k)!}.$$

Make sure you understand why. This answer is called the number of **permutations** of size k of a set of size n; it is sometimes denoted by $_nP_k$.

EXERCISE 25-12 Evaluate 3!, 7! (the highest one I know by heart), $_7P_3$, and $_5P_4$.

EXAMPLE 25-6 A special case is $_nP_n$ for any n, which equals $n!/0!$, or just $n!$. Do you see why this should be, based on Exercise 25-5?

EXAMPLE 25-7 The factorial has many interesting properties. Perhaps the most useful can be seen by writing it out:

$$n! = n \cdot (n-1) \cdot (n-2) \cdots 2 \cdot 1.$$

Now note that if you leave off the first n in the product, you will be left with $(n-1)!$. This means that for all n,

$$n! = n \cdot (n-1)!.$$

EXERCISE 25-13 Show that for any n and k, we have

$$n! = n \cdot (n-1) \cdots (n-k+1) \cdot (n-k)!$$

EXAMPLE 25-8 Here's a different kind of problem that often comes up with factorials. How many zeroes are there at the end of 103!?

Solution: Problems like this are pretty easy if you remember what the factorial means. We wish to know how many zeroes there are at the end of

$$103 \cdot 102 \cdot 101 \cdots 3 \cdot 2 \cdot 1.$$

Since each terminal zero is just a factor of 10, we should ask how many factors of ten there are. Since $10 = 2 \cdot 5$, there will be a 10 for each pair of a 2 and a 5 which divides 103!. Clearly there are more 2's than 5's, so for each 5 we will be able to find a 2. The number of 10's will thus equal the number of 5's.

So how many 5's are there? For each multiple of 5 there will be one; that is, one factor of 5 will divide 103! for the 5 which appears in the expansion, one for the 10, one for the 15, and so on. The number of such multiples of 5 less than or equal to 103 is the integer part of $103/5 = 20.6$, or 20. That is not the end of the story, however. For each multiple of $5^2 = 25$, there will be *two* factors of 5. We have already counted these once, so we need to count them one more time, adding in the integer part of $103/25$, or 4. The total is thus 24 5's, for 24 10's or **24** terminal zeros. If the number in question had been larger than $5^3 = 125$, we would have had to add in the multiples of 125 a third time, and so on for multiples of 5^4, 5^5, etc.

EXERCISE 25-14 What is the largest n such that 2^n divides 100!?

WARNING: The arrangements of Exercise 25-5 are *in a line*. In problems, sometimes you will have to consider things laid out in a circle as well. It doesn't seem like this makes any difference; you still have the same n things, and the same n places to put them. However, the key point is that with objects arranged in a circle, it is usually assumed that rotations of the circle don't matter. Thus the three arrangements below are all thought of as the same:

A   C   B

B   C   A   B   C   A

Why are these three apparently different arrangements considered to be the same? Consider what person A sees in each case: B on the right, C on the left. To A, the arrangement looks the same in all cases. If you consider what B and C see, you will see that the three cases are equivalent to them as well.

On the other hand, reflections *do* matter, since after a reflection, A sees B on her *left*! Thus

A

C   B

is different from the previous three. There are only two distinct circular arrangements of 3 objects.

If we count objects in a circle as we do objects in a line, we decide there are $n!$ arrangements. However, as shown above, these arrangements are not all different. Each distinct arrangement is counted n times, once for each rotation of the objects. To account for this, we must divide the number of arrangements by n, yielding $n!/n = (n-1)!$ distinct arrangements. (Compare this to our assertion that there are only two ways to arrange 3 objects.)

To complicate matters still further, think about a keychain with keys on it. When counting the number of arrangements of the keys on the chain, not only do the rotations of the chain not matter, but flipping the whole thing over doesn't matter either! Thus, even the two different circular arrangements are really the same for a three object keychain. There is only one fundamental arrangement of 3 objects on a keychain.

When dealing with keychains and other objects which can be flipped like this, you have to divide by an extra factor of 2, since each configuration and its flipped-over companion are indistinguishable.

EXAMPLE 25-9 In how many ways can 6 different keys be arranged on a keychain?

Solution: In a line, there would be 6! = 720 arrangements. In a circle, there are only 5! = 120. On a keychain, we need to divide this by 2, leaving only **60** possibilities.

EXERCISE 25-15 Figure out how many ways there are to arrange 4 keys on a keychain, then take your keychain and actually do it. Surprised that there are so few?

25.6 Mixing it Up

One thing remains before we can use our methods to solve a wide range of problems. This is really just an extension of the original discussion, but should probably be explained again. Consider the problem

> *In how many ways can Antoinette give one M&M each to two children if she has 3 different red, 4 different brown, and different 5 tan ones and the two children insist upon having M&M's of different colors?*

The point of this is that we can separate individual cases, find the number of ways for each, and then add them up. In this problem there are 6 cases: red-brown, brown-red, red-tan, tan-red, brown-tan, tan-brown. For red-brown we have $3 \cdot 4 = 12$ ways (and the same for brown-red), for red-tan $3 \cdot 5 = 15$ ways (same for tan-red), and for brown-tan $4 \cdot 5 = 20$ ways (same for tan-brown). The total is $2(12 + 15 + 20) = \mathbf{94}$.

Using casework we can go on to solve many problems.

EXAMPLE 25-10 How many odd numbers with middle digit 5 and no digit repeated are there between 20000 and 69999?

Solution: We can put the 5 in the middle first, and turn our attention to the last digit, which must be 1, 3, 7, or 9. If this last digit is 3, it restricts the first digit, which can be 2, 3, 4, or 6, while the first digit is unrestricted if the last digit is not 3. We thus consider two cases.

> *Case 1: Last digit 3.* Here there are only the possibilities 2, 4, and 6 for the first digit. The remaining two digits can be chosen from the 7 choices we haven't used in $7 \cdot 6$ ways. The total for this case is thus $3 \cdot 7 \cdot 1 \cdot 6 \cdot 1$. (The two 1's are the 5 in the middle digit, which has no choice, and the 3 in the last position.) Multiplying, we find a total of 126 numbers.

> *Case 2: Last digit not 3.* For the last digit we have the choices 1, 7, and 9, and for the first digit we have the four choices 2, 3, 4, and 6. Again, the remaining two digits may be picked in $7 \cdot 6$ ways, for a total of $4 \cdot 7 \cdot 1 \cdot 6 \cdot 3 = 504$.

To find the total number of numbers, we need to add the totals found by the two cases: $126 + 504 = \mathbf{630}$.

EXAMPLE 25-11 Many counting problems can be subtly changed by the **distinguishability** of the objects counted. Consider the problem:

> *In how many ways can two objects be put into two boxes?*

If the objects are distinguishable, there are four different ways: both in box 1, object A in box 1 and B in 2, B in 1 and A in 2, and both in 2. But if the objects are indistinguishable (meaning we can't tell the difference between them), the two middle choices are the same, and there are only three cases!

We can make it still worse by making the boxes themselves indistinguishable. In this case, "both in one box" is only one choice, since we don't care which box we are talking about. Similarly, "one in one box and one in the other" is a single choice, *even if the objects are themselves distinguishable.* Hence, with indistinguishable boxes there are only two possibilities, whether or not the objects are distinguishable. Try to use distinguishability in the exercises which follow.

EXERCISE 25-16 In how many ways can three different babies be put in two different playpens? In two identical ones?

EXERCISE 25-17 In how many ways can three identical rattles be given to two different babies?

Problems are often less than explicit about distinguishable versus indistinguishable objects; you may have to go on context and common sense. Get some balls and boxes and try out these concepts. Count the arrangements when the boxes and/or the balls are distinguishable, then count those when the boxes and balls are not distinguishable. This will help make the foggy concept of distinguishability clearer.

25.7 Counting the Wrong Thing, Part I

In many cases, the best way to count something is to count something else which turns out to be simply related. In the first examples, the way to go is to count the things that we *don't* want, and subtract from the total number of possibilities to get the number we do want.

EXAMPLE 25-12 The 54-member Council for Security and Cooperation in Europe wishes to choose 3 member states for different leadership positions. The L lobby decrees that at least one of Lithuania, Lichtenstein, Latvia, and Luxembourg must be chosen. In how many ways can the committee be selected?

Solution: The simplest approach is to count the number of choices of the offices *without* choosing any of the L countries. Then there are 50 states and 3 different positions, making $50 \cdot 49 \cdot 48$ choices. We wish to subtract this from the number of committees which can be formed without restriction, or $54 \cdot 53 \cdot 52$. The committees left are those which satisfy the L lobby. The result is just $\mathbf{54 \cdot 53 \cdot 52 - 50 \cdot 49 \cdot 48}$.

EXERCISE 25-18 How many ordered (i.e. the order of the books matters) sets of three of the eight *Anne of Green Gables* books are there if we insist that *Anne of Avonlea* be one?

EXERCISE 25-19 What fraction of four letter "words" contain a repeated letter?

These problems can also be attacked by splitting them into cases, but our new approach is much faster.

25.8 Counting the Wrong Thing, Part II

A second way to count something other than what we actually want is by the creative use of **overcounting**. In overcounting, we intentionally count more things than we really want, and get rid of the excess cases at the end.

EXAMPLE 25-13   In how many ways can Cleopatra choose 3 of the 5 colors of M&M's to eat?

Solution: The key here is the recognition that the order in which she picks the colors does not matter. Suppose we pretend that it does; then the answer will be, by Exercise 25-11, $5 \cdot 4 \cdot 3$. If order does not matter, however, then we have over-counted badly. For example, we have counted red-tan-brown and brown-tan-red as different, when in fact they are the same if order does not matter. In both cases, we have the same combination of colors: red, brown, and tan.

How many times have we counted this combination in our "order matters" count? We have counted every arrangement of the combination red-tan-brown, and we know from Exercise 25-11 that there are $3 \cdot 2 \cdot 1$ such arrangements.

For every combination, we have the same problem—each one has been counted $3 \cdot 2 \cdot 1$ times. Thus to get the true number of combinations, we must divide our original number, $5 \cdot 4 \cdot 3$, by $3 \cdot 2 \cdot 1$ to get

$$\frac{5 \cdot 4 \cdot 3}{3 \cdot 2 \cdot 1} = \mathbf{10}.$$

EXERCISE 25-20   In how many ways can Ulysses choose 4 of the 11 Confederate states for attack?

EXERCISE 25-21   Verify that the answers of the two previous problems satisfy

$$\frac{n!}{k! \, (n-k)!}, \tag{25.1}$$

where n is the number of objects to be chosen from and k is the number to choose.

EXERCISE 25-22   Prove that the number of ways to choose k objects from a set of n, ignoring order, is given by the expression (25.1).

This result is the number of **combinations** of k objects from a set of n objects. It is denoted by $\binom{n}{k}$, or sometimes by ${}_nC_k$. MAKE SURE YOU UNDERSTAND THESE LAST EXERCISES! The problem of picking a combination of objects from another set is the most fundamental one in counting. To make sure you understand the formula of Exercise 25-21, we present here some more examples.

EXAMPLE 25-14 In how many ways can a three-person subcommittee be chosen from a five-person committee?

Solution: The number we want is just $\binom{5}{3}$, which is evaluated as

$$\frac{5!}{3!\,2!} = \frac{5 \cdot 4 \cdot 3!}{3!\,2!} = \frac{5 \cdot 4}{2 \cdot 1} = \mathbf{10}.$$

Observe that the expansion property of factorials has been used in the first equality; if you don't follow this, go back and look at Exercise 25-13.

EXERCISE 25-23 In how many ways can a three-person subcommittee be chosen from a five-person committee if a particular person must be on the subcommittee?

EXERCISE 25-24 How many ways are there to pick no objects from a set of n objects? Does the formula give what you expect?

EXERCISE 25-25 In how many ways can Catherine choose two nuts and two bolts if she has eight nuts and six bolts?

EXAMPLE 25-15 In how many distinguishably different ways can a pair of indistinguishable dice come up?

Solution: We might at first think the answer was 6 times 6, since each die has 6 possibilities. But here we would be counting 4-2 and 2-4 as different outcomes, when they are, for this purpose, the same. Thus, we count in the following way. If the faces of the two dice are different, we can choose 2 of the 6 possibilities for the faces in $\binom{6}{2} = 15$ ways. If they are the same, we can choose the face in $\binom{6}{1} = 6$ ways. The total number of ways is thus **21**.

The quantity $\binom{n}{k}$ is often pronounced "n choose k," because it is the number of ways to choose k things from a set of n. Since the expression for $\binom{n}{k}$ involves factorials, we can use the simplifying tactic for factorials, as described in Exercise 25 and used above in Example 25-14.

EXAMPLE 25-16 A set of points is chosen on the circumference of a circle s the number of different triangles with all three vertices among the points i to the number of pentagons with all five vertices in the set. How many po there? (Mandelbrot #3)

Solution: This is very simple using basic counting. We form triangles by just choosing three vertices from among the points, so the number of triangles that can be drawn from n points is just $\binom{n}{3}$. Similarly the number of pentagons is $\binom{n}{5}$. Thus we have

$$\frac{n!}{5!\,(n-5)!} = \frac{n!}{3!\,(n-3)!}.$$

We can cancel the two $n!$'s, and rearranging yields

$$\frac{(n-3)!}{(n-5)!} = \frac{5!}{3!}.$$

But $(n-3)! = (n-3)(n-4)\cdot(n-5)!$, so we have

$$\frac{(n-3)!}{(n-5)!} = \frac{(n-3)(n-4)(n-5)!}{(n-5)!} = (n-3)(n-4) = 20,$$

and we can easily solve the quadratic to find $n = \mathbf{8}$. (The quadratic also has the root $n = -1$, but this is clearly extraneous, since there can't be a negative number of points.)

EXERCISE 25-26   The previous example showed that

$$\binom{8}{5} = \binom{8}{3}.$$

﹒   'rm

$$\binom{n}{k} = \binom{n}{n-k}$$

Try some different n's and k's and see if this holds generally. in the form (25.1) to see why or why not. (It should become

In the last exercise we proved our first **combinatorial identity**, namely that for all n and k,

$$\binom{n}{k} = \binom{n}{n-k}.$$

This is easy to see using the formula for $\binom{n}{k}$, but is there a deeper reason that it holds? For combinatorial identities, there usually is. Here the reason is that to choose k things from a set of n, we could just as well choose the $n-k$ things we *don't* want! Once you realize this, the identity is obvious, and very easy to remember.

WARNING: Don't confuse combinations with permutations! The thing to remember is that with permutations, *order matters*. So if you want a triple dip cone but don't care about the order of the flavors, the number of cones you can make is a problem in combinations. On the other hand, if you're picky about which flavor is on top and which is on bottom, the number of cones you can make is a problem in permutations.

In general rearrangements, the overcounting concept is still useful. For example, suppose we want to find in how many ways the word LINGUINI can be rearranged. We might immediately think the answer is 8!, since there are 8 letters in the word. The problem is that we are overcounting. The three I's are distinct; call them I_1, I_2, and I_3. We have counted, for example, $UNI_1LI_3GI_2N$, $UNI_2LI_1GI_3N$, $UNI_3LI_1GI_2N$, and so on as *different* words, when they are actually the same! Though distinct, the I's are indistinguishable.

Among the 8! arrangements, each has been written 3! times by ordering the I's in 3! ways. Similarly, each word has been formed 2! times by the orderings of the two N's. Dividing out by all these repetitions, since we only want one copy of each arrangement in the end, the final answer is $\dfrac{8!}{3!\,2!}$.

EXERCISE 25-27 In how many ways can the word RAMANUJAN be rearranged? How about MINIMIZATION?

EXERCISE 25-28 Prove the general formula: the number of rearrangements of a word consisting of k_1 copies of letter 1, k_2 copies of letter 2, and so on up to k_j copies of letter j, with n total letters, is

$$\frac{n!}{k_1!\,k_2!\,\cdots k_j!}.$$

25.9   Doing it Another Way

When you have become comfortable with counting problems, a good exercise is to do problems in more than one way. This helps you stay flexible and not get locked into one mode of solving. For example, on page 304 we showed that $\binom{n}{k} = \binom{n}{n-k}$ in two ways, each of which illuminated a different side of the identity.

EXAMPLE 25-17   As an example, let's find another way to count the arrangements of LINGUINI, done in one way in Section 25.7. This time, we will not resort to overcounting. Instead, we will rid ourselves of the repeated letters first by choosing final positions for them. Of the eight positions (the number of letters in LINGUINI), we take three for the I's; then of the remaining five, choose two for the N's. So far, then, the product is $\binom{8}{3}\binom{5}{2}$. The remaining three letters are not repeated, so we can arrange them in the three remaining spaces in 3! ways. The final answer is thus

$$\binom{8}{3}\binom{5}{2}3!$$

EXERCISE 25-29   Verify that the answer to Exercise 25-17 agrees with our previous answer to this problem.

EXERCISE 25-30   Which method is better suited to proving the general result, as stated in Exercise 25-28?

Always keep in mind the possibility that there may be a clearer, faster, or more intuitive way to approach a counting problem. And occasionally, counting something in two ways will give you a beautiful identity, as we will see on page 330.

25.10   The Binomial Theorem

We've already seen the expansion of $(x+y)^2$ and $(x+y)^3$, but what about higher powers, like $(x+y)^5$? Is there an easier way to expand this product without multiplying repeatedly? Let's write the product out as

$$(x+y)(x+y)(x+y)(x+y)(x+y).$$

Now we see that any term in the product can be formed by selecting an x or a y from each $(x+y)$. Thus we form x^5 by taking an x from each $(x+y)$. Since there is only one way to take an x from each term, there is only one x^5 in the product. However, there are 5 ways we can choose one y and four x's, forming $x^4 y$, because there are 5 $(x+y)$'s to choose the single y from. Hence, there is a $5x^4 y$ term in our expansion of $(x+y)^5$.

Moving on, there are $\binom{5}{2} = 10$ ways we can choose 2 y's from among the $(x+y)$'s, so there is a $10x^3 y^2$ term. Likewise we can easily determine the other three terms and:

$$(x+y)^5 = x^5 + 5x^4 y + 10x^3 y^2 + 10x^2 y^3 + 5xy^4 + y^5.$$

For a quick check, we can let $x = y = 1$ in the above equation. Is the resulting equation true? If not, then our expansion is incorrect.

So can we write an expression for the expansion of $(x+y)^n$, where n is any positive integer? Clearly there is an x^n term. Since we can pick one y and $(n-1)$ x's from the n $(x+y)$ terms in $\binom{n}{1}$ ways, there is a $\binom{n}{1}x^{n-1}y$ term. We can just continue in this manner until we have the expansion

$$(x+y)^n = \binom{n}{0}x^n + \binom{n}{1}x^{n-1}y + \binom{n}{2}x^{n-2}y^2 + \cdots + \binom{n}{n-1}xy^{n-1} + \binom{n}{n}y^n.$$

Notice that we put the $\binom{n}{0}$ and $\binom{n}{n}$ in the first and last terms to make the pattern complete.

This expansion is known as the **Binomial Theorem**, and it is the quickest way to evaluate powers of binomial expressions.

EXAMPLE 25-18   Write the Binomial Theorem using summation notation.

Solution: We want the summation representing $(x+y)^n$ to go from 0 to n, as the powers of x and y cover that range. Notice that in each term of the expansion, the power of y is always the same as bottom number in the combination. Furthermore the sum of the exponents of x and y is always n. Thus, if we let the power of y be i, then x must be raised to $n-i$ power and we can express each term as $\binom{n}{i}x^{n-i}y^i$. Finally, we can write the expansion as

$$(x+y)^n = \sum_{i=0}^{n} \binom{n}{i}x^{n-i}y^i.$$

EXAMPLE 25-19   Find the constant term of the expansion of $\left(x^2 - \frac{2}{x}\right)^6$.

Solution: Using the Binomial Theorem, the ith term is

$$\binom{6}{i}(x^2)^{6-i}\left(-\frac{2}{x}\right)^i = \binom{6}{i}\frac{(-2)^i x^{12-2i}}{x^i}.$$

(Notice that we include the negative sign with the second term!)

For the constant term, we must have the x's on top cancel those on the bottom, or $12 - 2i = i$. Thus, we find $i = 4$, and our term is $\binom{6}{4}(-2)^4 = 15 \cdot 16 = \mathbf{240}$.

Problems to Solve for Chapter 25

457. In how many different ways can a student guess a complete set of answers to a five-item true/false quiz? (MATHCOUNTS 1985)

458. How many factors of 2^{95} are there which are greater than $1,000,000$? (MATHCOUNTS 1984)

459. If $n = 100$, find the value of
$$\frac{(n+1)!}{(n-1)!}.$$

(MATHCOUNTS 1988)

460. What is the units digit of the sum $1! + 2! + 3! + \cdots + 14! + 15!$? (MATHCOUNTS 1985)

461. In a round-robin tournament, each of six softball teams plays each other team exactly once. How many softball games are needed? (MATHCOUNTS 1991)

462. Evaluate $\dfrac{\binom{10}{8}\binom{6}{2}}{\binom{7}{4}}$. (MAΘ 1992)

463. We are given 5 lines and two circles in a plane. What is the maximum number of possible intersection points among these seven figures? (MAΘ 1990)

464. A yogurt shop has four different flavors and six different toppings. If a customer wanted to get one flavor and two different toppings, how many combinations could she get? (MATHCOUNTS 1990)

465. Numbers that read the same forward and backward are called palindromes. How many three-digit numbers are palindromes? (MATHCOUNTS 1992)

466. If $\frac{a!}{b!}$ is a multiple of 4 but not a multiple of 8, then what is the maximum value of $a - b$? (Mandelbrot #2)

467. How many odd positive integers are factors of 480? (MATHCOUNTS 1989)

468. Less than 50 people are at a party. Each person shakes everyone else's hand. If there is an odd number of total handshakes at the party, what is the largest number of people that could be at the party? (Mandelbrot #1)

469. How many lines are determined by 12 points in a plane, no three of which are collinear? (AHSME 1952) (That is, how many lines are formed if all possible lines through two of the points are drawn?)

470. In how many ways can four identical red chips and two identical white chips be arranged in a circle? (MATHCOUNTS 1992)

471. How many ways can 5 books be arranged on a shelf if 2 of the books must remain together? (MATHCOUNTS 1984)

472. What is the sum of all integers less than 100 which have exactly 12 divisors? (Mandelbrot #1)

473. At the end of a professional bowling tournament, the top 5 bowlers have a playoff. First #5 bowls #4. The loser receives fifth prize and the winner bowls #3 in another game. The loser of this game receives fourth prize and the winner bowls #2. The loser of this game receives third prize and the winner bowls #1. The winner of this game gets first prize and the loser gets second prize. In how many orders can bowlers #1 through #5 receive the prizes? (AHSME 1988)

474. If $A = \{1, 2, 3\}$ and $B = \{a, b, c, d\}$ how many different functions are there that assign one element of B to each element of A? (MATHCOUNTS 1987)

475. *Palindromes*, like 23432, read the same forward and backward. Find the sum of all four-digit positive integer palindromes. (Mandelbrot #3)

476. Find the greatest n for which 12^n evenly divides 20!. (Mandelbrot #1)

477. A new school has exactly 1000 lockers and 1000 students. On the first day of school, the first student enters the school and opens all the lockers. The second student then enters and closes every locker with an even number. The third student will 'reverse' every third locker (if closed, it will be opened and if open, it will be closed). The fourth student will reverse every fourth locker and so on, until all 1000 students have entered and reversed the proper lockers. Which lockers will be open at the end? (MAΘ 1992)

Chapter 26

Statistics and Probability

26.1 Statistics

Suppose we want to compare the income of Americans to the income of British citizens. How can we do this? We could just list everybody's income in each country and compare our two lists. There are over a quarter of a billion people in the United States, so this would take a long, long time. Or we could just take a few people from each country and compare them. This, too, would be a bad idea, because we might take the richest people from one country and the poorest from the other and thus draw incorrect conclusions about the relative incomes of the citizens of the two countries.

There are a few simple ways to get a sound comparison of the incomes. We can find which income occurs *most often* in each country. This is called the **mode**. We could find the difference between the lowest and the highest income of a country. This gives the **range** of the incomes. The income which is the exact middle of all incomes is the **median**. By the middle, we mean that if we listed all the incomes from lowest to highest, the median is the one precisely in the middle.

Perhaps the best way to compare the incomes of the two nations is to compare how much income there is *per person* in each country. The income per person is called the **average** or **arithmetic mean** of the incomes in the country.

How do we evaluate the average? The income per person is found by just adding up all the incomes and dividing by the number of people! So the average of, say, 4, 6, and 11 is $(4 + 6 + 11)/3 = 7$.

Similar to the arithmetic mean of a set of numbers, we can define a **geometric**

mean. Instead of adding the three numbers and dividing by three, we multiply the numbers together and take the cube root. Thus if there are three people whose incomes are 4, 6, and 9, we find the geometric mean as $x = \sqrt[3]{4 \cdot 6 \cdot 9} = \sqrt[3]{216} = 6$. Similarly, for any set of n numbers, the geometric mean is the nth root of the product of the numbers.

EXAMPLE 26-1 Show that the arithmetic and geometric means of three different positive numbers are larger than the smallest of the three and smaller than the largest.

Solution: Let the numbers be $a < b < c$ and the arithmetic mean be A. We then have

$$A = \frac{a+b+c}{3} < \frac{c+c+c}{3} = c$$

and

$$A = \frac{a+b+c}{3} > \frac{a+a+a}{3} = a.$$

Letting the geometric mean be G, we similarly have

$$a = \sqrt[3]{a^3} < \sqrt[3]{abc} = G = \sqrt[3]{abc} < \sqrt[3]{c^3} = c.$$

Note that we have just used $a < b$ and $b < c$ repeatedly.

The number of times an element appears in a set of elements is the **frequency** of that number. The frequencies of all the elements in a set are often displayed as a chart or graph. Such a display of frequencies is called a **histogram**.

EXAMPLE 26-2 Find the mode, median, arithmetic mean, range, and geometric mean of the following set of numbers: 2, 4, 4, 5, 6, 10.

Solution: The mode is the number which appears most often, or **4**. The median is the number which is in the middle of the list when the numbers are listed from smallest to largest. We have a problem here. Since there is an even number of numbers, none of the numbers is in the exact middle. When this occurs, the median is the average of the middle two numbers. Since the middle two numbers are 4 and 5, the median is $(4+5)/2 = \mathbf{4.5}$. For the average we have

$$\text{Arithmetic mean} = \frac{2+4+4+5+6+10}{6} = \frac{\mathbf{31}}{\mathbf{6}}.$$

The difference between the largest and the smallest number is $10 - 2 = 8$, which gives us the range. Finally, we have

$$\text{Geometric mean} = \sqrt[6]{(2)(4)(4)(5)(6)(10)} = \sqrt[6]{(2^7)(3)(5^2)} = 2\sqrt[6]{150}.$$

EXAMPLE 26-3 A student has an average score of 80 on her first four tests. What must she score on the next test to raise her average to 82?

Solution: The average of her first four scores is the sum of the scores on the tests divided by 4. Since the average of the first four tests is 80, the sum of the four scores is $80 \cdot 4 = 320$. Letting her score on the 5th test be x, the sum of all five scores is $320 + x$ and we thus want

$$\frac{320 + x}{5} = 82.$$

Solving for x, we find $x = 90$, so she needs a **90** on her third test to raise her average to 82.

EXERCISE 26-1 The arithmetic mean of 12 scores is 82. When the highest and lowest scores are removed, the new mean becomes 84. If the highest of the 12 scores is 98, what is the lowest score? (MATHCOUNTS 1991)

EXERCISE 26-2 Twenty-five students have a combined average of 84 on a test, while another group of 20 students has a combined average of 66. Find the overall average. (MATHCOUNTS 1988)

26.2 Probability and Common Sense

Once you really know how to count, **probability** is not too hard. The probability of an event A is a little hard to define, but it is basically *the fraction of possible outcomes which correspond to A*. This probability is often denoted $P(A)$. For example, the probability of getting a head when you flip a coin is 1/2, because of the two equally likely outcomes, one is a head. A probability can be a decimal as well as a fraction; the probability 1/2 can just as well be written 0.5. Do the following exercises using common sense.

EXAMPLE 26-4   If a box contains two yellow balls and one red, what is the probability of drawing out the red one if one ball is drawn at random?

    Solution: There are three possible balls which can be chosen, and one of them is the desired red color. Thus, the probability is **1/3**. This is often written as $P(\text{red}) = 1/3$.

EXERCISE 26-3   If a box contains two yellow balls and one red, what is the probability of drawing out a yellow?

EXAMPLE 26-5   If a box contains two yellow balls and one red, what is the probability of drawing a red and a yellow if two balls are drawn?

    Solution: One way to do the problem is to say that there are $\binom{3}{2} = 3$ ways to choose two balls, and two ways to choose a yellow and a red, so the probability is **2/3**. However, another way is equally good.

    We use the fact that for any event A, the probability of A happening plus the probability of A not happening is 1, since either A occurs or it doesn't. Thus, we can write

$$P(A) = 1 - P(\text{not } A).$$

Here, we say that the probability of getting a red and a yellow is 1 minus the probability of getting both yellows. But this is the same as leaving the red behind, which clearly has probability 1/3, since the red is one of three balls which could be left behind. We then have

$$P(\text{red-yellow}) = 1 - P(\text{yellow-yellow}) = 1 - P(\text{red left}) = 1 - \frac{1}{3} = \frac{2}{3}.$$

EXERCISE 26-4   If a card is drawn from a deck of playing cards (jokers ignored as usual), what is the probability that it is

    i. black?

    ii. a spade?

    iii. a spade face card?

    iv. any face card?

    v. the ace of spades?

All there really is to probability is figuring out how to count first all possible outcomes, then all desired outcomes. Then just divide the latter by the former. Clearly a probability is always positive. It is also always between 0 and 1, since the number of ways for one outcome cannot be greater than the total number for all outcomes. Moreover, the sum of the probabilities of all possible outcomes is always 1, because the sum of the ways to get all the individual outcomes should equal the total number of ways the event can occur. (We have used this fact in Example 26-5 above.)

EXAMPLE 26-6 John and Jayne each choose a number (not necessarily different) from 1 to 10 inclusive. What is the probability that they each pick a number greater than 7?

Solution: They can each pick a number greater than 7 in 3 ways. Thus, the total number of ways they can both pick a number greater than 7 is $3 \cdot 3 = 9$. The total number of ways they can pick their numbers is $10 \cdot 10 = 100$. Hence, there are 9 desirable outcomes out of 100 possible, for a probability of **9/100**. (After reading the next section, come back and try this with multiplication of probabilities.)

EXAMPLE 26-7 What is the probability that a five-card poker hand contains exactly two aces?

Solution: The number of desired hands is found by choosing the two aces, in $\binom{4}{2}$ ways, then choosing the other three cards (which can't be aces), in $\binom{48}{3}$ ways. The total number of possible hands is found by choosing five cards from the deck of 52, in $\binom{52}{5}$ ways. Thus the probability of having exactly two aces is

$$\frac{\binom{4}{2}\binom{48}{3}}{\binom{52}{5}}.$$

EXERCISE 26-5 If Sapphira randomly chooses a 4 digit number (not beginning with zero) what is the probability that all four digits will be distinct? (MAΘ 1990)

EXAMPLE 26-8 Let's examine a more complicated probability problem. What is the probability that a five-card poker hand has exactly two cards of the same value, but no other cards duplicated?

Solution: First we pick the number which will be duplicated; we can do this in $\binom{13}{1}$ ways. Then we can pick two of the four cards of that number in $\binom{4}{2}$ ways. To fill out the hand, we then need three cards, all of different number, so we can choose 3 of the remaining 12 numbers in $\binom{12}{3}$ ways, and for each can choose one of the four suits in $\binom{4}{1}$ ways. Then the total number of ways is given by

$$\binom{13}{1}\binom{4}{2}\binom{12}{3}\binom{4}{1}\binom{4}{1}\binom{4}{1}.$$

To find the probability, we need to divide this by the total number of ways to choose a poker hand. Since this is just picking 5 cards from a set of 52, the number is $\binom{52}{5}$. The probability of getting a hand of the type we desire is the monstrous

$$\frac{\binom{13}{1}\binom{4}{2}\binom{12}{3}\binom{4}{1}\binom{4}{1}\binom{4}{1}}{\binom{52}{5}}.$$

Can you simplify this using factorials?

Just ask the questions: How many configurations are there that I want? How many are there in total?

26.3 Multiplying Probabilities

One very useful way to treat probabilities uses the multiplication principle of counting. Consider two events, A and B, which have no effect on each other, for example getting heads on two different coin flips. Such events we call **uncorrelated**. What is the probability of both A and B occurring? In the coin case, clearly there are four ways for the coins to come up: HH, HT, TH, TT, and only one of them is the one we want, HH. Thus the probability of getting two heads is 1/4. Note, though, that this is equal to the square of 1/2, the probability of each head individually.

It turns out that this is generally true: the probability of both A and B occurring, if A and B are purely uncorrelated events, is equal to the product of the probabilities of A and B individually. Why? Suppose the probability of A is N_A/T_A, where N_A is the number of desired outcomes and T_A is the total number. Similarly the probability for B is N_B/T_B. How many total outcomes are there for both experiments? By the multiplication principle of counting, there are $T_A T_B$, so long as the events have no effect on each other. How many desired outcomes? For the same reason, $N_A N_B$. Thus the probability of both occurring is $N_A N_B/T_A T_B$, which is just the product of the two probabilities.

EXAMPLE 26-9   Find the probability of rolling a 12 with two six-sided dice.

Solution: We could do this as follows: there is only 1 way to get a 12 (6-6), while there are 36 total possibilities (anything-anything). Thus the probability is 1/36. However, we can also use the multiplication rule for probability as follows. The only possible roll which yields a sum of 12 is 6-6. The probability of a 6 on the first die is obviously 1/6, the probability of 6 on the second die is 1/6. Since the two dice are uncorrelated, the probability of both occurring is the product, or $(1/6)(1/6) = \mathbf{1/36}$.

EXERCISE 26-6   A Flo Hyman spike puts the ball away 60% of the time. What is the probability that her first spike on a given point is returned and her second is not?

EXAMPLE 26-10   Three six-sided dice are rolled. What is the probability that at least one comes up with a 5 or 6?

Solution: You might think we need to separately consider the possibilities that one, two, or all three of the dice come up 5 or 6. However, all we really have to consider is the probability that *none* of the dice comes up 5 or 6, then subtract this from 1! The probability of a single die not coming up 5 or 6 is 2/3. Moreover, the dice are uncorrelated, so multiplication applies and we have

$$P(\text{at least one 5 or 6}) = 1 - P(\text{no 5 or 6}) = 1 - (2/3)(2/3)(2/3) = \mathbf{19/27}.$$

This is yet another problem where using $P(A) = 1 - P(\text{not } A)$ is a powerful simplification.

WARNING: Probabilities can only be multiplied when the events are *completely uncorrelated!*

EXAMPLE 26-11   Two cards are drawn in order from a standard deck of cards. What is the probability that the first is a spade and the second is a heart?

Solution: Since there are 13 spades among the 52 hearts, the probability that the first is a spade is $13/52 = 1/4$. Of the remaining 51 cards, 13 are hearts, so the probability of picking a heart second is 13/51. Hence, the desired probability is $(1/4)(13/51) = \mathbf{13/204}$.

EXERCISE 26-7 A box contains three red balls and three green. Two balls are chosen. What is the probability that a red is chosen first, then a green?

EXERCISE 26-8 A box contains three red balls and three green. Two balls are chosen. What is the probability that one red and one green are chosen? Note how this is different from the prior question.

26.4 Casework

Many many many many problems in both counting and probability come down to the evaluation of several cases in which the desired outcome occurs. We find the probability that each case occurs, and the overall probability is the sum of these. We will solidify this concept here by examining some common types of probability problems which use cases.

EXAMPLE 26-12 There is a 20% chance it will rain today. If it rains, there is a 10% chance that we will be allowed to go outside; otherwise, there is an 80% chance we will be able to go outside. What is the probability that we will be allowed to go outside? (MAΘ 1992)

Solution: We split this into the case that it rains and the case that it doesn't. The probability that it rains and we go outside is $(0.20)(0.10) = 0.02$. The probability that it doesn't rain and we go outside is $(1 - 0.20)(0.80) = 0.64$. The overall probability that we go outside is then the sum of these, or $0.64 + 0.02 = \mathbf{0.66}$.

Many case-type problems are more complicated, though. A very standard type is:

   Find the probability of rolling a 6 if two six-sided dice are rolled.

Solution: First consider all possible ways in which a 6 can arise: 1-5, 2-4, 3-3, 4-2, 5-1. There are 5 different cases to consider. However, for each case we are looking at a configuration which can only occur in one way. Since there are 36 total possible configurations, each configuration has probability 1/36, so that the 5 configurations which yield a 6 add up to make probability 5/36.

EXERCISE 26-9 Find the probabilities of all rolls, 2 through 12. Is there a pattern to help you remember these?

A much more interesting extension is to three dice. For example,

What is the probability of rolling a 12 if three six-sided dice are rolled?

Solution: Now we will have some nontrivial cases. Let's consider the first two dice as a unit, and the third by itself. Then the configurations which yield 12 are 6-6, 7-5, 8-4, 9-3, 10-2, 11-1. Using the results of Exercise 26-9 and the multiplication principle, we can write down the probability of each case. For 6-6 it is $(5/36)(1/6)$, since the probability of a 6 with two dice is 5/36 and with one die the probability of a 6 is 1/6. The rest of the cases are done just as easily, and we can then add the probabilities for all the cases to get

$$P(\text{6-6}) + P(\text{7-5}) + P(\text{8-4}) + P(\text{9-3}) + P(\text{10-2}) + P(\text{11-1}) =$$
$$\frac{5}{36}\cdot\frac{1}{6} + \frac{6}{36}\cdot\frac{1}{6} + \frac{5}{36}\cdot\frac{1}{6} + \frac{4}{36}\cdot\frac{1}{6} + \frac{3}{36}\cdot\frac{1}{6} + \frac{2}{36}\cdot\frac{1}{6} = \frac{25}{216}.$$

26.5   Odds

Because people like to have codes of their own that no one else understands, bettors have come up with a different way of expressing probability. It is called **odds**, and results in those strange numbers which fill the TV screen when the Kentucky Derby comes on. To put it simply, the odds of an event is the ratio of the probability it does not happen to the probability that it does. So take the flip of a coin, for instance. The probability of a head is 1/2, the probability of anything else is 1/2, and the odds of a head are thus 1/2 : 1/2, or 1 : 1. (Odds almost never contain fractions.) We read this as "1 to 1."

EXERCISE 26-10   Is an event with 2 : 1 odds or 1 : 2 odds more likely to occur?

EXERCISE 26-11   What are the odds against getting a 1 in one roll of a six-sided die?

EXERCISE 26-12   If 10% of the game cards in a sweepstakes are winners, what are the odds against winning?

EXERCISE 26-13   If a horse has a 7 in 100 chance of winning, what are the odds of its winning? (Be careful.)

A common mistake is to reverse the order of odds, forgetting which probability should go first. This is often determined by the context of the problem or the language used. We have introduced odds here as the odds against an event occurring, since this is typically the way most gamblers use them. In this case 100 to 1 (100 : 1) is very bad odds, and it is the probability of the event *not* happening which comes first. When we speak of the odds in *favor* of an event, the odds are exactly the opposite. Our event with odds 100 : 1 against becomes an event with odds 1 : 100 in favor of occurring. If facing a question involving odds, make sure you know which is asked for, odds against or odds in favor.

26.6 What Did You Expect?

Antoinette has really rotten luck. Every week for a year she played the lottery, and never won a thing. Terrible luck. Or is it?

To see whether Antoinette's luck is really so bad, we need to see what the average winnings are. Suppose the prizes in each lottery total $500,000, and 10,000,000 people play each week. Then per person, the average winning is $500,000/10,000,000=$0.05 for each lottery. Thus if Antoinette plays for a year, or 52 weeks, her expected earnings are only $2.60; suddenly her luck doesn't seem so bad.

This is the essence of **expected value**, the average amount that one can expect to get from some activity in which the result depends on chance. To find the expected value, all you need to do is take all the possible outcomes, multiply each by the probability of its happening, and add up the results.

EXAMPLE 26-13 Ignatius plays a game in which he chooses at random from a penny, a nickel, a dime, and a quarter. How much can he pay to play and still break even?

Solution: The amount you can pay to play a game and still hope to break even is exactly the expected value. In this game, Ignatius chooses each coin with probability 1/4, so his expected value is $(1/4)(1) + (1/4)(5) + (1/4)(10) + (1/4)(25) = \mathbf{10.25}$ cents.

EXERCISE 26-14 What is the expected value of a Michael Jordan shot if 43% are 2-pointers, 6% are 3-pointers, and the rest are misses (0 points)?

EXERCISE 26-15 What is the expected value of buying stock in a small company if the stock will fail with probability 1/2, be worth $1 with probability 1/3, and be worth $10 with probability 1/6? Would you buy a share for $2.50?

One thing to remember is that the expected value is not necessarily the most likely result in one event; it is simply the average result if the event were to take place many times. For example, suppose three coins are flipped. The expected number of heads is 1.5; obviously this is not a very likely outcome!

Problems to Solve for Chapter 26

478. A basketball player scores an average of 18.6 points per game for five games. How many points must he score in the next game to raise his average to 20 points per game? (Mandelbrot #1)

479. What is the average of 7 numbers if the average of the first two is 9 and the average of the last 5 is 16? (MATHCOUNTS 1986)

480. 42 is the arithmetic mean of a group of 30 numbers. If two numbers, 82 and 44, are removed, then what is the arithmetic mean of the remaining group of numbers? (MAΘ 1987)

481. Two numbers x and y have a geometric mean of 12 and an arithmetic mean of 12.5. Find $x^2 + y^2$. (MATHCOUNTS 1992)

482. Joan's average through five math tests was m. After a sixth test her average was n. If the teacher then decides to double the weight of the last test, what will Joan's average be? (MAΘ 1992)

483. The ace of hearts, the ace of clubs, the ace of diamonds, and the ace of spades are face down on a table. Two different cards are selected at random from the set of four cards. What is the probability that at least one of the cards is a red ace? (MATHCOUNTS 1985)

484. In a raffle 20 tickets are sold. Two prizes will be given. A student buys 2 tickets. What is the probability that this student wins at least one prize? (MATHCOUNTS 1988)

485. A blue urn contains 4 black marbles and two blue marbles. A black urn contains 4 black marbles and 11 blue marbles. One marble is drawn at random from each of the two urns. What is the probability that both of the marbles drawn are blue? (MATHCOUNTS 1988)

486. A teacher with a math class of 20 students randomly pairs the students to take a test. What is the probability that Camilla and Cameron, two students in the class, are paired with each other? (MATHCOUNTS 1991)

487. If there are 3 boys and 4 girls in a group and two are chosen to give a report, what is the probability that one boy and one girl are chosen? (MATHCOUNTS 1986)

488. The odds are 7 to 15 against horse Car Naggy winning the third race at Upson Downs. What is the probability that a different horse will win? (MAΘ 1987)

489. The probability of rain on any given day in Atlanta is 20%. After how many days would you expect it to have rained on 30 days? (MATHCOUNTS 1991)

490. The probability that a baseball player gets a hit is 3/10. Find the probability that she gets 2 hits in 4 at bats in her next game. (MAΘ 1991)

491. Two digits between 1 and 9, inclusive, are selected at random. The same digit may be selected twice. What is the probability that their product is a multiple of 3? (MAΘ 1987)

492. If five standard fair dice are tossed simultaneously, what is the probability that the outcome has a sum greater than 28? (MATHCOUNTS 1989)

493. Eight first-graders, 4 girls and 4 boys, arrange themselves at random around a merry-go-round. What is the probability that boys and girls will be seated alternately? (MAΘ 1987)

494. A secretary writes letters to 8 different people and addresses 8 envelopes with the people's addresses. He randomly puts the letters in the envelopes. What is the probability that he gets exactly 6 letters in the correct envelopes? (MAΘ 1992)

495. The integers from 1 to 10, inclusive, are partitioned at random into two sets of five elements each. What is the probability that 1 and 2 are in the same set? (MAΘ 1992)

496. Ashley, Bob, Carol, and Doug are rescued from a desert island by a pirate who forces them to play a game. Each of the four, in alphabetical order by first names, is forced to roll two dice. If the total on the two dice is either 8 or 9, the person rolling the dice is forced to walk the plank. The game stops as soon as one player loses or after all have rolled the dice once. What is the probability that Doug survives? (MAΘ 1990)

497. Instead of using two standard cubical dice in a board game, three standard cubical dice are used so that the game goes more quickly. In the regular game, doubles are needed to get out of the 'pit'. In the revised game, doubles or triples will get you out. How many times as likely is it for a player to get out of the 'pit' on one toss under the new rules as compared to the old rules? (MATHCOUNTS 1987)

498. Rocky and Bullwinkle are playing Risk. Rocky rolls one six sided die, while Bullwinkle rolls two of them. What is the probability that Rocky's roll is greater than or equal to Bullwinkle's larger number? (Mandelbrot #2)

499. Richard is hitchhiking from Decatur, AL, to Amherst, VA. The probability that Richard will see a car within the next 20 minutes is 609/625. What is the probability that he will see a car within the next 5 minutes? Assume that the probability of seeing a car at any moment is uniform (the same) for the entire 20 minutes. (Mandelbrot #2)

─the BIG PICTURE─

An interesting aspect of probability is that it is extremely difficult to define in a satisfying way. For example, what does it mean that the probability of a coin coming up heads is 1/2?

A naïve answer to this question is that if we were to do the identical experiment many, many times, we would expect for number of heads to approach being half the total number of flips: "It comes up heads half the time." However, this definition is lacking, because it contains the word *expect*. We have to include *expect*, because it doesn't *have* to happen this way; we could just keep on getting heads forever. All we can say is that we expect it to happen. But if we are talking about what we *expect* to happen, we are talking about probability again! The attempt at a definition has led us into a circle.

The logical circle can be shown more clearly by rewriting things in rigorous form. Our expectation that the number of heads will tend toward half the total number means that

> with probability 1, the number of heads will tend toward half the total number of flips.

So all we have done is defined probability in terms of probability!

Can you do better? Mathematicians have been forced to go to extreme levels of rigor to consider probability. They define a quantity in a certain way, and show that it satisfies all the intuitive requirements of a probability, and then use that. But the real definition of probability must be left to the intuition. After all, the number of heads *will* tend to half the total... at least, most of the time.

Chapter 27

Sets

27.1   Some Definitions

A **set** is a collection of objects. For example, the set of all past Presidents of the United States, the set of all real numbers, and the set of all copies of this textbook are all valid sets. A set is usually denoted by placing the objects in the set inside a pair of curly braces; thus the set of even positive integers less than 10 is given by

$$\{2, 4, 6, 8\}.$$

Some sets are too long to specify in this way: for example, the set of Presidents, {Washington, Adams, Jefferson, Monroe, Madison, ... }. In such a case, we can write the set like this:

$$\{\, x \mid x \text{ is a former President} \,\}.$$

Here x is a **dummy variable**, which simply takes on all values specified by the condition after the vertical bar. Another example could be the set of all points in the Cartesian plane:

$$\{\, (x, y) \mid x \text{ and } y \text{ are real numbers} \,\}.$$

Here there are two dummy variables, x and y; the values that each can take must be specified.

Sets can have names, to make writing them simpler. For example, we could define P to be the set of former Presidents; when we wish to refer to the set, we can just write P rather than $\{\, x \mid x \text{ is a former President} \,\}$.

Each of the major types of numbers (see Chapter 8) has a special letter-like symbol which always refers to that set. The set of real numbers is denoted by $\mathbb{R}$, using a stylized R for "reals." Similarly, the set of complex numbers is written $\mathbb{C}$. Unfortunately, the symbol for the integers, $\mathbb{Z}$, was invented in Germany, so is based on a Z rather than an I. The rationals are denoted by $\mathbb{Q}$, where the Q stands for "quotients." Remember these; their use will become more and more common as you get into more advanced problems. Instead of saying "Find all real numbers x...", a problem might say "Find all $x \in \mathbb{R}$". Be ready.

An object in a set is called an **element** of the set. Thus Grover Cleveland is an element of $\{\, x \mid x \text{ is a former President} \,\}$, and π is an element of $\{\, x \mid x \text{ is a real number} \,\}$. We sometimes use the symbol $\in$ to denote being an element, so that we could rewrite one statement above as "Grover Cleveland $\in P$." A cross through the $\in$ just means **not**, so that Aaron Burr $\notin P$. Since a set is just a collection, it doesn't make any sense for one element to be in twice; each element in a set can occur only once. Similarly, the order in which we list the elements does not matter; $\{2, 6, 8, 4\}$ is the same set as $\{2, 4, 6, 8\}$.

The number of elements in a set is called the **size** of the set, and is denoted by the symbol #. Thus $\#\{2, 4, 6, 8\} = 4$, and $\#\{\, x \mid x \text{ is a former President} \,\} = 41$ at this writing. The size of a set is more formally called its **cardinality**.

EXERCISE 27-1 Write the set $\{2, 4, 6, 8\}$ using $\{\, x \mid \ldots \,\}$ notation and the set $\{\, F \mid F \text{ is an ex-Beatle} \,\}$ using $\{x, y, z\}$ notation.

27.2 Operating on Sets

Given two sets, in what ways can we form new sets from them? Let's consider the sets $A = \{2, 4, 6, 8\}$ and $B = \{2, 4, 5, 7\}$. One obvious way to get a new set which is related to A and B is to simply combine them, taking all the elements of each. The new set, which we'll call C, is $\{2, 4, 5, 6, 7, 8\}$. (Note that we don't write 2 and 4 twice, since duplications are not allowed. Also, note that we could have written the elements in any order we pleased; the way we actually did write them just looks nice.) We call the set C obtained in this way the **union** of A and B, and denote it by $A \cup B$.

EXERCISE 27-2   Given the set A above, what is $A \cup A$? Can you generalize to any set A?

EXERCISE 27-3   If $\#A = 8$, $\#B = 9$, and sets A and B have no elements in common, find $\#(A \cup B)$. (Try it on two fixed sets A and B if you need to.)

EXERCISE 27-4   Do the previous exercise over, this time assuming that A and B have 6 elements in common.

EXERCISE 27-5   Find the general formula: if set A contains a elements, set B contains b elements, and sets A and B have x elements in common, how many elements are there in $A \cup B$?

Another new set can be formed from A and B by taking only those elements common to both. Using the same A and B as above, the only elements in common are 2 and 4, so this new set, called the **intersection** of A and B, is just $\{2, 4\}$. The intersection of A and B is denoted by $A \cap B$.

EXAMPLE 27-1   Consider the sets $E = \{2, 4, 6, \ldots\}$ and $O = \{1, 3, 5, \ldots\}$. Then $E \cup O = \{1, 2, 3, \ldots\}$, which is the same as $\{\, x \mid x \text{ is a positive integer}\,\}$. On the other hand, $E \cap O$ is a set with no elements at all, because E and O have no elements in common! The set with no entries is called the **null set**, and is denoted by $\{\}$, or more often by the special symbol $\emptyset$.

A final set operation acts on one set only. Given the set of all Presidents, consider the smaller set of Presidents whose names began with M. The **complement** of this smaller set is everything in the larger set, the set of Presidents, but not in the smaller set: in this case, all Presidents whose names did not begin with M.

You may ask, "why do we claim this operation acts on one set only, when we needed two sets to define it?" The answer is that the larger set is usually taken for granted, as being obvious from context. Thus the complement of the set of odd integers is the set of even integers; we don't need to specify that the set of all integers is the larger set we're using. The complement of a set A is designated by $\overline{A}$.

27.3   Venn Diagrams

A useful way to think about sets is through **Venn diagrams**. The basic idea is to represent a set by a circle, as in the diagram below, where a set A is shown; the complement of the set is just as easily represented. For the complement, we don't need to color in the whole rest of our sheet of paper; the rectangle in which the circle is drawn represents "everything."

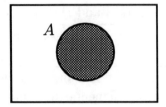
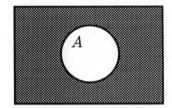

Using this representation, the intersection of two sets and their union can be easily depicted as well. Examine these diagrams, which show $A \cup B$ and $A \cap B$ for two sets A and B.

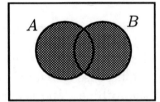
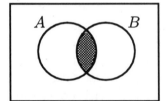

The method is especially important when we are considering three sets at the same time, because then the intersections and unions become too much to keep up with. In the Venn diagram, everything is clear. We have one circle for A, one for B, and one for C. Make sure you see the regions in the diagram that correspond to the intersections and unions of these three sets.

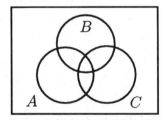

EXAMPLE 27-2   Draw a Venn diagram representing the set $\overline{A} \cap B$.

Solution: The answer is as simple as the diagram at right, where we have filled in $\overline{A}$ with vertical lines and B with horizontal. The desired set is the region covered by both horizontal and vertical lines.

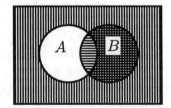

EXAMPLE 27-3   One common type of problem which you can solve using Venn diagrams is below.

> *At one hospital, there are 100 patients, all of whom have at least one of the following ailments: a cold, the flu, or an earache. 38 have a cold, 40 have the flu, and some number have earaches. If 17 have both colds and the flu, 10 have colds and earaches, 23 have the flu and earaches, and 7 have all three, how many have an earache?*

Note that to say someone has an earache and a cold is *not* to say that she doesn't have the flu as well; some people may be counted more than once in the breakdown above.

Solution: This seemingly complicated problem is simple when you consider a Venn diagram.

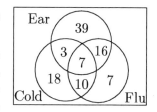

We work from the inside out. First, 7 have all three ailments; we place a 7 in the central space. Then, since 23 have both flu and an earache, with 7 already accounted for by having all three, there are 16 left to go in the space for flu and earache but not cold. We fill in the remaining two-ailment spaces similarly. Then we tackle the one-ailment spaces. We already have 33 flu victims, by counting all the people in the flu circle; thus there are $40 - 33 = 7$ people who have the flu only. We enter an 18 in the cold-only circle in the same way. Every patient must have one of the three diseases, so the number with earache only will be 100 minus all the numbers in the spaces, which comes out to 39. When everyone is accounted for, we can answer the original question: how many have earaches? We add up all the numbers in the earache circle, to get $39 + 3 + 7 + 16 = \mathbf{65}$.

In some problems of this type, you will also have to consider some number of people who are not in any of the sets; this corresponds to a number written outside of the three circles but inside the rectangle.

Note that this problem could be done just as well with pure equations, not using Venn diagrams at all. In fact, where there are four are more sets, Venn diagrams often are more trouble than they're worth. But for two or three sets, they provide a nice graphical approach to the solution.

27.4   Subsets

Any set which is wholly contained in another set is called a **subset** of that set. For example, the set of poodles is a subset of the set of all dogs, and the positive integers form a subset of the complex numbers. Similarly, $\{A, B\}$ and $\{A, C\}$ and $\{B\}$ are subsets of $\{A, B, C\}$. Being a subset is denoted by $\subset$. Thus we could write $\{\,x \mid x \text{ is a poodle}\,\} \subset \{\,y \mid y \text{ is a dog}\,\}$. Since the null set $\emptyset$ has no elements, it is automatically contained in any set: $\emptyset \subset A$ for any set A whatsoever. Similarly, a set is always a subset of itself.

EXERCISE 27-6   Write down all the subsets of {Barbie}. How many are there?

EXERCISE 27-7   Write down all the subsets of {Barbie, Ken}. How many are there?

EXERCISE 27-8   Write down all the subsets of {Barbie, Ken, Starshine}. How many are there?

EXERCISE 27-9   How many subsets does the null set have?

EXAMPLE 27-4   Do you see a pattern in the previous exercises? In fact, it is generally true that the number of subsets of a set with n elements is 2^n. Why? Let's treat this as a counting problem: in how many ways can a subset be formed of a set with n elements? Consider the first element. It has 2 possibilities: it can be in the subset or not. Consider the second element. It, too, has 2 possibilities: in or out. And so it goes; each element of the n contributes a factor of 2, so there are n factors of 2, for a total product of 2^n. This is an important result.

One incredible thing that can be done with the result that the number of subsets of A is $2^{\#A}$ is proving a beautiful combinatorial identity. We do it by counting the subsets in a different way. If you have read Chapter 25, you should know that the number of subsets of a set of size n which have 3 elements is $\binom{n}{3}$, since this is the number of ways to choose 3 elements from a set of n. Similarly, the number with 4 elements is $\binom{n}{4}$, the number with 0 elements is $\binom{n}{0}$, and so on. Thus the total number with any size, from 0 to n, is

$$\binom{n}{0} + \binom{n}{1} + \binom{n}{2} + \cdots + \binom{n}{n}.$$

But by Example 27-4, the total number is 2^n! Thus we have immediately proven that for any n,

$$\binom{n}{0} + \binom{n}{1} + \binom{n}{2} + \cdots + \binom{n}{n} = 2^n. \tag{27.1}$$

EXERCISE 27-10 Express the identity (27.1) in $\sum$ form.

EXERCISE 27-11 Convince yourself that (27.1) is valid by trying $n = 1$, $n = 3$, and $n = 5$.

EXERCISE 27-12 Go back through the argument with which we proved (27.1) one more time—it's worth understanding thoroughly.

Problems to Solve for Chapter 27

500. Find the number of solutions to $\{1, 2\} \in X \in \{1, 2, 3, 4, 5\}$, where X is a set. (AHSME 1972)

501. Using set notation, how can we describe this Venn diagram? (MAΘ 1992)

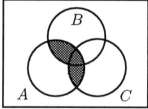

502. Set A contains 15 elements, set B contains 12 elements and the intersection of A and B contains 8 elements. How many elements belong to the union of A and B? (MATHCOUNTS 1986)

503. How many 3 element subsets can be formed from a set of 5 elements? (MATHCOUNTS 1989)

504. A is a set with N elements. For what value of N are there 11 times as many different subsets of A of size six as there are subsets of A of size three? (MATHCOUNTS 1988)

505. In one Berwyn high school, there are 75 students. If 30 students are studying Czech, 20 are studying Polish, 15 are studying German, 11 are studying Czech and Polish, 9 are studying Czech and German, 34 are not studying any language, and 4 are studying all three languages, then how many students are studying Polish and German?

506. How many k-element subsets of an n-element set are there which contain some particular element? How many subsets are there which do not contain the element? How many subsets are there in total? Prove the combinatorial identity $\binom{n-1}{k-1} + \binom{n-1}{k} = \binom{n}{k}$.

507. How many subsets of $\{\, n \mid n \text{ is a multiple of 3 less than } 100 \,\}$ are also subsets of $\{\, n \mid n \text{ is a multiple of 4 less than } 100 \,\}$?

—*the BIG PICTURE*—

In the early 1900's, a paradox arose in set theory which some felt threatened the entire idea of sets. Sometimes called **Russell's paradox**, the paradox starts with the fact that since a set is a collection of any type of objects whatsoever, some sets may contain themselves as elements. For example, a set A could be made which contained the numbers 1 and 2, and the set A: $A = \{1, 2, A\}$. A is a perfectly valid set for most purposes, though it does lead to weird things, as in

$$A = \{1, 2, A\} = \{1, 2, \{1, 2, A\}\} = \{1, 2, \{1, 2, \{1, 2, A\}\}\} = \cdots.$$

You might be tempted to disallow such a strange beast, but it turns out that sets which include other sets are essential to a useful and rigorous development of set theory.

So where is the paradox? Suppose we let M be *a set which consists of every set that does not contain itself.* Thus $A \notin M$ (because A contains itself), but $\{1, 2\} \in M$. The question is, is M in M? If M *is* in M, then we have a contradiction because M contains itself, and therefore is not in M. Things don't get any better when we try letting M not be in M, because then M does not contain itself, so by rights should be in M. Thus M is not in M, but M is also not not in M. (Give yourself a minute to sort all this out.)

Was the paradox ever resolved? Well... sort of. A tier system was proposed in which the first tier consists of sets which only contain objects (no sets); the second tier allows sets which contain tier 1 sets but no tier 2 sets; tier 3 sets can contain tier 1 and tier 2 sets, and so on. By placing M on some tier, and thus restricting the possible sets it can contain, we eliminate the paradox, though in a way which is not entirely satisfactory.

Chapter 28

Prove It

To many students, mathematics is no more than finding numerical answers to problems. However, there is much more. Being able to *prove* your assertions is at least as important as finding the answer. Unfortunately, most schools neglect proofs or confine them to geometry classes, when proofs are important to all fields of mathematics. Moreover, proofs are usually presented in a dry, methodical way to emphasize rigor, when real mathematical proofs are written with more words than equations.

28.1 Words, Words, Words

Proof problems and solutions have a special and subtle vocabulary of their own. Many of these terms confuse beginning students, so we'll go over them.

▷ When a problem asks us to solve something about **distinct** objects or numbers, it means that the objects or numbers in question are *all different*. For example, if we are asked to solve a question involving 3 distinct integers, the numbers cannot be 2, 3, and 2.

▷ When we say **without loss of generality**, we mean that we have chosen a specific case to solve, but the specific case really doesn't matter. By solving the assertion for that specific case, we prove it for all cases, as all cases are *qualitatively* the same; only the ordering of names or correlations is different.

EXAMPLE 28-1   Show that if $x + y + z = 7$ and x, y, and z are distinct positive integers, then one of these numbers must be 4.

Proof: Assume without loss of generality that $x < y < z$. We can do this since we know the numbers are distinct and it doesn't really matter which is which. (While $(1, 2, 4)$ and $(2, 1, 4)$ are considered different solutions, they still consist of the same three numbers.) If $x = 2$, the sum $x + y + z$ is at least $2 + 3 + 4 = 9$, which is too big. Thus $x = 1$. Similarly, if $y = 3$, the sum is at least $1 + 3 + 4 = 8$; thus, $y = 2$ and $z = 4$. Hence, one of the numbers (the largest) must always be 4. By using "without loss of generality" as we have, we have just named the largest integer z, the smallest x, and the other y. We can permute these labels in any way and the problem will be unchanged. Thus, all solutions can be found by permuting $(1, 2, 4)$.

EXAMPLE 28-2   Why can't we use "without loss of generality" as above on a problem involving $x + 2y + 3z = 1$?

Solution: The quantities in this problem are not interchangeable. Switching x and z yields $z + 2y + 3x = 1$, which is qualitatively different from the original $x + 2y + 3z = 1$. (For example, $(x, y, z) = (1, 0, 0)$ is a solution of one equation but not the other.) In the previous problem, switching x and z yields $z + y + x = 7$, which is not qualitatively different from $x + y + z = 7$. This is the heart of "without loss of generality"; changing the labels does not change the problem.

▷ In problems in which we are asked to **maximize** a quantity, we are actually asked to do two things. We must show that the maximum can be attained *and* that no value greater than that maximum can be attained. Just doing one of these is insufficient. The same, of course, holds for **minimization**.

EXAMPLE 28-3   Find the maximum value of $x + y$ if $x \leq 3$ and $y < 5$.

Solution: Clearly $x + y$ is always less than 9, since $x + y \leq 3 + 5$. However, 9 is *not* the maximum, since it is never attained! The true maximum is **8**, since that is the largest value which can be attained.

▷ A solution to a problem is called **trivial** if the numbers present in the problem have no use in determining that solution. Trivial solutions are those solutions which are blatantly obvious and have little mathematical value, so problems often ask the solver to find nontrivial solutions. For example, when solving the equation $x^2 + y^2 = z^2$, $(0,0,0)$ is a trivial solution. Generally, any solution in which all the variables equal 0 is a trivial solution. If on a test you are unsure whether a solution you have found is trivial or not, assume it is not trivial; if you had to think at all to find the solution, it probably isn't. As another example, when asked for the nontrivial factors of an integer, we want those factors besides 1 and the number itself.

▷ Sometimes proofs are so long that we want to break up the proof into smaller parts. After we prove each of these smaller parts, we combine them to complete the proof. In the text of a proof, these smaller parts are called **lemmas**. There aren't any proofs in this volume complicated enough to require lemmas, but there are some in the second volume. A proof is **rigorous** when the proof is complete with no unproven assumptions.

▷ A number is even **if and only if** it is divisible by two. Why do we say "if and only if" rather than just "if" or just "only if?" What is the difference? When we say a number is even *if* it is divisible by two, we do not exclude the possibility that a number which is not a multiple of two is even. By just saying a number is even *only if* it is divisible two, we don't say that all multiples of two are even. Only by combining the two in "if and only if" can we say both that a number must be a multiple of two to be even and that all multiples of two are even. Mathematicians often write "iff" rather than "if and only if," so don't assume it's a typographical error.

EXERCISE 28-1   Do you need "if," "only if," or "iff" in the following?

   i. A number ends with a 5... it is divisible by five.

   ii. An animal is a mammal... it is a human.

   iii. A figure is a circle... every point on it is a common distance from some center.

   iv. A number is an integer... it has no fractional part.

Proving facts involving if and only if usually requires two steps; the "if" and "only if" parts are generally proved separately. The examples at the end of this section will demonstrate this.

▷ That a number is a multiple of two is **necessary and sufficient** for the number to be even. "Necessary and sufficient" is just another way of saying "if and only if." By "necessary," we mean that it is necessary for a number to be a multiple of two in order to be even. As with "only if," this does not imply that all multiples of two are even. By "sufficient," we say that any multiple of two is even, but like "if," this does not exclude numbers which are not multiples of two from being even. Only by putting together both of these can we say all multiples of two and only multiples of two are even. Once again, proofs of facts involving necessary and sufficient usually involve proving the two separately.

EXAMPLE 28-4   Prove that the product of two integers is odd if and only if both of the integers are odd.

Proof: To show the "if" part, we write our odd integers as $2n + 1$ and $2m + 1$. The product of these is $(2n+1)(2m+1) = 4mn + 2m + 2n + 1$, which is odd because it isn't evenly divisible by two.

To show the "only if," we must show that the product of two even numbers and the product of an even number and an odd number are both even. First, letting the two even numbers be $2n$ and $2m$, the product is $4mn$, which is divisible by 2. Second, letting the even number be $2n$ and the odd $2m + 1$, the product is $(2n)(2m+1) = 4mn + 2n$, which is divisible by 2 and hence even. Thus the product of two integers is odd iff both the integers are odd.

EXAMPLE 28-5   Show that x being a multiple of 3 is a necessary and sufficient condition for x to be a solution of $\lfloor x/3 \rfloor - x/3 = 0$.

Proof: Write the equation as $x/3 = \lfloor x/3 \rfloor$. Since $\lfloor x/3 \rfloor$ is always an integer, $x/3$ must be an integer. Hence, it is necessary for x to be a multiple of 3. To show that it is sufficient that x be a multiple of 3, let $x = 3n$ for some integer n. Then $\lfloor x/3 \rfloor - x/3 = \lfloor n \rfloor - n = 0$, so all multiples of 3 are solutions to the equation $\lfloor x/3 \rfloor - x/3 = 0$.

28.2   Contradiction

Is too! Is not! Is too! Is not!

This is an age old argument of children everywhere. Suppose you are arguing that something "Is too!" The most obvious way to show that it is such is to show that it is indeed true; however, there is another way. Instead of showing that you are right, show that your adversary is wrong. If our opponent is wrong, then you must be right. This is the heart of contradiction.

A simple example of the use of contradiction is the proof on page 63 that there are infinitely many prime numbers. Rather than try to prove that there are infinitely many primes directly, we prove that the opposite is impossible—i.e., it is impossible that there is a *finite* number of primes.

EXERCISE 28-2   Take the time to go to page 63 and review the proof that there are infinitely many primes.

EXAMPLE 28-6   Prove that if x is a real solution to $x^5 + 3x^2 + 7x + 2 = 0$, then x must be negative.

Proof: First, $x = 0$ is clearly not a solution.   Second, if $x > 0$, then $x^5 + 3x^2 + 7x + 2$ is the sum of four positive terms and hence cannot be equal to zero.   Thus no positive x can be a solution to the equation.   Hence, we have shown by contradiction that if x is a solution to the given equation, it cannot be nonnegative, so any real solution x must be negative.

EXERCISE 28-3   Prove that if $a, b, c > 0$, then if $ax^2 + bx + c = 0$ has real solutions, both solutions are negative.

28.3   Converses Aren't Necessarily True

All dogs have noses; therefore, anything with a nose is a dog. Clearly this argument is ridiculous; however, people will often give arguments like this to prove mathematical facts.

Given a statement like "If an animal is a dog, then it has a nose," the **converse** of the statement is "If an animal has a nose, then it is a dog." Notice that we have just swapped the positions of "dog" and "nose;" that is what the converse is. The

inverse is "If an animal is not a dog, then it does not have a nose"; we have just negated "nose" and "dog." The **contrapositive** is "If an animal does not have a nose, the animal is not a dog." Here we have both swapped "dog" and "nose" and negated them.

From our examples, it is clear that if a statement is true, its converse and inverse are not necessarily true. Indeed, the converse and inverse of our sample statement about dogs' noses are quite ridiculous. The contrapositive of a true statement, however, is always true. Do you see why?

While it important to understand that the contrapositive of a statement is always true, it is equally important to see that the converse may or may not be true. Hence, when asked to prove a statement which is the converse of a true statement, the original statement is irrelevant. You must prove the converse separately.

EXAMPLE 28-7 What are the converse, inverse, and contrapositive of the statement, "If Jim is outside, it is raining?" Which of these must be true if the statement is true?

Solution: The converse is "If it is raining, Jim is outside." The inverse is "If Jim is not outside, it is not raining." The contrapositive is "If it is not raining, Jim is not outside." The contrapositive is the only one which must be true if the statement is true.

28.4 Mathematical Induction

Mathematical induction is a powerful tool when we are asked to prove something is true for *integers*. It works like this. Suppose we are asked to prove that a given assertion is true for all positive integers. First, we show that it is true for 1 (or some other **base case**, often 0). Second, we show that if it is true for some integer k, then it must be true for the number $k + 1$. This is the **inductive step**. Having proved this we argue that, since it is true for 1, it must be true for $1 + 1 = 2$. Since it is true for 2, it is true for $2 + 1 = 3$, and so on. Thus the assertion is true for all positive integers.

For example, let's show that

$$1 + 2 + 3 + \cdots + n = \frac{n(n + 1)}{2}.$$

First, we show it is true when $n = 1$. This is obvious, as

$$1 = \frac{1(1+1)}{2}.$$

Now, we show that if it is true for k, it must also be true for $k + 1$. If the assertion is true for k, we have

$$1 + 2 + 3 + \cdots + k = \frac{k(k+1)}{2}.$$

Now, we must evaluate the sum of the integers from 1 to $k + 1$:

$$
\begin{aligned}
1 + \cdots + k + (k+1) = (1 + \cdots + k) + (k+1) &= \frac{k(k+1)}{2} + (k+1) \\
&= \frac{k}{2}(k+1) + (k+1) \\
&= \left(\frac{k}{2} + 1\right)(k+1) \\
&= \frac{(k+1+1)(k+1)}{2}.
\end{aligned}
$$

Thus, we have shown that if

$$1 + 2 + 3 + \cdots + n = \frac{n(n+1)}{2}$$

is true for $n = k$, then it is true for $n = k + 1$. Since it is true for $n = 1$, it is therefore true for 2, 3, 4, ..., that is, all positive integers.

Ordinarily when using induction, we don't have to explain "Since it is true for..." We must merely prove the initial case, prove the inductive step, then assert that the induction is complete. The following example is a model of the use of induction as it should appear in texts, or on test papers.

EXAMPLE 28-8   Show that for all positive integers n,

$$7 + 6 \cdot 7 + 6 \cdot 7^2 + 6 \cdot 7^3 + \cdots + 6 \cdot 7^n = 7^{n+1}.$$

Proof: For $n = 1$, we have $7 + 6 \cdot 7 = 49 = 7^{1+1}$, so the assertion is true for $n = 1$. If the assertion is true for $n = k$, we have

$$7 + 6 \cdot 7 + 6 \cdot 7^2 + 6 \cdot 7^3 + \cdots + 6 \cdot 7^k = 7^{k+1}.$$

Thus,

$$7 + 6 \cdot 7 + \cdots + 6 \cdot 7^{k+1} = \left(7 + 6 \cdot 7 + \cdots + 6 \cdot 7^k\right) + 6 \cdot 7^{k+1} \; = \; 7^{k+1} + 6 \cdot 7^{k+1}$$
$$= \; (1+6)7^{k+1}$$
$$= \; 7^{k+1+1}$$

This proves the inductive step and our induction is complete.

EXERCISE 28-4 Consider the following "proof" that every person in the world is the same height. Step one: In a group of 1, every person is the same height. Step 2: Given that in any group of k people the people are all the same height, we show that any group of $k + 1$ people must consist of people who are all the same height. We do this as follows. Given a group of $k + 1$ people, we remove one. The other k must be the same height, since they are a group of k people. Now replace the removed person and take someone else out. This also leaves a group of k people of the same height including the first removed person. This person is then the same height as the other k. Hence, any group of $k + 1$ people is a group of people who are all the same height. This completes the inductive step, so all people are the same height.

Clearly something is wrong with this. What?

28.5   Shooting Holes in Pigeons

Consider a flock of $n + 1$ pigeons. Due to space constraints, the pigeons' home only has n holes (bear with us). If the flock flies home for the summer, there must be at least one hole with 2 or more pigeons in it. Do you see why?

This is the simplest statement of the **Pigeonhole Principle**. (It is also called **Dirichlet's Principle**, probably because he was the first to realize that such an obvious theorem could be useful.) In fact, the Principle is highly useful in math, especially in nonobvious settings.

EXAMPLE 28-9 Given 7 points on a line segment of length 1, prove that there must exist two of the points separated by no more than 1/6.

Proof: Divide the line segment into six equal length segments. By the Pi-geonhole Principle, two of the points must lie on one of these segments (including endpoints). These two points will be at most 1/6 apart, because they lie on a segment of length 1/6.

The hardest part of applying the Principle, besides realizing that it might be useful to the problem at hand, is determining the pigeonholes. They will almost invariably be simple, like dividing an interval into equal pieces or a square into equal squares.

The version of the Principle we are using is a little too weak for general use. We can easily strengthen it by modification. Consider a flock of $2n + 1$ pigeons, with the same n holes. Now there must be some hole with at least *three* pigeons. The general statement and the easy proof are as follows.

> **The Pigeonhole Principle.** Given $kn + 1$ objects which are in n boxes, there must be some box with at least $k + 1$ objects.
>
> *Proof:* We use the principle of proof by contradiction. Suppose that the n boxes each have k or fewer objects. The total number of objects is then less than or equal to nk. But the total number is given to be $nk + 1$, so this gives $nk + 1 \leq nk$, a contradiction. So our original supposition that there was no box with $k + 1$ or more objects must be false.

The Pigeonhole Principle crops up in a surprising variety of disguises. With some experience, you should learn to identify them.

EXERCISE 28-5 A group of n people are selecting entrees at a restaurant. All the entrees are either pasta, seafood, beef, chicken, or vegetarian. Find the smallest possible n such that we can be sure that at least 3 people have dishes from the same category. Prove your answer.

28.6   Convincing But Wrong

When you compare a proof you have written for a problem to one offered as the "right" proof, you will often find that yours is different from the proposed solution. However, don't assume your proof is wrong. Unlike "find the answer" questions, proofs have many different right answers.

Unfortunately, they also have many wrong ones. And no matter how convincing it is, a wrong proof is still wrong. For this reason, if your proof differs from the "correct" solution, don't automatically assume your proof is just a different way to solve the problem. Challenge your solution; check each link in your chain of reasoning to make sure it is sound.

In this section we discuss convincing but wrong arguments. We'll begin by proving that $-1 = 1$, starting from $1 + 1 = 2$. Our steps are as follows: $1 + 1 = 2$, so $1 - 2 = -1$, so $(1 - 2)^2 = (-1)^2$, so $(1 - 2)^2 = 1$, so $\sqrt{(1 - 2)^2} = \sqrt{1}$, so $1 - 2 = 1$, so $-1 = 1$. Clearly our conclusion, $-1 = 1$, is wrong, but our premise, $1 + 1 = 2$, is correct. So one of our steps must be faulty. Analyzing our "proof" closely, we see that our erroneous step is going from $\sqrt{(1 - 2)^2} = \sqrt{1}$ to $1 - 2 = 1$. We have taken the negative square root on the left rather than the positive square root. The moral of the story? It is easy to hide a wrong step amidst a barrage of correct ones.

Convincing but wrong proofs often include showing patterns without proving them. Recognizing a pattern is essential to problem solving, but noting that a pattern exists does not constitute a proof.

For example, suppose we are asked to find a closed form for

$$2^0 + 2^1 + 2^2 + \cdots + 2^n.$$

(A **closed form** for a sum is one which can be immediately evaluated by plugging in the variable; there can be no summations left.) If we evaluate the sum for $n = 1$, 2, and 3, we find that the answers are $2^2 - 1$, $2^3 - 1$, and $2^4 - 1$, respectively. From these results, we might try to deduce that a general closed form for the sum is $2^{n+1} - 1$. But this is no proof. Seeing a pattern of this type is important in *finding* a general rule, but not in *proving* it.

A common mistake in wrong proofs is **circular reasoning**. Circular reasoning occurs when we use a statement to prove itself. This may sound easy to avoid, but as the following examples show, a circular assumption can be buried very deeply; in working a complex problem it is easy to forget which statements you know and which you are trying to prove.

EXAMPLE 28-10   What's wrong with the following "proof"?

> *Suppose 5 women and 5 men are seated at a round table such that each person sits between 2 people of the opposite sex. We shall prove that if we number the chairs from 1 to 10 in order, a woman must be seated in chair 1.*

> *If a woman is in chair 1, a man must be in chair 2, so a woman must be in chair 3, and so forth, until we conclude that a man is in chair 10. Since chair 10 is next to chair 1, a woman must be in chair 1.*

Solution: We wish to show that a woman is in chair 1, but our first step in the erroneous proof *assumes* that a woman is in chair 1. We are guilty of circular reasoning—we must not in any step assume what we are trying to prove is true.

EXAMPLE 28-11   What's wrong with this proof that if $|x| + x > 0$, then $x > 0$?

> *Since $|x| = x$, then $|x| + x = 2x$. Thus $2x > 0$, so $x > 0$.*

Solution: This example shows that circular reasoning can be used to prove a true statement incorrectly. Our first step in the "proof" is $|x| = x$; but this is only true if $x \geq 0$! Thus in writing $|x| = x$, we assume that $x \geq 0$, which is what we are trying to prove. Again we are guilty of circular reasoning. (Among the problems at the end of this chapter, the reader is challenged to find a sound proof for the assertion of this problem.)

EXERCISE 28-6   Find what's wrong with the following proof and provide a sound alternative.

> *There are 21 students in a ten minute class. Each student sleeps for a total of 1 minute during the class. Prove that there is some moment when at least three students are asleep.*
>
> *Proof: Two students sleep during the first minute, two during the second, and so on, for a total of 20 students sleeping for a minute during the 10 minute class. The remaining student must sleep during one of these minutes as well, so there must be 3 students sleeping during the same minute.*

Problems to Solve for Chapter 28

508. Prove that if n is an integer satisfying $n^4 + 4n^3 + 3n^2 + n + 4000 = 0$, then n must be even.

509. In one of the examples in this chapter, we showed that if x is a real solution to $x^5 + 3x^2 + 7x + 2 = 0$, then x must be negative. Why can't we say that x is a solution to this equation if and only if x is negative?

510. Show that for all integers n greater than 2, $1 + 2 + 3 + \cdots + n$ is a composite number.

511. Given 11 points, no four of which are coplanar, each triangle formed by three of the points is given a letter A, B, C, or D. At most how many triangles must get the same letter? (Mandelbrot #1)

512. Show that if x/y and y/x are both integers, then $|x| = |y|$.

513. Explain the proposed paradox in the following story. Three men rent a hotel room. They are charged 15 dollars each. Later, the manager decides they should only have been charged 40 dollars for the room, so he gives 5 dollars to a messenger to give to the men. The messenger dishonestly keeps two dollars and gives each man 1 dollar. Each man has paid 14 dollars for the room and the messenger has 2 dollars, for a total of 44 dollars; however, the men originally paid 45 dollars for the room. Where's the other dollar?

514. Prove that if $|x| + x > 0$, then x must be positive.

515. Chairs are equally spaced around a table and numbered from 1 to $2n$. Prove that if every odd chair is directly opposite another odd numbered chair, then the number of chairs is a multiple of 4.

516. Prove that between any two consecutive multiples of 7, exclusive, there are exactly two multiples of three.

517. Given three lines through the origin, prove that there must be a pair of them which form an angle of less than or equal to 60°.

518. Show that

$$\frac{1}{1 \cdot 2} + \frac{1}{2 \cdot 3} + \cdots + \frac{1}{n \cdot (n+1)} = \frac{n}{n+1}.$$

519. Prove that a number has an odd number of distinct factors if and only if the number is a perfect square.

520. Three women are in a round-robin tennis tournament in which they each play each other player once. Prove that at least one player must lose one game and win one game.

521. Show that $(1 + 2 + 3 + \cdots + n)^2 = 1^3 + 2^3 + 3^3 + \cdots + n^3$.

522. A drawer contains 8 grey socks, 5 white socks, and 10 black socks. If socks are randomly taken from the drawer without replacement, how many must be taken to be sure that 4 socks of the same color have been taken? (MATHCOUNTS 1988)

523. A woman has written k letters and addressed k envelopes for them. She then randomly puts the letters in the envelopes. Show that the number of letters which are put in the proper envelope can be any number from 0 to k except $k - 1$.

524. Prove that $n^5 - n$ is divisible by 10 for all integers n.

525. Each of 6 points in space is connected to the other 5 points by line segments. Each segment thus formed is colored green or purple. Show that it is impossible to color all the segments without forming a triangle in which all three segments are the same color.

┌─ *the BIG PICTURE* ─

To mathematicians, a proof is more than just a confirmation of the truth of an already well-understood principle; it shows a true understanding of the principle, and conveys an aesthetic value.

For this reason, people interested in math delight in coming up with proof after proof of a result. Each new proof shows a different facet of the theorem, a geometric or algebraic or topological or analytic or differential facet. For example, Karl Friedrich Gauss, one of the greatest mathematicians ever, had around six different proofs for the Fundamental Theorem of Algebra (see page 105) and multiple proofs of other important theorems. Throughout history, proofs of the Pythagorean Theorem, proofs that the area of a circle is indeed πr^2, and proofs of the Angle Bisector Theorem have all enriched their subjects.

People have always sought to find the simplest, most elegant way to prove a theorem. The Mathematical Association of America's *Mathematics Magazine* even has a section devoted to this principle, in which a proof must consist only of a revealing diagram and a few equations. The most beautiful proof I know of the Pythagorean Theorem (shown on page 149), discovered by an ancient Hindu mathematician, consisted only of the diagram and one word: BEHOLD! Developing proofs of this type is an excellent exercise, but don't overdo it, or your proofs will soon be unreadable.

Chapter 29

Parting Shots

Here's a potpourri of problems, arranged very roughly by difficulty. Enjoy!

Problems to Solve for Chapter 29

526. Forgetful Jones Jr. forgot his first three exam scores. He did remember that his first score was 3 less than the second, and that the third grade was 11 more than the second. His impatient teacher told him that he needed a grade of 100 to raise his average to 81. What was his third exam grade? (MAΘ 1990)

527. A man born in the first half of the nineteenth century was x years old in the year x^2. In what year was he born? (AHSME 1954)

528. A floor, 9 feet by 12 feet, is to be tiled with 4 inch by 6 inch tiles. How many tiles are needed to cover the floor? (MATHCOUNTS 1991)

529. An organization of 100 people set up a telephone call system so that the initial contact person calls three people, each of whom calls three others, and so on, until all have been contacted. What is the maximum number of people who do not need to make a call? (MAΘ 1987)

530. How many distinct roots satisfy the equation $\sqrt{5-x} = x\sqrt{5-x}$? (AHSME 1958)

531. To swim a mile in a certain rectangular swimming pool, one must either swim the long length 80 times, or negotiate the perimeter of the pool 22 times. What is the number of square yards in the area of the swimming pool? (MATHCOUNTS 1986)

532. The radius a given circle is 1 inch, that of a second $\frac{1}{2}$ inch, that of a third $\frac{1}{4}$ inch and so on indefinitely. What is the sum of the areas of the circles? (AHSME 1953)

533. If $f(n) = \frac{1}{3}n(n+1)(n+2)$, then find $f(r) - f(r-1)$ in simplest form. (AHSME 1968)

534. Find all integers x so that $x^2 - 5x + 6$ is a positive prime number. (Mandelbrot #3)

535. The square of an integer is called a *perfect square*. If x is a perfect square, then find the next larger perfect square in terms of x. (AHSME 1979)

536. Angie has 6 sections of chain, each consisting of 4 links. If the cost of cutting one link open is 5 cents and the cost of welding it closed again is 20 cents, what is the least it would cost to have the six sections joined into a single chain 24 links long? (MATHCOUNTS 1989)

537. The length of rectangle R is 10% more than the side of square S. The width of the rectangle is 10% less than the side of the square. Find the ratio of the areas $R : S$. (AHSME 1955)

538. How many four-digit positive integers are squares of integers? (Mandelbrot #3)

539. If an iron ball 8 inches in diameter weighs 80 pounds, how many pounds does an iron ball 12 inches in diameter weigh? (MATHCOUNTS 1990)

540. An altitude h of a triangle is lengthened by a length m. How much must be taken from the corresponding base b so that the area of the new triangle is half that of the original triangle? (MAΘ 1992)

541. A company with 4 senior partners and 3 junior partners wanted to form a management committee which had at least two senior partners and at most one junior one. In how many different ways could the committee be formed? (ARML 1982)

542. An equilateral triangle is drawn with a side length a. A new equilateral triangle is formed by joining the midpoints of the sides of the first one. Then a third equilateral triangle is formed by joining the midpoints of the sides of the second; and so on forever. Find the limit of the sum of the perimeters of all the triangles thus drawn. (AHSME 1951)

543. Express the arithmetic mean of all integers from -101 through 100 as a fraction in lowest terms. (MATHCOUNTS 1990)

544. Find the sum of all the whole numbers from 0 to 10 which cannot represent the total number of intersections of five distinct coplanar lines. (MATHCOUNTS 1988)

545. The radiator of an automobile already contains 6 quarts of a 10% solution of antifreeze. How many quarts of pure antifreeze must be added to make a 20% antifreeze solution? (MAΘ 1990)

546. If you use 999 digits to write page numbers consecutively starting with 1, how many page numbers could you write? (MATHCOUNTS 1989)

547. A train 1000 feet long is going east at 20 mph. On a parallel track going west is another train going 40 mph. If the trains take 30 seconds to pass each other completely, how many feet long is the second train? (MATHCOUNTS 1988)

548. If $\dfrac{x}{y} = \dfrac{4y}{x} = z$, then find all possible values of z.

549. If $x + y = 7$ and $x^2 - y^2 = 21$, find $2x + 3y$. (MAΘ 1992)

550. The total cost to produce 10 units of a certain product is \$40, and for 20 units the total cost is \$70. The total cost is linearly related to the number of units produced. Find the total cost of producing 25 units. (MAΘ 1991)

551. The measures of the interior angles of a convex polygon of n sides are in arithmetic progression. If the common difference is $5°$ and the largest angle is $160°$, what is n? (AHSME 1968)

552. How many positive integers less than ten million have exactly 77 divisors? (ARML 1982)

553. From a two-digit number N we subtract the number with its digits reversed and find that the result is a positive perfect cube. For many such N is this true? (AHSME 1957)

554. If both x and y are integers, how many solutions are there of the equation $(x - 8)(x - 10) = 2^y$? (AHSME 1962)

555. Sam needs 5 different instruments for his band. He finds 5 people, each of whom can play two instruments. If no two people can play the same two instruments and each instrument can be played by exactly two people, in how many ways can Sam form his band from the 5 people? (Mandelbrot #1)

556. Let $x = \sqrt{2 + \sqrt{2}} - \sqrt{2 - \sqrt{2}}$. Find $384x^2 - x^8$. (MAΘ 1991)

557. A set of 17 points is chosen on the circumference of a circle. Find the maximum number of segments which can be drawn connecting pairs of points such that each segment intersects all others inside, not on, the circle. (Mandelbrot #3)

558. Find the solutions of $2^{2x} - 3^{2y} = 55$ in which x and y are integers. (AHSME 1961)

559. Find the largest integer N such that $N < \left(\sqrt{33 + \sqrt{128}} + \sqrt{2} - 8\right)^{-1}$. (ARML 1981)

560. The ratio of the interior angles of two regular polygons is $3 : 2$. How many such pairs are there? (AHSME 1962)

561. What is the degree measure of the acute angle formed by the hands of a clock at 3:20? (MATHCOUNTS 1992)

562. Two identical jars are filled with alcohol solutions, the ratio of the volume of alcohol to the volume of water being $p : 1$ in one and $q : 1$ in the other. If the entire contents of the two jars are mixed together, what is the ratio of the volume of alcohol to the volume of water in the mixture? (AHSME 1979)

563. Bill and Ted are playing a most excellent game. They begin with 59 sticks and each player on his turn removes at least one but no more than five sticks. The loser is the one forced to take the last stick. If Bill goes first, how many sticks should he take to be sure of winning? (Mandelbrot #2)

564. If fence posts are 2 feet apart, how many posts are needed to enclose a rectangular field which has length 20 feet and width 12 feet?

565. What is the first time between 4:00 and 5:00 that the hour hand and the minute hand are exactly $10°$ apart? (MATHCOUNTS 1991)

566. In a plane, four distinct lines intersect the interior of a circle forming regions within the circle. If m represents the maximum number of regions that can be formed and n represents the minimum number, find $m + n$. (MATHCOUNTS 1990)

567. Given that $\dfrac{2}{x} = \dfrac{y}{3} = \dfrac{x}{y}$, find x^3. (Mandelbrot #3)

568. Let K, in square units, be the area of a trapezoid such that the shorter base, the altitude, and the longer base, in that order, are in arithmetic progression. Which of the following must K be: an integer, a rational number, an irrational number? (AHSME 1966)

569. How many digits are in the product of 3,659,893,456,789,325,678 and 342,973,489,379,256? (AHSME 1969)

570. If the least common multiple of $(10!)(18!)$ and $(12!)(17!)$ is expressed in the form of

$a!\,b!/c!$, where a and b are two-digit numbers and c is a one-digit number, find abc. (MAΘ 1991)

571. Find x in terms of a, b, and c if $\dfrac{x}{a} = \dfrac{y}{b} = \dfrac{z}{c} = \dfrac{xyz}{x+y+z}$. (Mandelbrot #2)

572. Show that if the two roots of $ax^2 + 2bx + c = 0$ are the same, then a, b, and c form a geometric sequence. (AHSME 1955)

573. Given the sequence $10^{1/11}$, $10^{2/11}$, $10^{3/11}, \ldots, 10^{n/11}$, what is the smallest value of n such that the product of the first n members of this sequence exceeds $100,000$? (AHSME 1965)

574. A line with slope 6 bisects the area of the unit square with vertices $(0,0)$; $(0,1)$; $(1,1)$; and $(1,0)$. What is the y-intercept of this line? (Mandelbrot #2)

575. Show that among four points (no three of which are collinear) in the plane, no three of which form a right triangle, there exists at least one obtuse triangle. (Mandelbrot #3)

576. If a and b are positive real numbers and each of the equations $x^2 + ax + 2b = 0$ and $x^2 + 2bx + a = 0$ has real roots, then find the smallest possible value of $a + b$. (AHSME 1984)

577. Five points O, A, B, C, D are taken in order on a straight line with distances $OA = a$, $OB = b$, $OC = c$, and $OD = d$. P is a point on the line between B and C and such that $AP : PD = BP : PC$. Find OP in terms of a, b, c, d. (AHSME 1966)

578. A configuration is made of congruent regular hexagons, where each hexagon shares a side with another hexagon. What is the largest integer k, such that the figure cannot have k vertices? For example, this figure has 13 vertices. (Mandelbrot #1)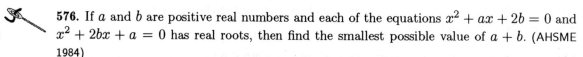

579. Suppose we are given n points in a plane, where $n \geq 4$ and no 3 of the points are collinear. If k distinct triangles are designated with vertices among the n points, show that no more than $k(n-3)$ of the $\binom{n}{4}$ groups of four points contain at least one of the designated triangles. (Mandelbrot #3)

580. Show that if r_1 and r_2 are the distinct real roots of $x^2 + px + 8 = 0$, then $|r_1 + r_2| > 4\sqrt{2}$. (AHSME 1967)

581. If $\{x\} = x - \lfloor x \rfloor$, show that for all real numbers x and y, $\{x+y\} = \{x\}$ only if y is an integer. (ARML 1981)

582. Arrange the three numbers x, $y = x^x$, $z = x^{(x^x)}$, with $.9 < x < 1.0$, in order of increasing magnitude. (AHSME 1968)

583. If (x, y) is a solution for the system of equations below, find the maximum value of $x^2 + y^2$. (MAΘ 1991)

$$2x^2 + 5xy + 3y^2 = 2$$
$$6x^2 + 8xy + 4y^2 = 3$$

584. In rectangle $ABCD$, $AB = 10$ and $BC = 15$. A point P inside the rectangle is such that $PB = 12$ and $PC = 9$. What is the length of PA? (ARML 1981)

585. We are given 4 bags of coins such that (a) all coins in a given bag weigh the same, and (b) the coins of a given bag weigh either 1, 2, or 3 ounces. Take 1 coin from bag 1, 3 coins from bag 2, 9 coins from bag 3, and 27 coins from bag 4. Weighing these 40 coins together on a scale yields a weight of 95 ounces. Determine the weight of a coin from each of the 4 bags. (ARML 1982)

586. The two lines DE and FG are both parallel to AB, and the 3 regions CDE, $DEGF$, and $FGBA$ have equal areas. Find CD/FA. (ARML 1982)

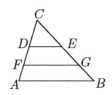

587. How many distinct solutions (a, b, c) are there to the equation $a^2 + bc = b^2 + ac$ if a, b, and c are integers between 1 and 5 inclusive? (Mandelbrot #2)

588. $ABCD$ is a square with side of unit length. Points E and F are taken respectively on sides AB and AD so that $AE = AF$ and the quadrilateral $CDFE$ has maximum area. What is this maximum area? (AHSME 1962)

Index

∅, 327
$\binom{n}{k}$, 302

AA similarity, 135
AAS congruency, 133
abscissa, 190
absolute value, 252
abstract algebra, 88, 276
altitude, 126
angle bisector, 125
Angle Bisector Theorem, 137
angle chasing, 176
angle of rotation, 229
angles, 111–122
    acute, 113
    alternate interior, 113
    central, 116
    complementary, 113
    corresponding, 113, 133
    exterior, 114
    in a triangle, 114
    inscribed, 116, 118
    marking, 114
    obtuse, 113
    reflex, 113
    remote interior, 114
    right, 113
    same-side interior, 113
    straight, 113

    supplementary, 113
    vertical, 113
angular velocity, 109
annulus, 183
apex, 220
apothem, 172
arc, 107
    length of, 115
    major, 107
    minor, 107
area, 179–185
    of a circle, 108
    of a circular segment, 115
    of a hexagon, 173
    of a parallelogram, 161
    of a rectangle, 163
    of a sector, 115
    of a square, 164
    of a trapezoid, 159
    of an octagon, 183
arithmetic mean, 286, 311
arithmetic series, 277
ASA congruency, 132
associativity, 271, 276
average, 311

base case, 339
Bell's Inequality, 269
Bell, J.S., 269

binary, 53
binary operations, 270
Binomial Theorem, 307
boxes, 215

$_nC_k$, 302
$\mathbb{C}$, 326
calculus, 188
Cardano, 88
cardinality of a set, 326
Cartesian coordinates, 190
ceiling function, 254
center
    in coordinates, 199
centroid, 124, 181
    in coordinates, 202, 203
chord, 107, 206
circle, 109
    area of, 108
    circumscribed, 126
    inscribed, 125
circles, 107–198
    concentric, 107
    plotting, 199
    secant to, 107
    sector of, 107
    segment of, 107
    tangent to, 107
circular reasoning, 122, 343
circular segment, 107
    area of, 115
circumcenter, 126
circumcircle, 126, 172
circumference, 108
circumscribed circle, 126
closed form, 343
coefficient, 22

collinearity, 111
combinations, 302
combinatorial identity, 305
commutativity, 271
comparison test, 281
complement, 327
completing the square, 74, 267
complex conjugate, 19
complex numbers, 17–20, 104
    as roots of quadratics, 76
composite numbers, 51
concentric circles, 107
concurrent, 124
cone, 220
congruency
    of triangles, 131–135
conjectures, 68
conjugate roots, 76
conjugate, complex, 19
constant, 22
continuous function, 253
contrapositive, 339
convergence, of a series, 281
converse, 165, 338
conversion factors, 40
coordinates, 189
coplanar, 212
corresponding angles, 133
cosecant, 139
cosine, 139
cotangent, 139
counting, 291–306
    circular arrangements, 298
    distinguishability and, 300
    multiplicative principle of, 292
cube, 213
cubic equations

solution of, 88
cylinder, 217

$d(n)$, 294
Dalton, John, 50
decibels, 16
degeneracy, 128
degree, 22
degrees, 112
Democritus, 50
denominator, 100
Descartes, Rene, 189
diagonal, 157, 169
diameter, 107
difference of squares, 73
dilation, 233
Dirichlet's Principle, 341
discriminant, 76
distance formula, 198
distance problems, 29
distinct, 334
distortion, 233
distributivity, 271
divergence, of a series, 281
divisibility, 51, 59
divisors, 51
    number of, 293
dodecahedron, 221
domain, 248
dummy variable, 282, 284, 325

$\in$, 326
Elements, Euclid's, 156
ellipse, 110, 233
equations
    linear, 22–32
    quadratic, 69–84
    systems of, 24

solving by elimination, 25
solving by substitution, 24
equilateral triangle
    area of, 148
equivalence relation, 274
Euclid, 156
Euler's identity, 98
Euler, Leonhard, 68
expected value, 320
exponents, 1–7
    base of, 1
    fractional, 4
    negative, 2
Exterior Angle Theorem, 114
extraneous roots, 79

factorial, 296
factoring, 70, 89–93, 272
Fermat's Last Theorem, 68
Fibonacci sequence, 285
fixed point, 229
floor function, 253
fractional part, 253
fractions, 100
    comparison of, 101
    converting to decimal, 100
    reduction of, 102
frequency, 312
functions, 246–257
    even, 251
    graphing, 247
    odd, 251
    transformations, 255
    with cases, 254
Fundamental Theorem of Algebra, 105

Galois, Evariste, 88
Gauss, K. F., 347

geometric mean, 286, 311
geometric series, 279
    infinite, 281
geometrical transformation, 228
Goldbach's conjecture, 68
great circle of a sphere, 212
greatest common factor, 63
greatest integer function, 253
group theory, 276

hexadecimal, 53
hexagon, 173
    area of, 173
hexahedron, 221
histogram, 312
HL congruency, 133
homothecy, 234
hypotenuse, 123

i, 17
icosahedron, 221
Ideal Gas Law, 50
identity, 272
if and only if, 336
iff, 336
Im, 19
image, 228
imaginary numbers, 104
    pure, 17
    square roots of, 83
imaginary part, 19
incenter, 125
incircle, 125, 172, 207
independent variable, 247
inequalities, 259–267
    absolute value, 265
    functions and, 265
    linear, 261

quadratic, 262
reciprocals and, 260
trivial, 266
inequality
    nonstrict, 259
    strict, 259
inradius, 125
inscribed circle, 125
integer, 99
    nonnegative, 99
interest, 45
intersection, 327
interval notation, 264
inverses, 273
irrational numbers, 103
    approximation of, 103

lateral surface area, 212
least common multiple, 64
lemmas, 336
lines, 111
    and coordinates, 191
    of symmetry, 231
    parallel, 113, 150, 196
    perpendicular, 113, 150, 196
    plotting, 197
    skew, 211
    slope of, 194
LL congruency, 133
logarithms, 13–14, 16
    and exponentials, 13
lowest terms, 102

map, 228
mathematical induction, 98, 285, 339
maximization, 335
median, 124, 166
    of a trapezoid, 158

median, statistical, 311
Mersenne numbers, 68
midpoint, 111
minimization, 335
minutes, 112
mode, 311
modular arithmetic, 55

Napier, John, 16
natural numbers, 99
necessary and sufficient, 337
nontrivial, 336
null set, 327
number theory, 51
numerator, 100

octagon
    area of, 183
octahedron, 221
    volume of, 223
operations, 270–273
    binary, 270
order of operations, 271
ordered pair, 24, 190
ordinate, 190
orthocenter, 127
orthogonal lines, 113
overcounting, 294, 301

$_nP_k$, 296
paradox, 290, 333
parallel lines, 113, 138, 150, 196
parallelepiped, 215
parallelogram, 160
    area of, 161
partial sums, 281
percent, 43
    increase or decrease, 45

perimeter, 124
permutation, 296
perpendicular bisector, 125
perpendicular lines, 113, 150, 196
π, 108
Pigeonhole Principle, 341
plane, 211
polar coordinates, 190
polygons, 169–174
    diagonals of, 169
    regular, 169
        area of, 172
        circumradius of, 172
        inradius of, 172
    similar, 138
polyhedron, 221
polynomials, 85, 252
    roots of, 105
power of a point, 205–209
prime factorization, 293
primes, 51
prism, 217
    right, 217
probability, 313–321, 324
    multiplication and, 316
proportionality
    constant of, 37
proportions, 36–46
    direct, 36
    inverse, 37
    joint, 37
    manipulation of, 39
pyramid, 219
Pythagorean Theorem, 128, 140, 149
Pythagorean triple, 130

Q, 326

quadrants, 190
quadratic formula, 75
quadrilaterals, 157–166
    circumscribed, 207
    concave, 157
    convex, 157
    diagonals of, 157
    orthodiagonal, 157
quantum mechanics, 269

$\mathbb{R}$, 326
radians, 112
radical, 4
    conjugate, 11
radius, 107
    in coordinates, 199
range, of a function, 249
range, statistical, 311
ratio, 36, 279
rational numbers, 9, 100
rationalizing denominators, 9
ray, 111
Re, 19
real numbers, 104
real part, 19
rectangle, 163
    area of, 163
recursion, 285
reflection, 192, 231
    in a point, 231
reflexivity, 274
relations, 273–275
relatively prime, 64
repeating decimals, 100
rhombus, 162
rigorous proof, 336
roots, 70, 85

    extraneous, 79
rotation, 192, 229
Russell's paradox, 333

$\sum$, 282
SA congruency, 133
SAS congruency, 132
SAS similarity, 136
secant (trigonometric), 139
secant to a circle, 205
seconds, 112
sector, 107
    area of, 115
segment, 111
segment, of a circle, 107
semiperimeter, 124
sequence, 277, 284
    recursive, 285
series, 277
    arithmetic, 277
      sum of, 278
    convergent, 281
    divergent, 281
    geometric, 279
      sum of, 280
    infinite, 280
sets, 325–331
    complement of, 327
    intersection of, 327
    size of, 326
    union of, 326
similarity
    area and, 179
    of polygons, 138
    of triangles, 135–138
similitude, 233
sine, 139

slant height, 219
slope, 194
slope-intercept form, 193
space, 211
sphere, 212
square, 164
    area of, 164
square root, 4
SSS congruency, 132, 136
statistics, 311–313
strict inequality, 259
subset, 330
summation notation, 282
surface area, 212
    of a box, 216
    of a cone, 220
    of a cube, 213
    of a cylinder, 218
    of a prism, 217
    of a pyramid, 219
    of a sphere, 212
symmetry, 231
    line of, 231
    point, 232
symmetry of a relation, 274

tangent (trigonometric), 139
tangent to a circle, 205
Tartaglia, 88
tetrahedron, 221
    volume of, 222
the BIG PICTURE, 16, 49, 68, 88, 98,
        110, 156, 188, 269, 276, 290,
        324, 333, 347
total surface area, 212
transcendental numbers, 104
transitivity, 274

translation, 191, 228
transversal line, 113
trapezoid, 158
    area, 159
    isosceles, 159
    median, 158
Triangle Inequality, 128
triangles, 123–153
    30°-60°-90°, 140
    45°-45°-90°, 140
    acute, 123
    altitude of, 126
    area, 135
    area of, 144
    centroid of, 124, 181
    circumcenter of, 126
    circumcircle of, 126
    circumradius of, 126
    congruency of, 131–135
    degenerate, 128
    equilateral, 123
      area of, 148
    in coordinates, 202
    incenter of, 125
    incircle of, 125
    inradius of, 144, 207
    isosceles, 123
    median of, 124, 166
    obtuse, 123
    orthocenter of, 127
    right, 123, 133
      circumcenter of, 127
      median of, 127
    scalene, 124
    similarity of, 135–138
trivial, 336
Trivial Inequality, 266

Uncertainty Principle, 269
union, 326

variable, 22
Venn diagrams, 327
volume, 212
    of a box, 216
    of a cone, 220
    of a cube, 213
    of a cylinder, 218
    of a prism, 217
    of a pyramid, 219
    of a sphere, 212
    of a tetrahedron, 222
    of an octahedron, 223

without loss of generality, 334
word problems, 28–32
work problems, 30
working backwards, 120

x-intercept, 192

y-intercept, 192

$\mathbb{Z}$, 326
Zeno's paradoxes, 290
zeroes, 70